An Anglican Covenant

An Anglican Covenant

Theological and Legal Considerations for a Global Debate

Norman Doe

CANTERBURY
PRESS

Norwich

© Norman Doe 2008

First published in 2008 by the Canterbury Press Norwich
(a publishing imprint of Hymns Ancient & Modern Limited,
a registered charity)
13–17 Long Lane, London EC1A 9PN

www.scm-canterburypress.co.uk

British Library Cataloguing in Publication data

A catalogue record for this book is available
from the British Library

ISBN 978-1-85311-904-0

Typeset by Regent Typesetting, London
Printed in the UK by
CPI William Clowes Beccles NR34 7TL

Contents

Preface   vii

Abbreviations   x

Introduction   1

Part 1   The Foundational Ideas of a Covenant

1   The Nature of a Covenant   13

     A Covenant is a Voluntary Relationship   14
     A Covenant is an Agreement   18
     A Covenant is an Exchange of Promises   22
     A Covenant Generates Commitments   26
     Conclusion   30

2   The Employment of a Covenant   31

     The Covenantal Character of Anglicanism   31
     The Use of Covenants in Anglicanism   35
     The Covenant in Scripture   41
     The Covenant in the Sacramental Tradition   44
     The Covenant in Reason and Experience   45
     Conclusion   51

3   The Purposes of a Covenant   53

     Unity   54
     Reconciliation, Recommitment and Trust   59
     Identity, Clarity and Understanding   61
     Order and Stability   63
     Mission and Witness   67
     Conclusion   70

Part 2   The Structure and Substance of a Covenant

4   The Form of a Covenant   73

     The Documentary Form of a Covenant   73
     Linguistic Form: Descriptive and Prescriptive Covenants   79

The Detail of a Covenant   86
Conclusion   90

5 The Subject-Matter of a Covenant   91

Common Identity   94
Obligations of Communion   97
Relationships of Communion   100
Autonomy and its Exercise   101
Matters of Common Concern   107
Conclusion   110

6 The Content of a Covenant   112

The Windsor Draft Covenant   113
The Nassau Draft Covenant   124
The St Andrews Draft Covenant   136
Conclusion   144

Part 3   The Implementation of a Covenant

7 The Process for a Covenant   149

The Evolution of a Process   150
Vocation: A Call to Covenant   153
Collaboration: Common Discernment   156
Negotiation: The Synthesis of Discordant Views   158
Education: Spiritual Preparation and Growth   161
Conclusion   164

8 The Adoption of a Covenant   166

Each Church Enacts a Communion Law   166
The Signatories to a Covenant   175
A Solemn Signature in a Liturgical Context   179
Conclusion   180

9 The Effects of a Covenant   182

Membership of the Anglican Communion   182
Covenants are Binding: *Pacta sunt servanda*   187
Discipline and Breach of Covenant   191
The Changeability of a Covenant   205
A Covenant and Ecclesiality   207
Conclusion   211

Conclusion   213
Bibliography   222
Index   239

Preface

In its *Windsor Report* (2004), the Lambeth Commission proposed the adoption by the churches of the Anglican Communion of an Anglican covenant. The Commission also offered a preliminary draft covenant. In January 2007, at Nassau, the Covenant Design Group produced a new draft, commended in February 2007 by the Primates' Meeting for discussion by the forty-four churches of the Communion. A further draft from the Covenant Design Group, meeting at St Andrew's House in London, was published in February 2008. The results of this worldwide process are to be considered at the Lambeth Conference 16 July to 4 August 2008. The debate is of outstanding historical significance in the development of the identity of the Communion, and of Anglicanism itself, as well as for the relations of its churches and their freedom of action in the world.

This book presents, explains and evaluates the proposals and draft covenants (including the St Andrews draft), the responses to both Windsor and Nassau, and the arguments in these responses for and against. It does so in terms of the theological and legal considerations which arise from these. It seems to me that nine key issues emerge from the proposals and the responses. A chapter is devoted to each. Throughout this study, covenant models (from covenantal and sacramental theology, and the practice of agreements in ecumenism and comparable international ecclesial communities) are suggested as a framework within which these issues might be approached. Time will tell how these issues will shape the debate at the Lambeth Conference and beyond.

The study aims to offer a balanced presentation of the proposals, drafts and responses, in relation to each of these issues, in what is hoped to be as objective and even-handed a manner as possible. I had the privilege of serving as a member of the Lambeth Commission, and in January 2008, following completion of the penultimate draft of this book, was appointed as a consultant to the Covenant Design Group for its London meeting. Consequently, doubtless for many I will not be seen to come to this as an unbiased investigator. However, this book is not intended as an apology for or defence of an Anglican covenant. The proposal has been made; draft covenants are in circulation; the Communion has embarked on discussion of them; this volume offers a framework for that discussion; and the Communion will make up its own mind.

The research carried out for this study yields evidence which favours those who support the proposals, but equally much of the research also substantiates the arguments of those who criticize the draft covenants (but accept the covenant principle). However, if it be felt by those who reject the principle (and the emerging drafts) that the evaluation of the arguments, when set against scripture, reason, and tradition, advocates too robustly for 'a' covenant or for a particular draft, this is because the research simply did not disclose extensive evidence to enable a stronger case in favour of their view. Similarly, if it is thought that the study strikes too crude a balance between theology and law, it is hoped that this also will be forgiven. This book is designed to stimulate not to foreclose debate around theology and law.

I owe a considerable debt of gratitude to a great many people who have given invaluable assistance to me in this project. The study has grown out of a dissertation for the degree of Master of Theology at the University of Oxford, and I am very grateful to my supervisor, Revd Timothy Bradshaw, Regents Park College, for his learning, encouragement and good humour, as well as to Revd Judith Maltby, Corpus Christi College, for her help with historical aspects of the study. My own colleagues at the Centre for Law and Religion, Cardiff Law School, have, as always, given me tremendous support, chiefly Eithne D'Auria, but also Anthony Jeremy, Russell Sandberg, the Revd Gareth Powell, Chancellor Mark Hill (an honorary professor at the Law School) and Dr Augur Pearce. Ideas have also grown from discussions with students on the Cardiff LLM in Canon Law, many of whom have direct experience of the issues with which the Anglican Communion is now grappling, notably Paul Colton (Bishop of Cork), Bernard Georges (Provincial Chancellor of the Indian Ocean), Stacy Sauls (Bishop of Lexington), and Harry Huskins (Executive Officer, Ontario Provincial Synod): I am deeply indebted to them.

Since the work of the Lambeth Commission was completed, I have kept in touch with the Revd Canon Gregory Cameron, Deputy Secretary General of the Anglican Communion, and the Revd Canon John Rees, Legal Adviser to the Anglican Consultative Council, both of whom have offered indispensable critical insights into the covenant project. Without the administrative assistance of my colleagues Sharron Alldred, Sarah Kennedy and Helen Calvert, staff at the postgraduate office at Cardiff Law School, the task of writing this book in a relatively short time would have been far more difficult than the pleasure it has proved. I owe a real debt of gratitude to SCM-Canterbury Press, particularly Christine Smith, Mary Matthews, Roger Ruston and Lesley Staff for their faith in this project. Last but not least, I should like to thank for their forbearance, kindness and constant support, my family, Heather and our children Rachel, Elizabeth and Edward. Needless to say, any errors in the book are solely my responsibility.

Norman Doe
Cardiff
Wales
15 February 2008

Abbreviations

AC	Appeal Cases
ACADC	Anglican Church of Australia, Draft Covenant (2006) submitted to the Covenant Design Group, Nassau 2007
ACC	Anglican Consultative Council
ACCT	Australian Churches Covenanting Together
ACN	Anglican Communion Network
ACNS	Anglican Communion News Service
AGI	Anglican Global Initiative
ALCA	Anglican-Lutheran Covenant, Australia
AMC:CS	*An Anglican-Methodist Covenant*, Common Statement of the Formal Conversations between the Methodist Church of Great Britain and the Church of England (London, 2001)
ARCIC	Anglican-Roman Catholic International Commission
Art.	Article
BCP	Book of Common Prayer
BWA	Baptist World Alliance
Can(s)	Canon(s)
CAPA	Council of Anglican Provinces of Africa
CAS	*A Scottish Response to the Windsor Report*, Changing Attitude Scotland (2005)
CCL	Roman Catholic Code of Canon Law 1983
CCM	Covenant for Communion in Mission, Inter-Anglican Standing Commission on Mission and Evangelism 2005
CCW	Covenanted Churches in Wales
CDG	Covenant Design Group
CIPRWR	Church of Ireland, Preliminary Response to the Windsor Report, Considered by the Standing Committee of the General Synod 2005
Cl.	Clause
CMS	Church Mission Society
CO	*Charta Oecumenica* 2001
Const.	Constitution
CPCE:LA	Community of Protestant Churches in Europe, Leuenberg Agreement
CPDMC	Constitutional Practice and Discipline of the Methodist Church, Great Britain (2002)

CPIO	Church of the Province of the Indian Ocean
CUACC	A Covenant Union of Anglican Churches in Concordat (2005)
CYTUN	Churches Together in Wales
DAZ	Douglas, I., and P. Zahl, *Understanding the Windsor Report* (New York, Church Publishing Inc., 2005)
Dioc.	Diocese
EccLJ	*Ecclesiastical Law Journal*
ECP	Episcopal Church in the Philippines
ECUSA	Episcopal Church USA (now TEC)
ELCA	Evangelical Lutheran Church in America
EVCF	Episcopal Voices of Central Florida
FOFAD	Bolt, P. G., M. D. Thompson and R. Tong (eds), *The Faith Once For All Delivered* (Camperdown, NSW, The Australian Church Record in conjunction with the Anglican League, 2005)
GS	General Synod
GSPN	A Statement from the Global South Primates, Nairobi, 2005
GSSC	Global South, Suggested Covenant, submitted to the Covenant Design Group, Nassau 2007
HBTG	House of Bishops Theological Group (Church of England)
IASCER	Inter-Anglican Standing Commission on Ecumenical Relations
IASCOME	Inter-Anglican Standing Commission on Mission and Evangelism
IATDC	Inter-Anglican Theological and Doctrinal Commission
IBC	International Bishops' Conference (Old Catholics)
IFSCCUCI	Inter-Faith Section of the Committee for Christian Unity, Church of Ireland
LARC	Lutheran-Anglican-Roman Catholic Covenant (Virginia, 1990)
LC	Lambeth Conference
LCRPR	Lambeth Commission Reception Process: Responses
LEP	Hooker, Richard, *Of the Laws of Ecclesiastical Polity*, ed. A. S. McGrade (Cambridge, Cambridge University Press, 1989)
LGCM	Lesbian and Gay Christian Movement
Linzey	Linzey, A., and R. Kirker (eds), *Gays and the Future of Anglicanism* (Winchester, O Books, 2005)
Lossky	Lossky, N., J. M. Bonino, J. Pobee, T. F. Stransky, G. Wainwright, and P. Webb (eds), *Dictionary of the Ecumenical Movement* (Geneva, WCC, 2002)
LQR	*Law Quarterly Review*
LWF	Lutheran World Federation
MCU	Modern Churchpeoples Union
MU	Mothers Union

NDC	Nassau Draft Covenant, of the Covenant Design Group meeting at Nassau, January 2007
NIFCON	Network for Interfaith Concerns (Anglican Communion)
NSWLR	New South Wales Law Reports
OED	*Oxford English Dictionary*
RCW	Response of the Church in Wales (2005)
Res.	Resolution
RHB	*Windsor Report*, A Report from the House of Bishops of the Church of England (2005)
RNDC	Response(s) to the Covenant Design Group Nassau Report and Draft Covenant
RPC	*Responding to a Proposal of a Covenant*, IATDC (2006)
RTT	*Repair the Tear: The Windsor Report – An Assessment and Call for Action* (Anglican Mainstream – UK and the Church of England Evangelical Council, 2005)
SADC	St Andrews Draft Covenant, of the Covenant Design Group meeting at St Andrew's House, London, 29 January to 2 February 2008
SAMS	South American Missionary Society in Canada
SBC	Southern Baptist Convention
SCOBA	Standing Conference of Canonical Orthodox Bishops in the Americas
SCOCCA	Standing Conference of Canonical Orthodox Churches of Australia
SECR	Scottish Episcopal Church Response (2005)
SOC	Statute of the Old Catholic Bishops
TAAC	*Towards an Anglican Covenant* (2006)
TCCG	*The Church Constitution Guide*, North American Mission Board, An Agency of the Southern Baptist Convention
TEC	Protestant Episcopal Church in the United States of America
TWR	Lambeth Commission on Communion, *The Windsor Report* (2004)
UOU	Union of Utrecht
Virginia Report	Virginia Report (of the Inter-Anglican Theological and Doctrinal Commission), *The Official Report of the Lambeth Conference 1998* (Harrisburg, 1999)
WAC	'The Windsor Action Covenant – Think Before You Sign', Progressive Episcopalians of Pittsburgh
WAEEC	*Women in the Episcopate*, Eames Commission (Toronto, 1998)
WARC	World Alliance of Reformed Churches
WCC	World Council of Churches
WDAC	Draft Anglican covenant, Appendix II, *The Windsor Report*
WMC	World Methodist Council

Introduction

The Anglican Communion is understood as a worldwide fellowship of forty-four autonomous churches in communion with the See of Canterbury. There is no body, at the global level, competent to make decisions binding on all the churches of the Communion. Its institutional instruments of communion (the Archbishop of Canterbury, Lambeth Conference, Anglican Consultative Council, and Primates' Meeting – formerly known as the instruments of unity) have moral authority but no global jurisdiction. The Communion has no worldwide system of canon law. Jurisdictional authority vests in each church, which has its own system of government and law. Nor are the churches of the Communion bound together by a formal agreement which spells out their mutual purposes, relations and commitments. Rather, communion between the churches is held together by 'bonds of affection' and a network of informal ties. Historically, the creative tension between autonomy and communion, and its adaptability to serve the gospel in a world of constant change, has been one among many of the achievements of Anglicanism.

However, events in recent years, especially those over issues of human sexuality, have put a severe strain on these bonds of affection. Events have moved quickly. In 1998 the Lambeth Conference classified 'homosexual practice as incompatible with Scripture' and pronounced that it 'cannot advise . . . ordaining those involved in same gender unions'.[1] In 2002, the Anglican Consultative Council advised provinces not to take controversial action in this matter without consulting the Anglican Communion.[2] In 2003, decisions were made in the Episcopal Church USA (then ECUSA, now TEC) to select a priest in a committed same sex relationship as one of its bishops, and in the Diocese of New Westminster, Canada, concerning the authorization of services for use in connection with same sex unions.[3] In October 2003, the primates warned that these actions threatened to 'tear the

1 LC 1998, Res. I.10(e).
2 ACC-12, Hong Kong (September 2002).
3 Lambeth Commission, Mandate, 1.

I

fabric of the Communion at its deepest level'.[4] The following month the consecration of the priest as bishop took place in TEC, an event described by the Anglican Communion News Service as 'one of the most controversial and momentous occasions in the history of the Anglican Communion'.[5] The Primates' Meeting in 2007 stated that: 'Since the controversial events of 2003, we have faced the reality of increased tension in the life of the Anglican Communion – tension so deep that the fabric of our common life together has been torn'.[6] The common life of the Communion will be a subject for discussion and debate at the Lambeth Conference in the summer of 2008.

As requested by the primates in October 2003, the Archbishop of Canterbury established the Lambeth Commission, on Communion,[7] to address among other things 'the legal and theological implications' of the decisions of the Episcopal Church (USA) and Diocese of New Westminster (Canada), and to make 'practical recommendations for maintaining the highest degree of communion that may be possible in the circumstances resulting from these decisions'.[8] By the time it met, the Commission had to address not only disregard for statements of the instruments of communion, but also declarations of impaired communion, external intervention in the affairs of provinces, and the effect of events on relations between Anglicans and their ecumenical partners.[9] In addition to short-term measures,[10] the Commission recommended in the long term the adoption of an Anglican covenant: for the churches of the Communion to collaborate in the creation of their own formal agreement which supports but does not replace the bonds of affection and commits them to an agreed framework for life together as members of a global family of churches. A preliminary draft of an Anglican covenant was offered by the Commission in its *Windsor Report* (2004): it deals with common identity, relationships and commitments of communion, the exercise of autonomy in communion, and the management of communion issues.[11]

---

4 Primates' Statement, 15/16-10-2003.

5 *Church Times*, 7-11-2003, 2.

6 *Communiqué*, 19-2-2007, para. 9: ACNS 4253.

7 The work of the Inter-Anglican Theological and Doctrinal Commission (IATDC), seeking since 2001 the development of a theology of communion, was suspended in order to release funds for the work of the Lambeth Commission: ACNS 4116 (23-2-2006).

8 Lambeth Commission, Mandate, 1 and 2.

9 The Lambeth Commission on Communion, *The Windsor Report* (hereafter TWR) (London, Anglican Communion Office, 2004), paras 22–41.

10 For moratoria, voluntary withdrawal from participation in the instruments of unity, and temporary provision of delegated pastoral oversight for dissenting groups, see TWR, Section D.

11 TWR, Appendix II, Proposal for the Anglican Covenant.

In setting out its reasoning behind the covenant proposal,[12] the Commission makes two basic points. First, at present there is no authoritative worldwide agreement which articulates the rights and responsibilities of Communion membership and provides a mechanism for their enforcement. Nor do the churches generally have legal provisions on inter-Anglican relations or on how to proceed in matters of common concern in the Communion.[13] Moreover, the principles of inter-church co-operation which the Communion has developed are unenforceable.[14] Consequently: 'how to make the principles of inter-Anglican relations more effective at the local ecclesial level' is 'a persistent problem in Anglicanism contributing directly to the present crisis'.[15] In other words, if tested the bonds of affection are unenforceable: the juridical category of autonomy prevails over the theological category of communion. Second, therefore, as an obvious mechanism for each church to render a formal agreement enforceable within it (as part of its commitment to communion), the Commission recommends that each church enact its own brief 'communion law',[16] to authorize its primate (or equivalent) to sign the covenant on behalf of that church and commit the church to adhere to the terms of the covenant,[17] in order: (a) to strengthen the bonds of unity; (b) to articulate what

12 At their meeting in 2001 the primates of the Anglican Communion considered a paper which proposed adoption of a covenant, with the primates as signatories: a 'concordat for incorporation by individual churches within their own canonical systems' seeking 'to increase the profile of communion, to define their inter-church relations, and for the resolution of inter-Anglican conflict'. The paper was subsequently published as: N. Doe, 'Canon law and communion', *Ecclesiastical Law Journal* 6 (2002) 241, esp. 262; *International Journal for the Study of the Christian Church* 3 (2003) 85, esp. 115.

13 TWR, para. 116: 'No church has a systematic body of "communion law" dealing with its relationship of communion with other member churches ... inter-Anglican relations are not a distinctive feature of provincial laws. This may be contrasted with the increasing bodies of ecumenical law in Anglican churches facilitating communion relations between Anglicans and non-Anglicans.'

14 TWR, para. 115: 'The principles about communion, autonomy, discernment in communion and inter-Anglican relations, enunciated at global level by the Instruments of Unity, have persuasive moral authority for individual churches; they do not have enforceable juridical authority unless incorporated in their legal systems (and generally they are not incorporated). This may be contrasted with the juridical experience of the particular church, in which enforceable canon law, the servant of the church, seeks to facilitate and order communion among its faithful.'

15 TWR, para. 117.

16 TWR, para. 118, n. 61.

17 TWR, para. 118; Draft Covenant (hereafter WDAC), Preamble: 'We, the churches of the Anglican Communion, in order to foster greater unity and to consolidate our understandings of communion, solemnly establish this Covenant, entered on our behalf by designated signatories and to which we shall adhere as authorized by laws enacted by each of our churches for these purposes, so that our communion may be made more visible and committed, and agree as follows ...'.

has to-date been assumed; (c) to make explicit and forceful the loyalty and bonds of affection which govern the relationships between the churches of the Communion.[18]

On publication of the *Windsor Report*, the Primates' Standing Committee set up a Reception Reference Group to receive and review responses to the Report from within the Communion and from ecumenical partners.[19] The Group received 322 responses and, on the basis of these, reported to the Primates' Meeting 2005 that: 'There seemed to be agreement and welcome for the principle of a covenant . . . However, a number felt more work had to be done on the Appendix "example" given in the Windsor Report before it would be acceptable'.[20] In turn, the Primates' Meeting, February 2005, recognized 'that serious questions about the content of the proposal for an Anglican covenant and the practicalities of its implementation mean that this is a longer term process'. Nevertheless, the primates commended the covenant as a project that should be given further consideration in the Provinces of the Communion between 2005 and the Lambeth Conference 2008. They requested the Archbishop of Canterbury to explore ways to implement this.[21] Subsequently, the Anglican Consultative Council noted the continued consideration of covenants for the Communion as commended by the *Windsor Report* and the Primates' Meeting.[22]

In March 2006, in a pastoral letter setting out his thinking on the Lambeth Conference 2008, the Archbishop of Canterbury stated: 'The controversies of recent years have spotlighted the difficulties we have as a Communion of making decisions in a corporate way. The *Windsor Report* raises this as a major question, and we shall need time to think about the Report's theological principles and its practical sugges-

---

18 TWR, paras 117, 118.

19 The Group was directed to ask two questions in relation to the covenant proposal: 'How would you evaluate the arguments for an Anglican covenant? How far do the elements in the possible draft represent an appropriate development of the existing life of the Anglican Communion?'

20 See Bibliography for the website address. Some expressed concern that adoption of the covenant would turn 'the Anglican Church into a "confessional" church', that the covenant should be 'less legalistic and more a statement of principle'; but others thought 'it should remain "a legal authorisation by each church for signing and solemnizing by the primates in a liturgical context"'.

21 Primates' Meeting, *Communiqué* 24-2-05, paras 8 and 9. The primates 'were glad to be reminded [by the Lambeth Commission] of the extensive precedents for covenants that many Anglican churches have established with ecumenical partners'. Also: 'even within our Communion the Chicago/Lambeth Quadrilateral has already been effectively operating as a form of covenant that secures our basic commitment to scripture, the Nicene Creed, the two Sacraments of the Gospel and the Historic Episcopate.' However, the primates were 'cautious of any development which would seem to imply the creation of an international jurisdiction which would override our proper provincial autonomy'.

22 ACC-13, Resolution 27: June 2005.

tions, particularly the idea of a Covenant for our Provinces, expressing our responsibility to and for each other.'[23] That same month, the Joint Standing Committee of the Anglican Consultative Council and the Primates' Meeting adopted a paper, *Towards an Anglican Covenant*, as a basis for discussion and reflection in the Communion, and requested the Archbishop of Canterbury in consultation with the Secretary General of the Anglican Communion to appoint a Task Group to initiate the process.[24]

June 2006 proved an important time for the covenant project. The 75th General Convention of the Episcopal Church in the USA passed a resolution, in 'demonstration of our commitment to mutual responsibility and interdependence in the Anglican Communion', to 'support the process of the development of an Anglican covenant that underscores our unity in faith, order, and common life in the service of God's mission'.[25] Later in the month the Archbishop of Canterbury issued a statement in which he expressed the opinion that '[t]he idea of a "covenant" between local Churches . . . seems to me the best way forward'.[26] July 2006 saw a report that the Episcopal Synod of the Church of Nigeria (Anglican Communion) had empowered 'the leadership of the Church . . . to give assent to the Anglican covenant'.[27] In September, a Global South primates' meeting endorsed the development of an Anglican covenant,[28] as did the Anglican Church of Burundi in October 2006.[29]

In January 2007, the Covenant Design Group appointed by the Archbishop of Canterbury, on behalf of the primates, met in the Bahamas at Nassau. The group discussed four areas related to the development of an Anglican covenant: its content, the process by which

---

23 ACNS 4127 (9-3-2006): 'Archbishop sets out thinking on Lambeth Conference 2008.'

24 The document was prepared by a small working party convened by the Deputy Secretary General of the Anglican Communion at the request of the Archbishop of Canterbury and the Secretary General and was intended to inform the deliberations of the Joint Standing Committee.

25 75th General Convention, TEC, Resolution A166: the Convention also directed the International Standing Committee of the Executive Council and the church's members on the ACC 'to follow the development processes of an Anglican Covenant in the Communion, and report regularly to the Executive Council as well as to the 76th General Convention', and appropriate bodies in TEC to serve as resources for the development of a covenant: http://gc2006/legislation

26 *The Challenge and Hope of being Anglican Today: A Reflection for the Bishops, Clergy and Faithful of the Anglican Communion* (27-6-2006): ACNS 4161.

27 ACNS 4162 (4-7-2006). The Lambeth Commission recommended adoption by the legislative and representative assembly of each church, not authorization by an episcopal synod: see Ch. 8.

28 Meeting at Kigali, *Communiqué*, ACNS 4193 (22-9-2006), para. 7.

29 ACNS 4202 (19-10-2006).

it would be received into the life of the Communion, the foundations on which a covenant might be built, and its own methods of working.[30] The Nassau group offered a new draft covenant dealing with: the life Anglicans share; commitment to the confession of the faith; life shared with others (the Anglican vocation); unity and common life; the unity of the Communion; and a declaration.[31] Subsequently, the Joint Standing Committee of the Anglican Consultative Council and the Primates' Meeting commended the work of the Covenant Design Group to the Primates' Meeting.[32] Among the documents used by the Group to shape its own draft covenant were drafts from the *Windsor Report*, Global South and Australia.

At Dar es Salaam, Tanzania, in February 2007, the Primates' Meeting commended the report and new draft covenant of the Nassau group for study and urged the churches of the Communion to submit an initial response to the draft by the end of 2007. On the basis of responses from thirteen churches in the Communion,[33] the Covenant Design Group, meeting in London 29 January to 2 February 2008, produced a new text, the St Andrews Draft Covenant, and accompanying documents.[34] The proposal is that this draft will be discussed at the Lambeth Conference 2008, so that the bishops may offer reflections and contributions. Following a further round of consultation, a final text will be presented to the Anglican Consultative Council (at ACC-14, in May 2009), and then, if adopted as definitive, offered to the churches for ratification. The covenant process will conclude when a definitive text is adopted or rejected finally through the synodical processes of the churches.[35]

---

30 ACNS 4252 (19-2-2007), Report of the Covenant Design Group.

31 Ibid.

32 ACNS 4250 (16-2-2007).

33 Namely, from Australia, Canada, England, Hong Kong, Ireland, New Zealand, Philippines, Scotland, Southern Africa, USA, Wales, West Indies, and the Lusitanian Church. Bodies within the churches responded, for example: in TEC, the Executive Council (on the basis of 500 responses to A Short Study Guide to Aid the Episcopal Church in Responding to the Draft Anglican Covenant as Prepared by the Covenant Design Group); in Australia, the Standing Committee of the General Synod (the General Synod itself did not comment on the response but recognized the importance of the covenant project, noted the committee response and asked the committee to facilitate further dialogue); Southern Africa, co-ordinated by the Vicar General (on the basis of responses from six dioceses); and England, the archbishops (on the basis of consultation with the House of Bishops, particularly its Theological Group, and the Archbishops' Council).

34 Report of the Second Meeting of the Covenant Design Group (London, February 2008): the Report contains a *Communiqué*, an Introduction, the Draft Covenant, a Draft Appendix, and a Commentary.

35 Primates' Meeting *Communiqué*, 19-2-2007, paras 15 and 16. The primates also: agreed to the establishment of a worldwide study of hermeneutics, on methods of inter-

Since publication of the *Windsor Report, Towards an Anglican Covenant*, and the Covenant Design Group Nassau Report leading up to its 2008 London meeting, responses to the covenant proposal have mushroomed: in consultations,[36] books,[37] journals,[38] and, from the Lambeth Reception Process, in reactions of churches, organizations, theological colleges, individual bishops, lawyers and theologians.[39] Initially, about a third supported the Windsor proposal and its draft covenant; a third supported the covenant principle but not the draft; and a third rejected both the principle and the draft.[40] Responses ranged from, for example (a) the proposal is 'pernicious: it brings us too close for Anglican comfort to the coercive and authoritarian structures of Rome'; through (b) the covenant would prevent 'unilateral innovation in future or at least make it clear what consequences followed from such unilateralism', but there should be 'caution . . . over [its] precise details'; to (c) '[t]he new covenanted fellowship . . . would balance autonomy with international responsibility', and reassure 'partners in the greater ecumenism'; if Anglicans are 'serious about belonging to an international body, this seems to be an excellent blueprint', to enable the Communion to be 'a functional international family'.[41] By January 2007, the Covenant Design Group noted at Nassau that: 'although in the papers submitted there was a great deal of concern about the nature of any covenant that might be put forward for adoption, very few of the respondents objected to the concept of covenant *per se*, but

preting the Bible (para. 8); affirmed continuation of the process of listening to the experiences of homosexuals (para. 13); expressed gratitude for the work of the Panel of Reference, established to supervise the adequacy of pastoral provisions for groups in dispute with their diocesan bishop (para. 14); and they agreed to establish a Pastoral Council, Pastoral Scheme and Primatial Vicar for those in the Episcopal Church alienated by recent developments (the latter was rejected by TEC).

36 See, for example, *Following Christ the Lord in Communion, Covenant and Mission*, An Anglican Consultation Hosted by the Anglican Communion Institute and Wycliffe Hall, Oxford, 2–6 July 2007.

37 For example: A. Linzey and R. Kirker (eds), *Gays and the Future of Anglicanism* (Winchester, O Books, 2005); P. G. Bolt, M. D. Thompson and R. Tong (eds), *The Faith Once For All Delivered* (Camperdown, NSW, The Australian Church Record in conjunction with the Anglican League, 2005); I. Douglas and P. Zahl, *Understanding the Windsor Report* (New York, Church Publishing Inc, 2005); and the essays in M. Chapman (ed.), *The Anglican Covenant: Unity and Diversity in the Anglican Communion* (London, T. & T. Clark, 2008).

38 See, for example, the studies in *Anglican Theological Review* 87 (2005) and in *International Journal for the Study of the Christian Church* 8.2 (2008) forthcoming May 2008.

39 http://www.anglicancommunion.org/commission/reception/report/index.cfm

40 TAAC, para. 2.

41 See respectively: *Church Times*, 29-10-04, 9; A Guide to the Windsor Report by an International Gathering from around the Anglican Communion meeting at Oxford, 19–21 October 2004; *Church Times*, 22-10-2004, 10.

rather saw the covenant as a moment of opportunity within the life of the Communion.[42] In February 2008, the Group commented that the provinces responding to Nassau 'all signalled a willingness to move forward, despite various concerns and questions' about the Nassau draft.[43]

The aim of the following chapters is to offer a rudimentary theological and juridical framework for this debate. The book proposes that nine key issues may be identified as critical to, and as a structural model for, the debate. They fall broadly into three basic categories: foundational ideas of a covenant (nature, employment and purposes); the structure and substance of a covenant (form, subjects and content); and the implementation of a covenant (process, adoption and effects). A chapter is devoted to each of the nine issues. First, the study examines the St Andrews report and draft covenant, comparing these with the Nassau proposals and those of the Lambeth Commission (and the draft covenant in the *Windsor Report*) and it sets out, arranges (in typological categories) and examines the responses to these.[44] Second, in order to sharpen the theological and legal considerations underlying the debate, the book proposes rudimentary yardsticks to evaluate the arguments for and against the proposals. It does so by seeking objectively to test the proposals and responses against classical Anglicanism and its criteria of: (a) scripture, in the light of covenantal theology; (b) tradition, in the light of sacramental theology as expressed canonically (for example baptismal covenant); and (c) reason, in the light of practical experience.[45]

Third, the book compares the Windsor and Nassau proposals, the responses to them, and the St Andrews proposal, with four sets of agreements which may be used as comparative models for the debate: (1) other covenants and agreements in Anglicanism, some historical,[46]

---

42 ACNS 4252 (19-2-2007), Report.

43 Commentary to SADC, para. 1.

44 A cautionary note is necessary about the responses. This study contains many quotations from these, in order for the respondents to speak for themselves. Throughout the book, often a quotation from a response is presented in the text with a reference to its source in a footnote. In the case of responses from dioceses, the quotation is not necessarily the view of the diocese but simply of those who fed the diocese with their own views which the diocese then submitted to the Lambeth Reception Group. The same also applies to the provincial consultation of late 2007 responding to the Nassau report and draft.

45 Richard Hooker placed these in the order: scripture, reason, and tradition: LEP, V.8.2. Some may see Hooker's sequence as signifying for him the relative importance of each.

46 Historical Anglican precedents include the 'Concordate' (1784) between the Diocese of Connecticut (now part of TEC) and Scottish bishops.

some contemporary and enjoying official recognition at a supra-provincial level,[47] and others, increasingly so, of a polemical nature created as a direct consequence of the events which gave rise to the Lambeth Commission,[48] as well as the doctrine of consensual compact in canon law, and what I argue is the 'unwritten covenant' of the current but non-binding global Anglican polity; (2) the experience of ecumenical agreements between churches of different traditions, particularly those involving Anglicans;[49] (3) the agreed instruments of other comparable international ecclesial communities, with particular reference to the Old Catholic Churches of the Union of Utrecht, Standing Conference of Orthodox Churches in the Americas, Lutheran World Federation, World Alliance of Reformed Churches, and Baptist World Alliance; and, where appropriate, (4) the use of concordats and other agreements in church–state relations (especially in Europe), in the light of international law principles on treaties. The book carries extensive footnotes to assist those involved in the debate who wish to consult the materials treated for the purpose of reference and comparison.

---

47 For example, the Covenant for Communion in Mission, of the Inter-Anglican Standing Commission on Mission and Evangelism (2005).

48 While these seek to serve the particular agendas of their authors, they are nonetheless interesting and useful examples of a covenantal approach to Anglican alliances: for example, the Agreement and Organisational Charter of the Anglican Communion Network (2003), and A Covenant Union of Anglican Churches in Concordat (2005).

49 For example, the Methodist-Anglican covenant 2001 in England; Anglican-Lutheran Covenant in Australia 2004; and *Charta Oecumenica* 2001 (between the Conference of European Churches and the Roman Catholic Council of European Bishops' Conferences).

Part 1

The Foundational Ideas of a Covenant

I

The Nature of a Covenant

Until now Anglicans have not needed to define the word 'covenant' for the purposes of their own ecclesial relationships in the Communion. However, they have done so in their ecumenical relations; typically, a covenant is an agreement with another church to share resources, ministry, worship and programmes of outreach.[1] For discussion of the proposed Anglican covenant, various criteria might be used to define 'covenant', such as its purposes, form, subject-matter, or effect: in this sense, each part of this book touches on the nature of a covenant.[2] This chapter, though, deals with the nature of a covenant in terms of its core character, and seeks a definition based on developments stimulated by the Lambeth Commission initiative.[3] The ideas which emerge present a covenant as an agreement, relational, voluntary, promissory and committed. These marks are then tested against scripture, tradition and reason. A clear understanding of the meanings of covenant is essential for the covenant dialogue, particularly so for the Lambeth Conference 2008, as neither the Covenant Design Group in its two reports nor the Primates' *communiqué* 2007 define covenant.[4] In biblical scholar-

---

1 See for example, *For the Sake of the Gospel: Mutual Recognition of Ordained Ministries in the Anglican and Uniting Churches in Australia* (2001) para. 8.3 (local covenants); compare para. 8.10: a 'concordat of communion' is an 'instrument designed to warrant or create full visible communion' at national level. See www.anglican.org.au/docs/FortheSakeofthe_Gospel2001.doc

2 For example, a covenant is an agreement which: aims at unity and common action (Ch. 3); deals with the subject of ecclesiastical relations (Ch. 6); or binds the parties to it (Ch. 9).

3 Several submissions from the provincial consultation in 2007 questioned whether 'covenant' was an appropriate title. In addressing these, the Covenant Design Group at London 2008 discussed alternatives, such as 'concordat' or 'common declaration', and 'finally returned to "covenant" as the best descriptor of the task ahead of us': Commentary, para. 5. See also M. Chapman (ed.), *The Anglican Covenant: Unity and Diversity in the Anglican Communion* (London, Mowbray, 2008) 25: 'it may even have been better to avoid a word which has such a complex and contested religious history.'

4 For the notion that 'the term "covenant" itself is fluid', and for examples of this fluidity (from informal agreement to solemn oath to formal contract), see A. K. Grieb, 'Interpreting the proposed Anglican Covenant through the Communiqué [of the Primates' Meeting, 2007], Episcopal News Service, 19 March 2007 (prepared for the House of Bishops, TEC).

ship, covenant has a range of meanings: relationship, obligation, oath, solemn promise, pact, compact, treaty, alliance, league, constitution, ordinance, agreement and pledge.[5] Interestingly, the Spanish translation of covenant in the Nassau draft is *pacto* (*Un Pacto Anglicano*) and the French, *pacte* (*Un Pacte Anglican*).[6]

A Covenant is a Voluntary Relationship

For the Lambeth Commission, communion is all about mutual relationships between churches (institutional or ecclesial communion) and between individual Christians (personal communion); it is expressed by community, equality, common life, interdependence, and mutual affection and respect.[7] In turn, a covenant would be a 'relational document' which deals with the relationships between the churches of the Communion on the model of a voluntary association.[8] Consequently, the Windsor draft covenant has a section on relationships of communion.[9] Similarly, for *Towards an Anglican Covenant*, 'covenant' is used to translate the nature of a wide variety of relationships. For example, in the Benedictine monastic tradition, members of communities would covenant with God, as their response to his call, to live a common life of discipline through which the true autonomy of each disciple could be realized. Above all, covenants originate in the initiative of God.[10] As the draft submitted to the Covenant Design Group meeting at Nassau by the Anglican Church of Australia refers implicitly to the covenant as freely entered,[11] so the Nassau draft itself speaks of 'the covenant relationship with other member churches', and employs 'covenant' as a verb, which itself underscores the relational aspect of covenanting.[12]

---

5 F. Brown, S. R. Driver, and C. A. Briggs, *A Hebrew and English Lexicon of the Old Testament* (1907). The Latin words *pactum* and *foedus* (in federal theology) and the French *alliance* commonly denote covenant in medieval and reformation theology: see for example, H. J. Hillerbrand (ed.), *The Oxford Encyclopedia of the Reformation*, Vol. I (Oxford, Oxford University Press, 1996) 444. Also F. L. Cross and E. A. Livingstone (eds), *The Oxford Dictionary of the Christian Church* (3rd edn revised, Oxford, Oxford University Press, 2005), 428: 'A bond entered voluntarily by two parties by which each pledges himself to do something for the other.'

6 www.anglicancommunion.org/commission/d_covenant

7 TWR, paras 48, 49.

8 See, respectively, TWR, paras 119, 118 and 12.

9 WDAC, Pt II.

10 TAAC, paras 13, 14

11 ACADC, Art. 18. See also the responses to TAAC, Noll (2006), 2: 'a covenant is relational by definition' and 'based on convictions'; and Ross (2006): 'Covenant is about relationship.'

12 NDC, Arts 1 and 6.6.

The same approach is employed with the St Andrews draft covenant,[13] on the basis that communion life in the Church reflects the communion of the divine life of the Trinity, and that the divine calling into communion is (according to scripture) furthered by God through the making of covenants (with Noah, Abraham, Israel and David).[14]

Several respondents agree. A covenant is a framework for relationships, not an instrument of control; it is a concrete means of unity expressing the importance of relationships – horizontal relationships within the church and vertical relationships with God.[15] For one respondent, a covenant should not just be among provinces but between provinces and God.[16] Moreover, a covenant is a voluntary expression of the *will* to maintain the bonds of unity, and would represent the 'voluntary' responsibility of self-restraint and mutual accountability.[17] The idea is neatly summarized by the Inter-Anglican Standing Commission on Mission and Evangelism (IASCOME): 'Covenants are relational'; they are fundamentally about relationships to which one gives oneself voluntarily, relational between those who are making the covenant and relational with and before God.[18] Though somewhat at odds with orthodox legal theory,[19] IASCOME also distinguishes covenants from contracts: covenants are free-will voluntary offerings from one to another while contracts are legally binding entities with an external locus of authority.[20] Several respondents agree that churches need to be very careful that entry to a covenant is voluntary.[21] Indeed,

---

13 SADC, Preamble: 'We . . . covenant together'; Cl. 3.2.5e: 'covenant relationship'.

14 Introduction to SADC, paras 1 and 2 (this was based on provincial submissions in 2007, particularly that of the Church of England).

15 Bishop Michael Doe (2006); Bishop P. Lynogh (2005); RCW (2005) 7: LCRPR; DAZ, 54–5 (Douglas); 32 (Zahl); V. Atta-Baffoe, 'The Anglican covenant: an African perspective', in Chapman (2008) 143: 'the effect of a covenant rests less on structures and instruments of the Communion and more on relationships across different peoples and cultures in service to the mission of God.'

16 Dioc. of Niagara (2005): LCRPR.

17 Dioc. of Saskatchewan; NIFCON (2005) para. 7: LCRPR; Radner (2005) 617.

18 IASCOME, CCM, p. 7.

19 While it is correct that contracts are binding in the sense that they are enforceable in the civil courts, they are also, like covenants, voluntarily entered: at common law a contract involuntarily entered renders the contract voidable: G. H. Treitel, *The Law of Contract* (11th edn, Thompson, Sweet & Maxwell, London, 2003) 363. This is also a fundamental of the canonical tradition; covenants have a binding character: see below Ch. 9.

20 IASCOME, CCM, p. 7. See also Wales, RNDC (June 2007): 'The idea of a covenant is opposed to that of contract'; covenant involves grace and inclusion, contracts, breaking relationships. Compare, however, K. Wilson, 'The Methodist idea of covenant', in Chapman (2008) 175: 'covenant' refers to 'a voluntary contractual relationship' but 'one will only understand the illuminating perspective of the covenant relationship of God and humankind . . . if it is filled out more sensitively'.

21 Sison (2006) 4: LCRPR.

some fear that the call to covenant at this time is tainted by duress and coercion rather than commitments which Anglicans can freely and honestly make with one another.[22] However, the Archbishop of Canterbury stresses that participation in a covenant must be a free decision by the churches: it would necessarily be an 'opt-in' matter.[23]

That covenant is relational is a biblical concept. It is commonly understood that in scripture covenant is relational, though 'covenant' is not always a synonym for 'relationship'.[24] Covenants establish a 'quasi-familial unity', with rites and cultic acts bringing covenant relationships into being; however, the means of union is not the rites but the agreement based on the pledge they represent.[25] In scripture, 'covenant' translates the Hebrew *berith* and the Greek *diatheke*. In the Old Testament, a covenant is a formalized relation between two parties, and, in the New Testament, Christians enter a new covenant relationship with God through Christ in the Spirit.[26] The salvific covenant issues from the sovereign, gracious, free initiative of God, and its acceptance on the part of humankind requires an inner disposition of the heart.[27] As part of its contribution to the Anglican covenant debate, the Inter-Anglican Theological and Doctrinal Commission

22 Kirker: Open Letter: LCRPR; G. Jones, '"Thy grace shall always prevent . . ."', in A. Linzey and R. Kirker (eds), *Gays and the Future of Anglicanism: Responses to the Windsor Report* (Winchester, O Books, 2005) 116 at 120: it is difficult to determine 'the extent provinces will be compelled to maintain communion via Canterbury, where they might not otherwise elect so to do'. See also M. McCord Adams, 'How to quench the spirit', *Church Times*, 29-10-2004, 9: a covenant would represent an 'institutional structure . . . too close for Anglican comfort to the coercive and authoritarian structures of Rome'.

23 Rowan Williams, *The Challenge and Hope of Being Anglican Today: A Reflection for the Bishops, Clergy and Faithful of the Anglican Communion* (27-06-2006): ACNS 4161: those churches that were prepared to take on a covenant 'as an expression of their responsibility to each other would limit their local freedoms for the sake of a wider witness; and some might not be willing to do this'.

24 P. Kalluveettil, *Declaration and Covenant* (Rome, Biblical Press Institute, 1982), 51, 91, 212: in one way or another it creates unity and community; 'Secular covenant actually means, "relation and obligation, commitment and action"; one cannot separate the idea of relationship from it.' 'The idea, "I am yours, and you are mine" underlies every covenant declaration. This implies a quasi-familial bond which makes sons and brothers. The act of accepting another as one's own reflects the basic idea of covenant: an attempt to extend the bond of blood beyond the kinship sphere, or, in other words, to make a partner one's own flesh and blood'; see also G. P. Hugenberger, *Marriage as a Covenant* (Leiden, E. J. Brill, 1994) 168.

25 D. J. McCarthy, *Old Testament Covenant: A Survey of Current Opinions* (Oxford, Oxford University Press, 1972) 33.

26 TAAC, para. 13; see also A. Goddard, 'Unity and diversity, communion and covenant', in Chapman (2008) 63.

27 ACCT, p. 2 (Biblical Basis of Covenant); P. A. Lillback, 'Covenant', in S. B. Ferguson and D. F. Wright (eds), *New Dictionary of Theology* (Leicester and Illinois, Inter-varsity Press, 1988) 173; Heb. 10.16; Jer. 31.31-34; Isa. 55.3.

focuses on the voluntary-relational elements of covenant in scripture: in the Old Testament, the covenant with Abraham is established on the initiative of God, through gracious and generous love and not on the basis of obligation. In the resultant 'covenant community', people are bound to God and to one another – 'covenant' is used to define the relationship between God and Israel. Moreover, for the Commission, once Anglicans talk of being in covenant with one another, they are reminded of participation in the covenant which God has made with us in Jesus Christ. Indeed: 'the horizontal relationship with one another is dependent, theologically and practically, on the vertical relationship with the creating, loving and reconciling God we know in Jesus and by the Spirit'.[28] This does not mean, however, that the creation of an Anglican covenant would be the development of a covenant between God and the churches of the Communion,[29] and some question the suitability of the title 'covenant' in the Anglican context.[30]

The notion of voluntary relationships based on proper disposition may also be significant for the Anglican covenant debate by virtue of its centrality in the sacramental covenants: in the baptismal covenant candidates experience (relational) adoption as children of God, an external sign of an inward reality, effective when combined with faith; the Eucharist expresses the covenant enacted by Christ at Calvary – in it the faithful are brought into closer communion, not only with the Lord, and with fellow worshippers, but also with the whole Church; and, canonically, marriage and ordination must be free and voluntary.[31]

Anglicans may find reassurance for the idea that a covenant is a voluntary relationship in the experiences of ecumenism and comparable global ecclesial communities. The *Charta Oecumenica* 2001 derives from the voluntary commitments of the participant churches. A new

---

28 *Responding to a Proposal of a Covenant* (October, 2006) (herafter RPC), para. 1.2, 1.3, 1.9, 1.11. See also TAAC, para. 13: Christians are in 'a new covenant relationship with God through the death and resurrection of Jesus, and in the gift of the Spirit'.

29 M. Davie, 'The rationale for the development of an Anglican Covenant', Church of England, General Synod, Agenda Paper, July 2007, Annex 3, commenting on the same idea in IATDC, RPC (October, 2006), para. 1.9: 'There is no sense, of course, that introducing the notion of "covenant" into talk of mutual relationships between Christians implies the establishment of a further "new covenant" over [that] inaugurated by Jesus Christ. Rather, all use of covenantal language in relation to the church today must be seen as a proposal for a specific kind of recommitment within that same covenant, in particular situations and in relation to particular communities.'

30 Southern Africa, RNDC (21-12-2007): it is 'a human attempt at managing unity'; see above n. 3.

31 Thirty-Nine Articles, Art. 27 (baptism); *The Eucharist: Sacrament of Unity*, An occasional paper of the House of Bishops of the Church of England (London, Church Publishing House, 2001); N. Doe, *Canon Law in the Anglican Communion* (Oxford, Clarendon Press, 1998) 128ff., 281.

relationship has been established in the form of a covenant in Anglican–Methodist dialogue. Relationality in the Lutheran-Anglican covenant (Australia) is expressed in mutual recognition of each church that the other belongs to the Church universal. The Australian churches treat their covenantal relationship as one in which the churches are partners on the ecumenical journey in an ongoing process of growing together (covenanting). The signatories were 'impelled' by the two experiences of faith and witness to enter the Lutheran-Anglican-Roman Catholic (Virginia) Covenant 1990. In the Southern Baptist tradition, a local 'covenant . . . defines the relational character of the church body . . . the believers' connectedness with each other'; in it the faithful intentionally define their covenant with God and with each other. Moreover, covenants do not disable other relations: the World Alliance of Reformed Churches does not restrict the relationships between a member church and other churches or with other inter-church bodies.[32] Voluntary relationships are also characteristic of church–state concordats.[33]

A Covenant is an Agreement

The Lambeth Commission does not expressly define a covenant as an agreement, but recommends that if a covenant emerges it must be based on 'agreement'.[34] The Windsor draft covenant simply provides that the churches 'agree' to its terms,[35] as does the draft submitted to the Covenant Design Group by the Anglican Church of Australia.[36] The Nassau report refers to the need for 'an appropriate measure of consent' to its draft and for a covenant to be 'accepted' by the churches as 'partners in this Anglican Covenant',[37] though the St Andrews

---

32 CO 2001, Preamble; AMC:CS (2001) para. 194; Australia: GS resolution, 78/04; ACCT, Preamble; LARC 1990, Preamble; *The Church Constitution Guide*, 6 (hereafter TCCG): North American Mission Board, a Southern Baptist Convention agency: the 'one another' passages in the New Testament indicate the relational character of Christian commitments; a covenant based on these would include relational statements; WARC, Const., Art., 1.3.

33 For the Roman Catholic Church, a concordat regulates relations of church and state in matters of common interest: H. Wagnon, *Concordats et droit international* (Gembloux, Éditions J. Duculot, 1935) 23.

34 TWR, para. 118: and that 'it is imperative for the Communion itself to own . . . the Covenant'.

35 WDAC, Preamble.

36 ACADC, Preamble.

37 Report, paras 8 and 10; NDC, Art. 7 (an expression taken from the Global South suggested covenant, Act of Inauguration Jointly Declared by Covenanting Member Churches of the Anglican Communion – hereafter GSSC – Art. 7 (Our Declaration)).

draft speaks of the churches as 'partakers in this Anglican covenant'.[38] However, *Towards an Anglican Covenant* treats a covenant as an agreed framework for common discernment; it emphasizes the need for an 'agreed text', for agreement in its implementation, and suggests that a covenant could indicate how 'agreement to disagree' might be reached.[39] That a covenant is an 'agreement' appears in a few responses to the proposals,[40] as does the notion that it could represent 'the mind of the Communion', or the 'intention' of each church to be part of the Communion.[41] One respondent considers that a covenant as an agreement (which could deal with matters of common concern) would represent the 'first constitution' of the Anglican Communion.[42] Similarly, the Inter-Anglican Standing Commission on Mission and Evangelism considers that 'a covenant is a serious and significant agreement'.[43] Some have mooted the idea of the development of individual covenants created unilaterally by churches offered to the Archbishop of Canterbury,[44] but others (perhaps paradoxically) fear that a covenant could undermine the consensual element in Anglicanism.[45]

In any event, these ideas resonate with common usage. A covenant is 'a mutual agreement between two or more persons to do or refrain from doing certain acts; a compact, contract, bargain; sometimes, the undertaking, pledge, or promise of one of the parties'.[46] In the Congregationalist tradition, a church covenant is the formal agreement made and subscribed by the members of a church in order to constitute themselves a distinct religious society.[47] Covenant in scripture has been seen as an agreement entered into by the Divine Being with some other being or persons.[48] However, the vertical salvific God–humankind covenant does not readily fit the agreement model; it is rather

---

38 SADC, Our Declaration.

39 TAAC, paras 3, 10, 22, 30.

40 Dioc. of Saskatchewan, sect. 4: LCRPR; see also Davie (2007): 'what is needed is for the churches . . . to reach agreement about what it means to live together as part of God's new covenant community and for them to formally recommit themselves to living in this way. It is this process of agreement and recommitment that the development of an Anglican covenant is intended to assist.'

41 HBTG (2005) 4.1.3: LCRPR.

42 J. Petre, 'Archbishop backs two-track Church to heal divisions', *Daily Telegraph* (19-5-2006).

43 IASCOME, p. 3.

44 A suggestion of the College of Bishops of the Scottish Episcopal Church, Letter of John Stuart, Secretary General to Gregory Cameron (5-12-2006), Response to TAAC.

45 R. A. Greer, 'No easy paths: was Trollope right?', in Linzey and Kirker (eds) (2005) 115.

46 OED, 'Covenant' (n), 1.

47 OED, 'Covenant' (n), 9.b.

48 OED, 'Covenant' (n), 7.

an agreement unilateral in creation but bilateral in accomplishment (grace–faith). Indeed, the Inter-Anglican Theological and Doctrinal Commission avoids the language of agreement in relation to biblical covenants, though it sees the covenant friendship with the Philippians as expressing a 'partnership' to spread the gospel.[49] Nevertheless, the so-called secular covenants in scripture have God as the guarantor of agreements between individuals, including leaders and their people;[50] a covenant could be a non-aggression pact between nations (Gen. 26.26–31), a bond to free slaves (Jer. 34.8–9), an agreement to stand guard (2 Kings 11.4), or a kind of bond (cf. Heb. 7.22; 8.6).

In ecumenical practice a covenant may be an agreement which 'gathers together in pilgrimage . . . churches and Christian communities' in which the parties 'agree', for example, collaboration for more visible unity.[51] The laws of Anglican churches sometimes employ the category 'covenant agreement'.[52] Member churches of international ecclesial communities associate on the basis of agreement. Those of the Lutheran World Federation *agree* in the proclamation of the Word of God, and *acceptance* of its constitution is a prerequisite for membership.[53] The constitution of the Standing Conference of Canonical Orthodox Bishops in the Americas treats itself as an 'agreement'.[54] Members of the Community of Protestant Churches in Europe associate in an 'agreement in the right teaching of the Gospel and in the right administration of the sacraments'.[55] In the Covenant Union of Anglican Churches in Concordat (2005) the signatories 'agree' 'to work together in the common cause of the Gospel'.[56] The scriptural

---

49 RPC, para. 1.5. See also Affirming Catholicism, Response to *Towards an Anglican Covenant* (13-12-2006): 'Further theological reflection is required on the nature of covenant and how a covenant between autonomous churches might differ from a covenant between God and his people.' For the same issue, see A. K. Grieb, 'Interpreting the proposed Anglican covenant through the communiqué [of the Primates' Meeting]', Episcopal News Service (19-3-2007).

50 That is, in agreements between individuals (Gen. 21.22ff.; 1 Kings 2.42–46), leaders who act as representatives of others (Gen. 14.13; 1 Kings 5.26; 2 Sam. 3.13), groups of people (Josh. 9.6), leaders and their subjects (2 Sam. 5.3; 1 Chron. 11.3), an individual and the representatives of a people (Josh. 2), and a priest and military leaders (2 Kings 11.4; 2 Chron. 23.1): Hugenberger (1994) 177.

51 ACCT, pp. 3,7: Covenanting Document, Part B. See generally N. Lossky *et al.* (eds), *Dictionary of the Ecumenical Movement* (Geneva, WCC, 2002) 264. For the TEC-Evangelical Lutheran Church in America concordat as an agreement, see ACNS 4045 (6-10-2005).

52 TEC, Constitution and Canons, Can. I.20.1.

53 LWF, Const., Art. III; Bylaws, 2.

54 SCOBA, Const., (1961), Preamble.

55 Leuenberg Agreement, Preamble, 2.

56 CUACC, Preamble.

concept of a covenant, as treaty-like,[57] is echoed in international law in which a treaty is: 'any international agreement in written form . . . whatever its particular designation (treaty, convention, . . . covenant, charter, statute, act . . . concordat . . . or any other appellation), concluded between two or more States or other subjects of international law and governed by international law'.[58]

However, there is a serious danger if emphasis on the agreement model brings the theological concept of covenant too close to that of a legal contract. Biblical scholars point out that a covenant is not a contract but a personal union pledged by symbol and/or oath: the relationship comes first.[59] Several respondents consider that a covenant will displace consensual relations in Anglicanism with contractual relations,[60] resulting in a legalistic ecclesiology, because, in 'a legal contract, the only pertinent relationship between the parties has to do with the specific matter outlined in the contract itself; there is no love between the parties'.[61] They therefore reject the analogy between covenant and contract: a contract is a bilateral agreement to perform an action which when performed ends the contractual relationship.[62] But for others, a covenant is not 'an enforceable contract, but one with moral authority'.[63] Nevertheless, if a covenant is an agreement, it is similar to a contract. In common usage, 'to covenant' means 'to enter into a covenant or formal agreement; to agree formally or solemnly; to contract'.[64] At common law most contracts take the form of an agreement manifesting mutual assent by each party, marked by offer and acceptance, an intention to create legal relations, the meeting of minds, and equality of bargaining power; in a contract the parties 'make the law for themselves'.[65]

---

57 See, for example, D. J. McCarthy, *Old Testament Covenant*.

58 International Law Commission, Yearbook (1962) ii. 161.

59 D. J. McCarthy, *Treaty and Covenant* (Rome, Biblical Press Institute, 1981) 297.

60 Modern Churchpeople's Union Response to TAAC (J. Clatworthy and P. Bagshaw) (Nov., 2006) 2.

61 H. T. Lewis, 'Covenant, contract and communion' (2005) 601, 604.

62 V. Strudwick (2006b) 'Towards an understanding of the type of Covenant needed for the Churches of the Anglican Communion' (unpublished paper: 2-2-2006); G. Cameron, 'Baby's First Steps: Can the Covenant Proposal Ever Walk?', in Chapman (2008) 35 at 41: the covenant 'is not a contract . . . a binding agreement that churches will perform this or deliver that'; nor is the covenant a confession or a code; see also Goddard 2008) 68.

63 Dioc. of Saskatoon (2006): LCRPR.

64 OED, 'Covenant' (v), 1.

65 A. G. Guest (ed.), *Anson's Law of Contract* (24th edn, Oxford, Clarendon Press, 1975) 1–4; E. A. Martin (ed.), *Oxford Dictionary of Law* (5th edn, Oxford, Oxford University Press, 2003) 114.

These contractual marks surface in contemporary church agreements.[66] The Anglican Consultative Council may alter its membership with the assent of two-thirds of the primates of the Communion.[67] The Memorandum of Agreement of the Anglican Communion Network (2003), which unites like-minded dioceses and congregations, is the result of its signatory bishops 'being of common mind' about their strategy for the current situation in TEC; they 'agree to associate' and this agreement may be amended by subsequent agreement.[68] Similarly, the agreement of the Community of Protestant Churches in Europe is based on a 'common understanding' of the gospel which enables churches party to it to engage in fellowship.[69] Membership of the World Alliance of Reformed Churches is conditional upon acceptance of scripture, as the supreme authority in matters of faith and life, and its Constitution.[70] In the Southern Baptist tradition, the parties 'intentionally define their covenant with God and with each other',[71] an agreement or mutual obligation, contracted deliberately and with solemnity.[72] Churches enter agreements on the basis of equality.[73] For the Roman Catholic Church, concordats are juridical 'agreements' to fulfil the respective objectives of church and state: a concordat is a law based on a union of wills.[74] All these instruments employ contract-like concepts and vocabulary.

A Covenant is an Exchange of Promises

The Lambeth Commission does not identify the promissory nature of a covenant; but it does consider that communion involves 'a covenant

---

66 Kilcoy Covenant (2001): the parties share a 'common intention'.

67 Const., Art. 3.a.

68 ACN: Memorandum of Agreement, Preamble; Organizational Charter, Preamble.

69 Leuenberg Agreement, Preamble.

70 WARC, Const., Art. II.1; By-Laws, I.1.

71 TCCG, p.6. For the 'one another passages', p. 8.

72 Piper, 'Why a church covenant?' (1993), http://www.desiringgod.org/library/ sermons

73 SCOBA, Const., Art. II(a)3: 'Autocephalous Churches, represented in the Standing Conference, are recognizing each other as equal sister Orthodox Churches with equal canonical rights.'

74 *Letter and Spirit: A Practical Guide to the Code of Canon Law*, The Canon Law Society of Great Britain and Ireland (Dublin, Veritas, 1995) para. 7 (p. 2); *The New Advent Catholic Encyclopedia*, 'Concordat': a concordat is 'an agreement, or union of wills . . . in regard to matters which in some way concern both the Church' and the state, 'possessing the force of a treaty entered into by both the ecclesiastical and civil power and to a certain degree binding upon both' (www.newadvent.org/cathen/04196a).

relation of binding mutual promises'.[75] Nor does the Windsor draft covenant contain explicit pledges. Indeed, the Covenant Design Group conceives of covenant as a means by which the churches would serve the great promises of God in Christ rather than as an exchange of promises between the churches, though its use of commitments in the St Andrews draft covenant has connotations of pledges.[76] However, the Australian draft submitted to the Group at its Nassau meeting uses the language of 'undertakings',[77] and *Towards an Anglican Covenant* proposes that, as the biblical covenant holds out a promise by God which is fulfilled in the faithful response of his people, so it seems appropriate that the churches build on the idea of a promise from God that we shall be led to truth and unity; and in the canonical tradition a covenant involves a promise given to commit to a certain course of action, to live in a relationship with the person to whom a binding promise is made.[78]

Responses to the proposals elicit few ideas of covenant as promissory. While one respondent suggests the adoption of a scriptural model of covenant in which the common feature appears to be a promise from God (which requires a response from those people who covenant obedience to him),[79] another thinks the Windsor draft covenant is about relationships on the basis of promises and law rather than communion.[80] One idea emerging following the Nassau report, is that a covenant, initiated by God, is about 'promise-making and promise-keeping in the world', and that 'communion [itself] . . . is the promise – the calling'.[81] A covenant is 'a promise to behave in a certain way,

---

75 TWR, para. 45.

76 CDG, Nassau Report, para. 16, and SADC, Cls.1.1,2.1,3.1; Martin (2003) 19: to affirm is 'to promise in solemn form to tell the truth while giving evidence or making an *affidavit*'; see also F. L. Cross and E. A. Livingstone (eds), *The Oxford Dictionary of the Christian Church* (3rd edn, revised, Oxford, Oxford University Press, 2005) 23.

77 ACADC, Art. 30: 'the undertakings made by entering into this covenant'; see also Arts 11 and 18.

78 TAAC, paras 13, 16, 20.

79 V. Strudwick, 'Toward an Understanding of the type of Covenant needed for the Churches of the Anglican Communion' (unpublished paper, 2006): 'The requirement will be to recognise a Scriptural promise, which in the context of our Anglican heritage we are committed to respond to in a particular way. The Scriptural promise of Our Lord which is set out in John 15 and 16 articulates an understanding of the Holy Spirit as enabling the created order to become what it was intended to be, and speaks of empowering the church in its life and worship by the release of creative activity, to engage in the search for truth and unity – an eschatological activity culminating in the Kingdom. The promise is to the Church, our obedience is to engage together in its life and worship, and the Covenant is an opportunity to declare that we recognise and commit ourselves, to this understanding and process.'

80 TEC, Sect. 4: LCRPR.

81 E. Radner, 'Steps towards the covenant', a presentation to the House of Bishops of

a solemn undertaking by one to adopt a particular attitude towards another'.[82] As such, the inclusion of a 'pattern' of affirmations in the Nassau draft covenant has been welcomed.[83] Indeed, the Concordat 1784 between the Diocese of Connecticut and the Scottish Bishops describes itself as a *bond* of peace in which the parties 'agree' to the terms of their communion relationship.[84]

On the one hand, the language of promises once more brings the covenant close to the notion of contract. Common usage sees a covenant as a promise, a testimony, a vow, and, sometimes, more than a promise but less than an oath.[85] If a covenant is promissory, it has much in common with a contract. In the canonical tradition, a contract (*pactum*) is an act with an acceptable purpose (*causa*) which involves at least two parties and is based on an undertaking and its acceptance.[86] At common law, a contract may be constituted out of nothing more than an exchange of promises; the law merely determines the circumstances in which a promise is legally binding.[87] The doctrine of consideration, which itself has canonical antecedents, provides that the promise must give something of value in return for that promise.[88] Consideration, the mutual exchange of promises, is a necessary element of contract.[89] As in theology,[90] in law a promise is a declaration or assurance that a certain state of affairs exists, or that its maker will do, or refrain from,

---

TEC on the proposed Anglican Covenant' (19-3-2007). See also Seitz (2007) for promises and pledges.

82 Cameron, in Chapman (2008) 43.

83 Australia, Standing Committee, RNDC (2007).

84 P. A. E. Thomas, 'Unity and concord: an early Anglican "Communion"', *Journal of Anglican Studies* (2004) 9 at 14: Concordat, Art. 6.

85 OED, 'Covenant': 1587 Golding, De Mornay, xxxiii. 541: 'The Gospels, the Acts, and the Epistles, all which together we calle the newe Couenant or the newe Testament'; 1643 Caryl, Sacr. Covt. 7: 'A Covenant . . . is more than a promise, and less than an Oath.' A covenant can be: 'A promise made to oneself, a solemn personal resolve, a vow' (Obs): c.1385 Chaucer, L.G.W. 688 Cleopatra: 'And in myn self this couenaunt made I tho, ffor right swich as ze feldyn wel or wo The same wolde I felen, life or dethe.'

86 A. W. B. Simpson, *A History of the Common Law of Contract* (Oxford, Clarendon Press, 1987) 386.

87 J. Poole, *Textbook on Contract* (6th edn, London, Oxford University Press, 2001) 1; Guest (1975) 2.

88 Simpson (1987) 375; *Wichals v Johns* (1599) Cro. Eliz. 703, Popham CJ (Fifoot, 400): 'each party's promise being a detriment as it was a "charge" upon him': 'there is a mutual promise, the one to the other: so that, if the plaintiff does not [perform his promise], the defendant may have his action against him; and a promise against a promise is a good consideration.'

89 Poole (2001) 13: 'Perhaps the consideration doctrine is no more than a trace of the Protestant work ethic in the common law: a rule against getting something for nothing.'

90 J. F. Childress, 'Promise', in J. F. Childress and J. MacQuarrie (eds), *A New Dictionary of Christian Ethics* (London, SCM Press, 1986) 505: it is 'a person's declaration [to] do or refrain from doing what has been specified'.

some specific act, conferring on the person to whom the promise is made a right to fulfilment of the declaration or assurance.[91]

On the other hand, the notion of a 'promise', 'pledge' or 'undertaking' is also a key element of biblical covenants. God takes the initiative with a conditional promise which specifies attainable blessings and sets out the terms for people to receive them; and humans accept or reject these. The covenant in scripture is a 'relationship of mutual commitment created by exchange of promises'.[92] In the Old Testament, the essence of covenant is captured in the summary promise of God: 'I will be your God, and you shall be my people' (Gen. 17.7; Exod. 6.7; 2 Cor. 6.16; Rev. 21.2–3).[93] The promissory element of the new covenant appears in the words of Jesus: 'If you abide in me and my words abide in you, ask for whatever you wish, and it will be done for you' (John 15.8). The new covenant promises the ability to keep covenants as one of its greatest benefits (2 Cor. 3.3–6; Heb. 8.10; 10.16; 13.20–21), which of course include justification and sanctification (Heb. 9.10–12; 10.15–18; 13.20–21).[94]

Needless to say, promises are key features of the baptismal covenant (in which the candidate undertakes fidelity to the faith), the marriage covenant (in which each party vows fidelity to the other), and the ordination covenant (in which the candidate promises to serve as an example to the flock of Christ).[95] They are also a feature of contemporary ecclesial agreements, such as the 'pledges' in the Covenant for Communion and Mission,[96] or the Covenant Union of Anglican Churches in Concordat (2005): the signatories 'pledge' to each other their mutual co-operation, support, discipline and accountability.[97] Much the same idea appears in ecumenical covenants, such as the Anglican-Lutheran Covenant in Australia in which the parties pledge to

---

91 Guest (1975) 2.

92 D. Tripp, 'Covenant', in G. S. Wakefield (ed.), *A Dictionary of Christian Spirituality* (London, SCM Press, 1983), 98; Hugenberger (1994) 169.

93 Lillback (1988) 173; see also IATDC, RPC (2006) para. 1.3: 'The covenant with Abraham is then dramatically developed as God fulfils a promise made in Genesis 15, namely that he would rescue Abraham's family from slavery in Egypt.'

94 Lillback (1988) 174.

95 Book of Common Prayer 1662, 263, 301, 553. See also OED: Book of Common Prayer 1549, Matrimony: 'So these persons may surely perfourme and kepe the vowe and covenaunt betwixt them made'; 1611 Bible, Gen. 21.27: 'And Abraham tooke sheepe and oxen, and gaue them unto Abimelech: and both of them made a couenent.' 1644 Direct. Publ. Worship in Scobell Acts and Ord. I.li (1658) 87: 'Who are now to be joined in the Honourable Estate of Marriage, the Covenant of their God.'

96 IASCOME, CCM, p. 9: 'we pledge ourselves' to, for example, recognize Jesus in each other's contexts and lives; to support one another in mission; and to encourage expressions of new life.

97 CUACC (2005), Art. I.

work together to develop joint participation in mission and witness; they 'solemnly covenant together' and 'undertake' to continue to work towards a Concordat for full communion and reconciliation of ministries.[98] Affirmations of will are standard usage for contracting parties in church–state concordats.[99]

A Covenant Generates Commitments

For the Lambeth Commission, theologically, communion clearly makes demands on all within it; it involves obligations, and corresponding rights.[100] Under the St Andrews draft covenant (like the Nassau text) the churches would 'commit' themselves to its objects; this echoes both the view of the Covenant Design Group that communion entails 'responsibilities' and the Windsor draft covenant which had a separate section on 'commitments of communion' – however, the Australian draft covenant, submitted to the Group for its meeting in 2007 did not expressly employ the language of 'commitment'.[101] *Towards an Anglican Covenant* clearly speaks of covenants in terms of commitment.[102] Several responses to the *Windsor Report* associate covenant with commitment: a covenant is an agreement which 'stretches' our mutual commitments, and would enable a fresh commitment.[103] Covenantal commitment is a necessary part of Christian discipleship: that is, learning to accept the constraints of living within a community the decisions of which may not be agreed by all, itself part of the baptismal vocation of dying to self and rising to a new life within the body of Christ.[104] Similarly, the consensual character of what unites the member churches in communion with one another implies certain obligations.[105] For the Archbishop of Canterbury a covenant would involve

---

98 ALCA, GS Res. 78/04; see also ACCT, p.11, Part C: The Future Pledge: the churches 'pledge', for example, 'to continue to discuss and articulate within our churches the meaning and significance of our involvement in the quest for a more visible expression of unity and the possibilities for further engagement in ecumenical partnership'.

99 Concordat between the Holy See and the Republic of Poland (1993), Art. 11: 'Les parties contractantes affirment leur volonté de collaborer pour défendre et respecter l'institution du mariage et de la famille, fondement de la société.'

100 TWR, para. 51.

101 For example, SADC, Cls. 1.2, 2.2, 3.2; NDC, Arts 3 (our commitment to confession of the faith), 4.4 and 5, and 6; WDAC, Pt. III; see also Introduction to SADC, para. 3 (for responsibilities).

102 TAAC, paras 16, 20: in civil law 'a covenant is a binding commitment to behave in certain ways'.

103 CPIO (2005) para. 7; Sudan, para. 3: LCRPR.

104 HBTG (2005) 3.7.2 (Rom. 6.1–14; 1 Cor. 12.12–26): LCRPR.

105 Greer (2005) 111.

formal commitments.[106] The 'pattern' of commitments in a covenant had been welcomed.[107]

These theological ideas have a distinct juridical dimension. The principle in the canonical tradition that a promise, with or without an oath, is binding,[108] has influenced both international law, in which a treaty is a source of *obligation*,[109] and the common law of contract,[110] in which the mere fact of a promise (or voluntary undertaking) produces obligation.[111] A promise is a surrender of freedom, and becomes an enforceable commitment if made for some good reason or consideration (classical view) and if it is relied upon (modern view).[112] In medieval common law, a mere unilateral promise if made under seal was actionable by writ of covenant.[113] More importantly, biblical scholarship defines a covenant as a 'mutual commitment created by exchange of promises', importing self-imposed obligations.[114] The covenantal promises of God, realized on fulfilment of certain conditions by humankind, put God under obligation.[115] The salvific covenant is sometimes seen as a community

---

106 Williams, 'Challenge and hope' (27-6-2006).

107 Australia, Standing Committee, RNDC (2007).

108 R. H. Helmholz, *The Canon Law and Ecclesiastical Jurisdiction from 597 to the 1640* (Oxford, Oxford University Press, 2004) 361 (esp. n.27). See also Roman Catholic *Code of Canon Law* 1983, c. 1290, and below Ch. 9 for *pacta sunt servanda*.

109 H. Thirlway, 'The sources of international law', in N. Evans (ed.), *International Law* (Oxford, Oxford University Press, 2003) 117 at 121–2: it is 'the basis for the binding nature of treaties. The whole point of making a binding agreement is that each of the parties should be able to rely on performance of the treaty by the other party or parties, even when such performance may have become onerous or unwelcome to such other party or parties. Thus a treaty is one of the most evident ways in which rules binding on two or more States may come into existence.'

110 Guest (1975) 2: '[a] promise is more than a mere statement of intention, for it imports a willingness on the part of the promisor to be bound to the person to whom it is made'; if the intention of the parties is to create an obligation between them (that is, to impose a duty on the promisor to fulfil the promise), this confers a right on the promisee to claim the fulfilment: this is a social, moral and legal obligation rooted not least in the expectation that the promise will be fulfilled.'

111 P. Fried, *Contract as Promise: A Theory of Contractual Obligation* (Cambridge, Mass. Harvard University Press, 1981) 14–17: 'there is a moral obligation inherent in promising which is derived from the social convention of creating expectations by one's undertaking.'

112 H. L. A. Hart, 'Are there any natural rights?', *Philosophical Review* 64 (1955) 175; P. S. Atiyah, *Promises, Morals and Law* (Oxford, Clarendon Press, 1981).

113 Guest (1975) 11.

114 Tripp (1983) 98; Hugenberger (1994) 169, 173: for self-imposed examples: Gen. 14.13; Exod. 23.32; Deut. 7.2.

115 J. D. Davis, *The Westminster Dictionary of the Bible* (Revised edn, London, Collins, 1944) 118; God says to Moses: 'Behold, I make a covenant. Before all your people I will do marvels such as have not been wrought in all the earth' (Exod. 34.10); and God says to David: 'I have made a covenant with my chosen one, I have sworn to David my servant, I will establish your descendants for ever, I will build your throne for

of justice characterized by obedience to live in the Spirit.[116] According to one respondent, as scriptural covenants are stipulative, so it is that stipulations in an Anglican covenant might be conceived as 'responses to a gift and flow from, and are co-ordinated with, those stipulations that provide the gracious inner nerve . . . of prior covenants'; they do not update or replace them, but live alongside them.[117] In sacramental theology too a personal covenant (such as in baptism) is a commitment of the individual soul to God.[118] The notion that covenant involves commitments is clearly recognized by the Inter-Anglican Theological and Doctrinal Commission.[119]

That a covenant is a commitment generated by promises is a key feature of Anglican agreements. The covenantal Lambeth Quadrilateral commits Anglicans to a series of normative practices: scripture is read; tradition is received; sacramental worship is practised; and the historic character of apostolic leadership is retained.[120] The Memorandum of Agreement of the Anglican Communion Network (2003) provides that the network is to be known for its commitment to evangelical faith and catholic order; and its Charter spells out its commitments: to propagate the gospel and the formation of disciples; to full membership in the Anglican Communion; and to work for the reunion of what it styles the Anglican diaspora in North America.[121] The same idea also surfaces in contemporary ecumenical covenants:

---

all generations' (Ps. 89.3–4). In the Old Testament, 'commitment' is a translation of the Hebrew *hesed*: 'loyalty' or 'steadfastness' in particular 'steadfast love': T. G. Watkin, 'The concept of commitment in law and legal science', in P. R. Beaumont (ed.), *Christian Perspectives on Human Rights and Legal Philosophy* (Carlisle, Paternoster Press, 1998) 95 (hereafter Watkin 1998); see also K. D. Sakenfeld, *Faithfulness in Action in Biblical Perspective* (Philadelphia, Fortress Press, 1985).

116 P. J. Gräbe, *New Covenant – New Community: The Significance of Biblical and Patristic Covenant Theology for Contemporary Understanding* (Carlisle, Paternoster Press, 2005) 214.

117 Seitz (2007).

118 Tripp (1983) 99: 'The covenant pattern of ideas is found in initiation, Jewish and Christian; instruction-decision-admission is the plan of Jewish proselyte baptism, adopted by the Christian baptismal liturgy. Renewal, re-affirmation, or appropriation of baptismal vows is typical of monastic, reforming or renewal movements.'

119 RPC (2006), paras.1.3: 'The prophets regularly call Israel back to the obligations of the covenant, obligations both to God and to one another'; see also 1.6 on covenant as involving obedience; and 1.8 on 're-commitment': see also Ch. 3 below.

120 TWR, para. 51, n. 21 (IATDC).

121 ACN: Organizational Charter, Arts III, IV. The draft constitution of the Anglican Global Initiative requires its members to be 'committed' to the purposes of this organization, the historic Anglican formularies as essential to Anglican identity, and the ultimate authority of the Holy Scriptures: Draft Const., Art. IV. See also A Covenant Statement of the House of Bishops, TEC, Camp Allen, Texas, 15-3-2005: para. 1 on its 'commitment to the Chicago-Lambeth Quadrilateral'.

the Anglican-Methodist Covenant and *Charta Oecumenica* consist of commitments, and in the Anglican-Lutheran Covenant in Australia the 'Anglican Church formally commits itself to enter into this Covenant with the Lutheran Church'.[122] The same applies to the agreements of international ecclesial communities. The constitution of the World Alliance of Reformed Churches commits the church parties (*inter alia*) to the purposes of the Alliance,[123] and that of the American Orthodox bishops commits their Conference to comply with its decisions.[124] In Protestant covenantal theology, a covenant is the mutual commitment of members of a gathered church.[125]

Finally, the idea of commitment to the Church universal is common in the laws of the churches of the Anglican Communion (more so than commitment to the Communion itself). Different images are used to convey the relationship. Some churches see themselves as '*a branch* of the One Holy Catholic and Apostolic Church of Christ'.[126] Others declare themselves 'an integral *portion* of the one Body of Christ composed of Churches which [are] united under the One Divine Head and in the fellowship of the One Holy Catholic and Apostolic Church',[127] or 'a partner ... in the universal Church'.[128] The understanding of the Church of England is that it *belongs* to the true and apostolic Church of Christ.[129] Equally, laws express the commitment of fidelity to catholicity and apostolicity in faith, sacraments and ministry.[130] Churches pledge themselves to uphold and propagate the Catholic and

---

122 AMC, Commitments, 1–6; CO, I–III; ALCA, GS Res. 78/04; see also ACCT, p. 2: the covenant requires 'a constant, solid commitment in the circumstances of life. Within the one faith community – the Body of Christ – there is a mutual responsibility and solidarity with one another for the fulfilment of this commitment.' The first assembly of the World Council of Churches 1948 stated: 'we have committed ourselves afresh to [God] and have covenanted with one another in constituting the World Council of Churches': Lossky *et al.* (2002) 264.

123 WARC, Const., Art. III (1–9): to further proclamation of the Word of God; to order life and worship in obedience to this; to further the work of evangelism, mission and stewardship; to help fellow member churches in the service of Christ; and to promote and defend religious and civil liberties wherever threatened throughout the world.

124 SCOBA, Const., Art. II(a)1: 'All decisions of the Conference shall require two-thirds approval of the member hierarchs present at a regular or special meeting to become binding on the Conference.'

125 Tripp (1983) 99.

126 Scottish Episcopal Church, Can. 1.1.

127 Canada, Const., Declaration of Principles, 1.

128 Anglican Church of Canada, Mission Statement.

129 Can. A1.

130 Indeed, it has been understood in civil law that: 'the identity of a religious community described as a Church must consist in the unity of its doctrines', which 'bind them together as one Christian community': *Free Church of Scotland (General Assembly) v Overtoun (Lord)* [1904] AC 515.

Apostolic faith and order.[131] The employment of guarantees expresses commitments in church–state concordats.[132]

Conclusion

The Windsor process does not yield a systematic theology of the nature of an ecclesial covenant. Nevertheless, it implies four basic *indicia*: a covenant is a voluntary relationship responsive to God embodied in an agreement involving an exchange of solemn promises which generate commitments. These definitional elements would not seem theologically exceptional. They appear in general ways as aspects of understandings of the salvific divine–human covenant, initiated by God promising committed (vertical) relations with humans (who may/may not accept or participate in it), and with (horizontal) consequences for human relations. It could be useful to see an ecclesial covenant as working within the framework of, but not the same as, the salvific covenant. Sacramental covenants, with similar vertical and horizontal aspects, are likewise voluntary, relational, promissory, committed and agreed (accepted). Though more horizontal than vertical, the same might be said of contemporary ecclesiastical Anglican agreements, ecumenical covenants and instruments of other comparable global church communities. However, an ecclesial covenant also emerges as both a theological and a juridical category. Covenants are not contracts, but they have a contractual dimension, sharing fundamental similarities with contracts; they are juridical vehicles for spiritual relationships. The challenge for the Communion is to develop an understanding of covenant which recognizes this, not thereby displacing the theological integrity of a covenant, but using the elements of scriptural, sacramental and ecclesiastical models as living theological definitions of covenant.

---

131 Australia, Const. I.I.1–3: 'The Anglican Church of Australia, being a part of the One Holy Catholic and Apostolic Church of Christ, holds the Christian Faith', receives the scriptures, and 'will ever obey the commands of Christ, teach His doctrine, administer His sacraments, follow and uphold His discipline and preserve the three orders of bishops, priests and deacons in the sacred ministry.'
132 Concordat between the Holy See and the Republic of Poland (1993) Art. 5.

2

The Employment of a Covenant

The proposal of the Lambeth Commission to use a covenant as a foundation for long-term relations between churches of the Anglican Communion presupposes that the figure of a covenant is consistent with the character of Anglicanism. This chapter explores whether this presupposition is sustainable.[1] Fundamentally, the matter is a question of observable fact rather than an issue of ecclesiastical policy. Several responses to the covenant proposals suggest that the use of a covenant would express the current consensual character of the Communion, but others consider that a covenant would be repugnant to the spirit of Anglicanism. The chapter tests these claims in the light of Anglican practice. Using the definition of covenant which emerged in Chapter 1, the following also deals with the incidence of the concept of covenant, and the range of covenantal models available, in scripture, the tradition of sacramental theology (for example, in baptism and marriage), and the experiences of the contemporary employment of covenants, concordats and other agreements in ecumenism and by comparable international church communities.

The Covenantal Character of Anglicanism

The Lambeth Commission proposes that communion at global level involves Anglicans sharing in 'double bonds of affection': those that flow from their shared status as children of God in Christ, and those that arise from their shared and inherited identity, which is the particular history of the churches to which they belong. This Communion is a relationship of 'covenantal affection'. That is: 'our mutual affection is not subject to whim and mood, but involves us in a covenant relation of binding mutual promises, with God in Christ and with one another'.[2] In this relationship, those saved by grace through faith in the

---

1 Prior to the Lambeth Conference in 2008, three of the four Instruments of Communion have affirmed the desirability of a covenant: Commentary to SADC, para. 4.

2 TWR, para. 45.

31

gospel are to live as a united family across traditional ethnic and other boundaries.[3] Rooted in the Trinitarian life and purposes of God, the covenantal relationship is the practical embodiment and fruit of the gospel,[4] in which unity, communion and holiness all belong together; it enables Anglicans (with all Christians), in 'mutual interdependence', to advance the mission of God. In the voluntary association that is the Anglican Communion, a *formal* covenant would seek to 'make explicit and forceful the . . . bonds of affection' and 'incarnate' the existing covenantal relationship.[5] *Towards an Anglican Covenant* also recognizes that the covenant relationship with God generates a covenantal relationship between his people, and that a formal covenant might articulate the principles of co-operation and interdependence, 'the bonds of affection', which hold the Communion together.[6]

The Covenant Design Group Nassau report maintains that by the grace of God Anglicans have been given the Communion of their churches through which to respond to God's larger calling in Christ (Acts 2.42); life together reflects the blessings of God in growing the Communion into a truly global family.[7] In other words, communion is the theological basis of any covenant.[8] These ideas resurface in the St Andrews report which also proposes a Trinitarian understanding of the foundations of communion so that life in the church is seen as 'caught up in the mystery of divine communion'.[9] Whereas the Windsor draft speaks of the Communion as a 'community', like the Nassau text the St Andrews draft covenant refers to it as a 'worldwide family of interdependent churches'.[10] However, unlike the draft submitted by the Anglican Church in Australia, the Nassau draft makes no mention of the 'bonds of affection' – but the St Andrews text does: each

---

3 Eph. 2.1–22: TWR, Section A (sub-heading) and para. 2.

4 1 Cor. 1.9; TWR, para. 4.

5 TWR, paras 1–3, 46, 119, 120. See Ch. 3 below for unity and identity as objects of a covenant.

6 TAAC, paras 1, 13.

7 Nassau Report, paras 15 and 16; see also TEC, Executive Council, RNDC (28-10-2007); and England, RNDC (21-12-2007): there is a need to link the Anglican Communion to the theme of creation (along the lines of TWR, para. 2).

8 E. Radner (Covenant Design Group member), 'Steps towards the covenant', a presentation to the House of Bishops of TEC (19-3-2007). See also CDG Commentary to SADC, para. 6: 'theologically, we believe it is correct to say that covenant emerges out of communion.'

9 Introduction to SADC, paras 1 and 2 (communion and covenant); para. 4 (church families); para. 7: life together reflects 'the blessings of God in growing our Communion into a truly global family'.

10 SADC, Cl. 2.1.2; and 2.1.1: communion is a gift of God; WDAC, Art. 7.1 (community); NDC, Art. 4.2 (a family bound together by the Holy Spirit who calls and enables Anglicans to live in mutual loyalty and service); Art. 4.1 (communion is a gift of God); see also WDAC, Art. 6; NDC, Art. 5.2.

church commits itself 'to have in mind that our bonds of affection and the love of Christ compel us always to seek the highest possible degree of communion'.[11] For the Inter-Anglican Theological and Doctrinal Commission too the notion of 'bonds of affection' remains central to any appropriate understanding of the shared communion in Anglicanism; indeed, it is out of this relational understanding of worldwide Anglicanism that the proposal for a covenant has now grown, and it is in this sense that the proposal should be understood.[12] According to some, communion itself *is* a covenant,[13] and the proposal for a covenant is an opportunity for the remaking of Anglicanism by developing a covenantal ecclesiology.[14]

Many responses agree with, and accept the value of, the proposition that relationships in the Anglican Communion are covenantal. Some applaud the proposal for an Anglican covenant, and consider it is high time that the Communion is held together by a concrete means of unity.[15] First, the basis of the idea is that Anglicans share a 'family likeness'; the Communion is characterized by 'a family-like mutuality'. Indeed, through globalization, pluralism, and the fall of colonialism, today the Communion is a 'multicultural family of churches' which has called into question often unexamined assumptions of what Anglicanism means.[16] Second, the idea of covenant reflects that Anglicans are part of a global family.[17] The Communion is an extended family, and each province is a nuclear family within the larger system; dispa-

---

11 SADC, Cl. 3.2.6; ACADC, Preamble. This was a point raised by the Joint Standing Committee of the Primates' Meeting and ACC in its discussion of the Nassau draft covenant.

12 RPC (2006), paras 1.10 and 1.11.

13 Grieb (2007); see also A Response to the Draft Anglican Covenant from the Standing Committee of the Diocese of Virginia: 'We affirm that we already have a covenant initiated by our gracious God, unmerited, unearned and undeserved, as revealed to us in Holy Scripture . . . The covenant we share with one another as a gift of the Triune God has been long expressed in the Nicene Creed and in the ancient baptismal confession of the Apostles' Creed.'

14 T. Dakin, 'Reflections on the Anglican covenant: some ecumenical and missional perspectives' (June 2007) (Anglican Institute Website): moreover: 'This would fundamentally affect the historical, "accidental", way in which Anglicanism identity has emerged and significantly change our understanding of the nature of episcopacy.'

15 A Statement of the Global South Primates, Nairobi, 27/28-1-2005 (hereafter GSPN (2005)) para. 12; and Bishop P. Lynogh (2005): LCRPR.

16 IATDC: http://www.aco.org/documents/iatdc/four questions/english.html; Mac-Dougall (2005) 12; DAZ, 6-18; and TEC, RNDC (28-10-2007): what was a colonial expression of Anglicanism is becoming a postcolonial worldwide communion characterized by globalization and pluralism.

17 Advent Letter, Archbishop of Canterbury, ACNS, 4354 (14-12-2007); see also J. Gladwin, 'The local and the universal and the meaning of Anglicanism: Kenya', in K. Stevenson (ed.), *A Fallible Church: Lambeth Essays* (London, Darton, Longman & Todd, 2008) 3 at 5 (on the variety of practices in the Anglican family).

rate groups have been held in harmony by a bond and covenant among Anglicans, and it is hoped that 'we might restore a sense of covenant to our common life'.[18] Third, many visualize the Communion as a voluntary association, and that what binds Anglicans together is at present purely consensual in character.[19] Throughout our lives, 'we enter into some kind of covenant . . . not only between God and the people of God, but also between ourselves and other human beings'; the notion of a covenant relationship accords with 'our own . . . experiences'.[20] But Anglicans need to ground this voluntary association of the churches in a theological vision of the Body of Christ as a communion in mission.[21] Consensual covenant is foundational in classical Anglicanism.[22]

For some respondents, however, the employment of a covenant is not the Anglican way, and is at odds with the spirit of Anglicanism: it would do away with the idea of a family, of federation, of communion that has characterized this global partnership of witness.[23] The covenant proposal, for 'a new polity' for the Communion, is 'one that translates the poetry of mutual affection and nostalgia for Canterbury into institutional structures that move in the direction of international canon law'.[24] Others criticize the use of a covenant on the basis that the Communion is not a single entity: technically, it is a fellowship which manifests itself in four Instruments, namely, the Archbishop of Canterbury, the Lambeth Conference, the Anglican Consultative Council and the Primates' Meeting. Rather, covenantal communion is found within local churches, but it is not the kind of communion that should be found in an international association of churches. A global covenant would represent the unity of man-made institutions and structures, a Babylonian unity which would fall under God's judgement. Instead, the way forward is a union through the Spirit with God and with one another, not denominational amalgamation.[25] The use of a covenant:

18 H. T. Lewis, 'Covenant, contract, and communion: reflections on a Post-Windsor Anglicanism', *Anglican Theological Review* 87 (2005) 601 at 602, 604, 607.

19 E. Radner, 'Freedom and covenant: the Miltonian analogy transfigured', *Anglican Theological Review* 87 (2005) 609 at 616; R. A. Greer, 'No easy paths: was Trollope right?', in Linzey and Kirker (eds) (2005) 100 at 109–10.

20 H. T. Lewis (2005) 602; CCW (2005) para. 2.4: LCRPR.

21 Church Mission Society (31-1-2005) (hereafter CMS (2005)): LCRPR.

22 Hooker, LEP, Bk. I.15.2: the church represents the natural inclination of people to 'sociable life' and their 'consent to some certain bonds of association'; also, 'as it is a society supernatural', 'that part of the bond of their association which belong to the church of God must be a law supernatural'; for know too: 'the fundamental law of any Christian polity originated in a divine-human covenantal agreement . . . on the model of the covenants made by God with Israel.'

23 British Columbia, s. 4; MacDougall (2005) 5, 14–15: LCRPR.

24 M. McCord Adams, 'Faithfulness in crisis', in Linzey and Kirker (eds) (2005) 70.

25 N. Cameron, 'The Windsor Report 2004: legal implications', FOFAD, 49; P. Adam,

represents a policy of containment; it is crisis-driven, a 'technical fix', a 'quick-fix'; it is an admission of the defeat of the bonds of affection, a marriage of convenience, not a well-thought-out plan.[26] While the rigour of an adoption process would suggest the proposal is a long-term matter (see Chapter 7), the Lambeth Commission itself concedes the project is in part crisis-driven.[27]

The Use of Covenants in Anglicanism

The Lambeth Commission does not offer historical precedents for its proposal,[28] but *Towards an Anglican Covenant* notes the *Concordate* of 1784, between Samuel Seabury, for the diocese of Connecticut, and the Scottish bishops to define the communion between those two ecclesial communities.[29] Several respondents, however, propose that the figure of a covenant is part of historical Anglican usage: since the time of Richard Hooker, Anglicanism has been covenantal.[30] The Inter-Anglican Theological and Doctrinal Commission considers that although the notion of covenant has not been prominent in Anglican traditions of polity and organization, the picture of the Church developed by the sixteenth-century reformers, and since, 'sets out models of church life for which "covenant" . . . may serve as a convenient,

'Communion: virtue or vice', ibid., 71 at 79: 'If we described ourselves as "The Anglican Mission", then we might worry less about our mutual relations, and more about serving God in the world. "Communion" as a self-description seems to promote unhelpful introspection'; D. B. Knox, 'Lambeth and reunion', ibid., 81 (John 17.21).

26 C. Hefling, 'A reasonable development?', in Linzey and Kirker (2005) 81 at 82; DAZ, 50ff: it is a reaction to the sociological, numerical and cultural changes in the Global South, secularization, selfishness, the changing face of Anglicanism, and loss of identity with Canterbury; TEC, s.4; SECR (2005) para. 4: LCRPR; DAZ, 53 (Zahl), 55 (Douglas).

27 TWR, para.119: the Communion 'cannot again afford . . . the crippling prospect of repeated worldwide inter-Anglican conflict': this is one of the reasons for the proposal.

28 For the movement of colonialism and mission in the historical development of Anglicanism worldwide, see K. Ward, *A History of Global Anglicanism* (Cambridge, Cambridge University Press, 2006).

29 TAAC, para. 14; see also para. 13 for covenants in Benedictinism. See P. H. E. Thomas, 'Unity and concord: an early Anglican "Communion"', *Journal of Anglican Studies* 21 (2004) 9–21 at 9. See also Radner (2007) for Covenant Agreements between TEC and various autonomous churches which once formed part of the missionary structures of the Episcopal Church (for example, Liberia, Mexico, Philippines).

30 H. T. Lewis (2005) 601. Indeed, Hooker saw the value of being 'in league of amity . . . to the end that when many are confederated each may make the other the more strong': LEP, I.10; *Church Discipline* I.4, 'Of the Formall cause of a Visible Church, the Church Covenant'; see also above n. 22.

accurate and evocative shorthand'.[31] One respondent suggests that the Articles of Religion represented an Anglican covenant before there was a Communion, forming the basis for ecumenical consensus among the Reformation churches.[32] The primates in 2005 also recognize that the Chicago-Lambeth Quadrilateral has effectively operated as a form of covenant that secures basic commitment to scripture, the Nicene Creed, the two gospel sacraments and the historic episcopate.[33] Others agree,[34] and covenants have been used in modern times to regulate inter-church relations.[35] Yet, for some, the history of covenants is not good,[36] and an Anglican covenant must not replicate the 'proto-covenant' of the Chicago-Lambeth Quadrilateral: it must be scriptural.[37] The St Andrews draft contains all four elements of the Quadrilateral.[38]

---

31 RPC (2006) para. 1.10; and J. E. Scully, 'Reflections on *Toward an Anglican Covenant*' (2007).

32 S. Noll, 'The global Anglican Communion: a blueprint' (2005) 2.

33 *Communiqué* 24-2-2005, para. 8. The Chicago–Lambeth Quadrilateral, also known as the Lambeth Quadrilateral, was approved by the Lambeth Conference in 1888 as stating from the Anglican standpoint the essentials for a reunited Christian Church. The text of the Articles is as follows: 'A. The Holy Scriptures of the Old and New Testaments, as "containing all things necessary to salvation", and as being the rule and ultimate standard of faith. B. The Apostles' Creed, as the Baptismal Symbol; and the Nicene Creed, as the sufficient statement of the Christian Faith. C. The two Sacraments ordained by Christ Himself – Baptism and the Supper of the Lord – ministered with unfailing use of Christ's Words of Institution, and of the elements ordained by Him. D. The Historic Episcopate, locally adapted in the methods of its administration to the varying needs of the nations and peoples called of God into the Unity of His Church.'

34 Noll (2005) 2: 'The Anglican Covenant concept can be traced back to the infancy of the Communion in 1886, with the so-called Lambeth Quadrilateral'; if not a covenant, 'it appears to be the Preamble to a Communion Covenant that was never enacted'; also Noll (2006): 'The idea of an Anglican Covenant . . . is implicit in the classical formularies'; see also MU (2004) p. 2: LCRPR.

35 W. Franklin, 'The Episcopal Church in the USA and the covenant: the place of the Chicago-Lambeth Quadrilateral', in M. Chapman (ed.), *The Anglican Covenant* (London, Mowbray, 2008) 101 at 102: covenants have been made between TEC and former missionary dioceses of that church including the Philippines, Mexico and Central America; and Grieb (2007); see also TEC, Constitution and Canons, Can. I.20.1: TEC, 'as a member of the Anglican Communion, has a relationship of full communion with those Churches in the historic episcopal succession and with whom it has entered into covenant agreements'.

36 CAS (2005) 2: 'The experience of the Scottish Episcopal Church is that Covenants can be used, and are used, to exclude and even to persecute'; that is, under the Presbyterian National Covenant 1638.

37 Dakin (2007). See also CDG Commentary to SADC, para. 8: this notes that questions have also been raised 'as to why the Lambeth Quadrilateral is not enough'.

38 SADC, Cl. 1.1; see also Commentary to SADC, on Section One.

The tacit covenant of global Anglicanism

The proposition of the Lambeth Commission that the communion Anglicans share is a relationship of covenantal affection does not appear explicitly in pronouncements of Lambeth Conferences about the nature of the Communion. For some respondents, however, the Communion has 'existing covenant relationships' in the principles of synodality and episcopacy, shared inheritances, and worldwide fellowship.[39] The point is a good one. It is clearly arguable that the current conventional principles operative at the global level, and enunciated in resolutions of Lambeth Conferences, are analogous to an unwritten or 'tacit covenant'.[40] Its terms are well known: the Communion is a fellowship of self-governing churches in a voluntary relationship of communion with Canterbury; they agree to assemble in fellowship under the moral authority of the instruments of Anglicanism: the instruments of faith (scripture, baptism and Eucharist, the historic episcopate, and common patterns of worship); and the institutional instruments (the Archbishop of Canterbury, Primates' Meeting, Lambeth Conference, and Anglican Consultative Council).[41] However, the analogy cannot be stretched too far. Several terms of this quasi-covenant rest on resolutions or undertakings (for example, to co-operate in mission, or to develop companion dioceses),[42] but these are not 'solemn promises'. The agreement involves commitments (for example to respect the autonomy of fellow churches),[43] but these commitments do not generate legally binding obligations. The institutional instruments and the principles agreed by them have no legal authority over each church; they do not bind legally: their authority is moral and not juridical.[44]

---

39 MU (2004) p. 2: LCRPR; also Vincent Strudwick, *Towards an Anglican Covenant: A Response from Inclusive Church* (20-11-2006), at www.inclusivechurch.net/articles (2006b): 'It is our understanding that what has held the Communion together is an unwritten Covenant, that we shall be led to truth and unity in response to God's promises, drawing on the holiness of our diversity in the fellowship.'

40 For this reason it may be classified as an 'episcopal concordat', in so far as the Conference is composed solely of bishops, though the Anglican Consultative Council too has affirmed many of these.

41 LC 1930, Res. 49: the Communion is 'a fellowship within the One Holy Catholic and Apostolic Church, of those duly constituted dioceses, provinces or regional Churches in communion with the See of Canterbury'; there are also of course obvious historical links between churches; LC 1998, Res. III.8; see also LC 1998, Res. III.1; LC 1998, Res. II.6: this 'reaffirms the primary authority of the Scriptures'.

42 LC 1988, Res. 47; LC 1998, Res. II.3.

43 LC 1878, Recommendation 1: this is one of the 'principles of church order'.

44 What might be styled the moral order covenant is summed up by the Lambeth Conference: churches are bound together 'not by a central legislative and executive authority, but by a mutual loyalty sustained through the common counsel of the bishops in conference' (LC 1930, Res. 48, 49).

The Lambeth Commission recognizes this.[45] What is novel about the Lambeth Commission proposal, however, is that a formal covenant will not solely be an episcopal but a synodical agreement, and that it would be enforceable.[46] Several also visualize the informal networks of the Communion in terms of tacit covenant.[47]

The doctrine of consensual compact

Individually, the churches of the Communion employ covenant concepts in self-understandings of their own ecclesiality (that is, what it means for them to be 'a church').[48] The concept surfaces in their legal instruments which describe a church, variously, as a 'covenanted', 'compactual' or 'consensual' community. First, each church represents the faithful coming together as: a family; one household of faith (bound together by the common traditions of doctrine, discipline and worship); a partnership; a voluntary society; or a community, constituted by a union.[49] As neither individual Christians nor groups of Christians can live to themselves alone, neighbouring dioceses from very early times associated themselves together in provinces and groups of provinces; dioceses recognize themselves as federated with one another in an association or regional church.[50] Many churches define themselves as a composite or union of dioceses.[51]

Second, therefore, a church is founded or constituted on the basis that the faithful: have covenanted with each other; or associated to

---

45 TWR, para. 115: 'The principles about communion, autonomy, discernment in communion and inter-Anglican relations, enunciated at the global level by the Instruments of Unity, have persuasive authority for individual churches; they do not have enforceable juridical authority unless incorporated in their legal systems (and generally they are not incorporated).'

46 See below Chs 8 and 9.

47 Bishop Michael Doe (2006). See also Bishop T. Brown (2006): prayer for one another, giving aid, and the gift of companion links between dioceses are illustrations of good relationships.

48 This is not the case with the Church of England; its polity is part of the law of the land.

49 Melanesia, Cans. A.1.A (family); Philippines, Const., Preamble (household of faith); New Zealand, Const., Preamble, 12 (partnership); Ceylon, Const., Preamble (voluntary society); Hong Kong, Const., Preamble (community); South India, Const., I (union).

50 Ceylon, Const. Preamble; Hong Kong, Const., Preamble: 'the entire Church, which comprehends the five aforesaid Dioceses', is 'a combination . . . of the several Dioceses.'

51 Hong Kong, Constitution, Preamble; Australia, RNDC (2007): the Anglican Church of Australia is a 'federation of autonomous dioceses united by a constitution'; for further discussion of this concept, see G. Blake, 'Diocesan autonomy and national coherence in the Anglican Church of Australia', Ecc LJ 10 (2008) 92.

consent and subscribe to the formation of a province and have so consented and subscribed; or agreed to a constitution for the purpose of associating together by voluntary compact; and in so doing the members shall remain one united and indivisible church.[52] Moreover, doctrinal formularies are adopted, received, and maintained by the institutional church through a corporate consensual pledge: 'we receive and maintain the Doctrine, Sacraments, and Discipline of Christ'.[53] A church is free 'to act in association with any Province . . . in such manner and for such purposes as shall be mutually agreed'.[54] These consensual acts of foundation or constitution are 'solemnly' decreed.[55]

Third, the law of the consensual ecclesial society is itself a compact: as 'it is expedient that the members of a Church . . . should . . . for its due government . . . and the ordering of its affairs, formally set forth the terms of the compact under which it is associated', so the people in synod assembled agree to establish its constitution or deed of association; the law is 'agreed to and set forth' but no new law is made unless it has received the concurrent assent of all orders of the church represented in synod.[56] The faithful consent to be bound by the compact.[57] The idea also appears in some state laws: church laws are 'deemed to be binding on the members . . . as if such members had mutually contracted and agreed to abide by and observe the same';[58] members associate under '[t]he binding effect of the "voluntary consensual compact"' which arises from a willingness to be bound to it; 'the consensual compact or contract is given the same effect, in relation to property matters, as if it were a common law contract'.[59] For the Lambeth Commission canon law, the servant of the Church, seeks to facilitate and order communion among its faithful.[60] As one respondent puts it, Anglicans are governed by canon law as well as by bonds of affection.[61]

---

52 New Zealand, Const., Preamble; Hong Kong, Const., Preamble; Nigeria, Const., I.2.

53 Southern Africa, Declaration of Fundamental Principles, 1870.

54 West Africa, Const., Art. III(c).

55 Hong Kong, Const., Preamble.

56 Southern Africa, Preliminary Resolutions, 1870, VI; Const., Preamble and Arts XXIV.13.

57 West Indies, Preparatory Declaration, 5.

58 Irish Church Act 1869.

59 Australia: *Scandrett v Dowling* [1992] 27 NSWLR 483; see generally N. Doe *Canon Law and the Anglican Communion* (Oxford, Clarendon Press, 1998) 19.

60 TWR, para. 115.

61 Bishop C. Epting, 2: LCRPR.

Formal covenants in contemporary Anglicanism

The Anglican Consultative Council has a covenant-like polity. It is organized on the basis of an agreed constitution which the Lambeth Conference 1968 submitted in draft to the member churches of the Anglican Communion for approval by a two-thirds majority.[62] The Council is conceived, variously, as a family, a community, an instrument for common action, a quasi-synodical body of laity, clergy and bishops, and an expression of synodical life at the global level.[63] Its consensual character is illustrated by the principle that its constitution may be amended only with the approval of two-thirds of the member churches.[64] The establishment and constitution of the Council is based on a global agreement between churches to associate together in a central body. It is the product of a multilateral communion act of the churches. The foundation of its constitution in consensual compact is also reflected in its status in English civil law.[65]

Second, since the *Windsor Report*, the House of Bishops of TEC has issued A Covenant Statement in which the bishops *inter alia* reaffirm their commitment both to the Chicago-Lambeth Quadrilateral 1888 and to serve Christ in communion with the other provinces of the Anglican family.[66] Similarly, the Canadian House of Bishops has 'committed' itself to respond as fully as possible to the primates' *communiqué* (2005), encourage moratoria (on services for same sex unions), 'affirm' adherence to the Lambeth Quadrilateral, and 'uphold' the Archbishop of Canterbury, Primates' Meeting, Lambeth Conference, and Anglican Consultative Council; they also affirm the Ten Principles of Partnership adopted by the Anglican Consultative Council in 1993 and the Anglican Cycle of Prayer as sources of unity in the cause of mission.[67]

---

62 LC 1968, Res. 69. The Council replaced the Lambeth Consultative Body (established after LC 1908, Res. 54) and also succeeded the Advisory Council on Missionary Strategy.

63 ACC – 1 Report, Preface, p. vii; Rt Revd Dr Chiwanga, Address, ACC – 12 Hong Kong, 2002; D. Hamid, 'Church, communion of churches and the Anglican Communion', *EccLJ* 6 (2002) 368.

64 ACC, Constitution, Art. 10; see also Guidelines for Meetings, 2.2.1: 'instrument of unity'.

65 See generally B. Georges, 'The Anglican Consultative Council' (Unpublished Dissertation Cardiff University 2006).

66 House of Bishops, Camp Allen, 15-3-2005: the covenant statement also expresses 'deep regret for the pain that others have experienced with respect to our actions at the General Convention of 2003' and offers 'our sincerest apology and repentance for having breached our bonds of affection by any failure to consult adequately with our Anglican partners before taking those actions'.

67 Statement of Commitment by the Bishops of the Anglican Church of Canada:

Third, several bodies have been formed recently to respond to the events which led to the Lambeth Commission. They are consensual bodies, variously styled networks, movements, or initiatives, and are organized on the basis of covenants, agreements, or concordats. The Anglican Communion Network, within TEC, styling itself a united missionary movement of Anglicans in fellowship with global Anglicanism, has six formal documents including a Memorandum of Agreement (2003) and an Organizational Charter (2004).[68] The Anglican Global Initiative, a not-for-profit association of churches, is organized on the basis of an agreed draft constitution (2004), which may be adopted 'if it becomes necessary'; provision is made for its possible incorporation in civil law.[69] Likewise, a Covenant Union of Anglican Churches in Concordat was entered in 2005 between the Church of Nigeria (Anglican Communion) and the Reformed Episcopal Church and the Anglican Province of America.[70] Finally, a Covenant for Communion and Mission, of the Inter-Anglican Standing Commission on Mission and Evangelism, an official commission of the Communion, has been published to provide a focus for binding the Communion together in a way rather different from that envisaged by the *Windsor Report*.[71]

The Covenant in Scripture

Needless to say, covenant is a fundamental concept in scripture, the history of theology, and the life of the Church.[72] God makes a covenant: with humankind for salvation through faith; with Noah that he be saved when the old world perished; with Abraham and his posterity, of which the token was circumcision; with the Israelites as a nation, of which a sign was the Sabbath and the Ten Commandments a commitment; with the Levites and Phineas for an everlasting priesthood; and with David, that his posterity should occupy his throne.[73]

ACNS 3971 (29-4-2005). See also: Covenant for the Church of England proposed by Anglican Mainstream (3-2-2007).

68 ACN, Memorandum of Agreement (2003): the signatories (bishops), mindful of 'the unfortunate divisions and canonical oppression within our Church, declare a need to establish a Network of Confessing Dioceses and Congregations'.

69 AGI, Draft Constitution, Arts II and III.

70 ACNS 4075 (17-11-2005) (hereafter CUACC (2005)).

71 IASCOME, p. 3.

72 P. A. Lillback, 'Covenant', in S. B. Ferguson and D. F. Wright (eds), *New Dictionary of Theology* (Leicester and Illinois, Intervarsity Press, 1988) 173.

73 Gen. 2.16, 17; Gen. 6.16; 9.12, 15, 16 (Noah); Gen. 13.17, 15.18, 17.2, 4, 7, 11, 13, 14, 19; 2 Kings 13.23; 1 Chron. 16.15–18 (Abraham); Exod. 31.16; Deut. 4.13, 23 (Israelites); Mal. 2.4, 8; Num. 25.12, 13 (Levites and Phineas); Ps. 89.20–28 (David).

The new covenant, administered by the spirit, based on faith, is for all nations, of which Christ is the mediator; human participation in this covenant through faithfulness becomes an expression of gratitude to God who in Christ redeems us.[74] And covenants are entered between humans.[75] These biblical covenants, the old covenant of works (law) and the new covenant of grace (gospel), are employed, typically in the Protestant tradition, both as an organizing principle in covenantal or federal theology and as the basis of ecclesiastical polity, as well as for monastic, reforming or renewal movements.[76] Their significance for ecclesial sociality is also recognized by Anglican theologians: the Church begins with the constitution of the people of God in the Old Testament Covenant; in continuation of this, through the life, death, and resurrection of Christ, in the new covenant the people of God are reconstituted as the Messianic community in which the blessing of God in Christ is realized for the coming kingdom.[77]

Unlike *Towards an Anglican Covenant*,[78] the Lambeth Commission does not suggest scriptural covenants as a possible model for its proposal, though it considers that the current covenantal relationship in Anglicanism has biblical foundations and that it represents 'the communion we have been given in Christ'.[79] By way of contrast, the Inter-Anglican Standing Commission on Mission and Evangelism finds inspiration for its Covenant for Communion in Mission in the scriptural figure of covenant.[80] On the one hand, for several respondents, scriptural models

---

74 John 7.39; Acts 2.32, 33; 2 Cor. 3.6–9; Gal. 4.21–31; Matt. 28.19, 20; Acts 10.44–47; Heb. 8.6 to 9.1; 10.15–17, 12.24. See also *The Mystery of Salvation: The Story of God's Gift*, A Report by the Doctrine Commission of the General Synod, Church of England (London, Church House Publishing, 1995) 107.

75 Gen. 21.27, 32; 1 Sam. 18.3;23.18; 1 Kings 20.34.

76 G. E. Mendenhall, *Law and Covenant in the Ancient Middle East and in Israel* (Pittsburgh, PA, 1954); A. Peel and L. H. Carlson (eds), *Writings of Robert Harrison and Robert Browne* (London, Allen & Unwin, 1953); D. H. Tripp, *The Renewal of the Covenant in the Methodist Tradition* (London, Epworth Press, 1969); D. Rees (ed.), *Consider Your Call: A Theology of the Monastic Life Today* (London, SPCK, 1978).

77 D. W. Hardy, *Finding the Church* (London, SCM Press, 2001), 27. Needless to say, the covenant between God and his people, the Jews, has not been superseded and remains in force.

78 TAAC, paras 13–16: in the New Testament, 'Christians claimed to be in a new covenant relationship with God through the death and resurrection of Jesus, and in the gift of the Spirit'; 'the covenant relationship with God generates a covenantal relationship between his people.'

79 TWR, Section A (sub-heading) and para. 2: it is, through the work of the Holy Spirit, 'an anticipatory sign' of the healing and restorative future which God wills for the world (Eph. 2.1–22).

80 IASCOME, p. 3: 'In Scripture, covenants are central in the Old Testament to God's relationship to Noah, Abraham, Moses and to the people of Israel. Jeremiah and Ezekiel foretell the coming of a new covenant – in which God will give God's people a new heart

are not helpful: there is no teaching of scripture on the model of organization for a worldwide association of churches; it would take a very creative mind to find from scripture any direct teaching on how a worldwide association of churches should arrange their connections on an organizational level.[81] Moreover, human covenants in scripture may not be worthy of emulation, whereas the God-initiated covenants are potentially useful models, not in 'a one-after-the-other logic' but in terms of 'a figural application'.[82]

On the other hand, the value of scriptural models is recognized by other respondents.[83] While there is no single scriptural covenant model, there is a pattern of covenanting, interlocking and co-operating, at once missional and reconciliatory – but precise forms in scripture should not be imitated slavishly as this could undercut the dynamic of covenanting.[84] Indeed, the Inter-Anglican Theological and Doctrinal Commission recognizes 'covenant' as a key term which emerges from Jewish and Christian writings to bring into sharp focus the whole understanding of God and the purposes of God. However, that is not to say that all uses of the word 'covenant' in current discussions necessarily imply that any covenants Anglicans might enter are somehow the *same* as the fundamental biblical covenant between God and his people. But, for the Commission, the ecclesiastical use of the word today carries, and honours, the memory of the biblical covenants. The

---

and new life and will walk with them, and they with him. In the New Testament Jesus inaugurates this New Covenant.'

81 P. Adam 'Communion, virtue or vice', in P. G. Bolt, M. O. Thompson and R. Tong (eds), *The Faith Once for All Delivered* (Camperdown, NSW, The Australian Church Record in conjunction with the Anglican League, 71 at 73f.; and M. D. Chapman, 'Introduction: what's going on in Anglicanism?', in Chapman (2008) 25: 'The model of covenant used is far closer to the agreements between churches in ecumenical discussion than to any Biblical model'; see also J. Barton, 'Covenant in the Bible and today', in Chapman (2008), 193 at 202: 'The background of the proposed inter-Anglican Covenant is not in fact biblical. It derives from the use of covenant language in the secular sphere, and in a number of modern inter-church agreements.'

82 Seitz (2007): summarizing those who object to the use of scriptural models, 'from the standpoint of the Bible, covenant is an inappropriate churchly commandeering of a biblical concept, and where there may be a fit, it is wrong'.

83 H. T. Lewis (2005) 602: moreover: '[i]t is impossible to study the Bible without grasping the importance of covenant' which characterizes 'the relationship between the God of Israel and the people of Israel'; and Jesus asserts that 'he is the very embodiment of the perfect covenant between God and humankind'; RCW (2005) 6: LCRPR.

84 Seitz (2007): 'It is not the task of those who undertake to compose a covenant, and those who obligate themselves, in Christ, to do what it asks, to imitate some precise form or event from within scripture's panoramic account. This would be an odd kind of Biblicism, and may explain in part why the New Testament can refer reflexively to a new covenant with all high seriousness, without getting caught up in the provision of inventive new forms. The same holds true for the Anglican Communion in our day. To do this would be to undercut the dynamic and personal character of covenanting.'

adoption of the covenant figure does not seek to introduce an alien notion into Anglicanism, but 'to draw from the deep scriptural roots in which Anglicanism has always rejoiced'.[85] Consequently, several responses to the Nassau draft covenant underscore the need to deploy biblical material in the development of the concept of a covenant for Anglicanism.[86] In turn, the London report of the Covenant Design Group employs a 'biblical framework' as the 'base and soil' for its draft covenant as well as a discussion of covenant in scripture.[87]

The Covenant in the Sacramental Tradition

Unlike the Lambeth Commission, several respondents recognize the concept of covenant in sacramental theology as a possible model for a covenant in Anglicanism. Some respondents see the Windsor proposal in the context of baptismal covenant.[88] Hooker understood that 'Baptism implieth a covenant or league between God and man'.[89] It is a covenant commanded by God (Matt. 28.18–20). Thus, on the basis of the baptismal promise to seek and serve Christ in all persons, loving our neighbours as ourselves, Anglicans already share a covenantal relationship.[90] Liturgical texts reflect this. Baptism is: a sign of entrance into the covenant of grace; a bond which God establishes; an outward visible sign of union with Christ in his death and resurrection; it is a community event, in which the candidate is accepted and sealed by God and incorporated into the Church; and, moreover, renewal of baptismal vows offers all communicants an opportunity for rededication to the covenant of faith.[91]

Connections may also be made between the covenantal nature of the Eucharist, in which the faithful partake of the blood of the new covenant, and the Anglican Communion as a eucharistic fellowship of churches.[92] The Communion is a covenantal community in so far as the

---

85 RPC (2006) paras 1.2 and 1.8; this is linked to the idea of Christians as 'a single family': para. 1.5.

86 England, RNDC (21-12-2007) for the need to root the covenant in 'biblical material'; see also Australia, RNDC (2007) suggesting the ACCT model (see below).

87 Commentary to SADC, para. 2; and Introduction, para. 2.

88 Ibid., 1.4; TEC, House of Bishops, Response, 12/13-1-2005: LCRPR.

89 LEP, V.64.4.

90 Via Media USA: http://www.remainepiscopal.org/Windsor1.html

91 North India, Const., I.I.II.8; Canada, The Book of Alternative Services (1985) 150; Wales, BCP (1984) 697; Gal. 3.27; Rom. 6.1–5; Australia, A Prayer Book for Australia (1995); New Zealand, A New Zealand Prayer Book (1989) 379; Diocese of Melbourne, Pastoral Handbook (1988) 20.

92 See, for example, Wales, BCP 1984, 13; DAZ, 30 (Douglas). See also Luke 22.17–20.

new covenant, marked by Jesus' breaking of his body and the shedding of his blood, is fundamental to its fellowship.[93] Similarly, a covenantal relationship is shared in holy matrimony by which the spouses are to keep the covenant made between them.[94] Further, one respondent considers that the burial office indicates the significance of a covenant concept in Anglicanism: it represents a 'dual covenant' in which people are committed to the care of God as a 'lamb of his own flock and a sheep of his own fold', and in which they are 'knit together . . . in one communion and fellowship . . . in paradise and on earth'.[95] The concept of covenant is also used with licences to minister.[96] Connections between an Anglican covenant and sacramental covenant were also suggested in the provincial consultation prior to the St Andrews report in 2008.[97]

The Covenant in Reason and Experience

Ecumenical covenants

The Lambeth Commission recognizes that the concept of the adoption of a covenant is not new in the ecumenical context. Anglican churches have commonly entered covenants with other churches to articulate their relationships of communion; these covenants provide very appropriate models from which Anglicans can learn much in their own development of inter-Anglican relations.[98] Both the Primates' Meeting and *Towards an Anglican Covenant* accept ecumenical covenants as valuable precedents for the use of covenant in Anglicanism,[99] as do many respondents. This is especially the case with respect to those covenants which have been entered by Anglicans with others,[100] a

---

93 IASCOME, p. 3.

94 BCP 1662: 'these persons may . . . perform and keep the vow and covenant betwixt them made'. See also Radner (2007): in a short survey of precedents for an Anglican covenant: 'human relations, such as marriage, are more than marginal to the discussion.'

95 H. T. Lewis (2005) 602.

96 Bishop Tom Brown, Dioc. of Wellington, 'A Covenant for the Anglican Communion – Response', considered by the CDG Nassau (undated) (Lambeth website): 'we use a form of Covenant agreement for all who hold a bishop's licence. This covenant is three-way between bishop, parish or other mission unit and the ordained or lay licenced minister' (the so-called 'diocesan covenant').

97 For example by Canada.

98 TWR, para. 119.

99 *Communiqué*, 24-2-2005, para. 8; TAAC, para. 15: the Bonn Agreement 1931 is cited as an example; also: in 1964 'the British Council of Churches made a covenant to work and pray for the inauguration of a union'.

100 Most Revd J. Marona, Episcopal Church of the Sudan (2005), para. 1; Church of

point highlighted in the provincial consultation leading up to the St Andrews report in 2008.[101] Covenants have proliferated recently as useful instruments in the ecumenical process, with separated parties solemnly binding themselves together for specific purposes; the use of covenants is valued to articulate common bonds and unity.[102] Indeed, for some, Anglicans have a *tradition* of covenants that help to clarify their relationships with other churches; thus, they ask why there should not be appropriate commitments which Anglicans can freely and honestly make with one another.[103] While some caution that care should be taken in labelling all ecumenical agreements 'covenants', they suggest that the unity *sought* in the Lambeth proposal is no different to that sought in ecumenism, though the communion practised may be in a different form.[104]

To be sure, the use of covenants, concordats, charters or other agreements is commonplace in the ecumenical field. However, what the Windsor reception process fails to disclose is the extensive incidence and diversity of such agreements. Some are bilateral, between a single Anglican church and another church, and articulate current practice: one Anglican-Methodist covenant endorses in a formal way (and seeks to go some way beyond) what is already a reality in many local situations.[105] Not unlike the Anglican-Lutheran Concordat of Agreement in the USA,[106] the Lutheran-Anglican covenant in Australia is a *national* covenant which enables further *regional* agreements to develop by stages.[107] A covenant may be tripartite,[108] or multipartite, between one

---

Ireland, Standing Committee of General Synod (25-1-2005) 7: LCRPR.

101 For example, Anglican–Lutheran agreements and the indigenous peoples' New Covenant 1994 (Canada); National Council of Churches in Australia (Australia). See also IASCER, Resolution 08.07.

102 Strudwick (2006).

103 IASCOME, p.3; DAZ, 54–5 (Douglas).

104 However, see Radner (2007): caution should be exercised in using ecumenical covenants as possible precedents: 'For these agreements still lack many ingredients we have assumed and indeed practised within the Anglican Communion as in fact *embodying* communion: not only mutually recognized ministries, and shared sacraments, but common and accountable counsel, the accountable (and in this sense "binding") sharing of resources including financial resources, and finally, the ultimate act of communion, martyrdom in the service of the other.'

105 *An Anglican-Methodist Covenant*, Common Statement of the Formal Conversations between the Methodist Church of Great Britain and the Church of England (2001) (AMC:CS (2001)) v.

106 *A Beginner's Guide to the Concordat of Agreement*, Office of Ecumenical and Interfaith Relations (2003): http://www.ecusa.anglican.org/6947_10580_ENG_HTM. htm

107 Australia: GS Resolution, 78/04(a),(b).

108 Such as the Lutheran-Anglican-Roman Catholic (Virginia) Covenant 1990.

Anglican church and many churches of different traditions.[109] Some trans-national covenants are entered by a number of Anglican churches and a group of churches from one other tradition.[110] In Australia, the Anglican Church is party to a covenant, involving fifteen churches, including Roman Catholic and Orthodox,[111] which enables options for co-operation and commitment dependent on what is possible between them at this stage of the ecumenical journey; the biblical motif of covenanting is used as a model.[112] Other covenants are continental, such as the European *Charta Oecumenica* (2001) between the Conference of European Churches and the (Roman Catholic) Council of European Bishops' Conferences which is a common commitment to dialogue and co-operation.[113] Finally, covenants may be local.[114]

The employment of covenants in other traditions

The Lambeth Commission and the responses do not identify the use of covenants or other agreements by comparable international ecclesial communities as possible precedents for an Anglican covenant. Nor do the critics identify these as potential yardsticks against which to challenge the covenant proposals and emerging draft texts. Yet, the models are particularly useful comparators for both supporters and critics, including those who argue that an Anglican covenant will threaten the autonomy of churches of the Communion, or function as a barrier to ecumenical advancement.[115] Other communities employ agreements

---

109 For example, the Covenant of Churches in Wales 1974: namely, the (Anglican) Church in Wales, Calvinistic Methodist Church of Wales or Presbyterian Church of Wales, Methodist Church, United Reformed Church of England and Wales (Congregational and Presbyterian), and Union of Welsh Independents.

110 The Anglican churches of Britain and Ireland and the Nordic and Baltic Lutheran churches have reached a common understanding of the Church, fundamental agreement in faith, and agreement on episcopacy, in the Porvoo Declaration. The parties are: Church of England, Church in Wales, Church of Ireland, and Scottish Episcopal Church, Evangelical-Lutheran Churches in Estonia, Finland, Iceland, Latvia, Lithuania, Church of Norway, Church of Denmark, and Church of Sweden.

111 ACCT, p. 4: The Covenanting Document, Part A, Declaration of Intent. The parties are: the Anglican Church of Australia, Antiochian Orthodox Church, Armenian Apostolic Church, Assyrian Church of the East, Church of Christ in Australia, Congregational Federation of Australia, Coptic Orthodox Church, Greek Orthodox Archdiocese of Australia, Lutheran Church of Australia, Religious Society of Friends, Roman Catholic Church in Australia, Romanian Orthodox Church, Salvation Army, Syrian Orthodox Church, Uniting Church in Australia.

112 ACCT, p. 2 (Biblical Basis of Covenant).

113 CO (2001) Preamble.

114 Such as the Kilcoy Covenant (Queensland, Australia) 2001.

115 See below Chs 6 and 9.

either to establish a body to co-ordinate community activities, or to establish the community itself and regulate relations within it.

Orthodoxy: In contrast to the Roman Catholic Church worldwide, governed not by a covenant but by a Code of Canon Law (1983) promulgated unilaterally by the Pope, but like the Anglican Communion, the Orthodox Church is understood as a family of self-governing churches, held together not by a centralized organization, but by the double bond of unity in the faith and communion in the sacraments. Each local church is 'autocephalous' or 'autonomous' yet in full communion with its 'sister churches' and gathered in one eucharistic community around the bishop.[116] The covenantal character of the unity between Orthodox churches may, at the inter-church level, be expressed in and organized on the basis of an agreement. For example, the hierarchs of several churches associate together in the Standing Conference of Canonical Orthodox Bishops in the Americas. Their constitution contains the 'theological foundation for the agreement'. The agreement expresses their 'common testimony' and enables them 'to actualize . . . unity in all those fields in which a common effort is required'. The purposes of the Conference are the consideration and resolution of common problems, the co-ordination of effort in matters of common concern, and the strengthening of that unity which is the essence of Christianity. The constitution preserves the jurisdictional autonomy of the member churches.[117]

Old Catholic Churches in the Union of Utrecht: These did 'something similar' to the Anglican covenant proposal in a statute of the International Old Catholic Bishops Conference (2000). This offers 'a common basis' for communion, and describes 'the kind of communion we are committed to and the obligations of the bishops in order to promote and to realize it'. The Conference unites the bishops of the churches as members of 'the same church-family': the statute 'can be seen as our "covenant" in which the ecclesiological identity of the Old Catholic churches is phrased', but each church remains 'autonomous and interdependent within the same communion'.[118]

---

116 T. Ware, *The Orthodox Church* (London, Penguin Books, 1963, reprinted 1991) 15; N. Lossky, 'The Orthodox churches', in P. Avis (ed.), *The Christian Church* (London, SPCK, 2002) 6.

117 SCOBA Constitution (1961): it recites Psalm 132.1 as its theological foundation; the parties are Greek, Antiochian, Serbian, Romanian, Bulgarian, Carpatho Russian, Ukrainian, Albanian; Constitution, Preamble. Art. II: 'No decision of the Conference shall interfere with the ecclesiastical jurisdiction of any of the Canonical Orthodox Churches, or any of the member Hierarchs.' See also Standing Conference of Canonical Orthodox Churches of Australia (SCOCCA).

118 J. A. O. L. Vercammen, Archbishop of Utrecht (25-1-2005): LCRPR: each church has its own law.

Lutheran World Federation: This is organized under its constitution, as 'a communion of churches which confess the triune God, agree in the proclamation of the Word of God and are united in pulpit and altar fellowship'. The Federation furthers united witness to the Gospel, strengthens the member churches in carrying out mission and in their efforts towards Christian unity worldwide, and seeks alleviation of human need, promotion of peace, human rights, social and economic justice, care for creation, and sharing resources. The Federation is an 'instrument of its autonomous member churches' and helps them 'to act jointly in common tasks'.[119]

World Alliance of Reformed Churches: The Alliance is a fellowship of Congregational, Presbyterian, Reformed and United churches.[120] Its present Constitution was adopted in 1970, and protects the autonomy of member churches.[121] To cure what some regard as 'a genius for division that is unique', the Alliance has embarked on a mission in unity project (1999–2005), recognizing that 'the present state of the Reformed Churches cannot be defended in the face of the witness of Scripture', to assist churches to overcome their divisions, to achieve unity in diversity and to strengthen their common witness in the modern world.[122]

Community of Protestant Churches in Europe: Lutheran and Reformed churches associate as a fellowship in the Leuenberg Agreement (1973). The agreement seems somewhat ambiguous as to its consequences for the freedom of member churches.[123]

World Methodist Council: A manifestation of a 'fellowship' of Methodists around the world, this is constituted on the basis of an agreed instrument which provides for a council which, at least once every ten

---

119 LWF, Const., Arts I–IV. In 2002 the LWF had 133 member churches, with 60 million members. The 'federal' concept is itself 'covenantal'.

120 WARC, Const., Preamble, Art. I.2: and those in the tradition of Valdes and Hus (predating the Reformation). It has 70 million members in 215 churches in 107 countries. Lossky (2002) 1217.

121 Const., Art. IV: 'None of these provisions shall limit the autonomy of any member church.'

122 Mission in Unity Project (1999–2005): The aims of the project are: to make churches more sharply aware of the present state of division and of the need for a concerted common response; to stimulate initiatives towards unity from within churches in selected countries and to promote models of unity in mission; and to contribute to developing a common theological understanding of unity in Reformed churches taking into account both the internal situation of the Reformed churches and the wider ecumenical context. Emphasis is placed on communication with churches, theological schools, church associations, youth fellowships, mission agencies, etc. 'Initiatives will not be imposed from above but developed contextually': http://warc.jalb.de/warcajsp/side.jsp?news_id+445&navi+27

123 CPLE:LA, Preamble. For the effects of the agreement on autonomy, see below Ch. 9.

years, must convene a World Methodist Conference. The Council has no legislative authority over the member churches.[124]

Baptist World Alliance: Its Constitution (2004) provides that the Alliance, extending over every part of the world, exists as an expression of the essential oneness of Baptist people in the Lord Jesus Christ, to impart inspiration to the fellowship, and to provide channels for sharing concerns and skills in witness and ministry. The Alliance 'recognizes the traditional autonomy and interdependence of Baptist churches and member bodies'.[125] Covenant has a central place in Baptist ecclesiology.[126]

Church–State Covenants: Covenants, concordats and other agreements have also proliferated in church–state relations within national borders.[127] In Europe, for example, agreements are entered to define church–state relations, to guarantee religious freedom, and to make provision for collaboration in matters of common concern. Protestant churches,[128] and the Roman Catholic Church, are parties to these agreements.[129] Agreements have also been established between alliances of

---

124 World Methodist Council (hereafter WMC), Constitution: CPDMC, pp. 782–3. The fellowship was formed when the first Ecumenical Methodist Conference was held in 1881 (London), and renamed the World Methodist Council in 1951 (at Oxford). Its constitution, drafted at Oxford 1951, was adopted at Janaluska 1956 and revised at Oslo 1961 and again at Denver 1971. For the Covenant Service in Methodism, see K. Wilson, 'The Methodist Idea of Covenant', in Chapman (2008) 175 at 185.

125 This is an international fellowship of 214 Baptist unions and conventions worldwide in 120 countries. Its goals are: '(1) To Unite Baptists Worldwide; (2) To lead in World Evangelization; (3) To Respond to People in Need; and (4) To defend Human Rights.' The Alliance has six regional or geographical fellowships for North America, Asia, Africa, Caribbean, Latin America, and Europe. For the concept of covenant in Baptist theology, see P. Fiddes, *Tracks and Traces: Baptist Identity in Church and Theology* (Carlisle, Paternoster Press, 2003): 'It was an early Baptist, John Smyth, who made the creative theological step of linking together the horizontal covenant and the vertical covenant; so in 1607 he defined the church as a visible community of saints where "two or three or more saints join together by covenant with God and themselves"' (p. 76).

126 Fiddes (2003).

127 See R. Puza and N. Doe (eds), *Religion and Law in Dialogue: Covenantal and Non-Covenantal Co-operation between State and Religion in Europe* (Leuven, Peeters, 2006).

128 In recent years in Germany agreements have been entered between the Protestant church and the state *länder*: Saxony-Anhalt (1993), Mecklenburg-West Pomerania (1994), Saxony (1994), Thuringia (1994) and Brandenburg (1996); as well as concordats with the Roman Catholic Church: Saxony (1996); Thuringia (1997); Mecklenburg-West Pomerania (1997), and Brandenburg (2003); and agreements with smaller religious communities (for example, in Lower Saxony there are agreements with the Free Religious Community of Lower Saxony (1970), the Evangelical Methodist Church in North West Germany (1978), the Association of Jewish Congregations of Lower Saxony (1983); and an agreement between the Federal Republic of Germany and the Central Council of Jews (2003).

129 There are concordats between the state and the Roman Catholic Church in Italy (1984), Poland (1993), Croatia (1996), Hungary (1997), Slovakia (2000), Slovenia (2001).

churches and the state.[130] Similarly, some state laws enable churches to enter 'covenants' to share church buildings.[131] Finally, in the secular international community states frequently employ treaties, covenants and other agreements to facilitate and regulate international affairs, as do non-governmental organizations.[132]

Conclusion

For some critics, the proposal to use a covenant as a foundation for long-term relations between churches of the Communion is at odds with the spirit of Anglicanism. Although correct insofar as the Communion does not have, and never has had, a formal global covenant, no further evidence is presented in the responses to support this position. The use of a covenant is not without precedent in scripture, tradition and reason. The Windsor proposition (and that of some supporters), that the 'bonds of affection' represent a relationship of covenantal communion (which might be articulated in a covenant), therefore, is not altogether unsound. The covenant figure is implicit in conventions presently operative at the global level, in the doctrine of consensual compact at the local level, and in the agreements of inter-Anglican organizations. It is also fundamental in scripture (in which the salvific covenant is inspirational as a special spiritual but not institutional model) and sacramental theology under which the covenants of the canonical rites provide helpful metaphors. Furthermore, covenants are commonplace in the ecumenical field and are used extensively by other international ecclesial communities (episcopal or not). These agreements provide useful models for both supporters and critics of the covenant proposals. They represent applied ecclesiology in conveying formally the theological experiences of these communities searching for a way to express structurally (and sometimes juridically) their communion, apostolicity and catholicity. The majority of these agreements seek explicitly to protect and enrich, not destroy, the autonomy of their member churches. Their survival and continued use appears to bear witness to their success in this respect. The use of a covenant by the Communion would not represent an original or radical innova-

---

130 Such as that in Poland with an alliance of the Lutheran, Orthodox, Polish Catholic, Evangelical Reformed, United Methodist, Old Catholic Mariavites Churches, and Baptist Union of Poland.

131 England and Wales: Sharing of Church Buildings Act 1969, s.1 (a covenant under seal).

132 For example, the International Federation of Red Cross and Red Crescent Societies has a constitution.

tion in ecclesiastical polity. The widespread use of such covenantal instruments among fellow Christians could underscore for Anglicans the conventionality or ordinariness of their own covenant proposals.

3

The Purposes of a Covenant

A covenant is not an end in itself but a means to an end.[1] Treatment of the concept of covenantal purposes discloses the goals which the Communion may intend to attain with a covenant, and necessitates discussion as to whether those goals are legitimate and the reasons for them acceptable.[2] Accordingly, clarity and agreement about purposes is essential for effective debate.[3] The Lambeth Commission proposes several ideas which indicate the purposes of, and reasons and justifications for, a covenant: most underlie what it describes as the 'overwhelming' case for adoption. They are based on the notion that the Communion has a 'responsibility' to attain these purposes, and that the covenant is a 'mechanism' to achieve them.[4] Some responses are cautious or critical, ranging from the idea that Anglicans need to be clear about purposes, which must be theologically motivated,[5] through, a covenant should state the purpose of the Communion,[6] to, a covenant would be divisive, and its actual aim is to control.[7] Indeed, in the canonical tradition, an agreement binds only if its purpose is legitimate.[8] The following identifies five basic ideas of purpose emerging from the debate thus far: unity; reconciliation, recommitment and trust; identity, clarity and understanding; order and stability; and mission and witness. Each one has its supporters, sceptics and critics. All

---

1 Grieb (2007): 'The idea of a covenant by itself is neutral. Everything depends on its purpose.'

2 Purpose is directly related to the effects of the covenant (see Ch. 9). In this chapter the 'purposes' of the covenant are treated as its strategic goals. These may be distinguished from the 'operational purposes' of a covenant which touch each topic treated in this book; each has its own operational purposes (for example, the purposes of the nature, form, subjects, substance, etc. of a covenant).

3 Without a coherent purpose: the covenantal intent is uncertain; compliance threatens to be formalistic; interpretation problematic; and there is no criterion against which to measure critically the effectiveness or otherwise of its administration.

4 TWR, para. 119.

5 Dioc. of Saskatoon (8-1-2006): LCRPR; and Noll (2005) 2.

6 Dioc. of Brisbane (16-12-2004) para. 2.7: LCRPR.

7 CAS (2005) 3: LCRPR; C. Lewis (2005) 149 at 152.

8 P. Vinogradoff, 'Reason and conscience', *LQR* 24 (1908) 382.

five purposes appear, with different emphases, in the St Andrews draft covenant, particularly that of mission.

Unity

For the Lambeth Commission, the principal aim of a covenant is unity: to enable and maintain life in communion; and the Windsor draft covenant provides that one of its objects is to foster greater unity.[9] *Towards an Anglican Covenant* recognizes that a covenant could serve a 'relational end', namely, the unity of the Communion as it becomes a genuinely global family of interdependent autonomous churches; and it could provide a fundamental basis of co-operation and action with one another and in relation to the whole Communion.[10] Many responses agree. They offer a range of types of unity. A covenant could consolidate ecclesial unity, give Anglicanism greater coherence, and balance unity with freedom.[11] It could provide a creative way of expressing a unity that is neither theoretical nor tyrannical, and offer unique opportunities for Anglicans to work more closely together, fostering the networks of relationships that form the lifeblood of the Communion.[12] This might result in a more unified Communion, sensitive and responsive to the needs of all its parts, which itself would represent an example to the whole world of how Christians can live and work together, no matter what challenges they encounter.[13] It might also express the responsibility of Anglicans to and for each other, and thereby prevent fragmentation within the Anglican Communion.[14] Like the Inter-Anglican Theological and Doctrinal Commission,[15] for the Covenant Design Group a covenant would seek to maintain the unity of the Spirit in the bond of peace, it would 'serve communion' and interdependence, enabling Anglicans to grow together as a

---

9 TWR, para. 119; WDAC, Preamble.

10 TAAC, paras 6, 8.

11 Province of Hong Kong (Hong Kong Sheng Kung Hui), para. 2.1: LCRPR; A. Goddard, 'Walking together? The future shape of the Anglican Communion' (2005) 6; E. Radner, 'Freedom and Covenant: the Miltonian analogy transfigured', *Anglican Theological Review* 87 (2005) 618. See below Ch. 9 for the possibility of types of Communion membership.

12 Advent Pastoral Letter from the Archbishop of Canterbury: HBTG (2005) 2.3.17; see also Affirming Catholicism, Reponse to TAAC (13-12-2006), para. 2; Dioc. of Saskatchewan, s. 4; RHB (2005) para. 4; MU (2004) p. 1: LCRPR; Davie (2007).

13 SAMS Canada (2005) p.2: LCRPR.

14 Archbishop of Canterbury, Pastoral Letter: ACNS 4127 (9-3-2005); IFSCCUCI (2004) p. 4: LCRPR; Sison (2006).

15 RPC, para. 1.8.

worldwide Communion to the full stature of Christ, and 'binding' the churches more closely together.[16] For several respondents the concepts of communion and covenant are inextricably linked; the latter may help to nurture the former by teaching Anglicans the habit and discipline of discerning and learning together, so that they consider others 'better than themselves' (Phil. 2.3).[17]

Many respondents, however, justifiably question the operational capacity of a covenant to unite: a covenant cannot manufacture unity as this is God-given.[18] They fear disunity if churches felt, in conscience, unable to adopt the covenant, or that a covenant might fragment the Communion by damaging the importance of both the local context to decision-making and the application of locally contextualized theological methods and biblical reflection.[19] Some consider that a covenant encourages a schismatic mindset, and that the notion of 'standing with' a group commits its signatories 'to supporting acts of others even if illegal, immoral, duplicitous, or schismatic'.[20] One respondent questions the legitimacy of a compromise to save an institution, and another argues that the actual purpose of a covenant, with particular issues in mind, is to function as 'a standing armistice' which masquerades as a covenant.[21] Some feel that a covenant would merely duplicate existing covenantal relationships (the baptismal covenant, creeds and eucharistic liturgies) and thereby dilute these ancient instruments of unity;[22] another view is simply to see the latter as relevant general

---

16 Commentary on SADC, paras 6 and 7, and SADC, Preamble and Section Three (unity); see also NDC, Art. 1, Preamble and Art. 7; see also Art. 5, Our Unity and Common Life and Art. 6, the Unity of the Communion. The NDC Preamble is similar to the GSSC Preamble. The draft covenant submitted to the Group by the Anglican Church in Australia provided (like the Windsor proposal) that the covenant would be entered 'to make explicit and more forceful the loyalty and bonds of affection which govern the relationships between the churches of the Communion': ACADC, Preamble.

17 Scully (2007) 2,8; Ross (2006): Lambeth Website. See also Southern Africa, RNDC (2007): a covenant must build unity and allow appropriate diversity.

18 B. Salier, 'John 17.21–23 and Christian unity', FOFAD, 87; MU (2004) 2: structures cannot meaningfully unite. See also Chapman, 'Introduction', The Anglican Covenant: Unity and Diversity in the Anglican Communion (London, Mowbray, 2008) 33: 'There is no substitute for worshipping, studying, learning, and eating together. Indeed, it may be that companionship is a better way forward than Covenant, and will lead to a far deeper sense of communion.'

19 CIPRWR (2005), 8: LCRPR; Modern Churchpeople's Union, Response to TAAC (Nov. 2006); CAS (2005) 3: LCRPR.

20 WAC (2005): LCRPR.

21 Radner (2005) 617; Baker (2004); see also F. T. Griswold, Epiphany Message from the Presiding Bishop TEC (Episcopal News Service 011305-2): a covenantal call to sacrifice may be too high a price to pay for unity.

22 Sharp (2007); see also Primates' Meeting, Points Raised: 'What is the value added by a covenant?'

precedents for an Anglican covenant. All of the foregoing fears provide real challenges for the advocates of a covenant, and they also emphasize the need for the constant reference to theology.

Nevertheless, the goal of unity is a persistent theme in the salvific covenant: God pledges himself to a spiritual union with humankind.[23] Similarly, in sacramental theology, through the baptismal covenant, by the Holy Spirit the baptized are united by adoption to be children of God; in the matrimonial covenant the spouses enter 'a mystical union that is betwixt Christ and his Church'; and in the ordination covenant candidates promise to maintain quietness, peace and love among all Christian people.[24] Classical covenantal theology also translates the goal of unity to ecclesiastical organizations whose agreements are designed to unite through mutual care and sharing.[25] For the early Reformers, the object of the 'covenant of human society' (*foedus humanae societatis*) was to address the disunity which resulted from the Fall.[26] The aim of organizational covenants, therefore, is to associate. As such, an ecclesiastical association is a 'symbiosis initiated by a special covenant (*pactum*) among the members for the purpose of bringing together and holding in common a particular interest'; members associate for *communicatio* to uphold 'the plan of social life set forth in covenanted agreements'.[27]

Moreover, unity is a purposive element in contemporary Anglican agreements.[28] For instance, the instruments of the Anglican Consulta-

---

23 Rom. 11.26–27.

24 Book of Common Prayer 1662, 263, 301, 553.

25 Hooker, LEP, Bk. I.10.1 and 4; see also A. S. McGrade (ed.), *Richard Hooker and the Construction of Christian Community* (Tempe, Ariz.: Medieval and Renaissance Studies, 1997).

26 For Eisermann (d. 1558), see J. Witte, *Law and Protestantism: The Legal Teachings of the Lutheran Reformation* (Cambridge, Cambridge University Press, 2002) 142–3.

27 Althusius, *Politica methodice digesta* (1603) 2.3, 4.8: the goal of social and political union is federal or covenantal, seeking communion (*communicatio*) through 'sharing' material and spiritual goods (*things*), labours and occupations (*services*), and pious discipline (*common rights*): O. O'Donovan and T. L. O'Donovan (eds), *From Irenaeus to Grotius: A Sourcebook in Christian Political Thought 100–1625* (Cambridge, Cambridge University Press, 1999) 757ff. These ideas are found in modern theological concepts of community, itself a unifying relationship between humans: to share experiences and to co-ordinate action for the common good, not with the 'rational order' of contractual relations, but with communion: J. Finnis, *Natural Law and Natural Rights* (Oxford, Clarendon Press, 1980) 135–144; and T. Gilby, *Between Community and Society: A Philosophy and Theology of the State* (London, Longmans Green & Co., 1953).

28 The same might be said of historical precedents. The primary object of the Concordat of 1784 (between the Diocese of Connecticut and the Scottish bishops) was 'to establish a bond of peace, and Holy Communion' between the two churches; and its organizational aim was to define their communion relationship: see P. H. E. Thomas 'Unity and concord: an early Anglican "Communion"', *Journal of Anglican Studies* 21 (2004) 9. See also D. S. Armentrout and R. B. Slocum (eds), *Documents of Witness: A*

tive Council provide for the object of the body, to advance the Christian religion,[29] as one of the instruments of unity in the Anglican Communion;[30] and they enable the exercise of provincial autonomy,[31] collaboration,[32] consensus,[33] and joint action.[34] The strategic goals of affiliation, unity and collaboration are also found in the draft constitution of the Anglican Global Initiative,[35] and in the Memorandum of Agreement and Organizational Charter of the Anglican Communion Network: to associate like-minded dioceses and congregations to engage in the common task of constituting a true and legitimate expression of the worldwide Anglican Communion.[36] The same ideas surface in the agreed vision of the Council of Anglican Provinces of Africa, which identifies a clear strategic goal for that body.[37] Ministerial covenants within churches also seek to nurture a 'working relationship' between the bishops, licensed ministers and the parish.[38]

History of the Episcopal Church (1782–1985) (New York, Church Hymnal Corporation, 1994) 14–17.

29 ACC, Const., Art. 2.

30 ACC, Guidelines for Meetings, 2.2.1.

31 ACC, Const., Art. 3.b: the right to appoint a member is a matter for the autonomous church.

32 ACC, Cons., Art. 10: referral to member churches for constitutional amendment; see Bylaws, 5 for collaboration between the Inter-Anglican Finance Committee and the Standing Committee.

33 Such as the right of the Primates' Meeting to veto a church membership application.

34 ACC, Bylaws, 4.

35 AGI, Draft Constitution (2004), Preamble: to 'affiliate and unite in love, holiness, and true godly fellowship through . . . Christ, Anglicans in Global South with Anglicans in North America and the United Kingdom as an authentic expression of the world-wide Anglican Communion'; Arts IV–X: '[t]o collaborate with members, ecumenical partners, non-Anglican churches, humanitarian organizations, governmental agencies, and non-governmental organizations . . . in . . . mission and ministry projects . . . to alleviate human need and to provide an effective means to spread the Gospel'.

36 ACN, Organizational Charter (2004) Arts I–X; Memorandum of Agreement (2003): 'to bring together those dioceses and congregations which hold the centrality and authority of Holy Scripture and . . . to be faithful in upholding and propagating the historic faith and order; pursuing the apostolic mission to a troubled and fallen church, nation and world'; That is: 'in co-operation' with the Archbishop of Canterbury and primates 'to participate in providing adequate episcopal oversight to congregations within ECUSA [TEC] that request it'.

37 CAPA (2005): works for 'a unified and self-sustaining Anglican Communion in Africa', providing 'holistic ministry' (to meet 'the spiritual needs of all people'); it seeks to achieve 'unity in diversity'. Its agreed functions spell out the practical aims of the organization (for example, 'share experience, consult and support each other' and 'confer about common responsibilities'); the council has 'governance organs' and is currently working on 'a strategic plan to guide its activities'.

38 Bishop T. Brown, 'A Covenant for the Anglican Communion: Response': Lambeth Website.

The adoption by proponents of an Anglican covenant of unity as one of its strategic objects is not exceptional. The goal of unity is conventional in the instruments of comparable international ecclesial communities. The Old Catholics' agreement aims to promote and to realize communion.[39] The constitution of the Standing Conference of Canonical Orthodox Bishops in the Americas seeks to enable the churches through the conference 'to actualize ... unity in all those fields in which a common effort is required' thereby 'strengthening ... Orthodox unity'.[40] One strategic goal of the constitution of the Lutheran World Federation is to unite the churches, strengthen them, and help them 'to act jointly in common tasks'.[41] Similar goals appear in the constitutions of the World Alliance of Reformed Churches,[42] the Southern Baptist Convention,[43] in which one purpose of a (local) church covenant is to associate Christians together to constitute a church,[44] the World Methodist Council,[45] and the Baptist World Alliance.[46] Needless to say, unity and co-operation are goals of ecumenical covenants such as the concordat between the Evangelical Lutheran Church of America and TEC, the Australian Churches Covenanting Together, the constitution of the Conference of European Churches, and the *Charta Oecumenica*.[47] Mutual co-operation is also a fundamental goal of church–state concordats.[48]

---

39 J. A. O. L. Vercammen, Archbishop of Utrecht (25-1-2005): LCRPR; see also C. B. Moss, *The Old Catholic Movement: Its Origins and History* (London, SPCK, 1964); and G. Huelin (ed.), *Old Catholics and Anglicans: 1931–1981* (Oxford, Oxford University Press, 1983).

40 SCOBA, Const., Preamble and Art. I.

41 LWF, Const., Arts I–III, V.

42 WARC, Const., Arts I.3 and III (1–9): they include: to unite the member churches in common service wherever needed and practicable; and to aid member churches which may be weak, oppressed or persecuted; and to contribute to the ecumenical movement.

43 Southern Baptist Convention, Const. (1845) Art. IV: 'Authority: While independent and sovereign in its own sphere, the Convention does not claim and will never attempt to exercise any authority over any other Baptist body, whether church, auxiliary organizations, associations, or convention.'

44 *The Baptist Faith and Message*, Sunday School Board (Nashville, Tenn., 1963) 12.

45 WMC, Constitution: CPDMC, pp. 782–3.

46 BWA, Bylaws of the General Council (2002).

47 Episcopal Church of the USA, Office of Ecumenism and Interfaith Relations, 'A beginner's guide to the Concordat of Agreement' (2003); ACCT, p. 4: The Covenanting Document, Part A, Declaration of Intent; Preamble of the Constitution of the Conference of European Churches (adopted 1992); CO (2001) Preamble: this aims 'to promote an ecumenical culture of dialogue and co-operation at all levels of church life, and to provide agreed criteria for this'.

48 Concordat between the Holy See and the Republic of Poland 1993, Preamble: harmonious relations.

Reconciliation, Recommitment and Trust

For the Lambeth Commission a covenant symbolizes the *trust* parties have in each other, an idea implicit in the Windsor draft covenant.[49] The idea is developed in *Towards an Anglican Covenant*: one 'important end' of a covenant is to assist the process of reconciliation post-Windsor; it can do so 'by focussing us on that which unites us, reaffirming our commitment to one another, and thereby helping to heal and strengthen the bonds of affection that have been damaged in recent years'; moreover, a covenant would represent a fundamental basis of trust.[50] Several respondents agree: a covenant provides 'an expression', or promotes 'a culture', of trust, the willingness to expose oneself to discussion of and 're-engagement' with Communion commitments.[51] This view is proposed because relationships of trust between member churches are the essential foundation of their fellowship; while a covenant should not take the place of the God-given bonds of communion it could offer an opportunity to renew Anglican relationships and to re-establish these after the damage of recent events.[52] Some consider that covenants are by nature reconciliatory.[53]

Many respondents doubt the ability of a covenant to achieve these goals: a covenant cannot force reconciliation; if trust is lacking, restoration of it by means of a covenant would be difficult; and for some, the proposal itself is based on mistrust.[54] Other critics concede that its workability depends upon trust, goodwill, conversation, and sharing, but churches must not have 'high expectations' about its impact.[55] As re-commitment is valued by the Inter-Anglican Theological and Doctrinal Commission, so the restoration of trust is a covenantal object recognized by both the Covenant Design Group and the Primates' Meeting in 2007.[56] One respondent argues that communion

---

49 TWR, para. 119; for example, WDAC, Arts 43, 5.2 and 3.

50 TAAC, paras 6, 8.

51 NIFCON (2005) para. 4; RCW (2005) 7; Bishop R. Ferris, Algoma Anglican Synod Office (Canadian bishop); Sudan, paras 3,4: LCRPR – Bishops/Diocese. See also Davie (2007): a covenant would address 'a lack of agreement, both in principle and in practice, among the churches of the Communion about what it means to be part of God's new covenant community and to live accordingly'.

52 Sudan, para. 4: LCRPR.

53 Seitz (2007): 'The inner nerve of covenanting is at once missional and reconciliatory.' Compare Wales, RNDC (2007): it is unclear whether the Nassau draft covenant is 'a means towards reconciliation or an expression of reconciliation'.

54 RTT (2005); Brisbane (2004) para. 4.3; MacDougall (2005) 17–18: LCRPR.

55 Diocese of Bendigo (2005); Diocese of Saskatoon (8-1-2006): LCRPR.

56 RPC, paras 1.9, 6.1; CDG, Nassau Report, paras 5, 6; *Communiqué*, 19-2-2007, para. 29: 'We believe that the establishment of a Covenant . . . in the longer term may lead to the trust required to re-establish our interdependent life.'

goes beyond polity, and derives from the trustworthiness of God; and so trust is a foundation of ecclesial communion, between and within churches: the Nassau draft covenant was a positive commitment to *trustworthiness*.[57] Some link the covenant project with re-establishing among Anglicans humility, generosity and hospitality, or returning Anglicanism to its foundation in the biblical gospel and apostolic faith and practice.[58] Others are critical: the Nassau report of the Covenant Design Group provides no evidence for its claim that the Communion would suffer irreparably if some measure of mutual and common commitment to the gospel was not reasserted in a short time.[59] For these, the Nassau draft covenant was an attempt to create structures of power which have no need for trust but which instead would crystallize distrust in juridical forms; the draft was not 'a new dawn of trust and mutual respect but a monument to the depth of conflict and the breakdown of relationships'.[60] Nevertheless, the Covenant Design Group at its London meeting in 2008 also recognized the importance of renewal as a covenant purpose, but not changing the character of the Anglican expression of Christian faith.[61]

The objects of reconciliation, renewal and trust are marks of the biblical covenants, as highlighted by the Inter-Anglican Theological and Doctrinal Commission.[62] These also mark the baptismal covenant (candidates receive the promises of a reconciling forgiveness of sin, and spiritual regeneration), the matrimonial covenant (in which mutual trust is essential), and the ordination covenant (in which a trust is placed in the candidate).[63] Similarly, in classical covenantal theology, a local church has a corporate covenant with God in order to mark a new relationship of trust between the faithful and God.[64] Inter-church

---

57 Radner (2007): 'polity' is defined as 'who tells whom what to do, or who gets to decide what and on what terms, and how it all gets organized'.

58 Cameron, in Chapman (2008) 35; S. Noll (2007).

59 Commenting on CDG Report, para. 8, Clatworthy, Bagshaw and Saxbee (May 2007) para. 2.2.

60 Ibid., para. 9: 'It will replace relationships of trust by relationships of constitutions and law.'

61 Introduction to SADC, para. 5; Commentary, para. 7: a covenant would enhance 'mutual trust'. Restoring trust was also seen as valuable by the Lusitanian church in the 2007 provincial consultation.

62 RPC, para. 1.2: 'the covenant established with [Abraham] was intended to be the means whereby God would address the problem of the human race and so of the entire created order.' See generally for example, G. E. Mendenhall, *Law and Covenant in the Ancient Middle East and in Israel* (Reprinted from The Biblical Archeologist, 17 Pittsburgh, PA, 1954).

63 Book of Common Prayer 1662, 263, 301, 553.

64 D. Tripp, 'Covenant' in G. D. Wakefield (ed.), *A Dictionary of Christian Spirituality* (London, SCM Press, 1983) 99.

agreements may have a penitential goal, like the Leuenberg Agreement of the Community of Protestant Churches in Europe: to confess the guilt and suffering that have accompanied and accompany the struggle for truth and unity in the church.[65] Ecumenical covenants too may seek: 'a new relationship' for the common confession of faith in Christ; 'renewal' of the will of churches to serve the mission of Christ; 'repentance' of the sin of division;[66] or renewal of commitment through the act of covenanting, which could be carried out in a spirit of penitence, and so be a witness to reconciliation.[67] Some respondents compare ecumenical covenants with the Anglican project: the former seek to foster new relationships; the latter seeks to re-establish an old relationship.[68] Church–state concordats often follow discord about the respective competences of the parties.[69]

Identity, Clarity and Understanding

For the Lambeth Commission a covenant: (a) 'incarnates communion' insofar as it provides a visible foundation around which Anglicans can gather to shape and protect their distinctive identity and mission; (b) provides an accessible resource for our ecumenical partners in their understanding of Anglicanism; and (c) puts into practice valuable lessons learnt from the experience of ecumenical agreements.[70] These ideas are elaborated in some responses. A covenant could be a significant educational tool to clarify Anglican ecclesiological identity, assist Anglican 'self-understanding' globally and locally, promote Anglican 'distinctiveness' within worldwide Christianity, and function as a 'visible foundation' of communion.[71] For the Primates' Meeting, one aim

---

65 CPCE:LA, Preamble, 1.

66 Church in Wales, Can. 1-5-1974.

67 ACCT, p. 3 (A Commitment to a Covenanting Process); CMU (1996) para. 43; AMC:CS (2001) paras 76, 194.

68 A. Perry 'From Waterloo to Windsor: the proposed Anglican Covenant in light of Anglican–Lutheran cooperation in Canada', Unpublished essay, Cardiff University (2007) 13.

69 See generally R. Puza and N. Doe (eds), *Religion and Law in Dialogue: Covenantal and Non-Covenantal Cooperation between State and Religion in Europe* (Leuven, Peeters, 2006).

70 TWR, para. 119; WDAC, Arts 1–5, especially Art. 4. See also Affirming Catholicism, Response to TAAC (13-12-2006) para. 9.

71 TAAC, para. 6; Strudwick (2006) (in affirming the historical relationship); CMS (2005); Goddard (2005) 6; E. Radner 'Freedom and covenant: the Miltonian analogy transfigured', *Anglican Theological Review* 87 (2005) 609 at 616; also MU (2004) 4–5: it would be 'good for visible, unified witness'; Southern Africa, RNDC (2007): a covenant has the potential 'to provide a confident articulation of Anglican identity'; see also Australia, RNDC (2007).

of the Lambeth Quadrilateral 'covenant' was to 'set forth to the world
. . . the identity of the . . . churches of the emerging Communion', but
the Covenant Design Group does not develop the notion of identity as
a covenant goal.[72] The critics do not deny the capacity of a covenant
to achieve these goals, though some argue that sharpening Anglican
identity might obstruct ecumenical dialogue.[73]

The Lambeth Commission also proposes the related goals of clarity
and understanding: the covenant would provide a basic framework for
an understanding of communion membership and what expectations
and commitments this generates.[74] Unlike the Nassau and St Andrews
draft covenants, the Windsor text itself provides that one of its objects
is to consolidate shared understandings of communion.[75] Similarly, for
Towards an Anglican Covenant a covenant could enable Anglicans
worldwide to understand and deepen their commitment to the beliefs,
history and practices they share in common and to develop these as
they engage together in mission.[76] Some responses, such as that of the
Inter-Anglican Standing Commission on Ecumenical Relations, con-
cur that a covenant would clarify the bonds of affection, understandings of core beliefs and practices, commitments and expectations (and
their strength), and give ecumenical partners a clearer understanding
of their Anglican partners.[77] Clarity is also recognized as important
by the Primates' Meeting 2007, in the Nassau report of the Covenant
Design Group (though in the St Andrews report it has less prominence),
and in submissions to that Group.[78]

---

72 Noll (2005) 2. The goal of identity is not conspicuous in the Nassau report of the
Group.

73 For example, NIFCON (2005) para. 7. See below Ch. 9.

74 TWR, para. 120: the idea is for churches to opt in rather than be excluded: see
below Ch. 9.

75 WDAC, Preamble.

76 TAAC, para. 9.

77 IASCER, Res. 08.07, 1: a covenant 'could lend greater coherence and credibility to
our life as a communion and to our ecumenical engagement'; see also Affirming Catholicism, Response to TAAC (13-12-2006), para. 1; SAMS Canada (2005) p. 4; and RTT
(2004) para. 55; Diocese of Saskatoon (8-1-2006); Most Revd J. Marona (Sudan), para.
2: LCRPR; Letter of Cardinal Walter Kasper to the Archbishop of Canterbury (17-12-
2004): the proposal of an Anglican Covenant is 'in line with the general thrust' of AR-
CIC. See also Bishop C. Epting (LCRPR) para. 2: a covenant could clarify 'who speaks
for Anglicanism on the world stage'; see also Bishop Hind, Church of England, General
Synod, Agenda Paper July 2007, GS 1661, Annex 2.

78 *Communiqué*, 19-2-2007, para. 29; CDG, Nassau Report, para. 4: a covenant
would 'articulate our common foundations'; M. Percy, Letter to the Secretary of the
Group (7-12-2006): 'the Communion will need to be reassured that the Covenant is not
a specifically targeted text that is directed against apparent pain or problems (i.e. is
neither palliative nor punitive), but . . . arises naturally and organically out of our common life, and expresses our desire to clarify and deepen our bonds of affection'.

The object of identity features in the biblical covenants (in which faith marks the believer), the baptismal covenant (in which the candidate is 'discerned from others' and grafted into the church), the marriage covenant (in which the spouses are joined in 'an honourable estate'), and the ordination covenant (in which the candidate is marked as a minister of God).[79] Similarly, the agreements of the Anglican Communion Network enable the network to 'be known for our commitment to evangelical faith and catholic order', and to be identified as a full member in the Communion.[80] Identity and understanding are shared characteristics of ecumenical covenants, to acknowledge the mutual identities of the partners as belonging to the Church universal,[81] and of the agreements of other church alliances. Thus the Old Catholics' agreement describes 'the ecclesiological identity' of the Old Catholic churches, and enables 'a local church to experience itself at the same time as . . . autonomous and interdependent', and that of the Lutheran World Federation likewise presents 'the self-understanding and the communion of member churches'.[82]

Order and Stability

The Lambeth Commission highlights several covenantal objects associated with order and stability in the Communion, namely to: (1) make explicit and more forceful the loyalty and bonds of affection which govern the relationships between the churches of the Communion;[83] (2) provide the weight of an international obligation; (3) underscore the commitment to public procedural multilateralism rather than unilateralism; (4) guard against the imperfections of ecclesial communion, human nature, and future conflict;[84] (5) promote peaceful life together,

---

79 Book of Common Prayer 1662, 263, 301, 553.

80 Core Purpose, Vision, and Core Values (2003); Organizational Charter, Arts I–X: that is, 'grounded in the classical Anglican formularies, and in submission to the moral and teaching authority of the Lambeth Conference and Primates Meeting'.

81 CPCE:LA, Arts 6, 37: the agreement expresses a 'common understanding of the Gospel' so far as this is required for fellowship.

82 Vercammen, Archbishop of Utrecht (25-1-2005): LCRPR; LWF Const., Arts I–III, V.

83 TWR, para. 118; their current unenforceability is seen as 'a persistent problem in Anglicanism contributing directly to the present crisis' (117). For enforceability, see below Ch. 8.

84 TWR, para. 119: the Communion 'cannot again afford, in every sense, the crippling prospect of repeated worldwide inter-Anglican conflict such as the current crisis. Given the imperfections of our communion and human nature, doubtless there will be more. It is our shared responsibility to have in place an agreed mechanism to enable and maintain life in communion and to prevent and manage communion disputes.'

which is a theological imperative of communion and God's will for the Communion;[85] (6) prevent and manage conflict and protect the Communion (and its ecumenical partnerships) from the effects of such conflict (allowing the parties to it to adjust their relationship and resolve disputes in the light of changing circumstances);[86] and (7) assist churches in their relations with the states in which they exist, when a church faces pressure from its host state(s) to adopt secular state standards in its ecclesial life and practice.[87] Similarly, *Towards an Anglican Covenant* recognizes that a covenant could provide what it sees as currently lacking in the Communion – an agreed framework for both common discernment and the prevention and resolution of conflict in the form of 'house rules' by which the family of churches wishes to live together for the development of a disciplined and fulfilling life in communion.[88] The Covenant Design Group also accepts the need for mutual commitment and discipline in a world and time of instability, conflict and fragmentation.[89]

The objects of order, stability, accountability and discipline have been the subject of considerable discussion among the respondents. As to order and stability, many suggest that a covenant would: balance autonomy with international responsibility; systematize elements of Communion life; protect ordered dialogue (by formalized consultation); prevent unilateral innovation or make clear the consequences of it.[90] A covenant could spell out the standards and expectations of the

---

85 TWR, para. 3.

86 In the ecumenical context, the crisis led to condemnation from the Russian Orthodox and Oriental Orthodox churches, and a statement from the Roman Catholic Church that the developments had created 'new and serious difficulties' in Anglican–Roman Catholic relations: see above, Introduction.

87 TWR, para. 119: an 'international Anglican covenant might provide powerful support to the church, in a dispute with the State, to reinforce and underpin its religious liberty within the State'. The Consultation of Legal Advisers (2002) has identified potential problem areas as to the 'Applicability of Civil Law standards to the Church': for example, clergy and secular employment law; recourse by church members to secular courts; marriage and polygamy; clergy and political activity. With the exception of the last, these seven objects are implicit in the Windsor draft covenant, particularly its principle of autonomy-in-communion: WDAC, Parts III–V. See below Ch. 6.

88 TAAC, paras 6–11.

89 Introduction to SADC, para. 4; see also Nassau Report, para. 15. See also ACADC, Part 6: 'By entering into communion . . . churches accept certain constraints upon the operation of the principles of autonomy and subsidiarity.' For accountability see more fully Chs 6 and 9 below.

90 *Church Times*, 22-10-2004, 10: 'if Anglicans are remotely serious about belonging to an international body, this seems to be an excellent blueprint', to enable the Communion to be 'a functional international family'; also Affirming Catholicism, Response to TAAC (13-12-2006) para. 1; NIFCON (2005): para. 4: that is, those aspects of it which have been 'in loose association with one another and until now have not needed to be defined with precision': LCRPR; A Guide to the Windsor Report, Commissioned by an

parties, helping them function together, through rules for engagement and communion.[91] A standard opinion is that every community needs rules to give order to its ideals, but at the same time balancing 'order and ardour', which involves a synthesis between freedom and mutual enslavement to one another in love – a covenant does not necessarily mean a straitjacket imposing uniformity and ending diversity.[92] Moreover, a covenant could establish ways in which Anglicans are accountable to one another (while respecting provincial autonomy), encourage mutual accountability and interdependence, and strengthen the currently 'weak and informal' decision-making structures.[93] Covenantal discipline is needed to combat our fallen nature, prevent or minimize conflict, advance a vision of the Communion at its best, and protect the Communion from itself at its worst.[94] The Archbishops of Canterbury and York have said of the Nassau draft covenant: 'It is not a tool for promoting schism or canonizing heightened intolerance, but an element in the continuing work of handling conflict without easy recourse to mutual condemnation'.[95] Several other responses to the Nassau text qualify the idea: a covenant could enhance mutual accountability *provided* it does not diminish legitimate diversity within the member

International Gathering from around the Anglican Communion meeting at Oxford 19–21 October 2004 (unpublished); Rt Revd Dr A. J. Malik (Pakistan): LCRPR.

91 SAMS Canada (2005) p. 2; and Anglican Frontier Mission, Response (31-1-2005); Bishop C. Epting, TEC, para. 2; Dioc. of Saskatoon (8-1-2006): LCRPR.

92 C. Sugden, 'An Anglican Communion covenant: a personal view'; G. Cameron, 'Ardour and order: can the bonds of affection survive?', Paper delivered at the conference of the Ecclesiastical Law Society, Liverpool, January 2007; A. Goddard, 'The Anglican covenant', a briefing paper for the Evangelical Group on General Synod: <http://www.fulcrum-anglican.org.uk//news/2007>

93 J. Kelsey (TEC Bishop): Statement (19-10-2004); see also Strudwick (2006); RTT (2004) para. 55; Dioc. of Saskatoon (8-1-2006): LCRPR: 'improve accountability'; MU (2004) pp. 2, 3: we should be 'more accountable to one another, less individualistic, negatively autonomous, more honest, consistent and transparent in what we want to achieve as a . . . Communion'; see also ACNS 4250 (17-2-2007): Primate of Australia: the Nassau draft provides mutual accountability.

94 Sudan, para. 4: 'Given our fallen human condition, we cannot regard the current crisis . . . as unique. We therefore see it very helpful to have an established mechanism to resolve serious disputes'; Westcott House: it might combat the tendency to extremism; Dioc. of Niagara; Rt Revd J. Malik: LCRPR; see also ACNS 404: R. Eames, 'The Anglican Communion: A Growing Reality' (5-10-2005); Bishop Hind, Church of England, General Synod, Agenda Paper July 2007, GS 1661, Annex 2; A. Perry, 'From Waterloo to Windsor' (2007) 16.

95 Church of England, General Synod, Agenda Paper July 2007, GS 1661, Annex 1: 'Whether or not a Covenant is adopted, the question of handling conflict will not go away . . . If we do not have a Covenant in the Communion, we will not be absolved from the imperative to manage our conflicts and tensions better than we have been doing.' See also Radner (2007): the covenant is about 'a positive commitment not a disciplinary exclusion'.

churches.[96] The Covenant Design Group at its London meeting 2008 reasserted the value of the principle of accountability.[97]

This is a crucial issue. For the critics, if a covenant represents a set of rules, and the power to enforce them, the Communion would become less free and necessarily more coercive, achieving uniformity at the expense of conviction and conscience.[98] Moreover, it might replace 'the bonds of affection' with 'the bondage of law', and inhibit the work of the Spirit, diversity in mission, and provincial autonomy.[99] The proper tools of communion are conversation, discussion, argument, and reasoning, but the proposal constitutes a move to mutual regulation away from being a family with its full range of rows and reconciliations.[100] Covenantal structures could place a bureaucratic and legalistic foundation at the heart of the Communion, put at risk inspired and prophetic initiatives in mission, threaten the comprehensiveness of Anglicanism, and lead to a centralized jurisdiction.[101] Furthermore, it is difficult to predict whether a covenant would prevent disputes between Anglicans, and it is unlikely to assist churches in their relations with their host states.[102]

Nevertheless, order is a mark of the salvific covenant (God commits himself to the faithful), baptismal covenant (candidates are to lead

---

96 Southern Africa, RNDC (2007): a covenant could seek 'appropriate mutual accountability, provided it neither diminishes legitimate diversity and autonomy, nor constrains Anglicanism's traditional ability to address new circumstances as they arise'; it may also have to acknowledge the need to set limits on 'the breadth of beliefs and practices'; see also TEC, RNDC (2007): 'At its best, an Anglican covenant can move the churches of the Anglican Communion to renew the sense of mutual responsibility and interdependence in the Body of Christ that has motivated life in the Communion in the past and leads us to higher levels of service to God's mission.'

97 Commentary to SADC, para. 8; see also SADC, Cl. 3.2.2 for 'mutual responsibility'.

98 LGCM (2005) para. 11: 'Is that what God is really willing for the Anglican Church?'; LCRPR; Modern Churchpeople's Union, Response to TAAC (November 2006). See also TEC, RNDC (2007): a covenant could be seen as a means to bring what is perceived to be a recalcitrant church into conformity with a particular set of norms in the Communion.

99 CIPRWR (2005) 11: autonomy 'ought not to be idolized but it deserves to be cherished: it may be a gift we have to offer to the whole Church of God'; see also RTT (2004) para. 20: LCRPR.

100 C. Hefling, 'A reasonable development?' in A. Linzey and R. Kirker (eds), Gays and the Future of Anglicanism (Winchester, O Books, 2005) 81 at 82–4; C. Lewis, 'On unimportance', in ibid. 149 at 152.

101 TAAC, paras 8, 11. See also Wales, RNDC (2007): 'an over-structuralised Communion will lead to loss of the present Anglican engagement with local issues and the promptings of the Holy Spirit' unless there are 'generous boundaries' to 'creative dissent'.

102 CIPRWR (2005) 8; Dioc. of Sydney (7-2-2005): LCRPR.

a committed life of fidelity), eucharistic covenant (the faithful must examine their consciences prior to admission), marriage covenant (spouses undertake 'to keep the vow and covenant between them'), and ordination covenant (candidates undertake faithful diligence). Likewise, stability is an object of the permanence of baptism, matrimony and ordination, and steadfastness is promised in each.[103] These are persistent themes in Protestant covenantal theology as applied to church organization.[104] Stability is also a central object in church–state concordats,[105] in the monastic covenant,[106] and in several inter-church agreements: the Lutheran World Federation is 'organized' under its constitution; and the Covenant Union of Anglican Churches in Concordat seeks to enable its members to work together in 'discipline and accountability'. Conflict prevention and resolution are aims of the constitution of the Standing Conference of Orthodox Bishops in the Americas, and of *Charta Oecumenica*,[107] as they are of church–state concordats.[108]

Mission and Witness

The Lambeth Commission proposes that a covenant would provide a unique opportunity for worldwide witness through the formality of ratification by the primates publicly assembled.[109] *Towards an Anglican Covenant* and the Inter-Anglican Theological and Doctrinal Commission too recognize that a covenant could clarify the mission of the churches and propose that it could serve the growth of the Communion.[110] On the one hand, many respondents see this as a legitimate purpose. A covenant could: help promote a theological vision of the

---

103 Baptism and ordination are indelible and marriage indissoluble until death; Book of Common Prayer 1662, 263, 301, 553. The Eucharist is a perpetual memorial until Christ's coming again.

104 J. Piper, 'Why a church covenant?' (1993) 5: 'what establishes the visible union of a group of believers into a church is that they make a covenant with each other to be the church.'

105 Concordat between the Holy See and the Republic of Poland (1993) Preamble: 'stable relations'.

106 H. Feiss, *Monastic Wisdom* (San Francisco, Harper, 1999) 145.

107 LWF, Const., Arts I–III, V; CUACC (2005), Arts 1, 2; SCOBA, Const., Art. 1.

108 Puza and Doe (2006) 259 (for example, in relation to restitution of church property).

109 TWR, para. 119; WDAC, Art. 7(4): this spells out a rudimentary understanding of the purposes of the Anglican Communion, and these include mission.

110 TAAC, paras 6, 11; IATDC, RPC, para. 2.3: 'The covenant as a vision for mission both stresses the importance of the work to be done and binds its members to one another for greater effectiveness in accomplishing it.'

Body of Christ as a communion in mission; manifest the importance of mission to the Communion; underline that mission requires co-operation; call the faithful to deeper spirituality in witness to common faith and heritage in the midst of diversity; and be a model to others in a fractious world.[111] Moreover, a covenant might provide *space* for rational debate on contentious issues, offering a safe place for conversation whether with God or others in the Anglican Communion.[112] Some suggest several missiological criteria to test the legitimacy of the proposals; for example, whether a covenant builds up the body of the Church, furthers its mission, deepens its holiness, enhances its witness, and nourishes the vitality by which it preserves, teaches and lives out the faith.[113]

On the other hand, the critics argue that a covenant might *exclude* people from the Kingdom of God; that it would promote the fiction that the Communion has a mission: mission belongs properly to the local church; that it would make the Communion too inward-looking thereby risking its apostolicity; and that it could frustrate *ubhuntu*: respect for human dignity, hospitality, and diversity.[114] Nevertheless, the Covenant Design Group concurs that a covenant could enhance mission, and this was a major issue emerging in the provincial consultation of 2007. Indeed, both the Nassau and St Andrews draft covenants promote mission as a fundamental object: the churches would enter the covenant 'to proclaim more effectively in our different contexts the Grace of God revealed in the Gospel', and to offer the love of God in responding to the needs of the world; like the draft submitted to the Group by the Anglican Church in Australia, there is special provision on the commitment to mission.[115] The idea is neatly summed up in the proposition that a covenant is a partnership for the proclamation of

---

111 See respectively, RHB (2005), para. 4; CMS (2005); Church of the Province of West Africa; CPIO (2005) para. 7; Rt Revd J. Malik; and IFSCCUCI (2004) 4–5: LCRPR. See also Global South Primates Meeting, Kigali *Communiqué*, 22-9-2006 (ACNS 4193), para. 7: 'an Anglican Covenant will demonstrate to the world that it is possible to be a truly global communion where differences are not affirmed at the expense of faith and truth but within a framework of a common confession of faith and mutual accountability.'

112 Strudwick (2006); Scully (2007) 1; RCW (2005) 6: LCRPR.

113 Clatworthy, Bagshaw and Saxbee (2007) para. 3.2.

114 FOFAD, 10-11; Wescott House: LCRPR; for *ubhuntu*, see Kevin Ward, 'African perspectives on episcopacy and sexuality', in Linzey and Kirker (2005) 243 at 244.

115 Introduction to SADC, para. 8; SADC, Preamble and Cl. 2.1 and 2.2; Nassau Report, para. 4; NDC, Art. 1, Preamble, Art. 4.4 and 4.5; see also Art. 4.2 (mission heritage) and 4.3 (common mission); ACADC, Part 4. The inclusion of mission has been welcomed by many (for example, Australia, RNDC (2007)).

the gospel;[116] mission is seen by some as a characteristic fundamental to the very nature of a covenant.[117]

In point of fact, mission and witness are purposive elements of the new covenant community (as depicted in scripture),[118] and the covenants of baptism (as a sign of profession), marriage (spouses live in witness to their union), and ordination (candidates promise to proclaim the gospel and serve as examples to the flock of Christ).[119] In modern covenantal theology, one aim of a covenant is to awaken a community to its mission; and covenanting is a response to the call of God.[120] The aim of the Covenant for Communion and Mission (2005) is to provide 'a fresh articulation of the principles and values that can serve to guide our cross-cultural and cross boundary relationships' among the mission agencies of the Communion.[121] Similarly, the draft constitution of the Anglican Global Initiative is driven not only by the present crisis but also by mission: its objects are to promote 'an authentic expression of the worldwide Anglican Communion' in mission and ministry projects, to provide an effective means to spread the gospel, and to plant churches and secure 'orthodox' episcopal oversight for dissenting parishes.[122] The Anglican Communion Network is a missionary movement, making disciples of Jesus Christ and (likewise) planting churches in North America.[123] Witness to mission is also an object in the agreement of the Community of Protestant Churches in Europe (to witness removal of divisions which bar the way to fellowship), the constitution of the World Alliance of Reformed Churches, and the Anglican–Lutheran concordat in the USA.[124]

---

116 Grieb (2007); see also Goddard (2007): a covenant should reflect a missional vision; and Dakin (2007) parts 3 and 8: 'the Covenant is a unique opportunity for the re-making of Anglicanism in which mission is both prior to the church and, through the Covenant, mission becomes intentionally constitutive of its very existence'; '[t]he purpose of any Anglican Covenant must be to release the economy of God's grace: to be the means by which people are blessed, in the fellowship of the covenant, to know more of the Covenantal, Missional and Scriptural God. The Anglican Covenant is therefore a way of generating and shaping missional capital.'

117 Seitz (2007): 'covenants are deeply personal, relational, missional, reconciliatory expressions of the will of the One God to save, to bring into fellowship, and to oblige'.

118 IATDC, RPC, para. 1.6: 'The new covenant community thus exists to set forward the mission of God in the power of the Spirit, and is therefore called to a shared, common life of holiness and reconciliation.'

119 Book of Common Prayer 1662, 263, 301, 553.

120 J. Piper, 'Why a church covenant?' (1993) 4, http://www.desiringgod.org/library/sermons.

121 IASCOME (2005), CCM, p. 3.

122 AGI, Draft Constitution (2004) Art. III.

123 ACN, Core Purpose, Vision, and Core Values (2003).

124 CPCE:LA, Arts 30–34; WARC, Const., Art. III (1–9); TEC–Evangelical Lutheran Church, Concordat of Agreement (2003).

Conclusion

The Lambeth Commission covenant proposal contains, explicitly and implicitly, five basic groups of ideas which may be understood to represent the strategic objects or purposes of a covenant: unity; reconciliation, recommitment and trust; identity, clarity and understanding; order and stability; and mission. Ideas emerging in the responses might be classified similarly. These covenantal goals are valued by many respondents. However, the critics question belief in the capacity of a covenant to realize unity, reconciliation, trust, and mission, and reject as unjustified the goals of order, discipline and accountability. When placed in a rudimentary way against scripture, tradition and reason, it would seem that each of the five goals is a feature of biblical, baptismal, marriage, ordination and (with the exception of discipline) ecumenical covenants. They are also standard goals valued by other international Christian communities, whose agreements moreover spell out clearly the Christian purposes of those global communities themselves. In contrast, the Lambeth process offers a less sophisticated (but since Nassau and St Andrews more missional) understanding of the purposes of the Anglican Communion as a global community.

Part 2

The Structure and Substance of a Covenant

4

The Form of a Covenant

The first issues to explore in this section, on the structure and substance of a covenant, are those which concern the form of a covenant: its quality, its language, and its quantity. The Lambeth Commission did not address questions of covenantal form in the text of the *Windsor Report*. However, *Towards an Anglican Covenant* recognizes that considerable thought has to be given to the form of the covenant.[1] The responses likewise treat the matter of form as one of real significance. Clarity about form is an essential part of the discourse in so far as the form of a covenant will send out signals about the very character of Anglicanism in the worldwide community of churches. As with other aspects of the covenant proposal, matters of form are also related to the nature and purposes of a covenant: form is conditioned by elements of these – as a covenant is promissory, so its form could be promissory, etc. The matter of form did not particularly engage the Covenant Design Group at Nassau or London. The following compares the form of the St Andrews, Nassau and Windsor draft covenants, the arguments in responses for and against such form, and it measures these against covenantal forms in scripture, tradition and reason, particularly those employed in ecumenical agreements and by other international ecclesial communities.[2]

The Documentary Form of a Covenant

As has already been seen, the Lambeth Commission proposes a written covenant to make explicit the 'bonds of affection' and to articulate what to-date has been assumed. It offers 'a preliminary draft', and implies that the document must be an accessible resource character-

---

1 TAAC, para. 17.
2 It also suggests that through the proposal to adopt a formal agreement, the Anglican Communion as an international body would seem to engage in the natural process of formal structuralization characteristic of the culture of most religious organizations.

ized by clarity.[3] The chair of the Commission has pointed out that the Windsor draft covenant itself was not written in stone, but is rather a tangible concept of how communion and living in communion could assume working reality.[4] *Towards an Anglican Covenant* also suggests a written form, but no additional reason is offered beyond the need to articulate existing principles.[5] The responses develop these ideas a little more fully. Several consider that the relations Anglicans have enjoyed until now have not needed to be defined with precision as the informal bonds of affection have been sufficient to sustain communion.[6] However, many argue that a formal covenant is necessary to codify Anglican assumptions about communion, and that a documentary covenant would reduce the scope for arbitrary decision-making.[7] Clarity of form and language, including definitional clarity and the avoidance of contentious terms, is valued in several responses, so that there is no doubt about that to which the parties are binding themselves.[8] The issues of documentary form and clarity do not expressly surface in the Nassau report of the Covenant Design Group or the documents of the Group from its London meeting.[9]

One suggestion in the responses is that a covenant should be 'synchronic' rather than 'diachronic' in form: the *Windsor Report* excessively emphasizes synchronic communion (with other contemporary Anglicans) and not the diachronic dimension of communion (with the catholic Church throughout history).[10] The Inter-Anglican Standing Commission on Ecumenical Relations advises a form grounded in Trinitarian theology and one which portrays a life for the churches together rooted in eucharistic communion as part of the Church universal; the suggestion was adopted by the Covenant Design Group at its London meeting.[11] Indeed, for some critics the language and thought-

---

3 TWR, paras 117, 118, 119 (also for 'ecumenical partners').

4 Eames: ACNS 4045 (6-10-2005); Barnett-Cowan (2004): the Windsor draft was in 'graph-form'.

5 TAAC, para. 1.

6 For example, IFSCCUCI (2004) p. 4: LCRPR.

7 Iglesia Anglicana del Cono Sur de America: LCRPR; Sugden (2007): Fulcrum Website.

8 TEC, s. 4; SAMS Canada (2005) p. 4; RTT (2004) para. 55; HBTG (2005); IFSC-CUCI p. 4: LCRPR.

9 But they are implicit in the notion of articulation of common foundations: NDC, Report, para. 4.

10 RTT (2004) para. 22; see also the Letter of Cardinal Kasper to Canterbury (17-12-2004): LCRPR.

11 IASCER, Responding to the Idea of a Covenant (8-12-2006) para. 4; emphasis on a Trinitarian foundation is also proposed by the Church of England in its response to the Nassau draft covenant and this now appears in the Introduction to SADC. See also Grieb (2007) on the idea that a covenant should reflect a theology of the Cross.

forms of the Windsor draft were insufficiently evangelical, too catholic, not properly grounded in Scripture, and too loyal to structures and organizational unity rather than to the apostolic faith.[12] Moreover, it was vulnerable to disputes over interpretation, with broadly worded provisions leaving loopholes for liberals and landmines for orthodox believers.[13] Similar criticisms were made of the Nassau text. The Primates' Meeting 2007 questioned the meaning of, for example, 'biblically derived' moral values (which churches should commit themselves to uphold), as did the Joint Standing Committee of the Primates' Meeting and Anglican Consultative Council in relation to 'member churches'.[14] These terms do not appear in the St Andrews draft covenant; but this too, like the Nassau text but unlike that submitted to the Covenant Design Group by the Australian church, has no definitions section.[15]

Even the scriptural covenants, which are to be 'written in the hearts of believers', have a documentary aspect: the Old Testament records (or testifies to) the spiritual reality underlying them, and the New Testament is understood theologically as a record of the new covenant.[16] Canonically, while candidates for baptism, marriage and ordination make oral undertakings, the terms of these covenants are recorded in the liturgical texts of Anglican churches in order to represent their 'public expression', not simply to protect linguistic forms but to provide conditions in which God's presence may be experienced.[17] As has already been seen, Anglicans increasingly formalize their agreements, and ecumenical covenants are codified to provide a visible symbol of unity.[18] The same can be said for the concordats of comparable international ecclesial communities in the documentary form of an 'agree-

12 R. Tong, 'How would the Anglican Church of Australia commit itself to an Anglican Covenant?', in P. G. Bolt, M. D. Thompson and R. Tong (eds), *The Faith Once For All Delivered* (Camperdown, NSW, 2005) 58–9. For scriptural elements of the draft, see below Ch. 6.

13 Bishop P. Epting (2005) para.4: LCRPR: such as 'essential' in Art. 13.3; providing hospitality to visitors from other provinces could be difficult to enforce.

14 Primates Meeting, Points raised in the Discussion of the Draft Text for an Anglican Covenant; NDC, Art. 2.2; Art. 3.1: they ask: 'Who assess the authenticity of any interpretation?'; see also Joint Standing Committee of the Primates and ACC, Points raised in Discussion of the Draft Text for an Anglican Covenant; see, respectively, NDC, Arts 3.1, 5, 5.2.III, 6.2.

15 But they are implicit in the notion of articulation of common foundations: NDC, Report, para. 4; ACADC, Part 1: this defines 'Anglican Communion', 'Instruments of Communion', 'The Member Churches', 'Member Church' and 'Reception'. TEC, RNDC (2007) proposes inclusion of a definitions section.

16 See for example, G. P. Hugenberger, *Marriage as a Covenant* (Leiden, E. J. Brill, 1994) 228 on documentary formulae in covenants.

17 New Zealand, Prayer Book 1989, xiii–xiv.

18 AMC:CS (2001) v: it endorses 'in a formal way what is already a reality in many local situations'.

ment', 'statute' or 'constitution'.[19] Indeed, the Southern Baptist tradition prescribes that local churches should have a written covenant to enable concrete agreement on church life: model covenants abound.[20] The consensual compacts of Anglican churches are also codified in constitutions and canons.[21]

Codification is commonly perceived in the sociology of religion as part of a normal process. Religious organizations, like their secular counterparts,[22] tend toward formal structures to fulfil their objects: they become socially institutionalized (and bureaucratized). Institutionalization (which may include the routinization of charisma) in turn generates theological dilemmas about: administrative order (elaboration of policy versus flexibility); delimination (concrete definition versus substitution of the letter for the spirit); power (conversion versus coercion); and expansion (structure versus communalism). The influences on institutionalization include both the accomplishment of major goals and the effects of conflict, each of which may necessitate greater visible organization.[23] In some respects, the Anglican covenant development exhibits the same tendency and tensions.[24] Some respondents imply that the covenant proposal reflects the modern 'demand' for greater accountability and transparency, the loss of deference in society, and the idea that the credibility of organized religion has to be earned. They suggest that the current crisis in Anglicanism has contributed to 'an erosion of trust in the church as an institution *worthy* of trust'; formal structures might restore that trust: 'Why should the church be any different?'[25] There is certainly some evidence that new

---

19 See Ch. 2 for the employment of these formal instruments.

20 R. Stanton Norman, *The Baptist Way: Distinctives of a Baptist Church* (Nashville, Tenn., Broadman and Holman, 2005) 118; see also C. W. Deweese, *Church Covenants* (Nashville, Tenn., Broadman, 1990); H. Webb, 'A new church covenant': http://www.lifeway.com/lwc/article_main_page/0,1703,A=161133&M=150036,00.html

21 N. Doe, *Canon Law in the Anglican Communion* (Oxford, Clarendon Press, 1998) 21f.

22 See, for example, C. Handy, *Understanding Organizations* (4th edn, London, Penguin Books, 1993) ch. 7; see also generally G. Morgan, *Images of Organization* (San Francisco, Barrett-Koehler, 1998).

23 K. A. Roberts, *Religion in Sociological Perspective* (2nd edn, Belmont, CA, Wadsworth, 1990) ch. 7; T. F. O'Dea, 'Five dilemmas in the institutionalization of religion', *Journal for the Scientific Study of Religion* (1961) 30.

24 Graham '"Our real witness": Windsor, public opinion and sexuality', in A. Linzey and F. Kirker (eds), *Gays and the Future of Anglicanism* (Winchester, O Books, 2005) 200: the crisis conveys '[a]n image of a church preoccupied with its own concerns, dimly aware of "poverty, violence . . . famine and injustice" outside its own walls, but seemingly incapable of breaking off from its own internal debates in order to respond'.

25 Graham (2005) 202. See also Cameron, in Chapman (2008) 42: the proposed covenant 'is not an attempt to develop a "Code"'; a code cannot cope with changing circumstances.

religious alliances tend toward institutionalization and formal structures.[26] Equally, it would not be difficult for the Communion to resist such trends and to retain its tacit covenant.

Debate about covenantal form has also raised the issue of confessionalism. *Towards an Anglican Covenant* points out that if a covenant contained a statement of Anglican doctrine this may be seen to alter the nature of the Communion towards that of a confessional family.[27] Anglicanism inclines to define its doctrine through liturgy rather than in confessions of faith.[28] There are those who consider that a covenant would help to express common faith and heritage, including biblical and credal faith.[29] Others contend that, for example, if the Articles of Religion were included in a covenant that would make the Communion 'confessional', or at least move the Communion towards confessionalism; according to one respondent, the Windsor draft covenant looks suspiciously like a 'confession'.[30] These concerns could be weighed against some sacramental covenants which are confessional in form,[31] but a non-confessional covenant would be more in line with the consensual compacts of churches which merely point to but do not spell out statements of belief in the historical and other formularies of the Church.[32] Sometimes, contemporary Anglican agreements are confessional, like those of some international ecclesial communities.[33]

---

26 See, for example, the constitutions of the World Council of Churches, the Australian National Council of Churches, and the Churches Together in Britain and Ireland; CAPA is also working on 'governance'.

27 TAAC, para. 5: it asks therefore: Should a covenant set out Anglican articles of belief?

28 Davie (2007). Moreover, 'when subscription is required to the [Thirty-Nine] Articles or other elements in the Anglican tradition, it should be required, and given, only in the context of a statement which gives the full range of our inheritance of faith and sets the Articles in their historical context': LC 1968, Res. 43.

29 CPIO (2005) para. 7; Goddard: Fulcrum Website; Sugden (2007): Fulcrum Website.

30 Noll (2007); Bishop P. Epting, para. 2: LCRPR. See also Chapman (2008) 97, 126.

31 Candidates at baptism, confirmation and ordination profess or declare the beliefs stated in the liturgical texts and in articles of religion.

32 See N. Doe, *Canon Law in the Anglican Communion* (Oxford, Clarendon Press, 1998) ch. 7.

33 For example, the Anglican Communion Network has 'a faithful statement of belief' and a practical 'renewed commitment' to it: Confession and Calling, Preface; CPCE:LA, Art. 37: 'The Agreement leaves intact the binding force of the confessions within the participating churches. It is not to be regarded as a new confession of faith. It sets forth a consensus reached about central matters, one which makes church fellowship possible between churches of different confessional positions. In accordance with this consensus the . . . churches . . . seek . . . a common witness and service and they pledge themselves to continue their common doctrinal discussions.' See also SBC – TCCG, 16: Sample Constitution, III: 'We affirm the Holy Bible as the inspired word of God and the basis for our

The Inter-Anglican Standing Commission on Ecumenical Relations is particularly keen that a covenant should not be confessional in form: a confessional covenant would have a major impact on ecumenical dialogue, with potentially negative consequences for many of the oldest relationships between Anglicans and others.[34] This anxiety is echoed by Affirming Catholicism and Inclusive Church: it would be alien to Anglicanism and likely to intensify strife.[35] The impractical nature of formulating a confessional covenant has also been highlighted.[36] In point of fact, the St Andrews draft covenant (like the Nassau text) does not systematically represent Anglican doctrine, though it has doctrinal elements and refers to the historic formularies.[37] It has been understood that the latter were included in the Nassau text not to establish a renewed Protestant confessionalism, but rather to acknowledge them as a historically accepted standard for common discernment and order, particularly with respect to scripture.[38] Some suggest that in the covenant debate a distinction must be made between a 'confessing' and 'confessional' church, and that historically Anglicanism has been both a confessing and confessional tradition: it has had a confessional element in the sense that the historic formularies declare where Anglicans stand and what they stand for.[39] The Covenant Design Group sought to avoid 'too precise formulations' for its St Andrews draft.[40]

---

beliefs. This church subscribes to the doctrinal statement of "The Baptist Faith and Message" as adopted by the Southern Baptist Convention in 1963. We voluntarily band ourselves together as a body of baptized believers . . . personally committed to sharing the good news of salvation to lost mankind. The ordinances of the church are believer's baptism and the Lord's Supper.'

34 IASCER, Responding to the Idea of an Anglican Covenant (8-12-2006) para. 14.

35 Response to TAAC (13-12-2006) para. 6; Strudwick (20-11-2006) sect. 1.

36 Cameron, in Chapman (2008) 43: 'The idea that a small group of people could write an exhaustive definition of Christianity to which 80 million Anglicans in all corners of the globe are expected to sign up is a very difficult task indeed.'

37 For example, SADC, Cls. 1.1.2 (formularies); 2.1.1 (communion is a gift of God). TEC and Wales, RNDC (2007) both comment that Art. 3 of the Nassau draft covenant appears to be confessional in form.

38 Radner (2007).

39 Davie (2007): that is a church which confesses Christ and the gospel, and 'a church which adheres to certain specific statements of belief'; he cites the Church of England Doctrine Commission Report *Believing in the Church* (London, 1981) 125. Davie argues that this means that: 'the development of a covenant will not mean a move from a non-confessional to a confessional Anglicanism or from a situation where everyone is accepted to a position where some begin to be excluded'; but a covenant might mean that the confessional basis of Anglicanism becomes more detailed with the forms of the acceptable expression of Anglican theology being more precisely defined; but the Communion will have to agree on this – it will not be imposed without consent.

40 Commentary to SADC, para. 11.

Linguistic Form: Descriptive and Prescriptive Covenants

The Lambeth Commission is of the view that its draft covenant is largely descriptive of existing principles.[41] This raises questions as to whether the form of a covenant should be descriptive, prescriptive, or both. *Towards an Anglican Covenant* recognizes that covenantal form could be: (a) descriptive: to articulate ecclesiology, to focus on that which unites Anglicans, and to help the Communion in self-understanding and ecumenical relationships; (b) prescriptive, to focus on the mutual commitments and represent the 'house rules' of the Communion; or (c) 'motivational', to commit the churches to common action, or 'aspirational', to speak of the Communion as it wishes to become.[42] However, the Inter-Anglican Theological and Doctrinal Commission considers that a balance needs to be struck: a form not merely consisting of conforming constitutions and canon law, but one which reflects interpersonal and relational elements prominent in the biblical examples of covenant combining narrative and vision with recitals (statements of past history, the present situation, and the desired future) and commitments (binding agreements between the partners to the covenant).[43] The Nassau report of the Covenant Design Group does not address questions of form beyond the claim that the strength of a covenant would be greater if it addressed broad principles; its draft is structured on the basis of affirmations, commitments and a declaration, but is considerably less 'juridical' than that submitted to the Group by the Anglican Church in Australia.[44] The matter did not seem to exercise the Group at its St Andrews London meeting.

A descriptive form

Towards an Anglican Covenant acknowledges that a 'lapidary' descriptive form may well be of educational importance and symbolical significance, and most churches should have little difficulty in signing up to such a covenant, so long as the text confines itself to widely established

41 TWR, para. 118.

42 TAAC, paras 6, 17: its treats a Covenant for Communion in Mission as of this type. Many in TEC would prefer this model: TEC, RNDC (2007).

43 RPC, para. 2.2. This also suggests that a covenant could usefully mention the issues that currently divide Anglicans, a view not shared by CDG, Report, para. 5. See also the response of MCU (November 2006) at 16: a covenant should be declaratory, affirmatory, aspirational (with commitments) and procedural.

44 Report 2007, para. 5. Also recommended by IASCER (8-12-2006); ACADC is modelled on the constitution of the Anglican Church in Australia.

and respected principles.[45] Several of the responses consider that the Windsor draft covenant is descriptive, a restatement or clarification of the existing situation, as the Lambeth Quadrilateral was descriptive.[46] Others advocate that a covenant should set out the existing life of the Communion and ought therefore to be more descriptive than prescriptive or 'dynamic'.[47] For some, that even a descriptive form would be uncontroversial is 'wishful thinking'.[48] One respondent proposes the Lausanne Covenant on world evangelization as a model to stress the missionary character of the Communion.[49]

In practice, most covenants have descriptive aspects. The Connecticut-Scottish Concordat 1784 describes agreement between the churches on the scriptural foundations of the faith.[50] The present tacit covenant of the Communion contains conventions that are declaratory, for example of 'universal custom'.[51] Ecumenical covenants commonly describe the ecclesial qualities which the parties recognize in each other: they do so in sections styled 'acknowledgements'.[52] Similarly, the instruments of international ecclesial communities have their descriptive aspects: in the Leuenberg Agreement 'the participating churches describe their common understanding of the Gospel insofar as this is required for establishing church fellowship between them'.[53] In the secular field, too, church–state concordats and other agreements often repeat fundamental provisions of constitutional law.[54] As a matter of fact, of the eighty-five separate provisions of the Windsor draft covenant approximately thirty-five are descriptive, for example that each church belongs to the One, Holy, Catholic and Apostolic Church of Jesus Christ, and that communion is a gift of God; and some are presumptive, for example that each church seeks to preach the Word

---

45 TAAC, para. 17.

46 Dioc. of Saskatoon (2006): LCRPR; Noll (2005) 2.

47 Dioc. of Brisbane (2004) para. 4.2; see also CIPRWR (2005) 8: LCRPR.

48 Dioc. of Ontario: LCRPR q. 4; see also RTT (2004) para. 54: 'the [draft] covenant's length, content and wording will undoubtedly provide a challenge.'

49 Noll (2005) 7–8. But the Lausanne Covenant 1974 has prescriptive aspects: for example, the pledges in Art. 7.

50 Art. I.

51 For example, LC 1897, Res. 7: this concerns the use of the title 'archbishop' for metropolitans.

52 The Anglican-Methodist Covenant in England employs 'affirmations' (and 'commitments'). In the Porvoo agreement the churches: recognize one another as churches belonging to the One, Holy, Catholic and Apostolic Church of Jesus Christ, and as truly participating in the apostolic mission of the whole people of God; they acknowledge that, in each of them, the Word of God is authentically preached, and the sacraments of baptism and the Eucharist are duly administered, that each shares in the common confession of the apostolic faith, and so on.

53 CPCE:LA, Art. 6.

54 R. Puza and N. Doe (eds), *Religion and Law in Dialogue* (Leuven, Peeters, 2006).

of God authentically, or that each church has the intention to listen, speak, act and strive to obey the gospel.[55] By way of comparison, the St Andrews draft covenant has thirty-six numbered clauses of which at least seventeen are broadly descriptive, typically in the affirmations (for example, that the origins of the Communion are in the Church of the Apostles);[56] and some are purposive (such as the Preamble).

A prescriptive form

Towards an Anglican Covenant states that a purely descriptive form would have 'limited impact' on churches and on their legal relationships with one another; this might, therefore, reduce its practical utility. The 'tone of the covenant is important': the Windsor covenant draft is 'juridical in style and character' and uses a register of canonical language to define the relationship between the churches of the Communion.[57] On the one hand, for several respondents, a prescriptive covenant could clarify commitments, develop 'rules for engagement', or provide 'rules of procedure'.[58] A prescriptive covenant could affirm the historic Anglican preference for unity-in-diversity, spell out commitments to living in community, and present international obligations.[59] A range of models is advocated: 'rule-oriented', constitutional (with first principles on polity), theological (*norma normans*, based on the authority of scripture), and promissory.[60] A covenant should not be merely motivational or aspirational, nor dominated by the language of conflict, but involve 'the real, risky stuff of commitment to life together'.[61] For some, the divine covenants in scripture have their prescriptive elements.[62]

On the other hand, many respondents argue that the language of a covenant should not be cast in a restrictive form. The more directive its text, the less acceptable it may prove. A simple covenant, affirming and exploring the desire to live and work together, would be more palatable than the detailed 'legalistic' document suggested by the Lambeth Commission, which cannot be seen as anything other than

---

55 Descriptive: WDAC, Arts 1.2,6.1; presumptive: ibid. Arts 1.4,4.3.
56 SADC, 2.1.1; compare NDC, Art. 4.1: the origins are in the 'undivided church'.
57 TAAC, paras 17, 18, 19.
58 Dioc. of Saskatoon (2006); Dioc. of Ontario, q. 4: LCRPR.
59 Sudan, para. 3; GSPN (2005) para. 3; MU (2004) p. 4: LCRPR.
60 Noll (2007); Strudwick (2006).
61 Scully (2007).
62 Seitz (2007); and Goddard, in Chapman (2008) 65: a key debate in covenant theology is whether God's covenants are unconditional or conditional on particular human responses.

canonical and juridical.[63] Others question the wisdom of using negative formulations in a covenant text because these would make it more
difficult to read and less than inspirational.[64] For Affirming Catholicism, an overly prescriptive covenant based on a juridical approach
might rule out the promotion of debate, conversation and serious discussion about difference.[65] Some, therefore, advocate a covenant with
clear and simple language (with active not passive verbs), motivational
rather than juridical.[66]

In view of these two approaches, it is instructive to explore precisely how innovative a juridical covenant would be, and in what ways
the St Andrews, Nassau and Windsor drafts are 'juridical' in terms of
form. The most common juridical formulae in the laws of churches
of the Anglican Communion, which seek to implement theological
ideas, are: *principles* (general propositions or maxims, sometimes
descriptive, sometimes prescriptive, which express fundamental values
and carry a 'dimension of weight'), *rules* (more particular provisions
which apply to specific circumstances and usually in the form 'If X,
then Y'), *rights* (entitlements), *duties* (obligations), and *norms* (directory or aspirational in character: 'ought'). Duties are cast in the form
of precepts (commands usually signified in the words 'shall/must') or
prohibitions ('shall not/must not'), whereas rights, being entitlements,
are permissive ('may'). Duties generate correlative rights, and *vice
versa*. These formulae are used by churches in their own legal systems.[67] Indeed, the dominant juridical regime in Anglican churches is
that of duties; within this, the dominant rights regime is that of correlative rights, not free-standing rights; this juristic technique has been
criticized.[68]

The Windsor draft covenant employs all of these juridical forms. For
example: that 'autonomy is the right of a church to self-government'
is a principle; the provision that 'if in episcopal office', 'no minister
. . . shall . . . unreasonably refuse any invitation to attend meetings

63 CIPRWR, 13; SECR (2005) para. 4; Diocese of Ontario, q. 4: LCRPR; Strudwick
(2006); Greer (2005) 115; C. Lewis, in Linzey and Kirker (2005) 149 at 152.

64 CCW (2005) para. 3: from Article 9 onwards a large number of double negatives
and legal terms (such as 'fiduciary duty' in Article 21) are included, giving the text the feel
of a legal contract rather than a covenant under the grace of God: LCRPR.

65 Response to TAAC (13-13-2006) para. 4.

66 Ross (2006): a juridical tone 'could be seen as more heavy verbiage from the West'.
See also Australia, RNDC (2007): this prefers a missiological rather than a structural
'canonical' covenant.

67 N. Doe, 'The principles of canon law: a focus of legal unity in Anglican-Roman
Catholic relations', *Ecclesiastical Law Journal* 5 (1999) 221.

68 N. Doe, 'Canonical approaches to human rights in Anglican churches', in M. Hill
(ed.), *Religious Liberty and Human Rights* (Cardiff, University of Wales Press, 2002)
185 at 200-204.

of the Instruments of Unity' is a rule; that a church 'shall pray for the needs of and with fellow member churches and their faithful' is a duty; that the Archbishop of Canterbury 'may issue guidance' in contentious matters, is a right; and that 'what touches all should be approved by all' is an aspirational norm.[69] Of the eighty-five separate provisions of the draft covenant (in its twenty-seven articles), approximately fifty are prescriptive. Thirty-eight provisions are in the form of precepts, and three provisions contain prohibitions.[70] However, each covenant precept which imposes a duty also generates a correlative entitlement, and each covenant right generates a corresponding duty.[71] Alternatively, therefore, the draft covenant may be understood as containing forty-one correlative rights (flowing from its precepts and prohibitions). The covenant also provides qualifications to some provisions, when a particular covenantal facility is available 'so far as is practicable', or 'subject to' or exercisable 'in accordance with' the law or discipline of a church.[72]

By way of comparison, principally but not exclusively in its commitments,[73] the St Andrews draft covenant (like the Nassau text) also contains: principles (that the historic episcopate is locally adapted in the methods of its administration); rules (that if a matter threatens the unity and mission of the Communion, a church must follow prescribed procedural elements); rights (such as that of ecclesial autonomy); duties (such as the solemn obligation to sustain eucharistic communion); and aspirational norms (such as that each church should share its material resources).[74] Of the thirty-six numbered provisions in the draft, at least eighteen are in the form of precepts (for example, that a church must have regard to the common good of the Communion).[75] Moreover, while prohibitions are not explicitly employed, each precept has an

---

69 See respectively, WDAC, Arts 18.2; 13.2; 15.3; 26.1; 20.3.

70 For precepts, see WDAC, Arts 7.4; 9.1; 10.1–2; 11.1–3; 12.1–4; 13.1; 14.1–3; 15.1–5; 16.1–4; 17.2; 20.3; 21.1–3; 22.3; 23.2,4; 25.1–2; 26.1; 27.1–3; for prohibitions: Arts 6.3: 9.2; 13.2.

71 For example, WDAC, Art. 14.1: that each church shall welcome the members of fellow churches entitles such members to the spiritual benefits available in the host church; Art. 20.1: the right of an autonomous church to regulate freely its internal domestic affairs implies a duty on the Communion and on each member church not to intervene in those affairs.

72 For example, WDAC, Arts 11.3; 12.4; 14.3; 15.2.

73 However, the language of 'shall', 'should', or 'may' is avoided (except in the Appendix). Rather, sometimes, conduct is presented as 'needed': for example, SADC, Cl. 3.2.3: controversial decisions 'need to be tested'.

74 SADC, Cls. 1.1.4, 3.2.5, 3.1.2, 1.2.3, 2.2.1; see also NDC, Arts 5.1, 6.5, 5.2, 6.4, 3.2, 4.4.

75 SADC, Cl. 3.2.1. Compare the twenty-six separate provisions in NDC of which at least thirteen are preceptive (e.g. Art. 6.1).

obvious prohibitive aspect.[76] Sometimes the covenantal affirmations contain a prescriptive element.[77] Some provisions are in the form of acknowledgements which too have a prescriptive dimension.[78] Unlike the Windsor draft, the St Andrews draft does not number juridical formulae within each of its sub-articles, perhaps failing to reflect the actual scope of its prescriptive side: these often contain quite distinct rules, rights and duties.[79] A feature of the draft, not appearing in the Windsor document, is the inclusion of justifications for particular provisions written into the clauses themselves.[80] At its 2007 meeting the Joint Standing Committee of the Primates' Meeting and ACC, discussing the Nassau text, considered that a covenant needs to 'avoid too much the language of "constitution" or "code"', as it 'cannot really be more than a set of aspirations',[81] and the committee criticized the text as too prescriptive in parts,[82] a criticism echoed by others.[83]

As was the case with the 1784 concordat,[84] and the current tacit covenant of the Communion,[85] prescription is a key feature of contemporary Anglican covenants: while predominantly aspirational, the Covenant for Communion in Mission contains 'pledges' and prescribes, for

---

76 For example, SADC, Cl. 1.2.1: commitments to act in continuity with the faith implicitly forbid the contrary; see also NDC, Art. 3.1.

77 For example, SADC, Cl. 3.1.3: the affirmation suggests that bishops should act as 'a visible sign of unity'; see also NDC, Art. 5.1.

78 For example, SADC, Cl. 2.1.3: that churches acknowledge that their common mission is 'a mission shared with other churches and traditions beyond this covenant' suggests that it *should* be shared; see also NDC, Art. 4.3.

79 For example, SADC, Cl. 1.2.4 contains at least six obvious duties involved in the handling of biblical texts (which could also be reconceived as twelve duties given that the duty bearers are both bishops and synods); see also NDC, Art. 3.3.

80 For example, SADC, Cl. 1.2.6: that churches are committed to pursue a common pilgrimage is so 'that people from all nations may . . . receive . . . life in the Lord Jesus Christ'; see also NDC, Art. 3.5.

81 Points Raised in Discussion of the Draft Text for an Anglican Covenant.

82 Namely: NDC, Art. 6.5 (on seeking guidance in matters of dispute).

83 Wales, RNDC (2007), particularly Art. 6. See also Southern Africa, RNDC (2007): an excessively prescriptive covenant will 'box in' the Holy Spirit; and Ireland, RNDC (2007).

84 Arts 4, 6: It recognizes that common life requires a degree of common worship such as 'is consistent with different Circumstances and Customs of Nations'; it is 'resolved' 'that a brotherly fellowship be henceforth maintained between the Episcopal Churches in Scotland and Connecticut, and such mutual Intercourse in Ecclesiastical correspondence carried on, when Opportunity offers, or necessity requires as may tend to the Support, and Edification of both Churches'.

85 See for example: LC 1908, Res. 62: 'it should be the recognised practice of the Churches' to admit Eastern Orthodox to communion; LC 1897, Res. 45: 'this Conference recognises the exclusive right of each bishop' to sanction additional services; LC 1958, Res. 125 on the duties of the laity; LC 1948, Res. 113: of a proposed experiment to ordain a deaconess as priest, 'the Conference feels bound to reply that in its opinion such an experiment would be against tradition and order'.

example, that Anglicans are to support one another in mission, share equitably God-given resources, and live into the promise of God's reconciliation.[86] The Agreement and Organizational Charter of the Anglican Communion Network, and the Covenant Union of Anglican Churches in Concordat, both use a juridical linguistic register.[87] While the prescriptive character of some ecumenical covenants is 'permissive',[88] most contain 'commitments' in the form of duties and correlative rights: to welcome members of the partner churches to receive sacramental and pastoral ministrations; to regard baptized members of the churches as members of the partner churches; and to welcome persons ordained as bishop, priest or deacon to serve in the ministry of the partner churches.[89] The same may be said of the instruments of international ecclesial fellowships. The constitution of the Standing Conference of Canonical Orthodox Bishops in the Americas requires the conference to meet twice annually for the mutual exchange of information and for decisive action and at other times for special needs.[90] The Old Catholic International Bishops' Conference statute requires the churches, for example, to 'maintain the catholicity, doctrine, and worship in apostolic succession', and no bishop may consecrate any person bishop for another church without approval of the conference.[91] And the constitution of the Lutheran World Federation prescribes that applicant churches must declare acceptance of the historical Lutheran confessional documents.[92] Needless to say, church–state concordats are predominantly prescriptive, spelling out the mutual rights and duties of the parties, though they too may contain descriptive elements.[93]

---

86 CCM, 9–10.

87 See also 'soft-law' agreements in international law: D. Shelton, 'International law and "relative normativity"', in Evans (ed.), *International Law* (2003) 145: international institutions increasingly adopt these which contain, for example, 'undertakings to endeavour to strive to co-operate'. See, for example, the Harare Declaration 1991 of the Commonwealth of Nations: this contains 'commitments' and 'pledges'.

88 ACCT, p. 1: it is 'permission-giving' but also contains 'commitments'; the *Charta Oecumenica* 2001 spells out mischiefs and curative commitments.

89 Wales, Can. 28-9-1995, Sched. 1; Lutheran-Anglican Covenant Australia (pledges, commitments).

90 SCOBA, Const., Art. V.1.

91 SOC (2000), B.Order, Art. 1.

92 LWF, Const., Art. V.

93 For example, Concordat between the Holy See and the Republic of Poland (1993): the parties are 'chacun dans leur ordre propre, indépendants et autonomes'.

The Detail of a Covenant

The Lambeth Commission did not address the issue of covenantal detail. However, *Towards an Anglican Covenant* warns that there can be no illusions: the detail of the covenant will determine the extent of its acceptability.[94] Thus, if a covenant were very detailed, it might prove too restrictive or inflexible to address unforeseen future challenges; if it were too general, it might commit the Communion to little or nothing; in either case, it would be inadequate.[95] Some ecumenical covenants are very short, like the Bonn Agreement of 1931 which has only three brief clauses,[96] but more recently they have tended to be longer.[97] For the Inter-Anglican Standing Commission on Ecumenical Relations, a covenant cannot be so general as to have no reality; there must be more than a commitment to listen to one another.[98] The Inter-Anglican Theological and Doctrinal Commission consider that an overly specific and detailed covenant tied entirely to the present controversies may not be much help in the future for the next set of issues that arises.[99] Similarly, the Covenant Design Group proposes that the covenant should not focus on particular issues, and its two drafts have about two-thirds the amount of detail as that in the Windsor draft.[100]

Several respondents argue that a covenant should be minimalist in content and focus on creating engagement, or delineating the minimum agreement possible, like the Lambeth Quadrilateral,[101] and ministerial

---

94 TAAC, para. 12: 'The length, structure and content of any covenant will depend in part on the relative weight' given to the three different sorts of relational, educational and institutional purposes.

95 TAAC, para. 5.

96 Bonn Agreement: '1. Each Communion recognizes the catholicity and independence of the other and maintains its own. 2. Each Communion agrees to admit members of the other Communion to participate in the Sacraments. 3. Full Communion does not require from either Communion the acceptance of all doctrinal opinion, sacramental devotion or liturgical practice characteristic of the other, but implies that each believes the other to hold all the essentials of the Christian faith.'

97 TAAC, para. 15: the term was explicitly used in 1964 when the British Council of Churches made a covenant to work and pray for the inauguration of a union; and this has become the model for many ecumenical covenants by separated parties seeking greater union, voluntarily submitting in a covenant for a common purpose.

98 IASCER, Responding to the Idea of a Covenant (8-12-2006), para. 14.

99 RPC, para. 2.2; see also the Modern Churchpeople's Union response to TAAC (Nov. 2006) Summary: a covenant 'should have the least content possible'.

100 NDC, Report, para. 5. See also Bishop Hind (11-6-2007), An Anglican Covenant, Annex 2 of Church of England General Synod Agenda Paper July 2007 (GS 1661): 'the Covenant must be strong and detailed enough to help the Anglican Communion understand the implications of "bonds of affection"'.

101 CIPRWR, 12; TEC, s. 4: LCRPR; Noll (2005) 2.

covenants employed increasingly today in member churches.[102] The Windsor draft covenant was too laboured, lengthy, detailed, ambiguous, complex, indigestible, and repetitious, respondents wondering whether the pressure of current events led to the inclusion of some detailed clauses to meet specific needs, thus diverting the covenant from its purpose in laying down common principles.[103] Too much detail will exacerbate misunderstandings.[104] For some, the form of a covenant could be based on the model of the Anglican formularies.[105] The Nassau text had been criticized as having excessive theological and legal jargon.[106]

It is instructive to compare the St Andrews, Nassau and Windsor drafts with similar instruments: the statute of Old Catholic Bishops in the Union of Utrecht has twenty-four articles over eight pages; *Charta Oecumenica*, twelve sections over eight pages; the Australian Churches Covenant, six pages; the Agreement, Organizational Charter and other documents of the Anglican Communion Network, ten pages; the Leuenberg Agreement, forty-nine articles over six pages; the Covenant for Communion in Mission, two pages, the Covenant Union of Anglican Churches in Concordat, eight articles on one page; the draft constitution of the Anglican Global Initiative, ten articles over three pages; the constitution of the Standing Conference of Canonical Orthodox Bishops in the Americas, seven articles over six pages; the constitution of the Lutheran World Federation, fourteen articles over eight pages; and the constitution of the World Alliance of Reformed Churches, twelve articles over seven pages. However, many of these comparable instruments, like the constitution of the Anglican Consultative Council,[107] are supplemented by additional documents. The Leuenberg Agreement and the constitutions of the Lutheran World Federation, World Alliance of Reformed Churches, and Standing Conference of Canonical Orthodox Bishops in the Americas, for instance, are all supplemented by more detailed bylaws.[108]

---

102 Bishop T. Brown: Lambeth Website.

103 DAZ, 57 (Zahl): 'Here is what I think it should have said: "As part of Christ's one, holy, catholic, and apostolic church, we promise not to do anything in the area of innovations in faith and morals without consulting with all our partners in communion." Period. That is all that is necessary, notwithstanding the theological "whereas" material backing up the first assertion of catholicity'; Dioc. of Ontario, q. 4; CCW (2005) para. 3; Sydney (7-2-2005): every baptism, confirmation and ordination candidate 'already solemnly affirms' the scriptures, creeds and formularies: LCRPR.

104 Scully (2006); see also Dakin (2007) para. 2.

105 Noll (2005) 5.

106 Southern Africa, RNDC (2007); see also Ireland, RNDC (2007): 'legislative structure'.

107 The Council is governed by a constitution, bylaws and guidelines.

108 Leuenberg Agreement, Art. VI (the agreement also identifies areas for further dis-

Indeed, some respondents consider that a shorter framework covenant should be supplemented by and elaborated in other texts, such as a more comprehensive code of practice, or other documentation.[109] First, some advocate an introductory theological text, developing that offered by the Covenant Design Group at Nassau.[110] In point of fact, the Group at its London meeting in 2008 offers a theological introduction to the St Andrews draft covenant which treats the relationship between communion and covenant.[111] Second, Windsor proposed that the Instruments of Communion set out formally their composition, functions, relations one with another;[112] there needs to be a clearer understanding of the expectations placed on provinces about the decisions of these bodies and the relationship between them; there is at the moment no clear demarcation indicating which responsibilities fall to which institution.[113] Currently, only the Anglican Consultative Council has a formal instrument of this type (its constitution), though this does not deal systematically with the relations of the Council to the Primates' Meeting or the Lambeth Conference.[114] The St Andrews draft covenant does not require the Instruments to set out formally their composition, functions and relations; instead, these are spelt out briefly in the covenant itself.[115]

Third, in similar vein, the Joint Standing Committee of the Primates and Anglican Consultative Council in 2007 raised the point on the Nassau draft that there might be less detail in the covenant text but a more detailed and separate schedule that clarifies procedures about submission of disputed matters to the Instruments of Communion.[116] Consequently, the St Andrews draft covenant now contains a framework procedure for the resolution of covenant disagreements and it requires the Instruments of Communion to create more detailed rules to implement these procedures.[117]

---

cussion); LWF, Const., Art. XIV.2; WARC, By-Laws, II.2.3; SOC, 'Rules'. See also Constitutional Charter of the Sovereign Military Hospitaller Order of St John of Jerusalem of Rhodes and of Malta (Rome, 1998).

109 Hong Kong, para. 2.2; CWW (2005) para. 3: LCRPR

110 England, RNDC (2007): it offers concrete suggestions for this.

111 Introduction to SADC.

112 WDAC, Art. 23.2.

113 TWR, para. 105–6.

114 See above Ch. 2 for the constitution of the Council.

115 But see Commentary to SADC, on Cl. 3.1.4: the text allows for 'the evolution of the Instruments'.

116 Points raised in Discussion of the Draft Text for an Anglican Covenant (on Art. 6.5).

117 SADC, Appendix; see more fully below Chs 6 and 9.

Finally, the Windsor draft covenant also recognizes the role of the principles of canon law common to the churches of the Communion.[118] The Anglican Communion Network of Legal Advisers of the Anglican Consultative Council is presently working on a statement of these.[119] The project, endorsed by the Primates' Meeting in 2002, was welcomed by the Lambeth Commission,[120] and by some respondents,[121] but is criticized by others.[122] Indeed, like the Nassau text, the St Andrews draft covenant commits the churches to seek a common mind about essential matters consistent with the canon law of the churches.[123] The

---

118 WDAC, Art. 17.1.

119 The Primates' Meeting 2001 considered a paper which was subsequently published: N. Doe, 'Canon law and communion', *EccLJ* 6 (2002) 241–263, esp. 262; *International Journal for the Study of the Christian Church* 3 (2003) 85–117, esp. 115. The paper proposed acknowledgement of the principles of canon law common to the churches of the Anglican Communion. At the meeting the primates endorsed the establishment of an Anglican Communion Consultation of Legal Advisers to test the hypothesis. The Consultation was held in March 2002, and concluded that 'there are principles of canon law common to the churches' of the Communion (see report by J. Rees, *EccLJ* 6 (2002) 399), a conclusion endorsed by the Primates' Meeting (April, 2002: see N. Doe, 'The common law of the Anglican Communion', *EccLJ* 7 (2003) 4). As recommended by that meeting, the Anglican Consultative Council (Hong Kong, September 2002) established the Anglican Communion Network of Legal Advisers to 'produce a statement of the principles'. This was further encouraged by the Primates' Statement, Lambeth (October, 2003), by the Lambeth Commission (*Windsor Report*, para. 114) and a group has met in Toronto (October, 2005) and Bahamas (April, 2006) to finalize a draft of these for submission to the Network (in 2008). For a working draft of the document, see www.acclawnet.co.uk: see also N. Doe and R. Sandberg, 'The "state of the union", a canonical perspective: principles of canon law in the Anglican Communion', *Sewanee Theological Review* 49 (2006) 234.

120 TWR, para. 114.

121 CIPRWR, 7: 'We are strongly supportive of this recommendation. We note however that such a Network was not envisaged in Resolution 13 of ACC 12 (September 2002) as a short term exercise but as a continuing and creative dialogue. We believe that the Church of Ireland should engage actively and urgently in the work of the Legal Advisers' Network but we urge that work in hand should not be rushed.' The work 'should be thorough and neither artificially curtailed nor seen as being pressed into service to deal with a single crisis'; see also Ceylon: LCRPR.

122 Jones (2005) 129–33: while the *ius commune* is not 'the same thing as a juridic bond . . . in appearance or intention', it 'arose through the accidents of British colonial history', and if so 'it is very poor theology'; its 'origin and authority . . . must have . . . theological underpinnings'; either it exists 'accidentally, or it is the necessary expression of a deeper coherence of which the Instruments of Unity are the clearest expressions the Communion has'; it '*should* be nothing more than the elaboration of the founding principles of Anglicanism's orthodox beliefs', 'the working out of some very elementary obligations that are then placed on member churches because they elect into the Communion': any 'notion that the *ius commune* might flourish in the Communion is naïve so long as such individuals continue to pay nothing more than lip service to some of the central beliefs of the apostolic faith'.

123 SADC, Cl. 3.2.4; see also NDC, Art. 6.3.

Primates' Meeting in 2007 also considered that in each church 'Canon Law should reflect and promote global Communion'.[124]

Conclusion

It is commonly understood that secular biblical covenants were in the form of a statement of the identity of their initiator, a recital of events leading to them, a statement of the relative obligations of the parties, and an invocation of divine sanctions.[125] The St Andrews, Nassau and Windsor draft covenants do not exactly follow this pattern. However, the Lambeth Commission recommendation for a written agreement has been both commended and criticized. Most respondents agree that the form of a covenant must be clear and precise, with a tone acceptable across the spectrum of ecclesiastical positions, and, on balance, it should not be confessional. The documentary model is consistent with scriptural covenants (if also 'written in the hearts' of its parties), sacramental covenants (which though orally undertaken are recorded in liturgical texts), and the experience of Anglican consensual compacts, ecumenism, and other international ecclesial bodies. Adoption of a documentary covenant may or may not be related to the normal organizational process of institutionalization within communities proposed in the sociology of religion. Respondents divide about the linguistic form of a covenant: for some, it should be descriptive, for others prescriptive. The impression is that a descriptive form presents itself as more theological than a prescriptive form which is perceived as juridical.[126] Actually, the St Andrews draft covenant (like the Nassau and Windsor texts) employs a variety of linguistic forms: descriptive and prescriptive, with the preceptive (rather than a negative) form prevalent. Indeed, all of the comparators used in this chapter indicate that prescriptiveness is a feature in the covenants of scripture, sacramental tradition, ecumenism, and other international ecclesial bodies.

---

124 Primates' Meeting, Points raised in Discussion of the Draft Text for an Anglican Covenant. See also Southern Africa, RNDC (2007): one view is that the development of a covenant text should be postponed until the principles of canon law project has been completed.

125 D. Tripp, 'Covenant' in G. S. Wakefield (ed.), *A Dictionary of Christian Spirituality* (London, SCM Press, 1983) 98.

126 The claim that any draft covenant is 'legalistic' cannot be sustained: a covenant could be 'juridical' without being 'legalistic': legalism – undue deference to law with the possible result of injustice – is an attribute of a positivist administration of a legal instrument, not a characteristic of its form or content.

5

The Subject-Matter of a Covenant

This chapter is a necessary preliminary to Chapter 6 which is a technical examination of the content of the St Andrews draft covenant, comparing this with the Nassau and Windsor texts. As has already been seen,[1] the Lambeth Commission understands communion as 'a relationship of covenantal affection' which involves biblical and divine foundations, unity and holiness, a whole range of relationships, and obligations within the context of interdependence.[2] The Commission also offers a detailed understanding of the autonomy of each church, not as independence or sovereignty, but as 'freedom-in-relation'.[3] In turn, these key ideas of communion and autonomy shape the subject-matter of the St Andrews, Nassau and Windsor draft covenants.

Part I of the Windsor draft covenant deals (largely descriptively) with the 'common identity' shared by the churches, the marks each church recognizes in one another. Part II treats the 'relationships of communion', their foundation, purpose and substance. Part III sets out 'commitments of communion', seeking to give meaning (prescriptively) to the obligations lying at the heart of communion. Part IV provides for the 'exercise of autonomy in communion', through a definition of autonomy, a statement of its proper exercise, and promotion of the values of diversity and mutual respect. Part V deals with the 'management of communion issues', and sets out practical ways in which matters of common concern can be handled 'in communion' by collaborative dialogue between local churches and the Instruments of Communion.[4]

While it fails to offer explicit and precise *reasons* for the inclusion of the subjects treated in its draft covenant, the Lambeth Commission implicitly recognizes the need for a formal treatment of these as matters upon which there *should* be agreement: it proposes that the

---

1 See above Ch. 2.

2 TWR, paras 1–11, 49, 51 and 52.

3 TWR, paras 72–86: see Ch. 6 for criticisms of the TWR understandings of autonomy.

4 See Ch. 6 for a detailed statement and discussion of the provisions of the draft covenant.

current absence of a mechanism which treats these matters has been a persistent problem in Anglicanism contributing directly to the present crisis.[5] Like the Commission, *Towards an Anglican Covenant* does not deal directly with the issue of covenantal subject-matter. However, as has already been seen, it does comment on the inclusion of a confessional statement, and it recognizes that a covenant should deal with the relationships between and mutual commitments of the churches of the Communion.[6] Many of the responses on subject-matter are implicit in comments about the purpose and form of a covenant. Some propose that a covenant should deal with those subjects treated in the Windsor draft. Others consider that a covenant should not treat all the subjects appearing in the draft. Several identify omissions from the draft covenant and argue for inclusion of additional matters.

Following its preamble, the Nassau draft covenant deals with: in Article 2, the life Anglicans share (in terms of common catholicity, apostolicity and confession of faith); in Article 3, the commitment to confession of the faith (on the churches' faithfulness to God in their various contexts); in Article 4, the life Anglicans share with others and the Anglican vocation (particularly the nature of communion and common mission); in Article 5, Anglican unity and common life (particularly autonomy and the Instruments of Communion); and, in Article 6, the unity of the Communion, which treats essential matters of common concern and their management, including matters of serious dispute at the global level of the Communion.[7] In outline, the subject-matter of the Nassau draft covenant corresponds broadly with that in the Windsor draft: Article 2 Nassau, with Part I Windsor, Article 3 with Part III, Article 4 with Part II, Article 5 (very roughly) with Part IV, and Article 6 with Part V. The subject-matter remains, the titles and order differ.

The St Andrews text is more streamlined: it deals with the same basic subjects but in three sets of provisions, on faith, mission and unity: the Anglican inheritance of faith (section one); the Anglican vocation (section two) and common life (section three).[8] On the one hand, the treatment of these subjects in the draft covenant does not reflect the *formal* subject-matter of the consensual compacts in the Com-

---

5 TWR, para. 118: this simply lists the subjects with which a covenant 'could deal'.

6 See above Ch. 1 (for relationships and commitments) and Ch. 4 (for confessional form).

7 According to Radner (2007) the draft could be understood to deal with teaching, mission and order, but these three main topics are 'somewhat obscured by a faulty enumeration in the text'.

8 CDG, Commentary to SADC, para. 3: it treats 'faith, mission and the maintenance of communion'.

munion operative at the local level of each church.[9] The draft covenant headings do not appear in the formal laws of churches; its provisions do not translate wholesale the local juridical order to the Communion plane.[10] On the other hand, however, each subject treated in the St Andrews draft (and the same applies to the Nassau and Windsor texts) mirrors at a deeper *substantive* level those subjects underlying the formal consensual compact of each church in terms of relations within that church (but not its relations with other Anglican churches).[11] Laws implicitly facilitate and order within the particular church: (1) the *common identity* of the faithful in their membership, ministry and mission; (2) the *commitments of communion*, in the distribution of rights and duties; (3) the network of *communion relationships* among the faithful manifested in common life and action (including shared participation in governance, collaboration in ministry, profession of the faith, participation in common worship, and accountability to church discipline);[12] (4) the *exercise of autonomy* by the constituent internal units of each church and at the same time their general supervision by central authorities at provincial or national level;[13] and (5) the *management of communion issues* of common concern *within* the units of the local church.[14] The treatment of such matters in a global covenant merely reflects broadly the ubiquity and persistence of these subjects as a normal part of ecclesial existence in Anglicanism.

---

9 See ACC – 4, 1979, Ontario: Guidelines for Provincial Constitutions: they should deal with: Pt 1: preamble and fundamental declarations; Pt 2: metropolitical authority and bishops, provincial assembly, liturgy, discipline, property, definitions, amendment; Pt 3: rules of order and procedure.

10 Typically, local laws deal in detailed rules with: the identity of a church (in fundamental declarations); territorial (province, diocese, parish) and institutional organization (composition and functions of synods and other bodies, legislative, executive and judicial); ministry (appointment, functions and discipline of bishops, clergy and lay officers); doctrine (proclamation, development, enforcement); public worship and liturgy (creation, administration and discipline), ritual (baptism, confirmation, communion, marriage and burial); property and finance; and, increasingly, ecumenism: see N. Doe, *Canon Law in the Anglican Communion* (Oxford, Clarendon Press, 1998).

11 The laws of churches do not deal with inter-Anglican relations: see TWR, para. 116: 'At present individual canonical systems are ambivalent to global communion, rarely centripetal (looking outward), mostly neutral (introvert) and sometimes centrifugal (keeping other provinces at a distance). For the canonical material, see N. Doe, 'Canon law and communion', *EccLJ* 6 (2002) 241.

12 For an analysis of the idea of the communion of the faithful in the corporate canonical life of the particular church, see the study on ecclesiology and law by E. Corecco, *Concilium* (1986) 3.

13 For example, provincial laws define, regulate and protect the autonomy of the diocese (and of the parish). For example, a province cannot interfere in the lawfully recognized affairs of a diocese.

14 The prevention and management of conflict is commonly treated in church laws.

Common Identity

That a covenant should deal with common identity is implicit in the views of those respondents who see clarity about identity as a legitimate covenantal object.[15] Identity in belief emerges as an important subject for treatment in a covenant. Several respondents suggest that a covenant should contain a concrete and unifying statement about the authority of scripture, or, more fully, a thorough affirmation of the primacy, unity, clarity, and sufficiency, of the Bible as the Word of God written: in this regard, Anglicans can learn from the Protestant Reformers.[16] Consequently, others propose that a covenant should include a *commitment* to the supremacy of scripture, the acceptance of the creeds and the threefold order, as the grounds for all other dialogues of faith, morals and the meaning of 'communion'.[17] Some contend that it should treat hermeneutics and the 'multivocality' of scripture.[18] The supremacy of scripture appears in the St Andrews draft covenant among the affirmations of common identity (as it did in the Nassau and Windsor texts), but it is not explicitly prescribed as a commitment of communion.[19]

Unlike the Windsor document but like the Nassau text, the St Andrews draft covenant does not deal with,[20] as a single formula, the classical Anglican trilogy of scripture, reason and tradition – a point raised by the Primates' Meeting in 2007, and by other respondents, including during the provincial consultation of 2007.[21] One theme

---

15 For example, Dioc. of Brisbane (2004); Myanmar, A.3: LCRPR. See also ACADC, Part 2: this contains fundamental declarations about Anglican identity; MCU, Response (November 2006) at 16; Australia, RNDC (2007): it is good for a covenant to focus on shared faith, ministry and mission; Wales, RNDC (2007): a covenant also needs to recognize that part of identity is the fact that churches are worshipping communities. For objects, see above Ch. 3.

16 Dioc. of Saskatchewan: LCRPR; Noll (2005) 4: who faced 'a similar challenge in the 16th century'; see also Noll (2006): 'The Covenant should include a section in which the Church affirms the Gospel of Jesus Christ as revealed through the testimony of the prophets and apostles' and should state that 'the Holy Scriptures of the Old and New Testaments are the Word of God written and contain all things necessary for salvation'.

17 Wesctott House (2005): LCRPR.

18 C. J. Sharp, 'Our Unity is in Christ' (2007): that is, guidance on interpretation of what is perceived as the many voices of scripture.

19 SADC, Cl. 1.1.2; see also NDC, Art. 2.1; WDAC, Art. 1.3.

20 Radner (2007): 'so confusing to so many in practice', these do not appear in the Nassau draft not because the elements of the triad are not in play, 'but because they are ordered within a more focused trajectory of discernment and authority'; compare WDAC, Art. 4.4.

21 Points Raised in Discussion of the [Nassau] Draft Text for an Anglican Covenant, Section 2; Noll (2005) 4: a covenant should deal with how to read scripture, and it needs

which emerged following the Windsor proposal was that a covenant should deal with the role of the historic Anglican formularies, in the light of modern and postmodern developments, especially the Thirty-Nine Articles of Religion and the Book of Common Prayer 1662. In this respect, one respondent considers that the Church of Nigeria in its recent constitutional amendment offers a way forward for a global Anglican covenant; namely: the church is 'in communion with those who uphold the historic faith, as expressed in the 1662 Book of Common Prayer, the Thirty-Nine Articles, and the Ordinal'. In other words, it is imperative that affirmation of the Thirty-Nine Articles should be a part of a covenant, because they 'enshrine within our tradition the Scripture principle . . . and endow it with the capacity for "local adaptation" which is necessary given the passage of time and the spread of the worldwide church'.[22] Somewhat more generally, the Inter-Anglican Theological and Doctrinal Commission maintains that a covenant should rehearse the theological tradition from which Anglicanism has developed.[23] Whereas the Windsor draft makes no mention of the Thirty-Nine Articles or Book of Common Prayer, the Nassau text names these and presents them as bearing witness to Christian truth historically.[24] The Primates' Meeting 2007, however, cautioned that a covenant might need to deal with 'the historic formularies without further detail' given the different value placed on them by churches.[25] So did the provincial consultation in 2007: in turn, the St Andrews draft covenant refers generally to 'the historic formularies' without naming them other than in a footnote.[26]

'to address the roles of reason and tradition' (along the lines of Hooker); moreover: 'The Covenant will also need to address the role of modern "higher" criticism, along the lines of Vatican I "Constitution on Divine Scripture". Renewed awareness of the shaping of Scriptural canon and the historic tradition of exegesis should allow expositors and theologians to move beyond the arid "assured results" of higher criticism or the carnival of postmodern "readings" to a more fruitful method of theological interpretation'; for Hooker, see LEP, V.8.2. See also Southern Africa, RNDC (2007): this expresses surprise at the absence of references in the Nassau text to scripture, reason and tradition.

22 Noll (2005) 5; see Nigeria, Const., Ch. 1.

23 IATDC Study of Communion (October 2006): see Michael Doe (2006); see also Clatworthy, Bagshaw and Saxbee (2007) 7.2: if there is to be a covenant, it should cherish classical Anglican method and its expression in Anglican polity.

24 NDC, Art. 2.5 (Australia, RNDC (2007) welcomes reference to the historic formularies). While WDAC makes no mention of them, these are treated in the principles of canon law common to the churches; see also Primates' Meeting 2007, Points Raised in Discussion of the Draft Text for an Anglican Covenant, Sect. 6: neither the Nassau nor Windsor drafts mention the place of the United Churches: 'Where do they stand in relation to the covenant? Do they have a place? Their position needs acknowledgement and mention'.

25 Points Raised in Discussion of the Draft of an Anglican Covenant, Sect. 2.

26 SADC, Cl. 1.1.2 and n. 4.

By way of contrast, common identity is not dealt with in the constitution of the Anglican Consultative Council,[27] whereas it is treated in the instruments of the Anglican Communion Network and the Anglican Global Initiative.[28] But these instruments do not spell out what the partners recognize and affirm 'in each other'. However, as with the Windsor draft (but less so with the St Andrews and Nassau texts), common identity is treated in ecumenical covenants: typically, the participating churches 'recognize', 'acknowledge', 'rejoice', or 'affirm',[29] *in each other* the marks of the One, Holy, Catholic and Apostolic Church; in Anglican–Lutheran relations, full communion means that each church believes the other to hold the essentials of the Christian faith.[30] Common identity (as mutual recognition) is treated indirectly in instruments of other international ecclesial communities, such as the Old Catholic Bishops, Lutheran World Federation, and World Alliance of Reformed Churches, and, confessionally, the Leuenberg Agreement of the Community of Protestant Churches in Europe.[31] Indeed, one provincial response to the Nassau draft covenant considers that it would be better to include in an Anglican covenant the ecumenical formula of mutual recognition (that is, what it recognizes in the *other* churches of the Communion, as was the case with the Windsor text) rather than each church affirming *its own identity*, as was the position in the Nassau text and is still the case in the St Andrews draft.[32]

---

27 Other than the provision which 'names' the council: ACC, Const., Art. 1.

28 The participants are identified by reference to what they claim is their promotion of classical Anglicanism: ACN, Organisational Charter, Preamble; AGI, Draft Constitution, Art. III.

29 For example, Covenant of the Churches in Wales 1975: 'We recognize in one another the same faith . . .'; Anglican-Lutheran Covenant, Australia: 'We acknowledge that in each other's ordained ministries gospel oversight and administration of the means of grace are authentic, and effective'; ACCT, Part A: 'We rejoice in all we have in common . . . We recognize one another as Communities of Faith, Hope and Love'; Anglican-Methodist Covenant (England), Affirmations, 1–7.

30 *Growth in Communion*, para. 45: the fundamental principle is that full communion between churches means that each church recognizes 'the catholicity and apostolicity of the other', 'believing the other to hold the essentials of the Christian faith'.

31 SOC, Preamble, 1; LWF, Const., Art. II: the member churches 'agree in the proclamation of the Word of God'; Art. I: they implicitly recognize in each other acceptance of the Confessions of the Lutheran Church; WARC, Const., Art. I.2: this recognizes that the member churches are 'in the tradition of Pierre Valdes and Jan Hus'; CPCE:LA, Arts 6, 29; see also SCOBA: the constitution contains no explicit statement of mutual recognition.

32 England, RNDC (2007).

Obligations of Communion

Many respondents argue that a covenant should (as with the St Andrews, Nassau and Windsor drafts) spell out the mutual commitments and expectations of the churches of the Communion, in order both to clarify them and to maintain communion.[33] It should also deal with expectations required towards the decisions of the Instruments of Communion (and their effect on member churches),[34] the marginalized (it should include a principle of inclusivity),[35] and the place of the Christian virtues in Communion relationships, as well as understanding difference, agreement to differ on scriptural interpretation, and the right to make decisions through personal prayer and conscience.[36] One opinion is that the Ten Principles of Partnership (formulated in 1993) need to be integrated into a covenant, namely: local initiative; mutuality; responsible stewardship; interdependence; cross-fertilization; integrity; transparency, solidarity; meeting together; and acting ecumenically.[37] Whereas the Windsor draft treats both the centrality of worship and the interchangeability of clergy,[38] the Nassau text does not: both matters were raised by the primates in 2007 and that of ministerial interchangeability by the Joint Standing Committee of the Primates' Meeting and Anglican Consultative Council.[39] While it does not deal with interchange of ministries, the St Andrews text now pro-

---

33 Dioc. of Saskatoon (2006); SAMS (2005) p. 2; Dioc. of Saskatchewan, s. 4: LCRPR.

34 HBTG (2005) 3.2.1; Sudan, para. 2: LCRPR.

35 CAS (2005) 4: 'We believe that being an inclusive church is fundamental to the gospel and to the mission of the Scottish Episcopal Church . . . if that inclusivity is challenged or diminished the very fabric of our church would be damaged . . . if the [SEC] were to lose its distinctive inclusivity, God would have little purpose for it'; but compare Ceylon: inclusivity is not an 'absolute value'; the limits of inclusivity need to be defined: LCRPR.

36 MU (2004) pp. 5–6: be patient and willing to understand another's beliefs; be open to different theological accents; recognize Christ's presence in all the faith-filled opinions, no matter how much we disagree with them; being honest about how we damage; keep issues in perspective; agreeing to differ in interpreting the gospel but to explore ways of communicating in the same spirit; believing everyone is loved unconditionally by God, instead of judging them, aim to share God's love and 'allow people to make their own decisions through personal prayer and conscience': LCRPR.

37 See TWR App. 3.5 for a full text of the Principles from Towards Dynamic Mission: Renewing the Church for Mission, Mission Issues and Strategy Advisory Group II (MISAG II) 1993; ACC-2, p. 53. For the suggestion, see Diocese of British Columbia, s. 4: LCRPR.

38 WDAC Arts 3.2 and 12.

39 Points Raised in Discussion of the Draft Text of an Anglican Covenant, Sects 3 and 4; Points Raised in Discussion of the Draft Text of an Anglican Covenant, Sect. 2; see also MCU, response (November 2006) 16 (a presumption of mutual recognition of orders).

vides for affirmations about shared patterns of common prayer and liturgical form as sustaining worship, faith and life together.[40]

Mission has emerged during the debate as an essential for treatment in a covenant. For many, the provisions on mission in the Windsor draft covenant were insufficient,[41] with no single reference to the great commission to evangelize the nations and no consideration of how the Church preaches the gospel to 'unreached peoples'.[42] On the other hand, one respondent considers that there may be no need for a covenant to deal with commitments to profess the faith because candidates in each church promise this in baptism, confirmation and ordination.[43] Like the submission to the Covenant Design Group by the Australian church, the Nassau draft covenant sought to rectify this, with its clauses on mission.[44] For some, however, this did not go far enough: a more overtly missional covenant should state the reality of the revealed mission of God, affirm how scripture continues to form the covenantal community in its mission (as well as its teaching, morals and social engagement), and present the Church as a covenantal community of disciples participating in *missio dei*.[45] The St Andrews text therefore elaborates a little more fully on mission.[46]

Indeed, commitments to a wide range of responsibilities are a central subject in the instruments of the Anglican Consultative Council, Anglican Communion Network, and Covenant Union of Anglican Churches in Concordat. Responsibilities of the Council of Anglican Provinces of Africa include: unity in diversity; respect for human dignity; teamwork (and interdependence); good governance; responsible

---

40 SADC, Cl. 1.1.5; see also Commentary to SADC, on Cl. 1.1.5.

41 WDAC, Art. 15.

42 Noll (2005) 7–8 (Mark 16.15–18): 'Rather than focus the Covenant on sacraments *per se*, I would urge the drafters to expound on the missionary character of the Church.' The Lausanne Covenant on world evangelization could be a model. It is not necessary to reinvent a distinctive Anglican mission theology and strategy for this; see also Noll (2006); see also Ross (2006) point 1.

43 Dioc. of Sydney (7-2-2005): LCRPR. Another opinion is that the Communion should somehow temper commitment by recognizing the pressures on bishops in the modern world: K. Ward, 'African perspectives on episcopacy and sexuality', in A. Linzey and R. Kirker (eds), *Gays and the Future of Anglicanism: Responses to the Windsor Report* (Winchester, O Books, 2005) 244: 'the actual place of a bishop in the community, with all the pressures and demands which that creates in different places and times, is not adequately expressed' in TWR.

44 NDC, Art. 4.3–5; see also ACADC, Part 4. This was welcomed in the consultations of 2007.

45 Dakin (2007) para. 4: it should also outline how leadership (especially episcopacy as 'covenantal persons') binds the local congregations to the covenant, and how the covenant would be witnessed among its own in the Anglican Communion and with those churches with perspectives sympathetic to the covenant.

46 SADC, Cls. 2.1.1–3.

stewardship; transparency and accountability; and sustainability.[47] In ecumenical covenants, commitments represent the prescriptive aspect of communion. For example, in Anglican–Lutheran relations: (a) subject to safeguards required by ecclesiastical discipline, members of one church may receive the sacraments in the other; (b) subject to invitation, bishops of one church may take part in the consecration of bishops in the other, to acknowledge the duty of mutual care and concern; and (c) subject to church regulation, a bishop, pastor/priest or deacon of one church may exercise liturgical functions in a congregation of the other if invited to do so; when requested, they may also provide pastoral care.[48]

By way of contrast, spiritual obligations of communion are less conspicuous in the instruments of other international ecclesial communities, though they frequently distribute commitments among their member churches. For example, the constitution of the World Alliance of Reformed Churches empowers its General Council to authorize member churches to establish regional organizations which are committed to promote the closest possible community and co-operation among the member churches in a particular area of the world.[49] In a manner rather more explicit than the St Andrews, Nassau and Windsor draft covenants,[50] the bylaws of the Alliance also provide that the Alliance shall be financed by contributions from member churches, gifts from individuals, congregations, organizations and other sources.[51]

---

47 ACC, Const., Art. 2: its objects 'shall be' to advance the Christian religion; ACN, Organizational Charter, Art. V: commitment to membership of the Communion; CUACC, Art. 2: the parties 'demonstrate their commitment to one another'; Arts 4 and 5: invitations to conduct episcopal ministry and reception of communicants; CAPA (2005): http://www.capa-hq.org

48 Cold Ash Statement (1983) of the Anglican-Lutheran Joint Working Group: *Growth in Communion*, para. 113; see also ibid. para. 45: full communion means: (a) communicant members of each church are able freely to communicate at the altar of the other; (b) there is 'freedom of ordained ministers' to officiate sacramentally in either church; (c) 'transferability of members; mutual recognition and interchangeability of ministries'; (d) freedom to use each other's liturgies; (e) freedom to participate in each other's ordinations and installations of clergy, including bishops; and (f) 'structures for consultation to express, strengthen and enable our common life, witness, and service, to the glory of God and the salvation of the world'. See also the Anglican-Methodist Covenant (England) which contains 'Affirmations and Commitments'; see also ARCIC, *Church as Communion* (1990) IV, 45.

49 WARC, Const. Art. IX.1; Bylaws, V: they are: European Area; Caribbean and North American Area; Southern African Area; Northeastern Asia Area; Latin American Area. See also the Statute of the Old Catholic Bishops, Preamble, 5: this speaks, for example, of 'the ecumenical self-obligation of the Union of Utrecht'.

50 SADC, Cl. 3.2.1; NDC, Art. 4.4; WDAC, Art. 15.4: each church shall offer its financial resources to assist other needy churches.

51 WARC, By-Laws, VI; the General Council and the Executive Committee 'may propose to the churches and to the Area Councils proportionate contributions'.

One aim of the Lutheran World Federation is to enable its churches to become more 'mutually committed', sharing mutual joys, sufferings and struggles, and the World Methodist Council is committed to, *inter alia*, advancing unity of theological and moral standards, upholding and relieving persecuted or needy Christian minorities, and arranging exchanges of preachers.[52]

Relationships of Communion

Those in favour of a covenant agree that it should deal with inter-Anglican relations.[53] It should contain a statement of communion, with an eschatological dimension, in order to consolidate, improve, or heal relationships.[54] A covenant should have provisions on membership of the Communion, the relationships between its churches and the universal Church, and the idea of communion as a gift of God.[55] Moreover, a covenant should deal with the purpose of the Anglican Communion itself, together with the associated beliefs and behavioural expectations in the Communion, or a formal statement of the vision of communion relationships.[56] These ideas are not exceptional. Collaborative relationships are treated by contemporary international Anglican agreements, but not relations of *communion*.[57] The Anglican Consultative Council is to facilitate the co-operative work of the member churches of the Anglican Communion; the Memorandum of Agreement of the Anglican Communion Network deals with co-operation with the Archbishop of Canterbury and the primates; and the Covenant Union of Anglican Churches in Concordat deals with the mutual co-operation of the parties. The Council of Anglican Provinces

---

52 Seventh Assembly: *Growth in Communion*, para. 220; LWF, 29; Report 19/29, para. 176; WMC, Constitution: CPDMC, pp. 782–3.

53 R. Eames, 'The Anglican Communion', two lectures delivered at the Virginia Seminary, USA: ACNS 4041 (5-10-2005) and ACNS 4045 (10-10-2005). See also ACADC, Part 5 on the gift of communion.

54 RCW (2005) 8; Rt Revd J. Malik, Pakistan; Myanmar, A.4; HBTG (2005) para. 3.4.2: LCRPR. See also England, NDC Response (2007): an introduction to a covenant should deal with the Trinitarian foundations of communion (on the basis of that employed in *The Church of the Triune God*, Cyprus Agreed Statement of the International Commission for Anglican-Orthodox Theological Dialogue (2007) paras 1–3).

55 MU (2004) p. 6; R. Turner, 'The Lambeth Proposed "Anglican Covenant" Considered' (November 2004) 1; Sudan, para. 4: LCRPR; see WDAC, Arts 1.1, 5.3, 7.2.

56 Diocese of Brisbane (2004) 2.7: LCRPR; Goddard (2005) 6.

57 See, however, A Covenant for Communion in Mission, Conclusion: 'We make this covenant in the promise of our mutual responsibility and interdependence in the Body of Christ.'

of Africa seeks to help Anglican Churches in Africa develop benefi-
cial relationships between themselves and the wider Anglican Communion, through a forum which enables sharing experiences, mutual
support, conferring about common responsibilities, and establishing
opportunities for collaboration and joint activities.[58]

By way of contrast, ecumenical covenants are more explicitly about
relationships of communion, or relationships which move towards communion, or full communion, and collaboration,[59] as are some instruments of other international ecclesial communities. In the Lutheran
World Federation communion finds its visible expression in pulpit and
altar fellowship, in common witness and service, in the joint fulfilment
of the missionary task and in openness to ecumenical co-operation,
dialogue, and community.[60] Often these instruments deal with the
purposes of the international fellowship, which, in contrast to the St
Andrews, Nassau and Windsor draft covenants, are commonly presented in some considerable detail.[61] The Leuenberg Agreement also
spells out the terms of the relationship between the member churches:
each church accords each other church fellowship in word and sacrament and strives for the fullest possible co-operation in witness and
service to the world.[62] However, the constitution of the Standing Conference of Orthodox Bishops in the Americas does not treat the nature
or terms of their communion.[63]

Autonomy and its Exercise

A standard contention is that a covenant should deal with the meaning
of autonomy, on the basis that as long as 'total autonomy' (presumably
in the form of unlimited independence) in the ecclesiological sense is a
reality, differences (as in this present crisis) will continue to be a threat

---

58 ACC, Const. Art. 2.a; ACN, Memorandum of Agreement, 8: to provide adequate
episcopacy for dissenting parishes; CUACC, Art. 1; CAPA (2005).

59 For example, Porvoo Agreement (communion); Covenant of the Churches in Wales
1975; LARC (1990), Preamble (movement toward communion); AMC:CS, Preamble: 'the
goal of full visible unity'; ACCT, Preamble (movement to full communion); CO, II
(collaboration).

60 Seventh Assembly: *Growth in Communion*, para. 220; LWF, 29; LWF Report
19/29, para. 176.

61 For example, WARC, Const., Art. III (1–9).

62 CPCE:LA, Arts 6, 29.

63 Compare the Roman Catholic Code of Canon Law 1983, c. 205: 'Those baptised
are in full communion with the Catholic Church here on earth who are joined (*iungun-
tur*) with Christ in his visible body, through the bonds of profession of faith, the sacraments and ecclesiastical governance.'

to any common expression of Anglicanism.[64] Moreover, it should deal with the exercise of autonomy, and respect for it, to balance power with responsibility.[65] The Windsor draft covenant is criticized for not having sufficient material on humility in searching scripture and tradition, diversity and respect for the integrity of differences, the role of conscience in acceptable diversity, and mutual listening.[66] Some relate respect for diversity to the virtue of patience and 'the Anglican virtue of un-decidability'.[67] While the St Andrews draft covenant (like the Nassau and Windsor texts) treats autonomy, listening and to a lesser extent diversity,[68] it does not explicitly deal with the extent to which a church may freely exercise its own conscience on contentious issues of common concern to the Communion.[69] Indeed, the Australian church submission to the Covenant Design Group at Nassau highlighted that a covenant should provide for the mutual maintenance of provincial autonomy with provincial preparedness to self-limitation (implicit in the conciliar tradition as reflected in synodical process); thus, a covenant should provide for churches to wait upon each other; consequently, its draft covenant has a separate part devoted to the exercise of autonomy.[70] Protection of autonomy and diversity also emerged as a major value in provincial responses to the Nassau text.[71] This led the St Andrews draft covenant (unlike the Nassau text) to include the central Windsor principle of autonomy-in-communion, in order to ensure that 'ecclesial communion does not submerge the responsible choices that

---

64 Eames (2005): ACNS 4045 (6-10-2005).

65 RHB (2005) para. 3; Dioc. of Brisbane (2004): LCRPR; *Church Times*, 22-10-2004, 10.

66 Strudwick (2005); see also MacDougall (2005) 19: difference can be 'a liability' but diversity 'an asset': for example 1 Cor. 12; Rom. 12; and A. Linzey, 'In defence of diversity', in Linzey and Kirker (2005) 181 for conscience. The treatment of diversity and its limits is commonly discussed in the context of autonomy: see, for example, Michael Doe (2006).

67 Percy (2006).

68 SADC Cls 3.1.2, 3.2.1 and 3.2.2 (autonomy), 3.2.3 (listening); NDC, Art. 6.2; WDAC, Arts 4.3 and 22.

69 It could include a provision, for example, that: 'Each church shall respect the conscientious decisions of all other member churches in essential matters of common concern'.

70 ACADC, Part. 6. See also Australia, RNDC (2007).

71 Wales, RNDC (2007): 'It is valuable to recognise the diversity that is the reality of the Anglican Church'; TEC, RNDC (2007): 'communion' means 'mutual participation' which 'in Anglicanism has historically embraced a shared commitment to theological breadth and comprehensiveness', and 'freedom in non-essential matters and humility in those matters where faithful Christians may err'; see also Southern Africa, RNDC (2007): a covenant must balance provincial autonomy and mutual accountability; and Ireland, RNDC (2007).

local churches must engage in order to be faithful to their calling by and under Christ'.[72]

Given their prominence in the report of the Lambeth Commission, and in responses to it, it is perhaps surprising to find no formal treatment of reception and *adiaphora* in the St Andrews, Nassau and Windsor draft covenants. The Commission defines reception,[73] and proposes a threefold model to test the acceptability of an authentic development of the faith, namely: theological debate and discussion; formal action; and increased consultation to see whether the formal action settles down and makes itself at home.[74] While many value the doctrine,[75] others question its utility,[76] but few suggest that reception should be treated in a covenant.[77] The Commission also connects autonomy and subsidiarity to *adiaphora*: churches are free to decide on non-essentials unless to do so would be scandalous and offensive.[78] While subsidiarity is treated in the Windsor draft covenant,[79] *adiaphora* is not, which for some respondents is a defect: a covenant could help to discern be-

---

72 Commentary to SADC, para. 11 and SADC, Cl. 3.1.2; see also TWR, para. 76; WDAC, Art. 21.

73 See TWR, paras 67–70: the process to determine whether a declaration, by an Instrument of Unity, or by a church in the exercise of its autonomy, is in harmony with the faith and the *consensus fidelium*.

74 TWR, para. 59; a possible covenantal formula could be, therefore: 'The development by a church or by the Communion shall be deemed authentic when tested by theological debate and discussion, formal action, and consultation which indicate the reception of that development as consistent with the faith and as not forbidden by the Communion.'

75 Noll (2006): 'The Covenant should affirm that the Church holds and teaches true doctrine in essential matters of salvation and in indifferent matters where specific, culturally conditioned judgements and applications are made.'

76 FOFAD14–15: 'No due process of the Anglican Communion will ever turn an error into the truth'; HBTG (2005) 1.3.5–6: 'The use of the doctrine of reception to defy the declared will of the Church is an attempt to exercise freedom of action without reference to the wider Church and is therefore unacceptable': LCRPR.

77 Clatworthy, Bagshaw and Saxbee (2007) 4.2, commenting on the Nassau draft: 'Similarly the requirement that novel and controversial issues be "tested by shared discernment in the life of the Church" is to be welcomed'; there may be 'a greater need for clarity as to what matters are appropriately discussed at a local and what at an international level. In this regard, the achievements of the Anglican Consultative Council are to be celebrated, not diminished.'

78 TWR, paras 38–39, 71, 77, 83, 87, 89, 93, 94: *adiaphora*: 'things which do not make a difference, matters regarded as non-essential, issues about which one can disagree without dividing the Church'; subsidiarity: 'the clearer it is that something is "indifferent" in terms of . . . central doctrine and ethics, the closer to the local level it can be decided; whereas the clearer it is that something is central, the wider must be the circle of consultation.'

79 WDAC, Art. 18.4: autonomy expresses subsidiarity: decision-making at the appropriate level.

tween essentials and *adiaphora*;[80] the concept might also prove useful for conflict resolution.[81] One respondent advocates the 'things necessary to salvation' principle as a more appropriate test.[82] *Towards an Anglican Covenant* also mooted inclusion of clauses on agreements to differ.[83] Interestingly, in relation to subsidiarity, the Inter-Anglican Theological and Doctrinal Commission propose three criteria to determine the level (local or global) at which decisions should be taken: intensity, extent and substance.[84] In turn, the draft covenant submitted by the Anglican Church in Australia to the Covenant Design Group at Nassau deals with autonomy (and the concept of self-limitation),[85] subsidiarity,[86] and reception,[87] all of which are defined. Indeed, the Australian response to the Nassau text proposed that a covenant might provide that a church should refrain from an innovation *unless* reception determines that there is no bar to that innovation (that is, unless two of the Instruments of Communion advise that there is no bar to the innovation).[88] In similar vein, the Inter-Anglican Standing Commission on Ecumenical Relations considers a covenant could provide a way to discern what matters are communion-breaking.[89] Like Windsor and Nassau, the St Andrews draft covenant deals with common discernment and disagreement.[90] Some respondents consider that a

---

80 TEC, s. 4; see also Sudan, para. 4: LCRPR.

81 CIPRWR (2005) 9–10; HBTG (2005) 1.4: whether a matter is *adiaphora* needs the widest possible discussion: LCRPR.

82 Bishop C. Epting, para. 1: LCRPR.

83 TAAC, para. 30.

84 RPC, para. 3.2: 'If a conflict became intense, it is less likely to be resolved easily at local level; if its scope is extensive, involving many people in multiple locations, a universal solution is probably required; if the matter is substantial rather than trivial or peripheral, a larger structural resolution seems indicated'. Australia, RNDC (2007) proposed that this threefold test be incorporated in a covenant.

85 ACADC, Part 6.17: 'Autonomy, the right of a church to self-government'; 5.6: 'Subject to the Fundamental Declarations and Ruling Principles, Member Churches have plenary authority and power to make canons, ordinances and rules for their own order and good government, and to administer their own affairs.'

86 ACADC, Part 6.17: 'the principle of subsidiarity, that decisions should be made as close to the local level as possible'.

87 ACADC, Part 1.1: '"Reception" means a process of testing whether a controversial development or action, not yet approved by the Anglican Communion but nevertheless arising within a province by legitimate processes, might gradually, over time, come to be accepted as an authentic development consistent with the faith as it has been received by the Anglican Communion.'

88 Australia, RNDC (2007).

89 IASCER (8-12-2006) 13: it commends the Agreed Statement of the International Anglican-Orthodox Theological Dialogue on Heresy, Schism and the Church as a useful resource here.

90 See below Ch. 6. The Archbishops of Canterbury and York have stated: 'It could be that a well-structured Covenant would help us not to treat every divisive matter with

covenant should also deal with the interpretation of scripture, and the St Andrews text (like Nassau and Windsor) touches upon this.[91]

The treatment of autonomy in comparable covenants is informative. In the ecumenical sphere, such as in Anglican–Lutheran dialogue, a covenanted communion relationship is understood as compatible with autonomy,[92] with diversity, which might be defined,[93] and with freedom.[94] Treatment of autonomy is also commonplace in the instruments of other international ecclesial communities.[95] For example, the statute of the international Old Catholic Bishops Conference provides for a 'relationship between autonomy of the local church (as to self-government in the broadest sense) and supra-local obligation of each church (as to the communion of local churches)'.[96] The autonomy of member churches is protected in the Standing Conference of Orthodox Bishops in the Americas,[97] the World Alliance of Reformed Churches,[98] the Southern Baptist Convention,[99] and the World Methodist Council.[100] Some instruments also deal with reception, which is

---

the same seriousness and enable us to discern what was really – theologically and ecclesially – at stake when disagreements arose': Church of England, General Synod, Agenda Paper, July 2007 (GS 1661) Annex 1.

91 Noll (2006): 'the Covenant should affirm that Scripture is to be interpreted in its plain and canonical sense, in consonance with the received reading of the historic Church'; SADC, Cl. 1.2.4; NDC, Art. 3.3; WDAC, Art. 10.2.

92 Cold Ash Statement (1983), *Growth in Communion*, para. 113: in 'this new relation, churches become interdependent while remaining autonomous'.

93 See S. Oppegaard and G. Cameron (eds), *Anglican-Lutheran Agreements: Regional and International Agreements 1972–2002* (Geneva, Lutheran World Federation and Anglican Consultative Council, 2004): *Growth in Communion*, para. 138: '[D]iversity is understood to be a desirable dimension of the catholicity of the Church, where judged to be genuine expressions of a faith held in common. A sufficient agreement in faith does not require us "to accept every doctrinal formulation characteristic of our distinctive traditions"'; the inset quotation is from the Porvoo Common Declaration, para. 33.

94 Waterloo Declaration, para. 7: *Growth in Communion*, para. 117: 'Full communion is understood as a relationship between two distinct churches or communions in which each maintains its own autonomy while recognising the catholicity and apostolicity of the other, and believing the other to hold the essentials of the Christian faith.'

95 LWF, Const., Art. IV.

96 Preamble, 4.1.

97 Const., Art. II(a)2: 'No decision of the Conference shall interfere with the ecclesiastical jurisdiction of any of the Canonical Orthodox Churches, or any of the member Hierarchs.'

98 Const., Art. IV: 'None of these provisions shall limit the autonomy of any member church.'

99 Const., Art. IV: 'While independent and sovereign in its own sphere, the Convention does not claim and will never attempt to exercise any authority over any Baptist body, whether church, auxiliary organizations, associations, or conventions.'

100 Constitution: CPDMC, pp. 782–3.

sometimes defined,[101] and with *adiaphora*,[102] which may be used in processes prior to covenanting.[103]

As to the meaning of autonomy, the Lambeth Commission proposes that, being the right to self-government, autonomy is a form of limited authority: it means that a church has 'the unfettered right to order and regulate its own local affairs'. However, decisions in mixed affairs, involving both internal (domestic) and external (common) matters, must be compatible with the standards of the wider community of which the autonomous body forms part: this is the Windsor principle of autonomy-in-communion, that autonomy denotes not unlimited freedom, but 'freedom-in-relation', subject to limits generated by the obligations of communion.[104] These ideas are consistent with understandings of autonomy in the Orthodox tradition,[105] international law,[106]

---

101 Old Catholics, Statute, Preamble, 4.2: 'The reception by a church is a manifestation that the decisions of the bishops, prepared and taken in a comprehensive conciliar process, have been initiated by the Spirit of God and correspond to the will of God for the mission of his Church. Reception therefore includes the participation and joint responsibility of the baptized (clergy and laity) in this process both within each local or national church (synods or other responsible organs) and within the Union of Utrecht as a whole. But being a process led by the Spirit of God, it cannot comprehensively, let alone conclusively, be put into juridical terms or mechanical finalization.'

102 Formula of Concord (Lutheran 1580), Art. 10: 'For settling also this controversy we unanimously believe, teach and confess that the ceremonies or church rites which are neither commanded nor forbidden in God's Word, but have been instituted alone for the sake of propriety and good order, are in and of themselves no divine worship, not even part of it'. however, 'in time of persecution, when a plain confession is required of us, we should not yield to the enemies in regard to such *adiaphora*'; 'no church should condemn another because one has less or more external ceremonies not commanded by God than the other, if otherwise there is agreement among them in doctrine and all its articles'; see M. D. Thompson, 'The concept of adiaphora and the Windsor Report', in P. G. Bolt, M. D. Thompson and R. Tong (eds), *The Faith Once For All Delivered* (Camperdown, NSW, Australian Church Record in conjunction with the Anglican League, 2005) 105–6.

103 CPCE:LA, Art. 5: this recognizes that in the covenanting process the churches learned 'to distinguish between the fundamental witness of the Reformation confessions of faith and their historically-conditioned thought forms'.

104 TWR, paras 72–86; for a robust defence of this understanding see A. Goddard, 'Unity and diversity, communion and covenant: theological, ecclesiological, political and missiological challenges for Anglicanism', in M. Chapman, *The Anglican Covenant* (London, Mowbray, 2008) 69; for criticisms of these ideas, see below Ch. 6.

105 J. H. Erickson, *The Challenge of Our Past: Studies in Orthodox Canon Law and Church History* (Crestwood, NY, St Vladimir's Seminary Press, 1991) 91–2, 110: 'In present-day Orthodox usage, a church is termed "autocephalous" [lit: 'self-headed'] if it possesses: (1) the right to resolve all internal problems on its own authority, independently of all other churches, and (2) the right to appoint its own bishops, among them the head of the church, without any obligatory expression of dependence on another church', but it is regarded by some as 'the spiritual counterpart of the sovereign nation-state'.

106 Compare: a sovereign body, as a general principle, has authority to legislate for the internal affairs of the territory in which it is located as well as for the external affairs of others in a community to which it is related but legally superior; the sovereignty of the UK

civil law,[107] and Anglican laws with their provisions on the autonomy of a province,[108] and the autonomy of the diocese.[109] It also represents the understanding of autonomy in the canon law of the Eastern Catholic Churches,[110] in which the exercise of autonomy by the churches is subject to limits in matters of faith, sacraments and ecclesial governance,[111] Roman Catholicism,[112] and Lutheranism.[113]

Matters of Common Concern

Like the Nassau and Windsor texts, the St Andrews draft covenant deals with the respective roles of the Instruments of Communion and structures for the management of communion issues in essential matters of common concern.[114] Several respondents who support the covenant principle agree that a covenant should have provisions on mechanisms for the management of matters of common concern and shared decision-making.[115] They agree, therefore, that it should address the institutional structures of the Communion, and the roles of the Instruments of Communion, including that of the office the Archbishop of Canterbury,[116] to which appointment might be offered to the

Parliament, for example, is understood to include the power to legislate, for instance, extra-territorially, but its authority may be limited by external laws when incorporated into UK law (for example, European law).

107 An obvious example is the competence of the Scottish Parliament: this has authority only on those matters devolved to it; it cannot legislate on reserved matters dealing with issues concerning the whole of the UK, of which Scotland is part. UK matters are reserved to the UK (Westminster) Parliament.

108 ACC-4, 1979, B: a province is a 'self-governing Church'.

109 West Africa, Const. Art. XXIII.1: a provincial synod recognizes for dioceses 'the greatest possible liberty compatible with the unity and good order of the Church . . . and to ensure the fullest consultation with them in matters of legislation'; dioceses are autonomous communities to the extent that diocesan authorities have jurisdiction over the affairs of the diocese (but not over affairs of concern to the wider provincial community); see also South East Asia, Const. Art. XVI; see N. Doe, *Canon Law in the Anglican Communion* (Oxford, Clarendon Press, 1998) 54–5.

110 See V. Pospishil, *Eastern Catholic Church Law* (New York, St Maron Publications, 1996).

111 Code of the Eastern Catholic Churches (1990), cc. 27–38, 56, 77, 79, 83, 112, 146, 600.

112 Code, cc. 581, 584, 585, 587, 598, 678: for example, autonomous religious institutes are subject to internal and external controls. See generally N. Doe, 'Communion and autonomy in Anglicanism': www.anglicancommunion.org/ecumenical/commissions/lambeth/documents/200402whatisitfor.pdf

113 The Lutheran World Federation as a Communion of Churches (Geneva, 2003) 22: 'There is no autonomy without interdependency.'

114 See below, Ch. 6.

115 For example, GSPN (2005) para. 12: LCRPR.

116 Bishop Epting (2005); HBTG (2005) para. 1.4; RHB (2005) para. 4: LCRPR.

whole Communion.[117] However, very many consider that a covenant should *not* provide for treatment of matters of common concern by way of a supra-provincial jurisdiction (see below Chapter 6).[118] Another argument is that, if there is to be a covenant, it should protect traditional Anglican inclusiveness by affirming open and respectful debate and should reject all attempts to foreclose debate or suppress an honest and informed seeking after truth; and it should not impose hierarchically determined conclusions on genuine differences of opinion.[119]

Some argue that the Primates' Meeting, as an executive of the Lambeth Conference, rather than the Anglican Consultative Council, is the most appropriate forum to deal with matters of common concern.[120] The consensus emerging in the provincial consultation, however, was for the Council to play a more central role than the primates.[121] According to the Primates' Meeting 2007, a covenant would need to deal with the authority and capacity of the Instruments of Communion and the balance between them.[122] The St Andrews draft covenant seeks to distribute functions relating to matters of common concern among the Instruments of Communion in order for them 'to work more corporately'.[123] However, the Inter-Anglican Theological and Doctrinal Commission consider that a covenant should identify a body charged with its interpretation.[124] The Windsor draft deals expressly with interpretation; the Nassau text does not do so, but the St

---

117 Noll (2005) 9: 'A Global Anglican Covenant will need to spell out the method by which a presiding primate is chosen and a way of admitting or excluding provinces other than the unilateral decision of a particular individual'; 'the theo-political position of the Archbishop of Canterbury presents an insuperable obstacle to a fully empowered Global Anglican Communion'; Noll suggests, therefore, that the presiding primate must be open to bishops from all regions; it would be gracious for the Church of England and the British Government 'to disestablish the office of the Archbishop of Canterbury and offer it to the worldwide Communion'.

118 For example, CIPRWR, 12; Dioc. of British Columbia, s. 2; Dioc. of Ontario, q. 4: LCRPR.

119 Clatworthy, Bagshaw and Saxbee (2007) 7.2: 'We suggest that the greatest protection for inclusivity may be found in faithful listening to the voice of God echoed in the voices of God's faithful people.'

120 Noll (2005) 8–10: along the lines of, for example, the Council of Anglican Provinces in Africa (CAPA) and the Council of Anglican Provinces in the Americas and Caribbean (CAPAC).

121 The view was held by, for example, Hong Kong, New Zealand, Scotland, Southern Africa, TEC, and Wales.

122 Points Raised in Discussion of the Draft text for an Anglican Covenant, Sect. 6.

123 Commentary to SADC, para. 8.

124 RPC, para. 3.3: 'any covenant requires an instrument to interpret it. There is no such thing as a self-interpreting covenant any more than there are self-interpreting scriptures. A covenant implies an interpretive body to decide on what level of polity it is best addressed and whether or to what extent it has been breached'; see also Grieb (2007), Scully (2007) 15 and Philippines (2005): LCRPR.

Andrews draft covenant seeks to do so in its Appendix.[125] Several suggest that further thought must be given, in the context of subsidiarity, to the proper limits of autonomy and to what matters may properly be debated and decided at local level, and to how such decisions might be made,[126] but a covenant should not be fixated on controlling disintegration and conflict resolution.[127]

Matters of common concern are a standard topic in contemporary Anglican instruments, which deal with the structural organization of the entity in question: a Covenant for Communion in Mission exhorts parties to meet to share common purpose; the Organizational Charter of the Anglican Communion Network provides for the composition, meetings and functions of its Convocations, Steering Committee, Council and officers; and the Covenant Union of Anglican Churches in Concordat provides for delegations of ministers and laity to attend the assemblies of the respective member church bodies.[128] Reaching a 'common mind',[129] and common decision-making on shared concerns, are also features of ecumenical covenants.[130] Similarly, instruments of comparable international ecclesial communities enable those communities or a representative global body within them (either those bodies composed solely of ordained persons or those with a mixture of ordained and lay persons): 'to act jointly in common tasks' (Lutheran World Federation);[131] to act 'in common service wherever needed and practicable' (World Alliance of Reformed Churches);[132] to engage in

125 WDAC, Art. 27; NDC, Art. 6.6 does not specify one instrument with authority to settle contested interpretations; the article only provides for determination of failures to fulfil 'the substance of the covenant as understood by the Councils of the Instruments of Communion'; under the Appendix of SADC, bodies charged with the resolution of covenant disagreements must engage in interpretation and the document implies that final authority to interpret will vest in the Anglican Consultative Council: see below Chs 6 and 9.

126 Clatworthy, Bagshaw and Saxbee (2007) 4.9.

127 Scully (2007) 12.

128 CCM, p.4; ACN, Organizational Charter, Art. V; CUACC, Arts 2 and 4.

129 Covenant of the Churches in Wales, Art. VII.

130 Cold Ash Statement (1983) of the Anglican-Lutheran Joint Working Group: *Growth in Communion*, para. 113: 'Full communion carries implications which go beyond sharing the same eucharist'; 'there should be recognised organs of regular consultation and communication, including episcopal collegiality, to express and strengthen the fellowship and enable common witness, life and service'; to be 'in full communion implies a community of life, an exchange and a commitment to one another in respect of major decisions on questions of faith, order and morals'.

131 LWF, Const., Arts III, IV, and VII: the Federation 'may take action in matters committed to it by the member churches'; it 'may act on behalf of one or more churches in such specific tasks as they commit to it'; and it 'may request individual churches to assume tasks on behalf of the entire Communion'; its Assembly has authority to 'give general direction to the work of the Federation'.

132 WARC, Const., Arts III, IV; By-Laws, II: its General Council meets ordinarily

'the consideration and resolution of common ecclesiastical problems' and 'the co-ordination of effort in matters of common concern' (Standing Conference of Orthodox Bishops in the Americas);[133] and 'to fulfil common tasks' and take decisions 'in all organizational or disciplinary matters concerning the maintenance of communion', including 'controversial matters of faith and principle' (Old Catholics' International Bishops' Conference).[134] Finally, church–state agreements treat matters of common concern.[135]

Conclusion

The subjects treated by the St Andrews, Nassau and Windsor draft covenants are common identity, the relationships and commitments of communion, the exercise of autonomy, and the management of communion issues; in the St Andrews process, these are summed up in faith, mission and unity. Politically, these subjects are dealt with because they are considered germane to the long-term resolution of events leading to the Lambeth Commission. Theologically, it is arguable that the subjects should be addressed because they deal with fundamental ecclesiological concerns about what it means to be a church, or, more particularly, to be a church within the body of Christ. Their inclusion also flows directly from a theology of covenant as an agreement designed to unite churches in stable relationships of commitment. Beyond this, it is difficult to identify theological reasons why these matters should be treated. However, many respondents agree that these are proper subjects for a covenant. Equally, some consider that the absence of provisions on scriptural interpretation, *adiaphora*, reception, the Christian virtues, and the purposes of the Communion, is a defect in the Windsor and Nassau drafts, and many oppose material on decision-making at Communion level. Nevertheless, that there is

---

once in every seven or eight years; it is convened and its programme is determined by the Executive Committee; it is empowered to make and administer policies and programmes in accordance with the purposes of the Alliance; to elect officers, members of the Executive Committee, Departments, Committees and Commissions; to adopt and amend a Constitution and By-Laws; to consider all matters brought before it by the member churches; to give oversight to the affairs of the Alliance.

133 SCOBA, Const., Art. I(c).

134 Old Catholic Bishops, Statute, Preamble, 6; Order, Art. 3.

135 Typically, with regard to the overlapping activities and interests of the state and religious organizations: protection of freedom of religion; church property; church autonomy; employment; chaplaincies; education; social welfare programmes: see R. Puza and N. Doe (eds), *Religion and Law in Dialogue: Covenantal and Non-Covenantal Cooperation between State and Religion in Europe* (Leuven, Peeters, 2006).

theological integrity in a covenantal treatment of these subjects may be proposed on the basis that they are not merely managerial topics but deeply spiritual concerns. As such, juridically, it is commonplace for agreements in ecumenism and other international ecclesial communities to address common identity (mutual acknowledgements), obligations of fellowship (mutual commitments), maintenance of autonomy (properly exercised), and the manner in which matters of common concern may be resolved (usually through the establishment of representative institutions at the international level).

6

The Content of a Covenant

The relationship between communion and autonomy in Anglicanism has been described as one of creative tension.[1] Communion is a theological category, and autonomy a juridical category, each reality drawing strength from the other.[2] The draft covenants which have been produced thus far seek to articulate and regularize this creative tension for the Anglican Communion in such a way that communion and autonomy share the same goals.[3] The following outlines, in chronological order, the key provisions of the Windsor 2004, Nassau 2007 and St Andrews 2008 draft covenants and, in the footnotes, indicates (illustratively not exhaustively) the provenance of the principles set out in their Articles, where appropriate identifying innovations; in all three texts, most provisions are taken from existing Anglican sources.[4] Unlike the *Windsor Report* (and its draft) but like the Nassau text, the St Andrews draft covenant indicates some of its sources.[5] As the chair of the Lambeth Commission stated as to the Windsor proposal,[6] the Covenant Design Group maintains that what is offered in its Nassau draft (and the St Andrews text is not dissimilar) is not 'the invention of

---

1 *Women in the Episcopate*, Eames Commission (Toronto, 1998) para. 36.

2 Virginia Report, LC 1998, Official Report, 36; Report of the Carrington Committee, in *The Lambeth Conference 1948* (London, 1948) 84: 'While all [provinces] are autonomous they are all interdependent, drawing inspiration each from all. They are not independent in any divisive sense, but are interlocked by ties that bind them one to another in a single faith and order, in a common loyalty to our Lord . . . as in an agreed purpose in world evangelism.'

3 For elements of this concept of unity in goals, see *The Truth Shall Make You Free, The Lambeth Conference 1988*, 104 (committee report).

4 The main sources are resolutions of the Lambeth Conference, reports, the laws of churches, and ideas adopted by Anglicans in ecumenical dialogue.

5 Indeed, the Primates' Meeting 2007 raised the point that citations might be given throughout the instrument so that its sources might more clearly be identified: Points Raised in Discussion of the Draft Text for an Anglican Covenant: General Points.

6 Archbishop Robin Eames: ACNS 4045 (6-10-2005): 'the Covenant proposal in Windsor is not the revolutionary document some commentators have described it'; it is 'not a threat to Provincial autonomy so jealously protected throughout the Communion' though 'it challenges traditional thinking on "bonds of affection" as the sole ingredient in relationships within our Communion'.

a new way of being Anglican, but a fresh restatement and assertion of the faith which we as Anglicans have received, and a commitment to interdependent life'.[7] However, for some respondents, there is no point in a covenant which does not make changes.[8] This chapter also compares the drafts and sets out respondents' arguments for and against the covenantal terms.[9]

The Windsor Draft Covenant

The Articles in Part I, on *common identity*, spell out those features of ecclesiality which each Anglican church recognizes in each other member church. The approach is one commonly used by Anglicans and their partners in ecumenical agreements.[10] Each member church belongs to the One, Holy, Catholic and Apostolic Church of Jesus Christ,[11] participates in the whole apostolic mission of the people of God,[12] affirms holy scripture, as containing all things necessary for salvation,[13] the rule and ultimate standard of faith,[14] holds the essentials of the apostolic faith,[15] as summed up in the creeds, and seeks to

7 Report, para. 12: the text is meant to be 'robust enough to express clear commitment in those areas of Anglican faith about which there has been most underlying concern in recent events, while at the same time being faithful and consistent with the declarations, formularies and commitments of Anglicanism as they have been received by our Churches. In this way, nothing which is commended in the draft text of the Covenant can be said to be "new"; it is rather an assertion of that understanding of the true Christian faith as it has been received in the Anglican Churches.' The IATDC too considers that a covenant should 'reflect the memory of the Anglican historical traditions and also summarize our present understanding of "the Anglican way"': RPC (October 2006) para. 2.3.

8 Clatworthy, Bagshaw and Saxbee (2007) para. 3.

9 The Primates' Meeting in 2005 considered that there were 'serious questions about the content' of the Windsor draft covenant: *Communiqué*, 24-2-2005, para. 9.

10 Typically for example, *Growth in Communion*: Anglican-Lutheran International Working Group (2000–2002) (Geneva, Lutheran World Federation, 2003) para. 45: 'Full communion is understood as a relationship between two distinct churches or communions in which each maintains its own autonomy while recognizing the catholicity and apostolicity of the other, and believing the other to hold all the essentials of the Christian faith.'

11 Art. 1.1: LC 1930, Res. 49. The laws of most churches make this claim for themselves: for example, Scottish Episcopal Church, can. 1.1.

12 Art. 1.2. See ARCIC, *Church as Communion* (1990) IV.45; see also LC 1998, Res. II.1(b)(ii).

13 Art. 1.3: Thirty-Nine Articles of Religion, Art. 6; LC 1888, Res. 11; LC 1998, Res. III.5.

14 Art. 1.4: LC 1888, Res. 11; LC 1920, Res. 9 (Lambeth Quadrilateral); LC 1998, Res. III.5.

15 Art. 1.4: This is adapted from formulae used in ecumenical agreements: as for example, n. 10; see, however, LC 1888, Res. 11 for the spirit of the formula.

preach God's Word authentically (Art. 1).[16] Each church recognizes in the other common sacraments and liturgical tradition (Art. 2), namely, that: each church holds and duly administers the sacraments of baptism and Eucharist as instituted by Christ,[17] and practises the common patterns of Anglican liturgical and ritual tradition,[18] as adapted to the needs of each generation and particular circumstances of each local ecclesial community.[19] Each church recognizes the common ministry and mission of the other (Art. 3), namely: the threefold ordained ministry of bishops, priests and deacons,[20] and the ministry of the laity,[21] as ministries given by God as instruments of his grace.[22] Each church shares a common understanding (Art. 4) of belonging to one another,[23] in mutual reciprocity and forbearance in the Body of Christ;[24] communion does not require acceptance by every church of all theological opinion, sacramental devotion, or liturgical practice that is characteristic of the other.[25] Every church has the intention to listen, speak, act and strive to obey the gospel, has the same concern for a conscientious interpretation of scripture, in the light of tradition and reason,[26] be in dialogue with those who dissent from that interpretation,[27] and heal divisions.[28] Each church shares a common autonomous polity with episcopal-synodical government (Art. 5).[29]

---

16 World Council of Churches, Report (1983).

17 Art. 2.1: LC 1888, Res. 11; LC 1920, Res. 9.

18 Art. 2.2: LC 1998, Res. III.8(f).

19 Art. 2.2: LC 1908, Res. 24, 27; for outreach to the youth, see LC 1998, Res. II.8(c).

20 Art. 3.1: LC 1888, Res. 11; Chicago-Lambeth Quadrilateral 1888.

21 Art. 3.1: LC 1958, Res. 94.

22 Art. 3.1: Porvoo Declaration. Also Art. 3.2: each church shares a common life of service in the apostolic mission entrusted by Christ, serving in the world his purposes of mission, justice and peace.

23 Art. 4.1: WAEEC, para. 36; ARCIC, *Church as Communion* (1990) IV.45.

24 Art. 4.1: ARCIC, *The Church as Communion* (1990) IV.45.

25 Art. 4.2: Bonn Agreement (1931).

26 Art. 4.3, 4: Chicago-Lambeth Quadrilateral (1886–8); Strudwick (2005) values the principle because the churches should commit themselves 'to respect the integrity and good faith of those whose search has led them to differing understandings in matters of importance in doctrine and ministry'.

27 Art. 4.4: LC 1998, Res. III.2(c); see also ACC-12, Res. 34.3. The provision is seen by some as 'an echo of Hooker': RCW (2005) 7.

28 Art. 4.4: see for example, Church of England, Canon A8; Rom. 15.5: forbearance. Some criticize the article as suggesting that reason and tradition are on a par with scripture: Church Society (2004) 4.3. Others propose that a covenant should mention how scripture can be interpreted under the guidance of the Holy Spirit: EVCF (2005) para. 4; but see TWR, paras 55, 57 and 61.

29 Art. 5: LC 1930, Res. 48. Art. 5.1: each member church is autonomous, episcopally led and synodically governed. Art. 5 also contains two propositions hitherto unarticulated: Decisions in each church are to be presumed as duly authorized within that church

Part II expresses the *relationships of communion*. Communion between Anglicans has a divine foundation (Art. 6): it is a gift of God (a communion of three persons), to all member churches,[30] and animated in the experience of God's work of redemption;[31] the divine call to communion[32] is inviolable and no member church may declare unilaterally irreversible broken communion with any fellow church.[33] In turn, churches share communion in terms of their common membership, relation and purpose (Art. 7): the Anglican Communion is a community of interdependent churches and consists of relations between each church, the See of Canterbury, and the fellowship of member churches worldwide;[34] each church acknowledges its Communion membership,[35] and is constituted by, exists in and receives fullness of life in its relations to the other member churches.[36] It also means that ordained and lay persons in each church are in personal communion with those of other member churches.[37] Each church shall serve the purposes of the Communion, which include: (a) achieving greater unity; (b) fostering and protecting a common mind in essential matters; and (c) proclaiming to the world in common witness the good news of the kingdom of God.[38] Each church also recognizes the process

---

but such decisions do not bind outside that church (5.2). Every church shares the same concern for good government for the fulfilment of its mission and for the common good of the Anglican Communion and the church universal (5.3): see also CMS (2005): Art. 5.3 recognizes that good government is for the fulfilment of mission; see also MU (2004) p.5: this criticizes the provision as it denies authority to the Communion.

30 Art. 6.1. See for example, Virginia Report, 24ff; WAEEC, 22, 23; LC 1998, Res. III.8(d). The article has been valued as 'the Trinitarian model must shape our ecclesiology': CPIO (2005) para. 6.

31 Art. 6.2. See Inter-Anglican Theological and Doctrinal Commission submission (see TWR, n. 21).

32 Art. 6.3. Virginia Report, 24, 26, 27; *Bishops in Communion* (2000) [Church of England] 6. The article has been understood as 'a very strong statement of communion': RCW (2005) 7.

33 Art. 6.3. The latter part of this sentence is an innovation (but see TWR, para. 29).

34 Art. 7.1. This reflects the models of bilateral communion with Canterbury (LC 1930, Res. 49), multipartite communion 'with all churches of the Anglican Communion' (for example Korea, Const., Fundamental Declaration), and communion with the community of churches (for example Hong Kong, Const., Preamble: the province is 'in communion with the Anglican Communion').

35 Art. 7.2. This surfaces in the constitutions of member churches.

36 Art. 7.2. See also Art. 8.3 below. This is a common feature of the perichoretic social doctrine of the Trinity as applied to human persons (for example L. Boff, *Trinity and Society* (London, Burnes & Oates 1988)) and is applied to churches: TWR, paras 51, 84.

37 Art. 7.3. For the notion of personal communion (such as between bishops), in addition to ecclesial communion, see, for example Virginia Report, 29.

38 Art. 7.4. See, for example LC 1998, Res. III.2(a). Remarkably, however, the Communion has not formally articulated its own strategic purposes: these ideas are, however,

and substance of communion (Art. 8): communion, never perfected until God's kingdom is all in all, involves unity, equality of status, and a common pilgrimage towards truth, each church in partnership with its fellow churches learning what it means to become interdependent and thus more fully a communion.[39]

The Windsor draft provides that communion involves responsibilities so that each church may be more fully completed in, through and by its relations with other member churches, having regard for their common good (Art. 8(3)).[40] The *commitments of communion* are set out in Part III. Each church has a commitment of loyalty to catholicity and the common good of the Anglican Communion (Art. 9); it must: act in a manner compatible both with its belonging to the One, Holy, Catholic and Apostolic Church, and with its membership of the Anglican Communion.[41] In all essential matters of common concern in the Anglican Communion, no member church shall act without consideration of the common good of the Communion and fundamental compliance with the Covenant.[42] Each church has obligations concerning the confession of the faith (Art. 10); it must: uphold and act compatibly with the catholic and apostolic faith, order and tradition,[43] and moral values and vision of humanity received by and developed in the fellowship of member churches;[44] and, primarily through its bishops, ensure that biblical texts are handled respectfully and coherently, building on our best traditions and scholarship believing that scriptural revelation must continue to illuminate, challenge and transform cultures, structures and ways of thinking.[45] Each church has sacramental commitments (Art.

---

implicit in the commitments set out in WDAC Part III, and they are commonly expressed as the purposes of individual churches: for example LC 1998, Res. II.6(c), New Zealand, Const., Preamble; Sudan, Declaration of Fundamental Principles, I; South East Asia, Const., Preamble; North India, Const. II.I.II.

39 Art. 8.1. WAEEC, para. 61. See also Art. 8.2: Communion subsists in the mutual acknowledgement by churches of their common identity.

40 For interdependence, see Virginia Report, 24ff. This is also taken again from Trinitarian doctrine (the idea that the divine communion manifests itself *ad extra*) as applied to human persons: see for example, W. Kasper, *The God of Jesus Christ* (Oxford, Blackwell, 1989) 289ff.

41 Art. 9.1.

42 Art. 9.2. LC 1978, Res. 11: 'The Conference advises member Churches not to take action regarding issues which are of concern to the whole Anglican Communion without consultation with' a Lambeth Conference or the Primates' Meeting. Some respondents criticize 'essential matters' as lacking clarity: Epting (2005).

43 Art. 10.1. See LC 1930, Res. 49 (faith and order); WAEEC, para. 35 (tradition).

44 Art. 10.1. See ARCIC, *Church as Communion*, IV.45. The reference to 'moral values' has been criticized as too vague: A. Pearce 'English ecclesiastical autonomy and the Windsor Report' (2005); Dioc. of Brisbane (2004) para. 4.5.

45 Art. 10.2. See LC 1998, Res. III.1(b). This has been criticized as promoting too

11), and must: maintain and administer the sacraments of baptism and eucharist;[46] welcome members of all other member churches to join in its own celebration of the sacraments; and enjoin its members to eucharistic sharing in a fellow church in accordance with the canonical discipline of that host church.[47] Each church has apostolic and ministerial commitments (Art. 12) to: uphold the historic threefold ministry of bishops, priests and deacons;[48] recognize the canonical validity of orders duly conferred in every member church;[49] welcome persons episcopally ordained in any member church to minister in the host church subject to the necessary consents required by and in accordance with the law of that church; and permit any person ordained in that church to seek ministry in any other member church subject to its law and discipline.[50] Each minister in each church, especially a bishop, shall be a visible sign of unity and maintain communion within each church and between it, the See of Canterbury and all other Communion churches (Art. 13).[51] Each host church has commitments to be hospitable to,

---

monarchical a concept of episcopacy and as neglecting the roles of scholars, theologians and the whole people of God: Epting (2005).

46 Art. 11.1. This surfaces in the laws of churches. See also LC 1888, Res. 11; LC 1998, Res. III.8(d).

47 Art. 11.2, 3. See *Growth in Communion*, para. 45.

48 Art. 12.1. See Ordinal (1662). This is common in the laws of churches: for example Korea, Fundamental Declarations.

49 Art. 12.2. WAEEC, para. 35; also a fundamental of full communion in ecumenical relations: see, for example *Growth in Communion*, para. 117. Currently, such recognition is a matter for the member church unilaterally. Several see the mutual recognition of orders as imperative (for example Epting, para. 2), but others favour exclusion of a provision on the matter because of difficulties over female ordination and its ecumenical insensitivity (for example CCW (2005) para. 3).

50 Art. 12.3,4. Introduction of formal duties to welcome and permit are new. The requirement of consents to minister is a standard feature of the laws of Anglican churches.

51 The following duties under Art. 13 are new: Art. 13.2: No minister, especially a bishop, shall: (a) act without due regard to or jeopardize the unity of the Communion; (b) neglect to co-operate with ministers, especially bishops, of member churches for the good of the Communion and Church universal; (c) unreasonably be the cause or focus of division and strife in their church or elsewhere in the Communion; (d) if in episcopal office, unreasonably refuse any invitation to attend meetings of the Instruments of Unity; 1 Cor. 12.25. This was welcomed by, for example, Sudan, para. 1, but criticized by G. Jones '"Thy grace shall always prevent . . ."', in A. Linzey and R. Kirker (eds), *Gays and the Future of Anglicanism: Responses to the Windsor Report* (Winchester, O Books, 2005) 124: it requires 'a level of obedience that affects an understanding of a transCommunion ecclesiology, one in which "the good of the Communion and Church universal" is now made an explicit focus of Anglican unity. Thus, Windsor spells out the practical understanding of building a new covenant on the basis of a shared understanding of apostolic ecclesiology, implications that are born of the Church of England's original and originating (for the Communion) claim to be catholic and reformed. It is, in short, an argument with real purchase on the theological questions.'

welcome and make available its ministrations to the members of fellow churches (Art. 14),[52] and to mission and prayer, including offering its spiritual, intellectual, and financial resources to assist with the needs of another church or of the Communion as a whole (Art. 15).[53] Each church has commitments in relation to the bonds of mutual loyalty (Art. 16), namely: in essential matters of common concern to the Communion place the interests and needs of the community of member churches before its own,[54] in such cases, make every effort to resolve disputes by reconciliation, mediation or other amicable and equitable means,[55] and to respect the counsels of the Archbishop of Canterbury, Primates' Meeting, Lambeth Conference, and Anglican Consultative Council,[56] and the principles of canon law common to the churches of the Anglican Communion.[57] Finally (Art. 17): each church recognizes that if a member church enters a relation of communion with a non-member church, this effects a relationship between each member church and the non-member,[58] to the extent provided in its laws and the regulatory instruments of the ecumenical partner;[59] and before a member church enters any agreement with a non-member church, that church shall consult the appropriate Instrument of Unity.[60] Article 17 has been heavily criticized.[61]

---

52 This formal statement is new in Anglicanism, but common in ecumenism (for example Porvoo Declaration); *Growth in Communion*, 45; Rom. 16.16; 1 Cor. 16.20; 1 Pet. 5.14.

53 WAEEC, para. 35; Art. 15.4: Gal. 5.13; 1 Thess. 5.11. For the idea in responses that mission requires co-operation, see, for example CMS (2005).

54 Art. 16.1. See ARCIC, *Church as Communion*, para. 45.

55 Art. 16.2: this is a fundamental principle of the canonical tradition; Rom. 14.19.

56 Art. 16.3: this is a current expectation (see E. Coleman (ed.), *Resolutions of the Twelve Lambeth Conferences 1867–1988* (Toronto, Anglican Book Center, 1992) viii).

57 Art. 16.4. See above p. 89.

58 Art. 17.1. This is new, but makes an important statement about the ecumenical intent of the Communion, though it reflects in spirit the duties which member churches have in their own laws to seek or restore visible unity with non-Anglican churches: see, for example, Jerusalem and the Middle East, Const., Art. 5(ii).

59 Art. 17.1. This is declaratory of current canonical practice in member churches.

60 Art. 17.2. This is new, but reflects the spirit of LC 1978, Res. 11; see also LC 1968, Res. 47.

61 Epting (2005): the requirement to consult an instrument of unity is 'much too broadly worded. Provinces enter into many varied kinds of ecumenical agreements all the time. It would be unwieldy and unnecessary, every time to have to consult globally. At most, perhaps we could say that "before a member church enters into any full communion agreement that church shall take counsel with the Inter-Anglican Standing Commission on Ecumenical Relations". For what would the "appropriate Instrument of Unity" be in such cases?' 'In addition, it will be important to parse the word "consult". Does this mean consultation which may yet result in disagreement or consultation which must lead to agreement before consultation can be said to have occurred?' See also CCW (2005) para. 3: the respondent suggests an alternative wording: 'Each church recognises that it

Part IV deals with the exercise of *autonomy in communion*.[62] First, under Article 18, autonomy is a fundamental principle of Anglicanism;[63] it is the right of a church to be self-governing.[64] An autonomous church has authority ordinarily to make decisions for itself in relation to its own affairs at its own level.[65] Autonomy expresses subsidiarity, that is decision-making at the appropriate level.[66] Autonomy is exercised by a church in the context of the wider community of which it forms part.[67] Second (Art. 19), each autonomous church exercises the right to order and regulate its own affairs through its own system of government and law, and shall be free from control by any decision of any ecclesiastical body external to itself,[68] in relation to its exclusively internal affairs unless that decision is authorized under or incorporated in its own law.[69] The validity within each autonomous church of any ecclesiastical act relating to such internal affairs is governed by the law of that church.[70] Third (under Art. 20), some affairs treated within each church may have a dual character and consist of mixed elements of internal (domestic) concern and of external (common) concern to

---

constitutes part only of the Church of Christ within its Province, and therefore: (1) will seek to enter into ever closer communion with other churches within its province for the furtherance of the work of God; and (2) will support other member churches in their ecumenical relationships, praying for and working with one another to further the unity of the Body of Christ.'

62 Art. 18.6: There are limits on the exercise of autonomy imposed by the relationships of communion, the acknowledgement of common identity, the commitments of communion, and the principles applicable to the management of communion affairs. The article was welcomed, for example, by RHB (2005) 2.2.1; Kelsey (2004); Radner (2005) 618; and DAZ, 45–46.

63 Art. 18.1. See LC 1930, Res. 48; LC 1978, Res. 21.3.

64 Art. 18.2. See, for example *Oxford English Dictionary* (2nd edn, Oxford, Oxford University Press, 1989), 'autonomy'.

65 Art. 18.3. This is autonomy as understood by ecumenical partners: see, for example Lutheran: *The Lutheran World Federation as a Communion* (Geneva, 2003); Roman Catholic: Code of Canon Law (1983) c. 586 (concerning religious institutes); Eastern Catholic: D. Motluk, 'The code of canons of the Eastern Catholic Churches', *Studia Canonica* 36 (2002) 189 at 196.

66 Art. 18.4. See Virginia Report, Ch. 4.

67 Art, 18.5. For example the Scottish Parliament cannot legislate on reserved matters, issues concerning the whole of the wider community of the UK, of which Scotland is part: UK matters are reserved to Westminster.

68 Art. 19.1,2. This surfaces in the laws of churches: for example North India, Const. I.IV4: 'an autonomous church and free from any control . . . external to itself'.

69 Art. 19.2. This is a statement of current canonical practices across the Communion.

70 Art. 19.3. This is an innovation, but probably an articulation of current canonical understanding.

the Anglican Communion.[71] Therefore, autonomy includes the right of a church to make decisions in those of its affairs which may also touch the Anglican Communion of which it forms part,[72] provided those decisions are compatible with the interests and standards of the wider Communion (as determined in accordance with Part V);[73] what touches all should be approved by all.[74] Article 20 attracted heavy criticism: it inappropriately invests an international network with a dignity which the New Testament reserves for a local church;[75] that a church should act compatibly with the Communion standards is too restrictive;[76] there are difficulties about *which* matters touch all and who decides these;[77] also it allows inactivity on contentious issues,[78] and effectively gives every church a veto over the actions of every other church.[79]

Each church must exercise its autonomy in communion (Art. 21): each church has a fiduciary duty to honour and not to breach the trust put in it by the Communion to exercise its autonomy in communion.[80] In essential matters of common concern, each church shall in its exercise of autonomy have regard to the common good of the Anglican Communion.[81] In such matters, prior to any action, each church must exercise its autonomy in communion through explanation, dialogue, consultation, discernment and agreement, in the community of inter-

---

71 Art. 20.1. See Virginia Report, 44; LC 1978, Res. 21.3.

72 Art. 20.2. See ACC-12, Res. 34.2: 'provincial authorities to have in mind the impact of their decisions within the wider Communion.'

73 Art. 20.2.

74 Art. 20.3. See also, for example ACC, Guidelines for Meetings, 3.2: the right to a voice. For the *quod omnes tangit* principle of the (conciliar) canonical tradition, see Y. Congar, 'Quod omnes tangit ab omnibus tractari et approbari debet', *Revue historique de droit français et étranger* 36 (1958) 210: its origin is a law of Justinian 531. See also Ten Principles of Partnership, *Towards Dynamic Mission: Renewing the Church for Mission*, Mission Issues and Strategy Advisory Group II (1993) Principle 8: 'What touches one member touches all'. See too Roman Catholic Code of Canon Law (1983) c. 119.3: 'what touches all as individuals must be approved by all'.

75 FOFAD, 33: in commenting on TWR paras 94, 95, 'the more important an issue is perceived to be the higher the level of decision that is necessary. Local congregations may decide matters of indifference but the Anglican Communion must be consulted on central issues of importance'; another problem is determining 'just what is a matter of indifference'.

76 Cameron (2005) 52.

77 Bishop Epting (2005): LCRPR.

78 Dioc. of Brisbane (2004) para. 4.5: LCRPR.

79 CCW (2005) para. 2.4: LCRPR.

80 Art. 21.1. TWR, para. 40. The fiduciary duty is derived from the canonical tradition of *good faith*.

81 Art. 21.2. See ACC-12, Res. 14.1: 'dioceses and individual bishops not to take unilateral actions . . . which would strain our communion'.

dependent churches with the appropriate Instrument of Unity.[82] Article 21 was criticized on the basis that any restriction on a national provincial synod arises out of historical relationships of fellowship; not a constitutional connection of jurisdiction, law and coercion.[83] Finally, under Article 22, diversity is a desirable dimension of the catholicity of the church, a feature of the historic development of Anglicanism, and inherent to the particularity of each member church.[84] Each autonomous church has the greatest possible liberty to order its life and affairs, appropriate to its Christian people in their geographical, cultural and historical context, compatible with the unity and good order of the Communion.[85] Each church must respect and maintain the autonomy of all churches in the Anglican Communion and must not permit any authority or person within it to intervene in the internal affairs of another member church without its consent.[86] Article 22 has been criticized because diversity of belief or morality is not allowed by the New Testament, though scriptural interpretation should always be done in a context of dialogue and discussion.[87]

Part V, on the *management of communion issues*, contains the greatest number of innovations. Under Article 23, communion issues are those essential matters of common concern to the member churches of the Communion, and include the affairs, actual and prospective decisions, of a member church which touch fundamentally the fellowship and mission of the Anglican Communion, the relations of its churches, and the compatibility of such decisions with the covenant

---

82 Art. 21.3. TWR, paras 67–70.

83 FOFAD, 32: 'Fidelity to the faith once for all delivered should be a primary duty of provincial synods. If this coincides with the health of the Anglican Communion well and good.' The attempt to draw a parallel between the law-making power of a province and a body in the secular world 'on which has been conferred subordinate and restricted legislative power' fails. First, no superior external Anglican body has conferred power on national provincial synods. It is not like the Parliament of the United Kingdom passing an imperial act granting independence to a former colony and granting law making powers to that new country. It is more akin to the people of the Thirteen Colonies putting together their own constitution for the United States of America. Second, to whom or what is the autonomous, independent and sovereign national province subordinate? It makes no legal sense. For TWR to say churches are 'autonomous' and 'not independent or sovereign', is 'playing with words'.

84 Art. 22.1. TWR, paras 36–37, 83, 86, 89. For support for the article see, for example ECP (2005).

85 Art. 22.3. This is a new formulation. See however the Vatican II document *Sacrosanctum concilium* (1963), and *De ecclesia eucharistia* (2003).

86 Art. 22.3. LC 1878, Recommendations 1.1; see also LC 1930, Res. 48 and LC 1988, Res. 72 which reaffirms 'the historical position of respect for diocesan boundaries and the authority of bishops within' them. See also ACC, Guidelines for Meetings, 4: order and respect in debate.

87 FAFOD, 30; see also 11–12.

and the unity and good order of the Communion. The Instruments of Unity must set out formally their composition, functions, relations with one with another, and procedures,[88] for matters arising under this Part. A matter is a communion affair if so designated by the relevant Instrument of Unity, where appropriate in dialogue with any member church involved in the matter, subject to the right of the Archbishop of Canterbury under Article 27. Article 24 sets out the basic functions of the Instruments of Unity.[89] Each church must designate a person to act as its own Anglican Communion Liaison Officer, appointed to defend the bonds of communion expressed in the covenant, and accountable to its central assembly; and it must have a system to identify and process within that church contentious communion affairs for submission to that Officer (Art. 25). Process in communion matters is as follows. On discernment by the Officer of any contentious communion affair, the Anglican Communion Liaison Officer must liaise with the primate and the Secretary General of the Anglican Communion. Following such liaison, the Officer or Secretary General may submit the matter to the Archbishop of Canterbury. The Archbishop may issue such guidance as he deems fit or, as appropriate, refer the matter to the Council of Advice (recommended by the *Report*) for guidance and, if necessary, the Primates' Meeting, the Anglican Consultative Council, or the Lambeth Conference to resolve the issue having regard to the common good of the Communion and compatibility with the covenant (Art. 26).[90]

---

88 This is recommended by TWR, Appendix I. For support for the article, see for example, HBTG (2005) 2.3.5.

89 The Article repeats the current position, namely: '(1) The Instruments of Unity serve in communion to discern our common mind in communion issues, and foster our interdependence and mutual accountability, but exercise no jurisdiction over autonomous member churches save to the limited extent provided in this Covenant and the laws of member churches. (2) The Archbishop of Canterbury enjoys a primacy of honour and is a personal sign of our unity and communion, and shall be assisted by a Council of Advice. (3) The Lambeth Conference, under the presidency of the Archbishop of Canterbury, expressing episcopal collegiality worldwide, gathers for common counsel, consultation and encouragement and to provide direction to the whole Communion. (4) The Anglican Consultative Council has such membership and functions as are prescribed by its constitution. (5) The Primates' Meeting, presided over by the Archbishop of Canterbury, assembles for mutual support and counsel, monitors global developments and exercises collegial responsibility in doctrinal, moral and pastoral matters'. For support see, for example, HBTG (2005) 2.3.13.

90 See LC 1998, Res. III.6 for recommendations for an enhanced role for the Primates' Meeting and the ACC in cases of exceptional emergency incapable of internal resolution in a province (exercised by way of guidance and in consultation), and reaffirmation of Canterbury's role as a sign of unity. For support for the idea of a 'steer' from Canterbury on behalf of the Communion see Strudwick (2006).

The Instruments may exercise 'in communion' this limited jurisdiction, of conflict resolution, under carefully prescribed and exceptional conditions, respecting the autonomy of each church; the matter in question must be a contentious (Art. 26) communion issue (Art. 23), that is: an essential matter of common concern which touches fundamentally the fellowship and mission of the Communion, and which jeopardizes its unity and good order.[91] This reference model is currently employed in the laws of a number of Anglican churches.[92] The draft covenant contains no provision for the expulsion of churches (unlike the instruments of other global ecclesial communities):[93] it is an opt-in scheme. Nor does the covenant create a general competence on the part of the Archbishop of Canterbury to issue binding decisions unilaterally. However, under Article 27, the Archbishop of Canterbury must decide all questions of interpretation of the covenant, consulting the (recommended) Council of Advice, and seeking the advice of any other body as he deems appropriate. If approved by the Joint Standing Committee of the Primates' Meeting and Anglican Consultative Council, the decision of the Archbishop shall be regarded as authoritative in the Communion until altered in like manner. The Council of Advice must carry out periodic reviews of the administration of the covenant for submission to the Archbishop of Canterbury who must act upon such reviews as he deems appropriate, so that the member churches may more completely embrace the life in communion to which all are called by the Lord Jesus Christ.

Part V attracted most criticism. On the one hand, Article 26 goes too far: in strengthening the Instruments of Unity it creeps towards papacy.[94] The appointment of an Anglican Communion liaison officer in each church is undesirable in principle and would be awkward in practice.[95] An enhanced role for the Archbishop of Canterbury and the Primates' Meeting would change the nature and structure of authority in Anglicanism – the proposal is too erastian, hierarchical and institutional, at odds with autonomy and democracy, and it is unclear as

---

91 If the matter were *adiaphora* (things which do not make a difference: TWR, para. 87) or one amenable to a process of reception (TWR, paras 68–70), the local church remains free to act.

92 In matters of doctrine or liturgy: see, for example, Central Africa, Const., Art. V; Uganda, Const., Art. II; South East Asia, Const., Fundamental Declarations, 4ff.; Southern Africa, Can. 41.

93 See below Ch. 9. Several respondents value the absence of a provision for suspension or expulsion from the Communion: see, for example, Inclusive Church.

94 Church Society (2004) 6.3; see also Rwanda (2005): LCRPR.

95 SECR (2005) para. 4: LCRPR.

to whom the Instruments of Unity are accountable.[96] Moreover, the Lambeth Conference should not become a governing body, nor the Primates' Meeting its standing committee; and the Council of Advice is unhelpful.[97] Article 26 would result in the centralization of power, usurp the functions of local synods, bishops and the Anglican Consultative Council, and oblige churches to submit innovations in theology or ethics to the Instruments of Unity on pain of censure.[98] Article 27 also smacks of papacy, is inconsistent with synodical government, and would lead to interventionism.[99] On the other hand, some criticize Article 26 because it does not go far enough: the New Testament mentions no territorial obstacles to the promotion of the gospel; and the Article insufficiently involves the laity in decision-making on Communion issues – an Anglican congress or synod would be a better mechanism to resolve contentious issues.[100]

The Nassau Draft Covenant

The preamble to the Nassau draft covenant (which is more missiological than the Windsor preamble), provides in Article 1 that the churches of the Anglican Communion,[101] under the Lordship of Jesus Christ, solemnly covenant together in order (1) to proclaim more effectively in their different contexts the grace of God revealed in the gospel; (2) to offer the love of God in responding to the needs of the world; (3) to maintain the unity of the Spirit in the bond of peace; and (4) to grow up together as a worldwide Communion to the full stature of Christ.[102] The preamble met with general approval in the provincial

---

96 CIPRWR, 12; Hughes (2004) III.B; Radner (2005) 610; Church Society (2004) para. 2.3; RCW (2005) 8, CAS (2005) 3; Dioc. of Saskatoon: LCRPR.

97 RCW (2005) 6: LCRPR.

98 Dioc. of Columbia, s. 2; Hughes (2004) III.C; M. McCord Adams 'Faithfulness in Crisis', in A. Linzey and R. Kirker (eds.), *Gays and the Future of Anglicanism: Responses to the Windsor Report* (Winchester, O Books, 2005) 70.

99 Dioc. of Ontario, q.4; CAS (2005) 2; Church Society (2004) 6.3; Pearce (2005) 10.

100 Dioc. of Bendigo (2005); GSPN; Tong (2005) 58–9; Diocese of British Columbia, s. 4: LCRPR.

101 The preamble in WDAC simply provided that the objects of covenanting are 'to foster greater unity and to consolidate our understandings of communion . . . so that our communion may be made more visible and committed'. Noll (2007) argues that the preamble should include the notion that the covenant is entered to proclaim more effectively 'the saving love of God for a fallen world accomplished through the death and resurrection of . . . Christ'.

102 The scriptural texts cited are: Ps. 127.1–2; Ezek. 37.1–14; Mark 1.1; John 10.10; Rom. 5.1–5; Eph. 4.1–16 (also cited by TWR, para. 2 as to the purposes and benefits of communion), Rev. 2–3.

consultation of late 2007,[103] though the use of scriptural references at the head of each Article was severely criticized.[104]

Article 2, on the life Anglicans share,[105] presents (like but less fully than the Windsor document) those features of common catholicity, apostolicity and confession of faith which each member church, and the Communion as a whole, affirms about itself.[106] Each member church is part of the One, Holy, Catholic and Apostolic Church,[107] worshipping the one God, Father, Son and Holy Spirit (Art. 2.1).[108] It affirms that it professes the *faith* which is (1) uniquely revealed in the holy scriptures (a) as containing all things necessary for salvation, and (b) as being the rule and ultimate standard of faith,[109] and (2) set forth in the catholic creeds, which faith the Church is called upon to proclaim afresh in each generation (Art. 2.2).[110] The churches must affirm that they hold and duly administer the two sacraments ordained of Christ himself, baptism and Lord's Supper,[111] ministered with the unfailing use of Christ's words of institution, and of the elements ordered by him (Art. 2.3),[112] and that they participate in the apostolic mission of the whole people of God (Art. 2.4).[113] Each church must affirm that, led by the Holy Spirit, it has borne witness to Christian truth in its

103 However, Australia, RNDC (2007) suggests the deletion of 'up' in (4); and England, RNDC (2007) criticizes (4): it suggests only Anglican churches can attain the full stature of Christ.

104 For example RNDC Australia, England, Wales, Southern Africa, and TEC all questioned why these references were included in the text of the draft covenant.

105 The scriptural texts cited are Deut. 6.4–7; Lev. 19.9–10; Amos 5.14–15, 24; Matt. 25, 28.16–20; 1 Cor. 15.3–11; Phil. 2.1–11; 1 Tim. 3.15–16; Heb. 13.1–17.

106 The approach is common in ecumenical agreements. See above n. 10. However, Australia, RNDC (2007) proposed deletion of the formula 'and the Communion as a whole', suggesting that only each church should be required to recognize these marks in itself.

107 See WDAC, Art. 1.1; LC 1930, Res. 49. The laws of most churches make this claim for themselves: for example Scottish Episcopal Church, Can. 1.1.

108 Source given by NDC, n. 1: the Preface, Declaration of Assent, Canon C15, Church of England.

109 NDC, Art. 2.2; see WDAC, Art. 1.3; LC 1888, Res. 11; LC 1920, Res. 9; LC 1998, Res. III.5; NDC, n. 2: Lambeth Quadrilateral 1888. The inclusion of the article is supported by Noll (2006): he adds that the churches should affirm that scripture is to be interpreted in its plain and canonical sense in accordance with the received reading of the historic Church. However, Southern Africa, NDC Response (2007) suggests that the centrality of scripture is inadequately expressed in the article.

110 NDC source, n. 3: Preface, Declaration of Assent, Can. C15, Church of England. The inclusion of this formula is supported by some: see, for example Clatworthy *et al.* (2007) para. 4.5.

111 WDAC, Art. 2.1: LC 1888, Res. 11; LC 1920, Res. 9.

112 NDC source, n. 4: cf. Chicago-Lambeth Quadrilateral 1886/1888; Preface, Declaration of Assent, Can. C15, Church of England.

113 WDAC, Art. 1.2. See ARCIC, *Church as Communion*, IV.45: see also LC 1998, Res. II.1(b)(ii). NDC gives no source.

historic formularies, the Thirty-Nine Articles of Religion, the 1662 Book of Common Prayer, and the Ordering of Bishops, Priests, and Deacons (Art. 2.5) – no reference to these was made in the Windsor text.[114] It also affirms its loyalty to this inheritance of faith as our inspiration and guidance under God in bringing the grace and truth of Christ to this generation and making him known to our societies and nations (Art. 2.6).[115] Some suggest that care must be taken in the reference to the historical formularies as not all provinces place great value on them (particularly if in a covenant they are given 'quasi-scriptural status' or are treated as 'definitive').[116] Others feel the article should more clearly reflect the Lambeth Quadrilateral.[117]

Like the Windsor text, Nassau Article 3, on the commitment of churches to confession of the faith,[118] requires the churches (in seeking to be faithful to God in their various contexts) to uphold and act in continuity and consistency with the catholic and apostolic faith, order and tradition,[119] biblically derived moral values and the vision of humanity received by and developed in the communion of member churches (Art. 3.1).[120] As in the Windsor text, there is a responsibility

---

114 The provision did not appear in WDAC (but see WDAC, Art. 2.2, and LC 1998, Res. III.8(f)). NDC, Art. 2.5, n. 5: 'This is not meant to exclude other Books of Common Prayer and Ordinals duly administered for use throughout the Anglican Communion, but acknowledges the foundational nature of the Book of Common Prayer 1662 in the life of the Communion'. The Nassau provision is welcomed by Noll (2006).

115 NDC, Art. 2.6, n. 6: Cf., Preface, Declaration of Assent, Can. C15, Church of England.

116 Joint Standing Committee of the Primates' Meeting and ACC, Points Raised (2007), sect. 2; Primates Meeting 2007, Points Raised, sect. 2(5); see also Sharp (2007), Noll (2007), and Wales, RNDC (2007) and TEC, RNDC (2007). Australia, RNDC (2007) suggests describing the historic formularies under the title 'inheritance of faith' (see S. Sykes, 'The Anglican character', in I. Bunting (ed.), *Celebrating the Anglican Way* (London, Hodder & Stoughton, 1996) 21–32 at 23.

117 See the RNDC of: Australia (2007): this also suggests the text of the Quadrilateral should be included in the covenant; and TEC and Wales which suggest moving the material on the historic episcopate from Art. 5 to Art. 2.

118 The scriptural texts cited are: Deut. 30.11–14; Ps. 126; Mark 10.26–27; Luke 1.37,36–55; John 8.32, 14.15–17; 1 Cor. 11.23–26; 2 Tim. 3.10—4.5. TEC, RNDC (2007) suggests that Art. 3 is extra-credal and confessional and is out of place in the draft covenant.

119 WDAC, Art. 10.1 (though the NDC expression 'biblically derived' does not appear here). See LC 1930, Res. 49 (faith and order); WAEEC, para. 35 (tradition). England, RNDC (2007) proposes inserting another commitment: 'Uphold and proclaim a pattern of Christian moral reasoning and discipline that is rooted in, and answerable to, the teaching of Holy Scripture and the Catholic tradition, and that reflects the renewal of humanity and the whole created order through the death and resurrection of Christ and the holiness that in consequence God gives to, and requires of, His people.'

120 WDAC, Art. 10.1. See ARCIC, *Church as Communion*, IV.45. For the need for greater clarity of 'biblically derived moral values' see, for example Sharp (2007); Noll (2007) proposes that a provision should be included to the effect that biblical texts are to

on each church to seek in all things to uphold the solemn obligation to sustain eucharistic communion,[121] welcoming members of all other member churches to join in its own celebration, and encouraging its members to participate in the Eucharist in a member church in accordance with the canonical discipline of that host church (Art. 3.2).[122] Some suggest greater clarification of this provision.[123] In addition, the Article provides that churches must ensure that biblical texts are handled faithfully, respectfully, comprehensively and coherently; this is achieved primarily through the teaching and initiative of bishops and synods,[124] and building on the best scholarship, believing that scriptural revelation must continue to illuminate, challenge and transform cultures, structures and ways of thinking (Art. 3.3).[125] Unlike the Windsor document, there is a commitment to nurture and respond to prophetic and faithful leadership and ministry, and to assist fellow churches as courageous witnesses to the transformative power of the gospel in the world (Art. 3.4).[126] Moreover, the churches must pursue a common pilgrimage towards truth,[127] so that all peoples from all nations may be free and receive the new and abundant life in the Lord Jesus Christ (Art. 3.5).[128]

Under Article 4, on the Anglican vocation and life shared with others,[129] each church affirms that communion is a gift of God:[130] that his people from east and west, north and south, may together declare his glory and be a sign of the kingdom of God.[131] The churches

---

be interpreted in their plain and canonical sense. See also Ch. 5 above for other criticisms of this expression.

121 WDAC, Art. 11.1. This surfaces in the laws of churches. See also LC 1888, Res. 11; LC 1998, Res. III.8(d).

122 WDAC, Art. 11.2, 3. See *Growth in Communion*, para. 45.

123 Joint Standing Committee of the Primates' Meeting and ACC, Points Raised (2007), sect. 3.2: it needs clarification.

124 Australia, RNDC (2007): this suggests that 'primarily through the teaching and initiative of bishops and synods' should be replaced with 'acknowledging the teaching responsibility of bishops and the deliberations of synods'.

125 WDAC, Art. 10.2. See LC 1998, Res. III.1(b).

126 The rough equivalent in WDAC is its Art. 7.4.

127 WDAC, Art. 8.1. WAEEC, para. 61.

128 Australia, RNDC (2007): this suggests that Art. 3.5 be changed to require that each church is to 'seek to discern truth with other members of the Communion that peoples from all nations may receive the new and abundant life in the Lord Jesus Christ and truly be free'.

129 The scriptural texts cited are: Jer. 31.31–34; Ezek. 36.22–28; Matt. 28.16–20; John 17.20, 24; 2 Cor. 8–9; Eph. 2.11—3.21; Jas 1.22–27.

130 WDAC, Art. 6.1. See above, n. 30. This is welcomed by TEC, RNDC (2007). Southern Africa, RNDC (2007) suggests this be altered: 'communion is a gift of God, and that God's people from all over the world are called to declare God's glory' and be a sign of God's kingdom.

131 Compare WDAC, Art. 7.4(a).

acknowledge gratefully the gracious providence of God extended to Anglicans down the ages, their origins in the undivided Church, the rich history of the church in Britain and Ireland shaped particularly by the Reformation, and their growth into a global communion through the various mission initiatives (Art. 4.1).[132] The churches affirm that, as the Communion continues to develop into a worldwide family of interdependent churches,[133] they face challenges and opportunities for mission at local, regional, and international levels. Unlike Windsor, the Nassau draft has an affirmation that the churches cherish their faith and mission heritage as offering unique opportunities for mission collaboration, for discovery of the life of the whole gospel and for reconciliation and shared mission with the church throughout the world (Art. 4.2).[134] Consequently, the member churches acknowledge that their common mission[135] is one shared with other churches and traditions not party to this covenant;[136] it is with all the saints that Anglicans will comprehend the fuller dimensions of Christ's redemptive and immeasurable love (Art. 4.3).[137] Article 4 also has a commitment to answer the call of God to share in his healing and reconciling mission for the blessed but broken and hurting world, and with mutual accountability, to share God-given resources and material resources for this task (Art. 4.4).[138] In this mission, which is the mission of Christ,[139] the churches commit themselves to proclaim the good news of the kingdom of God; to teach, baptize and nurture new believers; to respond to human need by loving service; to seek to transform unjust

---

132 TWR, para. 47; see also LC 1930, Encyclical Letter: the Communion is a 'commonwealth of Churches without a central constitution'. England, RNDC (2007) suggests that 'undivided church' should be replaced with 'the church of the apostles and the ancient common tradition'.

133 WDAC, Art. 7.1: this spoke of a 'community' of interdependent churches consisting of relations between each church, the See of Canterbury and the fellowship of member churches worldwide. See above, n. 34.

134 WDAC, Art. 15.1 and (for co-operation) 15.2.

135 WDAC, Art. 3.2. See also, for example LC 1878, Res. 15.

136 ACADC, Part 4, 9. This does not go as far as WDAC, Art. 17: see above n. 58. JSC of the Primates and ACC, Points Raised (2007), sect. 4: Art. 4 should explain how this vocation differs from that of other churches. England, RNDC (2007) criticizes 'not party to this covenant' as too negative.

137 WDAC, Art. 8.1: communion is 'never perfected until God's Kingdom is all in all'.

138 WDAC, Art. 15.4 (as to spiritual and material resources). See above n. 53.

139 NDC, Art. 4.5, n. 7: Cf. the five marks of Mission as set out in the MISSIO Report 1999, building on work at ACC-6 and ACC-8. There is no equivalent in WDAC. Australia, RNDC (2007) suggests inclusion of: 'The member churches affirm that they enter into this covenant in order that their common mission might thereby be enriched and magnified to the glory of God. The mission of the church, which is the Mission of Christ, is to proclaim the good news of the Kingdom of God . . .'

structures of society; and to strive to safeguard the integrity of creation and to sustain and renew the life of the earth (Art. 4.5).[140] The provisions on mission, and their improvement on the Windsor text, have been welcomed by many.[141]

Under Article 5, on Anglican unity and common life,[142] the churches affirm the historic episcopate, locally adapted in the methods of its administration to the varying needs of the nations and peoples called by God into the unity of his church,[143] and the central role of bishops as custodians of faith (a formula which has been criticized),[144] leaders in mission, and as a visible sign of unity (Art. 5.1).[145] Under Article 5.2 (as in the Windsor draft), the churches also affirm the place of the four Instruments of Communion which serve to discern a common mind in communion issues, and to foster interdependence and mutual accountability in Christ.[146] In a manner similar to but less fully than the Windsor draft, each church orders and regulates its own affairs through its own system of government and law and is therefore described as autonomous.[147] The churches of the Communion are bound together, not juridically by a central legislative or executive

---

140 ACADC, Part. 4, 8. See also Anglican Church in Aotearoa, New Zealand, and Polynesia, Const., Preamble. This is a much fuller treatment of mission than in WDAC, Art. 3.2 (serving in the world Christ's purposes of mission, justice and peace).

141 Noll (2006), who also suggests the article be renamed 'Our Call to Mission', and the addition of the words: each church commits itself 'to present Jesus Christ in the power of the Holy Spirit so that men and women come to put their faith in God through him, to accept him as their Saviour and to serve him as their King in the fellowship of his Church'. Compare Sharp (2007): 'If this Covenant is to serve as a juridical tool to enforce orthodoxy, then these kinds of rhetorical gestures do not belong here and serve only to confuse the genre of the document'.

142 The scriptural texts cited are: Num. 11.16–20; Luke 22.14–27; Acts 2.43–47; 4.32–35; 1 Cor. 11.23–26; 1 Pet. 4.7–11; 5.1–11.

143 NDC, Art. 5.1, n. 8: cf. the Chicago-Lambeth Quadrilateral 1886/1888. WDAC, Art. 12.1 commits churches to uphold the historic threefold ministry of bishops, priests and deacons.

144 This commonly surfaces in the laws of churches. Australia, RNDC (2007) suggests that the formula should be 'guardians and teachers of the faith' and 'signs of unity'; England, RNDC (2007) suggests that this should include a reference to 'the personal, collegial and communal' manner in which episcopacy is exercised'; Wales, RNDC (2007) comments that the formula should be 'bishops in synods' are guardians, etc; TEC, RNDC (2007) argues that the formula diminishes the role of the laity in discerning God's word.

145 WDAC, Art. 13.1; TWR, paras 63–6.

146 WDAC, Art. 24.1 (verbatim). See also TWR, Appendix 1. England, RNDC (2007) suggests: 'We affirm the place of the four Instruments of Communion as instruments of unity and means of communion which serve to discern our common mind in Communion issues, and to foster our interdependence and mutual accountability in Christ.'

147 WDAC, Art. 19.1 (first part); LC 1978, Res. 21.3; Virginia Report, 44.

body, but by the Holy Spirit who calls and enables them to live in mutual loyalty and service.[148]

Moreover, under Article 5 (as in the Windsor text), on the four Instruments of Communion, the Archbishop of Canterbury, with whose See Anglicans have historically been in communion, is accorded a primacy of honour and respect as first among equals (*primus inter pares*); the Archbishop calls the Lambeth Conference and Primates' Meeting, and presides at the Anglican Consultative Council (Art. 5.2.I).[149] (Some suggest an enhancement of the primacy of Canterbury.[150]) The Lambeth Conference (at which the Archbishop of Canterbury presides), expressing episcopal collegiality worldwide, gathers the bishops for common counsel, consultation and encouragement,[151] and serves as an instrument in guarding the faith and unity of the Communion (Art. 5.2.II).[152] The Primates' Meeting, presided over by the Archbishop of Canterbury, assembles for mutual support and counsel, monitors global developments and works in full collaboration in doctrinal, moral and pastoral matters that have Communion-wide implications (Art. 5.2.III).[153] The Anglican Consultative Council, a body representative of bishops, clergy and laity of the churches, co-ordinates aspects of international Anglican ecumenical and mission

---

148 LC 1930, Res. 49(c). England, RNDC (2007): this suggests an alteration following the affirmation of autonomy: 'However, we recognize that we are bound together, not juridically by a central legislative or executive authority, but by the Holy Spirit who calls and enables us to preach and live out the gospel in mutual loyalty and service.'

149 TWR, para. 99. NDC, Art. 5.2.I. This is a lot fuller than WDAC, Art. 24.2.

150 McPartlan (2006): the first among the bishops only takes a decision in agreement with the other bishops who take no important decisions without the agreement of the first among them; J. Borelli and J. H. Erickson (eds), *The Quest for Unity: Orthodox and Catholics in Dialogue* (Crestwood/Washington DC, St Vladimir's Seminary Press/US Catholic Conference, 1996) 142, n. 53. Apostolic Canon 34 provides: 'The bishops of every nation/region ought to know who is the first one among them, and to esteem him as their head, and not to do any great thing without his consent; but every one to manage the affairs that belong to his own diocese and the territory subject to it. But let him [that is, he who is first] not do anything without the consent of all the other [bishops]; for it is by this means that there will be unanimity, and God will be glorified through Christ in the Holy Spirit.'

151 WDAC, Art. 24.3 (verbatim).

152 TWR, paras 100–102; see also TWR, Appendix 1(3): the Conference as 'guardian' of unity and teaching; and 1(4): the proposal for LC resolutions to be categorized, for example, on matters which 'touch upon the definition of Anglicanism' or 'the authentic proclamation of the Gospel' – these should be subject to a distinctive procedure to demonstrate their differentiated status and therefore for the special attention of the Communion. Neither WDAC nor NDC make such distinctions.

153 WDAC, Art. 24.5 (verbatim, except WDAC 'exercises collegial responsibility' is replaced with 'works in full collaboration', and NDC adds 'that have Communion-wide implications'). See TWR, Appendix 1(5) and, for example LC 1998, Res. III.6.

work (Art. 5.3.IV).[154] The Article has been criticized as not enabling closer co-operation between the instruments, failing to strengthen the authority of the Anglican Consultative Council, obstructing the creation of additional instruments, and implying that political consensus is the same as spiritual unity.[155] It has also been criticized as giving too magisterial a role to the Primates' Meeting.[156]

Like the Windsor text, under Article 6 of the Nassau draft covenant, on the unity of the Communion,[157] each church commits itself in matters of common concern, to have regard to the common good of the Communion in the exercise of its autonomy,[158] and to support the work of the Instruments of Communion with the spiritual and material resources available to it (Art. 6.1).[159] Each church must spend time with openness, and patience,[160] in matters of theological debate and discernment, to listen and to study with one another in order to comprehend the will of God (Art. 6.1).[161] Such study and debate is an essential feature of the life of the Church as it seeks to be led by the Spirit into all truth and to proclaim the gospel afresh in each generation (Art. 6.2). Unlike the Windsor text, the Nassau draft covenant recognizes that some issues, which are perceived as controversial or new when they arise, may well evoke a deeper understanding of the implications of the revelation of God; others may prove to be distractions or even obstacles to the faith: all therefore need to be tested by shared discernment in the life of the Church (Art. 6.2).[162]

As with Windsor, there is a duty upon each church to seek with other member churches, through the shared councils of the church,[163]

---

154 Compare WDAC, Art. 24.4: the ACC has 'such membership and functions as are prescribed by its constitution'. The ACC constitution is considerably wider in scope than NDC, Art. 5.3.IV. The Primates' Meeting 2007 raised the point that the description of the work of the ACC needs to be expanded.

155 Primates' Meeting, *Communiqué* (2007) para. 18; Joint Standing Committee of the Primates Meeting and ACC, Points Raised (2007) sect. 6.4; Dioc. of Virginia, Standing Committee, Response to NDC: Fulcrum website; Sharp (2007).

156 RNDC of: TEC and Wales: the fallibility of the instruments should be recognized.

157 The scriptural texts cited are: Neh. 2.17,18; Matt. 18.15–18; 1 Cor. 12; 2 Cor. 4.1–18, 13.5–10; Gal. 6.1–10.

158 WDAC, Art. 21.2 (and Arts 5.3, 9.2, 16.1). For sources, see above n. 81.

159 WDAC, Art. 16.3: each church is to 'respect' the counsels of the instruments (and Art. 15.4).

160 WDAC, Art. 4.1 (forbearance); for sources, see above n. 24.

161 WDAC, Art. 21.3; TWR, paras 67–70.

162 This is *broadly* in line with TWR, paras 68–70 (on reception). Australia, RNDC (2007): this suggests that Art. 6.2 should be moved to an explanatory note to the covenant.

163 Australia, RNDC (2007): this should also refer to 'ecumenical consultation'.

a common mind about matters of essential concern,[164] consistent with the scriptures, common standards of faith,[165] and the canon law,[166] of the member churches (Art. 6.3). Each church must heed the counsel of the Instruments of Communion in matters which threaten the unity of the Communion and the effectiveness of its mission (Art. 6.4).[167] While the Instruments of the Communion have no juridical or executive authority in the member churches,[168] the churches recognize them as bodies by which their common life in Christ is articulated and sustained, and which therefore carry a moral authority which commands our respect (Art. 6.4). A member church must seek the guidance of the Instruments of Communion, where there are matters in serious dispute among the churches that cannot be resolved by mutual admonition and counsel (Art. 6.5). In such cases, each church must submit the matter to the Primates' Meeting. If the primates believe that the matter is not one for which a common mind has been articulated, they will seek it with the other instruments and their councils. Finally, on this basis, the primates will offer guidance and direction (Art. 5.5),[169] unlike the Windsor draft covenant, under which in limited cases the Instruments of Unity enjoyed a jurisdiction of conflict resolution.

According to the Nassau text, and unlike the Windsor text (which did not deal with exclusion), the churches acknowledge that in the most extreme circumstances, where a member church chooses not to fulfil the substance of the covenant as understood by the councils of the Instruments of Communion, they will consider that such a church will have relinquished for itself the force and meaning of the purposes of the covenant. Consequently, a process of restoration and renewal will be required to re-establish their covenant relationship with that other member church (Art. 6.6).[170] Some have pointed out that if the covenant ends up giving more power to the Primates' Meeting or to the

---

164 This is similar to WDAC, Art. 23.3.

165 This is similar to WDAC, Art. 9.1.

166 WDAC, Art. 16.4: this requires the churches 'to respect the principles of canon law common to the churches of the Anglican Communion'. See above Ch. 4. Australia, RNDC (2007) suggests deletion of the reference to canon law.

167 For a broad equivalent, see WDAC, Arts 20.2 and 23. Australia, RNDC (2007): 'heed' is ambiguous (and could mean 'abide by') and should be replaced with 'listen to and consider'.

168 ACADC, Part 5. See also WDAC, Art. 19.2: each church shall be free from control by any decision of any ecclesiastical body external to itself in relation to its exclusively internal affairs unless that decision is authorized under or incorporated in its own law. See generally N. Doe, *Canon Law in the Anglican Communion* (Oxford, Clarendon Press, 1998) 343–50 for the status of decisions of the instruments of communion.

169 This does not go as far as WDAC, Art. 6 which gives an authority of guidance to Canterbury and a power of resolution to the appropriate instrument of communion.

170 This goes further than WDAC which did not deal with covenantal breach.

office of the Archbishop of Canterbury than they currently possess this will be because that is what the churches have decided should happen. The covenant will reflect this decision. It will not have created it.[171] Under the declaration,[172] with joy and firm resolve, the signatories declare 'our churches to be partners in this Anglican Covenant, releasing ourselves for fruitful service and binding ourselves more closely in the truth and love of Christ, to whom with the Father and the Holy Spirit be glory for ever. Amen' (Art. 7).[173]

On the one hand, several respondents support the thrust of Article 6. It accords with the Pauline injunction that those in communion through their mutual participation in the life of the Trinity should be of one mind (Phil. 2.2). The primates would simply be exercising a role proper to their senior episcopal office, as they do in their own churches as chief pastors and teachers, consulting with clergy and laity. Moreover, worries about dominance by conservative bishops are unfounded (they all have one vote and must reach a consensus); the churches of the Global South have come of age and the North must get used to this. Indeed, Article 6 does not mean that the primates will have unlimited authority to determine the mind of the Communion; they will be subject to both substantive and procedural limits: their decisions must be consistent with scripture, common standards of faith and the canon laws of the churches (6.3); where a common mind does not exist, they will have to seek it with the other instruments (6.5.2); and they will have no authority to decide unilaterally what the mind of the Communion is on any given topic.[174] Furthermore, the requirements of openness, study and patience in matters of theological debate, and that novel and controversial matters be tested by discernment, are welcomed.[175] Article 6 is not new but merely attempts to lay out how affairs have been developing in fact in the last decade of life in the Communion in counsel.[176]

On the other hand, most respondents have offered a bombardment of criticisms. First, Article 6 is characterized by silences, ambiguities and evasions, begging questions of definition, interpretation, and implementation; and the concept of the Communion having a common mind is delusory. Second, no party should be obliged to do more than to ask a question and to listen to the answer. Moreover, no test has

---

171 Davie (2007).

172 The scriptural texts cited are: Pss 46; 72.18, 19; 150; Acts 10.34–44; 2 Cor. 13.13; Jude 24–25.

173 No such declaration appears in WDAC.

174 Davie (2007) 14–16.

175 Clatworthy *et al.* (2007) para. 4.2.

176 Radner (2007).

been included to determine what is 'essential' – it is therefore presumed that any signatory could instigate a complaint, and the result of this would be for Communion institutions to focus on disputes and not on the building up of the body. Third, to vest jurisdiction in the Primates' Meeting would override autonomy.[177] The meeting is unrepresentative of the wider church and granting it a measure of juridical authority over the Communion should be resisted,[178] as at odds with both the principle of synodical government,[179] and the function of church leaders to convince, not to instruct so as to block initiatives for mission.[180] Fourth, Article 6 demands that a member church violates its own constitution and canons (but how this is so is unclear) as well as the classical Anglican principle of diversity.[181] Lastly, since the Lambeth Conference meets once a decade, seeking a common mind with it would take too long; so, the Primates' Meeting could be a standing committee of the Lambeth Conference.[182] The Article would render the Primates' Meeting superior to the Lambeth Conference and the ACC.[183] Sim-

177 Clatworthy et al. (2007) para. 4: what is held in common is not a matter of discernment; if something is disputed, there is no common mind; it is merely a euphemism for majority opinion of the Primates (6.5); there needs to be greater clarity about what 'common mind' means and transparency as to how a majority is determined; would each primate have one vote, or would votes be weighted according to nominal membership? Would 50%+1 be sufficient majority or would 100% be required? Also, while a voluntary co-ordination of canon laws is acceptable, a central authority empowered to amend the laws of churches is not.

178 Sharp (2007); see also Clatworthy et al. (2007) paras 4.8 and 10: this is inconsistent with the ecclesiology of the Church as 'the blessed company of all the faithful' (BCP 1662), whereas the structures of the Communion are actually shouldered by the laity, particularly financially; international institutions should be made more accountable to the laity; see also Bartel (2007) III.

179 Joint Standing Committee of the Primates' Meeting and ACC 2007, Points Raised, sect. 6.5.

180 S. Hensman, 'Love and witness in a broken world' (2007).

181 Bartel (2007): An international tribunal would not be more reliable in 'tracking the truth' than the traditional polity of the Anglican Communion; such a tribunal would be vulnerable to pressure from hardliners; concentrating power in the instruments of unity is at odds with the commitment of the draft covenant to the open, communal pursuit of truth. The traditional Anglican respect for diversity in doctrines, interpretations and ways of life are not an obstacle to the mission of the Communion, but central to it. The polity the Communion should have is one it has had from the beginning: 'entrusting decisions on reception of innovations in faith and practice to the synodical processes of the individual provinces'.

182 Joint Standing Committee of the Primates' Meeting and ACC 2007, Points Raised, sect. 6.5.2.

183 Clatworthy et al. (2007) para. 4.7; Dioc. of Virginia, Standing Committee Response to NDC: Fulcrum Website. See also Chapman (2008) 29: 'what the drafting group should focus on is creating some form of Anglican Representative Council which would command respect and to which member churches would be content to delegate their sovereignty.'

ilar opposition to an enhanced authority for the Primates' Meeting emerged in the provincial consultation of 2007.[184]

For the critics, therefore, a form of jurisdiction needs to be found and acknowledged which is capable (a) of defining and safeguarding the full range and limit of authentic and faithful human responses to the gospel and (b) of being responsible for the necessary processes of dialogue and open listening between those who differ within those limits.[185] As such, when disputes arise the Instruments of Communion should (where appropriate to the issue) be able to establish clear and careful consultative processes, publicly seeking, receiving and sharing advice. Timetables, once established, should be maintained and the processes should be as transparent as possible. At no time should there be an attempt to use power or the threat of sanctions to pre-empt the course of debate. Rather, there should be a rigorous and lengthy process of testing, discernment and reception of perceived developments in faith and order. Consequently, member churches must be able to test innovations in practice as part of their autonomous loyalty to the inheritance of faith. Past decisions must be liable to be re-opened when information, circumstances and understandings change. Moreover, church leaders have a particular responsibility to enable debate on the basis that no one has absolute certainty, no truth is so well established as to be beyond all question, and that all disputants may learn from those with whom they disagree.[186]

The Anglican Church of Australia has proposed an alternative scheme to Article 6. When a church considers that a voluntary self-limitation of its authority is warranted, it should seek the guidance of the Instruments of Communion by submitting its proposal to the Primates' Meeting. If the primates believe the matter is not one for which a common mind has been articulated, they should refer the proposal to the other instruments for advice and guidance. The Primates' Meeting should then report its own response together with those of the other Instruments of Communion to the church in question. That church should refrain unless the responses of at least two Instruments

---

184 RNDC of, for example Australia: the instruments generally should have only a guiding and moral role rather than a semi-juridical or executive authority; Southern Africa: there was 'universal disquiet' about the Primates' Meeting proposal; TEC: 'Most Episcopalians do not want to see the development of a synodical decision-making body in the Anglican Communion. They would prefer communion based on relationships and shared participation in service to God's mission'; however, others see lack of such a body as contributing to current discord; some would like to see the Joint Standing Committee of the Primates' Meeting and ACC as 'authorized to oversee the decision-making process'.

185 Faith and Order Advisory Group: CCU/FO/06/33, para. 22.

186 Clatworthy et al. (2007) para. 10.

of Communion indicate that there is no bar.[187] In a similar vein, the Church of England suggests that a covenant should commit each church to heed the counsel of the Instruments of Communion which therefore should carry a spiritual, pastoral and doctrinal authority which commands respect. Each church should also submit matters in serious dispute that cannot be resolved by mutual admonition and counsel to the primates so that they can offer guidance on how they may be resolved. Such guidance should be based either on the existing position of the Communion or after the development of a common mind through consultation with the local churches of the Communion, their bishops and the other Instruments of Communion.[188]

The St Andrews Draft Covenant

Modelled on Nassau, the preamble to the St Andrews draft covenant provides that the churches of the Anglican Communion,[189] under the Lordship of Jesus Christ, solemnly covenant together in affirmations and commitments. As the people of God drawn from 'every nation, tribe, people and language',[190] the churches covenant in order (1) to proclaim more effectively in their different contexts the grace of God revealed in the gospel; (2) to offer the love of God in responding to the needs of the world; (3) to maintain the unity of the Spirit in the bond of peace; and (4) to grow up together with all God's people to the full stature of Christ.[191]

The Anglican inheritance of faith[192]

Clause 1.1 presents (like Nassau but less fully than Windsor) those characteristics which each church of the Communion affirms about

187 Australia, RNDC (2007).

188 England, RNDC (2007): this also suggests that the churches commit themselves 'to refrain from intervening in the life of other Anglican churches except in extraordinary circumstances where such intervention has been specifically authorized by the relevant Instrument of Communion'; Ireland, RNDC, Proposed Redraft (2007), Art. 3: each church is 'to heed the Instruments of Communion where there are matters in serious dispute . . . that cannot be resolved by mutual admonition and counsel'.

189 The formula 'the churches of the Anglican Communion' signifies the churches recognized in the Schedule of Membership of the ACC: Commentary to SADC.

190 SADC, source, n. 1; Rev. 7.9.

191 Unlike NDC, no scriptural verses are cited before the preamble. These had been criticized in the provincial consultation 2007 and dropped by the Covenant Design Group: see Commentary to SADC.

192 SADC, Section One. This replaced the NDC title. Unlike NDC, no scripture verses are cited.

itself.[193] Each church affirms its communion in the One, Holy, Catholic and Apostolic Church,[194] worshipping the one God, Father, Son and Holy Spirit.[195] Each church affirms that, reliant on the Holy Spirit, it professes the *faith* which is (1) uniquely revealed in the holy scriptures of the Old and New Testaments (a) as containing all things necessary for salvation, and (b) as being the rule and ultimate standard of faith,[196] and (2) set forth in the catholic creeds, to which the historic formularies of the Church of England bear significant witness,[197] which faith the Church is called upon to proclaim afresh in each generation.[198] Each church affirms that it holds and duly administers the two sacraments ordained by Christ himself, baptism and the Supper of the Lord,[199] ministered with the unfailing use of Christ's words of institution, and of the elements ordered by him.[200] Next, each church affirms that it upholds the historic episcopate, locally adapted in the methods of its administration to the varying needs of the nations and peoples called of God into the unity of his Church.[201] It affirms that shared patterns of common prayer and liturgy form, sustain and nourish the worship of God, faith and life together,[202] that it participates in the apostolic

---

193 The idea is that signatories need to affirm (a) their own self-understanding and not (b) their view of other churches: Commentary to SADC. England, RNDC (2007) had proposed (b), which is an approach used in ecumenical agreements: see above n. 10. The NDC idea of recognizing these marks in the Communion also has been dropped on the basis of Australia, RNDC (2007).

194 See WDAC, Art. 1.1; LC 1930, Res. 49. The laws of most churches make this claim for themselves: for example, Scottish Episcopal Church, Can. 1.1.

195 SADC, Cl. 1.1.1; source, n. 2: the Preface, Declaration of Assent, Canon C15, Church of England. The NDC affirmation that it 'is part' of the Church universal is dropped.

196 SADC, Cl. 1.1.2; source, n. 3: Lambeth Quadrilateral; see also NDC, Art. 2.2; see WDAC, Art. 1.3; LC 1888, Res. 11; LC 1920, Res. 9; LC 1998, Res. III.5.

197 SADC, n. 4: the Thirty-Nine Articles of Religion, 1662 Book of Common Prayer, and Ordering of Bishops, Priests, and Deacons. These were mentioned in NDC, Art. 2.5, but not in WDAC. The reason for the change is that some churches do not formally recognize the Thirty-Nine Articles.

198 SADC, Cl. 1.1.2; source, n. 5: Preface, Declaration of Assent, Can. C15, Church of England.

199 WDAC, Art. 2.1: LC 1888, Res. 11; LC 1920, Res. 9. The clause is not 'an exhaustive treatment of sacramental theology or to resolve questions about the nature or number of the sacraments'; for this reason the express wording of the Lambeth Quadrilateral is used: Commentary to SADC.

200 SADC, Cl. 1.1.3; source, n. 6: Chicago-Lambeth Quadrilateral 1886/1888; Preface, Declaration of Assent, Can. C15, Church of England; this is modelled on NDC, Art. 2.3.

201 SADC, Cl. 1.1.4, source: Chicago-Lambeth Quadrilateral 1886/1888; NDC, Art. 5.1.

202 SADC, Cl. 1.1.5. This was not in NDC. The clause is designed to underline 'the importance of common prayer as one of the defining characteristics of Anglicanism': Commentary to SADC.

mission of the whole people of God, and that this mission is shared with other churches and traditions beyond the Anglican covenant.[203]

Second, like the Windsor text and modelled on Nassau, in living out the inheritance of faith together in varying contexts,[204] each church of the Communion commits itself to uphold and act in continuity and consonance with Scripture and the catholic and apostolic faith, order and tradition.[205] It also commits itself to uphold and proclaim a pattern of Christian theological and moral reasoning and discipline; this pattern must satisfy two tests: (a) it must be rooted in and answerable to the teaching of Holy Scripture and the catholic tradition; and (b) it must reflect the renewal of humanity and the whole created order through the death and resurrection of Christ and the holiness that in consequence God gives to and requires of his people.[206] Each church must seek in all things to uphold the solemn obligation to sustain eucharistic communion,[207] in accordance with existing canonical disciplines as Anglicans strive under God for the fuller realization of the communion of all churches.[208] Each church must ensure that biblical texts are handled faithfully, respectfully, comprehensively and coherently; this is achieved primarily through the teaching and initiative of bishops and synods, and building on habits and disciplines of Bible study across the Church and on rigorous scholarship, believing that scriptural revelation must continue to illuminate, challenge and transform cultures, structures and ways of thinking.[209] There is a commitment to nurture and respond to prophetic and faithful leadership and ministry and mission to equip God's people to be courageous witnesses to the power of the gospel in the world.[210] Moreover, the churches must pursue a common pilgrimage with other churches of the Communion to discern truth, so that peoples from all nations may truly be set free to receive the new and abundant life in Christ.[211]

---

203 SADC, Cl. 1.1.6, modelled on NDC, Art. 4.3, ACADC, Part. 4, 9 and points raised in England, RNDC (2007). NDC, Art. 2.6 has been dropped.

204 SADC, 1.2; the NDC scriptural references have been dropped.

205 SADC, Cl. 1.2.1; modelled on the first part of NDC, Art. 3.1.

206 SADC, Cl. 1.2.2; this is largely based on England, RNDC (2007) and a substantial revision of NDC, Art. 3.1; see also WADC, Art. 10.1.

207 WDAC, Art. 11.1. See also LC 1888, Res. 11; LC 1998, Res. III.8(d).

208 SADC, Cl. 1.2.3. The idea is that there is an obligation to sustain eucharistic communion 'even where there is conscientious objection': Commentary to SADC. The clause replaces NDC, Art. 3.2: members of fellow churches were entitled to join in celebrations in the host church. For ecumenical models, see *Growth in Communion*, para. 45.

209 SADC, Cl. 1.2.4; NDC, Art. 3.3; WDAC, Art. 10.2. See LC 1998, Res. III.1(b).

210 SADC, Cl. 1.2.5; NDC, Art. 3.4. The rough equivalent in WDAC is its Art. 7.4.

211 SADC, Cl. 1.2.6. This revises NDC, Art. 3.5, and is based on Australia, RNDC (2007).

Life Anglicans share with others: the Anglican vocation[212]

This section has no exact parallel in Windsor, but is modelled on Nassau. First, each church affirms that communion is a gift of God:[213] that his people from east and west, north and south, may together declare his glory and be a sign of God's reign.[214] The churches acknowledge gratefully the gracious providence of God extended to Anglicans down the ages, their origins in the Church of the Apostles, the ancient common traditions, the rich history of the Church in Britain and Ireland shaped by the Reformation, and their growth into a global communion through the expanding missionary work of the Church.[215] Each church affirms the ongoing mission work of the Communion, and that, as the Communion continues to develop into a worldwide family of interdependent churches, it embraces challenges and opportunities for mission at local, regional, and international levels; moreover, it cherishes the faith and mission heritage as offering Anglicans distinctive opportunities for mission collaboration.[216] In turn, it affirms that a common mission is shared with other churches and traditions beyond this covenant; it is with all the saints that we will comprehend the fuller dimensions of Christ's redemptive and immeasurable love.[217]

Second, each church commits itself to answer the call of God to evangelization and to share in his healing and reconciling mission for the blessed but broken, hurting and fallen world, and, with mutual accountability, to share God-given resources and material resources for this task.[218] In this mission, which is the mission of Christ,[219] each church undertakes to proclaim the good news of the kingdom of God; to teach, baptize and nurture new believers; to respond to human need by loving service; to seek to transform unjust structures of society; and to strive to safeguard the integrity of creation and to sustain and renew the life of the earth.[220]

---

212 SADC, Section Two. The NDC scriptural references have been removed.

213 SADC, Cl. 2.1.1; NDC, Art. 4.1; WDAC, Art. 6.1.

214 Compare WDAC, Art. 7.4(a).

215 SADC, Cl. 2.1.1. Compare NDC, Art. 4.1: the 'undivided church'; the article was modified on the suggestion of England, RNDC (2007); TWR, para. 47.

216 SADC, Cl. 2.1.2; a revised version of NDC, Art. 4.2; see also WDAC, Art. 15.1 and for co-operation 15.2, but compare WDAC, Art. 7.1: 'community'.

217 SADC, Cl. 2.1.3; NDC, Art. 4.3; ACADC, Part 4, 9. WDAC, Art. 3.2 (and LC 1878, Res. 15).

218 SADC, Cl. 2.2.1; NDC, Art. 4.1; WDAC, Art. 15.4 (as to spiritual and material resources).

219 SADC, Cl. 2.2.2 (NDC, Art. 4.2), n. 8: Cf. the five marks of Mission as set out in the MISSIO Report 1999, building on work at ACC-6 and ACC-8. There is no equivalent in WDAC.

220 ACADC, Part. 4, 8. See also Anglican Church in Aotearoa, New Zealand, and

Anglican unity and common life[221]

First, each church affirms that by its participation in baptism and Eucharist we are incorporated into the one body of the Church of Jesus Christ to pursue all things that make for peace and build up a common life.[222] Second, each church affirms its resolve to live in a communion of churches. Each church is episcopally led and synodically governed, orders and regulates its own affairs and its local responsibility for mission through its own system of government and law and is therefore described as autonomous-in-communion.[223] The churches of the Communion are not bound together by a central legislative, executive or judicial authority.[224] Trusting in the Holy Spirit, who calls and enables us to live in mutual affection, commitment and service, the churches seek to affirm their common life through those Instruments of Communion by which the churches are enabled to develop a common mind.[225] Third, each church affirms the central role of bishops as custodians of faith and teachers of faith,[226] leaders in mission, and as a visible sign of unity, representing the universal Church to the local, and the local to the universal. Episcopal ministry is exercised personally, collegially and within and for the eucharistic community.[227] The churches receive and maintain the historic threefold ministry of bishops, priests and deacons, ordained for service in the Church of God, as they call all the baptized into the mission of Christ.[228]

Fourth, the churches affirm the importance of Instruments in the Anglican Communion to assist in the discernment, articulation and exercise of their shared faith and common life and mission. In addition to the many and varied links which sustain their life together, the

---

Polynesia, Constitution, Preamble. This is a much fuller treatment of mission than in WDAC, Art. 3.2 (serving in the world Christ's purposes of mission, justice and peace).

221 The NDC scriptural texts have been removed.

222 SADC, Cl. 3.1.1. This is new and did not appear in NDC.

223 SADC, Cl. 3.1.2; NDC, Art. 5.2 simply spoke of churches as autonomous; for the autonomy-in-communion principle, see TWR, para. 76 and WDAC, Arts 18–22.

224 SADC, Cl. 3.1.2; based on NDC, Art. 5.2 and LC 1930, Res. 49(c); and England, RNDC (2007).

225 SADC, Cl. 3.1.2; this modifies NDC, Art. 5.1 which repeated WDAC, Art. 24.1 (verbatim). See also TWR, Appendix 1 and England, RNDC (2007).

226 This is commonly found in the laws of churches.

227 SADC, Cl. 3.1.3; this elaborates on NDC, Art. 5.1. The Commentary to SADC makes specific reference here to TWR, paras 64 and the IATDC Report, *Communion, Conflict and Hope* (forthcoming 2008), Appendix 2, 'The Anglican Way: The Significance of the Episcopal Office for the Communion of the Church'.

228 SADC, Cl. 3.1.3; this was not in NDC. For the threefold ministry, see WDAC, Arts 3.1 and 12.1.

churches acknowledge four particular Instruments which co-operate in the service of communion.[229] The Archbishop of Canterbury, with whose See Anglicans have historically been in communion, is accorded a primacy of honour and respect as first amongst equals (*primus inter pares*); as a focus of unity, the Archbishop gathers the Lambeth Conference and Primates' Meeting, and presides in the Anglican Consultative Council.[230] The Lambeth Conference, expressing episcopal collegiality worldwide, gathers the bishops for common counsel, consultation and encouragement,[231] and serves as an instrument in guarding the faith and unity of the Communion,[232] and equipping the saints for the work of ministry and mission.[233] The Anglican Consultative Council is comprised of laity, clergy and bishops representative of provincial synods. It facilitates the co-operative work of the church of the Communion, co-ordinates aspects of international Anglican ecumenical and mission work, calls the churches into mutual responsibility and interdependence, and advises on developing provincial structures.[234] The Primates' Meeting is called by the Archbishop of Canterbury for mutual support, prayer and counsel. The primates and moderators are called to work as representatives of their provinces in collaboration with one another in mission and in doctrinal, moral and pastoral matters that have Communion-wide implications.[235]

In turn, acknowledging their interdependent life, each church of the Communion commits itself to six basic obligations.[236] First, it must have regard to the common good of the Communion in the exercise of

---

229 ADC, Cl. 3.1.4; it develops the first sentence of NDC, Art. 5.2. The clause seeks to meet fears about the 'canonisation' of the Instruments, to allow for their evolution, and to recognize more informal links (such as diocesan and parochial partnerships): Commentary to SADC.

230 SADC, Cl. 3.1.4.I; NDC, Art. 5.2.I; TWR, para. 99. The Instruments are listed in this way to reflect their historical and chronological development: Commentary to SADC.

231 WDAC, Art. 24.3 (verbatim).

232 SADC, Cl. 3.1.4.II; NDC, Art. 5.2.II; TWR, paras 100–102; see also TWR, Appendix 1(3): the Conference as 'guardian' of unity and teaching; and 1(4): the proposal for LC resolutions to be categorized, for example on matters which 'touch upon the definition of Anglicanism' or 'the authentic proclamation of the Gospel' – these should be subject to a distinctive procedure to demonstrate their differentiated status. Neither SADC, NDC nor WDAC make such distinctions.

233 SADC, Cl. 3.1.4.II, n. 10: Eph. 4.12.

234 SADC, 3.1.4.III; n. 11: the objects of the ACC as set out in Art. 2 of its Constitution.

235 SADC, 3.1.4.IV; NDC, Art. 5.2.III; this elaborates on WDAC, Art. 24.5. It is also designed to reflect TWR, para. 104 and Appendix 1(5). See also, for example LC 1998, Res. III.6.

236 The NDC scriptural texts are dropped.

its autonomy,[237] and to support the work of the Instruments of Communion with the spiritual and material resources available to it.[238] Second, each church is to respect the constitutional autonomy of all of the churches of the Communion, while upholding the interdependent life and mutual responsibility of the churches, and the responsibility of each church to the Communion as a whole.[239] Third, each church must spend time with openness, and patience,[240] in matters of theological debate and reflection, and listen, pray and study with one another in order to comprehend the will of God.[241] Such prayer, study and debate is an essential feature of the life of the Church as it seeks to be led by the Spirit into all truth and to proclaim the gospel afresh in each generation. Some issues, which are perceived as controversial or new when they arise, may well evoke a deeper understanding of the implications of the revelation of God; others may prove to be distractions or even obstacles to the faith: all therefore need to be tested by shared discernment in the life of the Church.[242] Fourth, there is a duty upon each church to seek with other churches, through the shared councils of the Communion,[243] a common mind about matters understood to be of essential concern,[244] consistent with the scriptures, common standards of faith,[245] and the canon law,[246] of the churches.

Fifth, each church is to act with diligence, care and caution in respect to actions, either proposed or enacted, at a provincial or local level, which, in its own view or the expressed view of any province or in the view of any one of the Instruments of Communion, are deemed to threaten the unity of the Communion and the effectiveness or cred-

---

237 NDC, Art. 6.1, but the reference to 'essential matters of common concern' is removed; WDAC, Art. 21.2 (and Arts 5.3, 9.2, 16.1).

238 SADC, Cl. 3.2.1; NDC, Art. 6.1; WDAC, Art. 16.3 each church is to 'respect' the counsels of the instruments (and Art. 15.4).

239 SADC, Cl. 3.2.2 and n. 12: Schedule, *Communiqué*, Primates' Meeting 2007 (Dar es Salaam). This is also reminiscent of WDAC, Art. 22.3, but it does not appear in NDC.

240 SADC, Cl. 3.2.3; NDC, Art. 6.2; WDAC, Art. 4.1 (forbearance); for sources, see above n. 160.

241 SADC, Cl. 3.2.3. The reference to prayer was not in NDC, Art. 6.2; see also WDAC, Art. 21.3; TWR, paras 67–70.

242 SADC, Cl. 3.2.3, modelled on NDC, Art. 6.2. This is *broadly* in line with TWR, paras 68–70.

243 SADC, Cl. 3.2.4; NDC, Art. 6.2 was wider: through 'the Church's shared councils'.

244 SADC, Cl. 3.2.4; modelled on NDC, Art. 6.3. This is similar to WDAC, Art. 23.3.

245 SADC, Cl. 3.2.4; modelled on NDC, Art. 6.3. This is similar to WDAC, Art. 9.1.

246 Compare WDAC, Art. 16.4: this required the churches 'to respect the principles of canon law common to the churches of the Anglican Communion'. See above Ch. 4.

ibility of its mission.[247] Unlike the process in the Nassau text,[248] each church must consent to five principles and procedural elements,[249] namely: (a) *consultation*: to undertake wide consultation with the other churches of the Communion and with the Instruments and Commissions of the Communion;[250] (b) *evaluation*: to accept the legitimacy of processes for communion-wide evaluation which any of the Instruments may commission;[251] (c) *mediation*: to be ready to participate in mediated conversation between parties, which may be in conflict;[252] (d) *respect for requests*: to be willing to receive from the Instruments a request to adopt a particular course of action in respect of the matter under dispute (on the basis of their moral authority which commands respect);[253] and (e) *autonomy*: any request would not be binding on a church unless recognized as such by that church.[254]

However, commitment to the covenant entails an acknowledgement that in the most extreme circumstances, where a church chooses not to adopt the request of the Instruments of Communion, that decision may be understood by that church itself, or by resolution of the Instruments of Communion, as a relinquishment by that church of the force and meaning of the purposes of the covenant, until they re-establish their covenant relationship with other churches of the Communion.[255]

---

247 SADC, Cl. 3.2.5. NDC, Art. 6 proved the most contentious section of the Nassau draft, requiring the greatest attention of CDG and it has been 'considerably rewritten' in order to achieve commitment to a common life which also respects the principle of provincial autonomy; there is 'no intention to erect a centralised jurisdiction' and the Instruments of Communion 'cannot dictate with juridical force on the internal affairs of any Province': Commentary to SADC. Compare NDC, Art. 6.4: each church must heed the counsel of the Instruments of Communion in matters which threaten the unity of the Communion and the effectiveness of its mission. For a broad equivalent, WDAC, Arts 20.2, 23.

248 And its provisions in Art. 6.5.

249 The elements set out in Cl. 3.2.5 'are not intended to form a sequential process, but to be elements which can all be active and present at any stage in the process of common discernment and reconciliation': Commentary to SADC.

250 SADC, Cl. 3.2.5.a. This was not in NDC.

251 SADC, Cl. 3.2.5.b: in accordance with procedures appended to the covenant.

252 SADC, Cl. 3.2.5.c: in accordance with procedures appended to the covenant.

253 SADC, Cl. 3.2.5.d: moreover: 'While the Instruments of Communion have no legislative, executive or judicial authority in our Provinces, except where provided in their own laws, we recognize them as those bodies by which our common life in Christ is articulated and sustained, and which therefore carry a moral authority which commands our respect.' This is modelled on the second sentence of NDC, Art. 6.4. See also WDAC, Art. 19.2: each church shall be free from control by any decision of any ecclesiastical body external to itself in relation to its exclusively internal affairs unless that decision is authorized under or incorporated in its own law.

254 SADC, Cl. 3.2.5.e. This accords with the principle of autonomy.

255 SADC, Cl. 3.2.5.e; modelled on NDC, Art. 6.6. The clause is a recognition that communion 'cannot be sustained in extreme circumstances where a Church or Province

Framework procedures for the resolution of covenant disagreements, which implement these principles and procedural elements, are contained in an Appendix to the draft covenant, and these are discussed in Chapter 9.[256] Sixth, each church commits itself to have in mind that the Anglican bonds of affection and the love of Christ compel Anglicans always to seek the highest possible degree of communion.[257]

Finally, under the declaration, with joy and firm resolve, the signatories declare 'our churches to be partakers in this Anglican Covenant, releasing ourselves for fruitful service and binding ourselves more closely in the truth and love of Christ, to whom with the Father and the Holy Spirit be glory for ever. Amen'.[258] The declaration ends with a quotation from scripture: 'Now may the God of Peace, who brought again from the dead our Lord Jesus, the great shepherd of the sheep, by the blood of the eternal covenant, make you complete in everything good so that you may do his will, working among us that which is pleasing in his sight, through Jesus Christ, to whom be the glory forever and ever. Amen' (Hebrews, 13.20, 21).[259]

Conclusion

Generally, of the eighty-five separate provisions of the Windsor draft covenant, contained in its twenty-seven articles, fifty-nine are derived from existing Anglican texts, and twenty-six are 'new' formulations, but themselves either adapted from existing ecumenical models (and applied to the Anglican context) or based (explicitly or implicitly) on the recommendations of the Lambeth Commission. As with the Nassau text, of the thirty-eight separate provisions of the St Andrews draft covenant, approximately twenty-five are sourced similarly. On the one hand, all three drafts are understood by many respondents to restate classical Anglicanism and to represent a basic framework, to enable life in communion, by spelling out the expectations (for the first time in a single document) as to what communion means for the member churches. On the other hand, many respondents contest whether the Windsor and Nassau draft covenants protect the free exercise of autonomy (and thereby enable diversity). Similarly, the Windsor principle of

---

were to act in a way which rejects the interdependence of the Communion's life': Commentary on SADC.

256 This is a 'tentative draft' which will need 'careful analysis': Commentary to SADC.

257 SADC, Cl. 3.2.6. This does not appear in NDC.

258 SADC, Our Declaration. NDC, Art. 7. No such declaration appears in WDAC.

259 This passage did not appear in the NDC declaration.

'autonomy-in-communion', implicit in the Nassau text, but explicit in the St Andrews draft, is welcomed by many, in striking a balance and protecting the Communion as a family, in relation to matters of fundamental concern to the whole community of churches, especially those with a potential for division. However, the Windsor and Nassau draft covenants were highly contested where they innovate most, in relation to the management of communion issues. Here too the respondents were divided. Most were anxious about vesting determinative authority in the Primates' Meeting, and many favoured an advisory authority in the primates, and a determinative authority, if at all, in the Anglican Consultative Council on the basis that this is consistent with synodical government. Nevertheless, many welcome provision for a very limited ministry for the Instruments of Communion in serious cases of disagreement about essential matters of common concern which represent a substantial risk to the unity and mission of the Communion. The St Andrews draft covenant seeks to strike this very balance.

Part 3

The Implementation of a Covenant

7

The Process for a Covenant

The process for consideration of a covenant for the Anglican Communion has now reached a critical stage, prior to the Lambeth Conference 2008. The Lambeth Commission recommended a covenanting process in 2004 consisting of two basic parts: preparation (which is considered in this chapter) and adoption (which is considered in the next chapter). The Reception Reference Group presented a brief summary of responses to the covenant proposal to the Primates' Meeting 2005 which itself requested the Archbishop of Canterbury to orchestrate consideration of the proposal by the member churches of the Communion before the Lambeth Conference 2008. The Joint Standing Committee of the Anglican Consultative Council and the Primates' Meeting endorsed an outline timetable for this in 2006. The Covenant Design Group produced its Nassau draft text in 2007, and, following consultation around the Communion, its St Andrews draft in February 2008. On the basis of these, five key principles emerge as useful guideposts for the covenanting process: evolution, vocation, collaboration, negotiation, and education. They might also be understood to represent *conditions* for both the acceptability of the process and for entry into or adoption of a covenant. This chapter places these principles or conditions against the experiences afforded by covenanting processes in scripture, sacramental theology, ecumenism and the experiences of comparable international ecclesial bodies. It proposes that phases in the covenanting process may be understood to have a pneumatological dimension as 'an act of communion', and for some, the process for a covenant is almost as important as the end result.[1]

---

1 V. Strudwick, 'Toward an understanding of the type of Covenant needed for the Churches of the Anglican Communion' (2006): in so far as it provides an opportunity for greater understanding to develop between provinces, dioceses and individual Anglicans; see also Scully (2007) who welcomes 'the notion of a covenanting process that would help to keep us in mutual conversation'.

The Evolution of a Process

For the Lambeth Commission, it was imperative for the Communion itself to own and be responsible for the development of a covenant. It suggested a long-term process, conducted in an educative context, to enable the Communion to engage in real debate and agreement on its adoption as a solemn witness to communion. The Commission proposed: discussion and approval of a first draft by the primates; submission to the member churches and the Anglican Consultative Council for consultation and reception; final approval by the primates; legal authorization by each church for signing; and a solemn signature by the primates in a liturgical context.[2]

In 2006, the Joint Standing Committee of the Anglican Consultative Council and the Primates' Meeting adopted a 'modified version' of this process, with five phases: formulate a draft; test the draft; agree the text; implement the text; and monitor its implementation. It did so, on the recommendation in *Towards an Anglican Covenant*,[3] and suggested that provinces, Communion commissions and networks, theological institutions and all with an interest,[4] be invited to respond to the questions set out in the paper.[5] It also adopted the Windsor principle that the Communion must own the process as an act of communion characterized by collaboration, participation and transparency, balancing the promotion of particular interests and shared common interests.[6] Phase one (one year) would be carried out (for task completion and

---

2 TWR, para. 118.

3 TAAC, Introduction, and para. 34: the Committee requested the Secretary General, in consultation with the Archbishop of Canterbury, to move to 'the appointment of a Task Group to work on the proposal': this seems to be at odds with para. 23: see below n. 7.

4 TAAC, para. 23: the following are listed: the International Anglican Doctrinal and Theological Commission, International Anglican Standing Commission on Mission and Evangelism, Anglican Communion Network of Legal Advisers, ecumenical commissions, and Global South.

5 TAAC, 3: the Committee addressed six questions: (i) Is the concept of an Anglican covenant still viable? (ii) What form of covenant is best suited to the needs of the Communion at the present time? (iii) Who will be responsible for the preparation of a draft text? (iv) How will the Provinces and Instruments of Communion be participants in the generation of a text? (v) What method of implementation will be adopted, or how might this method be best discerned? (vi) What sort of timetable is desirable for the covenant project?

6 TAAC, para. 22: 'Any process by which a possible Covenant might be drafted, tested, agreed, implemented and monitored should of itself be an act of communion so that in the fullest sense the instrument is made by and for the Communion. Consequently, the process ought to be characterised by collaborative dialogue, equal participation, and transparent objectivity.'

cost-effectiveness) by a small Covenant Drafting Group of ten, reflecting diversity in terms of geography, culture and church tradition. The Archbishop of Canterbury should appoint the Group, in consultation with the Secretary General of the Anglican Communion,[7] to formulate a draft, or several draft options, with explanations (the cases for and against such draft(s) and how the draft(s) would work in practice).[8] The Group would submit its work to a joint meeting of the Joint Standing Committee and the Primates' Meeting itself in 2007.[9] In phases two and three (three to five years), each church would be asked, in relation to the draft(s): (i) to invite comment from within that church; (ii) to collate the feedback; and (iii) to return the feedback to the Group for it to consider and formulate another text (or texts) for consideration by the Lambeth Conference in 2008. A further revised draft could be brought to the Anglican Consultative Council in conjunction with a meeting of the primates in 2009.[10] For phase four (two to three years),[11] the Committee considered that there were at least two options: adoption by each church on the basis of legislation enacted by it;[12] or, the Anglican Consultative Council could adopt the covenant and incorporate it into its constitution (that is, no adoption by each church) subject to ratification by two-thirds of the member churches of the Council (in accordance with its constitution).[13] Finally, phase five, monitoring administration of the covenant, was suggested by Windsor.[14]

The Covenant Design Group met in Nassau in January 2007 and produced a report and single draft covenant. It encouraged commitment (in the form of 'an appropriate measure of consent') to the fundamental shape of its draft, and recommended that the primates consider and commend the text to the provinces for study and response.[15] The Group report and draft covenant were received by the Joint Standing Committee of the Anglican Consultative Council and Primates' Meeting in February 2007 which also informed the primates that it commended the work for further study and reflection. In turn, the Primates' Meeting (in the same month) received the report and draft.

---

7 TAAC, para. 23; see, however, above, n. 3.

8 Southern Africa, RNDC (2007): this suggests that the Covenant Design Group should offer different optional texts of a covenant and explain the options with each.

9 TAAC, para. 23: this accords in its essentials with the TWR, para. 118 recommendation.

10 TAAC, para. 24.

11 TAAC, para. 25.

12 As recommended by TWR, para. 118. See below Ch. 8.

13 See ACC Const., Art. 10. The responses do not address this possibility.

14 TAAC, para. 26; see also WDAC, Art. 27.3: by the (proposed) Council of Advice.

15 Report, paras 8, 9 and 10.

Both the Joint Standing Committee and the Primates' Meeting discussed, commented upon and suggested amendments to the Nassau text. The Primates' Meeting requested the Archbishop of Canterbury to prepare on its behalf a letter commending the report and the draft covenant to the provinces for study and response.[16] As a result, the provinces were invited to submit an initial response to the Nassau text through the Anglican Communion Office by the end of 2007 so that a revised version could be discussed at the Lambeth Conference in 2008. Thirteen provincial responses were available to the Group for its London meeting. The Group formulated its second draft, the St Andrews text, in February 2008, and a further round of consultation is due to follow after discussion at the Lambeth Conference,[17] with a final text presented to ACC-14 in May 2009 which, if adopted as definitive, will be offered to provinces for ratification through their synodical processes.[18]

Several criticisms have been made of the process.[19] First, that of timescale: some respondents argue that since Windsor the process has been accelerated. This does not give churches the time to debate the matter meaningfully. Rather, a period of conceptualizing (about what is needed) is required prior to drafting. As such, the process should wait until the Inter-Anglican Theological and Doctrinal Commission has completed its work on Anglican ecclesiology and the theology of communion. It has also been pointed out that the process must respect the synodical timetables of the member churches. Moreover, a rapid development could violate the participatory nature of decision-making in Anglicanism (and could marginalize the laity).[20] Second, the drafting bodies: some argue that drafting should be in the hands of the Anglican Consultative Council, or an Anglican Congress, or that choice of process should itself be debated.[21] Nevertheless, the Covenant

---

16 ACNS 16-2-2007; Primates' Meeting *Communiqué* 19-2-2007, para. 15.

17 CDG *Communiqué* (2008) para. 4: it is hoped that bishops will study the SADC in their preparation for the Conference, consulting dioceses and sharing reflections at the Conference; proposals on adoption will be presented to the Joint Standing Committee of the ACC and primates in March 2008.

18 Primates' Meeting, *Communiqué*, 19-2-2007, para. 16.

19 Following Windsor, the issue of process attracted little comment; see however, Dioc. of Bendigo (2005); Dioc. of Niagara: LCRPR: a timetable is essential and delay should be avoided.

20 Grieb (2007): this suggests for TEC a five-year period of fasting from full participation in the covenant process; Scully (2007) sect. 1; the point is also made that the Virginia Report process is incomplete. For respecting provincial timetables, see Perry (2007) and Bagshaw (2007). Similar criticisms emerged in responses to the Nassau draft: see Wales and Canada (the process is too hurried) and Southern Africa (the process is being driven too quickly by current disagreements).

21 RCW (2005) 7 (ACC); Dioc. of British Columbia, s. 4 (Anglican Congress): LCRPR.

Design Group adopted the majority of points raised in the provincial consultation of 2007 and incorporated these in the St Andrews draft covenant.[22] Indeed, most are agreed that evolution of a text is important, emerging organically out of common life in the Communion.[23]

Vocation: A Call to Covenant

Anglicans embrace the idea that the churches of the Anglican Communion are joined in the communion of God through Christ by the gracious power of the Holy Spirit.[24] A key aspect of pneumatology[25] is the interaction of the work of the Holy Spirit – the mysterious invisible power, energy or breath of God which guides, directs and rules[26] – and the human spirit (or soul), breathed into humankind at creation.[27] The Spirit is 'poured out' on, 'distributed' or 'given' to, and 'dwells' in,[28] believers; they 'receive', 'have', or are 'filled' with the Holy Spirit, so they live, walk and serve 'in the Spirit'.[29] However, neither the Lambeth Commission nor *Towards an Anglican Covenant* identifies the potential pneumatological aspects of the covenant process for Anglicans, or the possibility of a call to covenant – though the Commission did recognize the divine call to communion, as do many respondents.[30]

While no respondent offers a systematic pneumatological approach to the covenanting process, vocation has emerged as an important

---

22 See the Commentary to SADC and Ch. 6 above, especially the footnotes.

23 Dioc. of Brisbane (2004) para. 4.2: Anglicans must allow for the covenant 'to evolve as the Communion itself changes'; Percy (2006) para. 2; MU (2004) p. 5: LCRPR.

24 LC 1998, Res. III.8(d).

25 Pneumatology: 'the theology of the Holy Spirit': J. A. Komonchak, M. Collins, and D. A. Lane (eds), *The New Dictionary of Theology* (Dublin, Gill & Macmillan, 1987) 488; 'a way of talking about God active in the world and *in our experience*': A. E. McGrath (ed.), *The Blackwell Encyclopaedia of Modern Christian Thought* (Oxford, Blackwell, 1993) 448.

26 N. Lossky, J. M. Bonino, J. Pobee, T. F. Stransky, G. Wainwright, and P. Webb (eds), *Dictionary of the Ecumenical Movement* (hereafter Lossky) (Geneva, WCC, 2002) 534: the Spirit is 'the divine power working in the church'; A. Schmemann, *Of Water and the Spirit* (New York, St Vladimir Seminary Press, 1976) 107.

27 Gen. 2.7; see generally J. Macquarrie, *Paths in Spirituality* (2nd edn, London, SCM Press, 1992) 40–21, 153: spirituality involves 'the perfecting of personal being'.

28 For example Acts 2.17f.; 10.45; Heb. 2.4; 2 Cor. 1.22.

29 For example 1 Cor. 2.12, 14.16; Gal. 3.14, 5.16; 5.25; Acts 1.8; 2.4, 2.38, 9.17.

30 TWR, para. 4: God has 'called [us] into the fellowship [*koinonia*, 'communion'] of his Son' (1 Cor. 1.9); and para. 45: 'All those called by the gospel of Jesus Christ and set apart by God's gift of baptism are incorporated into the communion of the Body of Christ'. See also WAEEC, para. 29: 'God wills the full communion of all humankind with himself and among all peoples'. TAAC recognizes that biblical covenants originate in the initiative of God (para. 13). See also, for example, DAZ, 18 (Douglas).

issue. On the one hand, it is people who provide the call to covenant: the process could involve the Archbishop of Canterbury 'calling on all churches of the Communion . . . to . . . move towards the development and acceptance of an Anglican Covenant'.[31] On the other hand, some suggest that it is for the Communion to discern whether God is calling Anglicans to covenant one with another: time should be given for prayer to determine this.[32] In this sense, the process might have an eschatological dimension: 'the goal of the Anglican Communion remains the in-breaking of the kingdom of God which we journey towards'.[33] Covenanting might be understood as an aspect of this call. However, some speculate that the Spirit might oppose adoption of a covenant.[34] According to the Inter-Anglican Theological and Doctrinal Commission, the covenanting process is about how the churches of the Communion relate to each other in their common vocation to discern the will of God for the life of the Communion.[35] While the Covenant Design Group recognizes the divine call to communion,[36] it does not relate this to its covenanting process; nor do the primates.

Needless to say, the concept of a call to covenant is already familiar to Anglicans. The Covenant for Communion in Mission provides that it signifies a common call to share in the healing and reconciling mission of God to the world; and its preamble reminds Anglicans that as Christians they are called to share their relationships in the mission of God to the wider world. The Anglican Communion Network sees itself as called to its work, but the Covenant Union of Anglican Churches in Concordat does not present its parties as having been called by God into their covenanted relationship.[37] Indeed, theologically and canonically, vocation is a precondition for entry into the baptismal covenant, itself a 'Christian calling'; and God 'calls' men and women

---

31 HBTG (2005) 4.1.2: LCRPR; see also Noll (2005) 2,11: a covenant is 'being called for by thoughtful observers' of Anglicanism, particularly the Global South.

32 Rwanda (2005) para. 7: at least with regard to the purposes and content of a covenant: LCRPR.

33 RCW (2005) 9: LCRPR.

34 H. T. Lewis, 'Covenant, contract, and communion: reflections on a Post-Windsor Anglicanism', *Anglican Theological Review* 87 (2005) 607: 'It would appear that those who are threatened by the winds of change, by the spirit that blows "where it listeth", by that Spirit who would lead us into all truth, are seeking refuge in canonical and legal manoeuvres to ensure that their agenda is advanced'; but he hopes that 'we might restore a sense of covenant to our common life'.

35 RPC, paras 4.1, 5.1.

36 Nassau Report, para. 14; Introduction to SADC, paras 1–2.

37 CCM, Preamble; ACN: Confession and Calling, I.3, II.6; CUACC, Art. 1 (which simply recognizes that they 'are working together') and Art. 6.

to the married state.[38] The ordination covenant may provide a model to discern and test a call to covenant: no one receives holy orders unless called, tried, examined and admitted according to the rite of ordination.[39] Entry to the ordination covenant is an initiative of God, discerned through a deep inner conviction in which prayer is critical, and the call is tested by the Church as part of a spiritual process.[40] There is a point of contact here with the scriptural idiom of 'cutting a covenant', which symbolizes that a covenant involves spiritual sacrifice, a point acknowledged by *Towards an Anglican Covenant*.[41]

Lessons from the ecumenical field underscore for Anglicans the value of pneumatic understandings of covenanting processes. Reliance on the Holy Spirit, to inspire a 'common calling',[42] is a central pillar of ecumenical covenanting. For instance, the Lutheran–Anglican–Roman Catholic (Virginia) Covenant 1990 is based not only on the parties having felt 'impelled' by 'powerful experiences' to covenant together, but also on recognition that the Spirit 'calls us to ... consensus so that we can advance toward the goal of unity willed by Christ'; it has a section styled 'A Call into Covenant' and the bishops in turn call on their respective faithful to commit to the terms of the covenant.[43] Interim ecumenical covenants also sometimes reflect the belief that God will guide the churches into fuller covenanted relationships.[44] The vocational aspect of covenanting is less evident in the instruments of other international ecclesial communities. However, members of the Community of Protestant Churches in Europe understand that they 'have been *led* closer together' to a new covenanted relationship. The Australian Orthodox alliance is based on a 'vision' to pursue a closer and more substantial co-operation between the local sister churches

---

38 Matt. 28.18–20; for example, Canada, BCP 1962, 540 (adult baptism) and Wales, BCP 1984, 736 (marriage).

39 For example, Church of England, Canon C1(1); CIC, cc.232, 1009, 1029.

40 For example TEC, *Book of Common Prayer* (1979) 577; *A New Zealand Prayer Book* (1989) 887: ordination occurs with the assent of the people; Church of England: Ministry Division, Guidance: Summary of Criteria for Selection for Ministry (2005): the selection conference aim is 'to search our God's will for the future of the candidates' and 'his Church'; thus: 'times set aside for worship and meditation are ... central to the whole conference'.

41 G. P. Hugenberger, *Marriage as a Covenant* (Leiden, E. J. Brill, 1994) 195; P. A. Lillback, 'Covenant', in S. B. Ferguson and D. F. Wright (eds), *New Dictionary of Theology* (Leicester and Illinois, Intervarsity Press, 1988): see, for example Gen. 15.7–21; Ps. 50.5; TAAC, para. 13: covenants 'originate in the initiative of God, and elicit the costly sacrifice of faithful response by his covenant people to his work'.

42 Conference of European Churches, Constitution, Preamble.

43 LARC 1990: that is, the Common Declaration of the Archbishop of Canterbury and the Pope in 1982 and the prayer of Jesus for unity.

44 Covenant of Churches in Wales 1975.

with a view towards the more conclusive confrontation of common problems. The Baptist World Alliance recognizes that 'in the providence of God, the time has come' to enter an agreement and its purposes are agreed 'under the guidance of the Holy Spirit'. Similarly, in the Southern Baptist tradition, covenanting awakens the community to its mission and it is 'by the help of the Spirit' that church communities covenant 'to overcome the divisions which impair their witness'.[45]

Collaboration: Common Discernment

Common discernment is of great importance to the Lambeth Commission in its treatment of communion as a 'process' which involves collaboration and consultation.[46] These are also pivotal to the covenanting process recommended by both the Commission and *Towards an Anglican Covenant*.[47] They are also recognized as important in the responses to the proposal: time should be given for consultation in the process; drawing up a covenant will itself deepen relationships among the churches; and, the process might help churches to 're-engage' with each other.[48] Importantly, the process should be conciliar, with input from representatives of the churches, not simply the primates and bishops, but also clergy and laity including 'ordinary Anglicans'.[49] Transparency and dialogue are essential elements of the process which should be in the nature of a conversation – reasonable, tolerant and open; the strength of a covenant depends on the depth of its roots.[50] Some feel that electronic responses should be invited from provinces at each stage to increase participation in the process.[51] For others, part of the value of the covenant process is that it will enable the Communion to move away from its historic Anglo-centric character by owning a

---

45 CPCE:LA, Preamble, Arts 4, 5; Standing Conference of Canonical Orthodox Churches of Australia: this was 'a vision of Archbishop Stylianos' in 1975: http://home. it.net.au/~jgrapsas/pages/sccoca.htm; BWA, Preamble to the Constitution of 1905; Piper (1993).

46 See also the Ten Principles for Partnership (1993), Principle 7: 'Transparency involves openness and honesty with one another . . . Information needs to be fully shared with one another.'

47 See above pp. 150–1.

48 Rwanda (2005) para 7; Vercammen (2005); Ferris: LCRPR.

49 For conciliarity in the current debate on communion, see Radner (2005) 618; Dioc. of Brisbane (2004) para. 4.2; Dioc. of British Columbia: LCRPR, s. 4.

50 Affirming Catholicism (2006) 5; Strudwick (2006): deliberations must be 'open, accessible and consultative', and that minutes of the Covenant Design Group be put on the internet; Scully (2007) sect. 3; see also Bartel (2007) sect. 4; MCU (2006): provinces should at the very least be encouraged to consult their dioceses.

51 Bishop Brown (2006) para. 2.8.

covenantal self-understanding developed across the provinces.[52] Others see a need to consult ecumenical partners, and indeed the matter has been considered, for example, by the Anglican–Lutheran International Commission.[53]

On the other hand, for many the process will take too long: a covenant will take years to draw up, or even, given the need for synodical process in each church, generations may pass before a covenant text is approved.[54] Some also argue that the process might show how little Anglicans share, or, worse still, that it will be divisive, with infighting among the instruments of unity; the political realities of divergence militate against agreement about its terms.[55] Others urge that the process must not take too long,[56] or that it should be driven by the widest possible representation, such as a global Anglican gathering more representative than the Lambeth Conference,[57] or, in contrast, that the covenant should be developed around the Archbishop of Canterbury.[58] As we have seen, both the Covenant Design Group, and the Primates' Meeting 2007,[59] proposed extensive consultation to generate the confidence of the Communion; thirteen provinces responded in the provincial consultation of 2007.

Collaboration and consultation are also canonical aspects of the process of admission to the sacramental covenants. Parental agreement should be obtained before an infant is baptized, and, if the parents reside in another parish, consultation should take place with the minister of that parish before proceeding with baptism.[60] In some churches, when a party to a proposed marriage covenant has a former spouse still living, there must be consultation with the bishop for advice on

---

52 Goddard (2006): Fulcrum Website.

53 Dioc. of Saskatoon (8-1-2006): LCRPR; see also IASCER (2006) para. 3; Affirming Catholicism (2006) para. 8; for Lutheran input, see ACNS 4291 (31-5-2007), *Communiqué*, White Point, Nova Scotia, Canada.

54 Crosslinks (An International Mission Agency) (2005) (years); Tong (2005) 59 (generations). See also A. Perry, 'From Waterloo to Windsor: the proposed Anglican covenant in light of Anglican-Lutheran co-operation in Canada' (2006) 15: 'even the process of approval of a Covenant is likely to take an absolute minimum of three or four years, to allow two meetings of its three-year cycle for the General Synod to consult with the dioceses and internal provinces'; the Waterloo declaration is still being implemented by legislation six years after adoption by the Lutheran and Anglican churches in Canada. The same point is made by Scully (2007) sect. 5.

55 Dioc. of Niagara: LCRPR; Hughes (2004) III.C; Tong (2005) 58.

56 Ross (2006) para. 6.

57 Archbishop Jongonkulu Ndungane: ACNS 4213 (16-11-2006); see also Scully (2007).

58 Bishop Brown (2006) para. 2.7.

59 Nassau Report, para 8; Primates *Communiqué*, 19-2-2007, para. 16.

60 LC 1948, Res. 108; see, for example England, Can. B22(5); Southern Africa, Can. 35.5.

whether the marriage should be solemnized.[61] While the decision to ordain vests in the bishop, prior to ordination there is collaboration with local congregations and consultation with selectors.[62] The Covenant for Communion in Mission provides several principles which may be used to guide Anglicans as they collaborate in the covenanting process.[63] Needless to say, persistence in collaboration has been critical to ecumenical covenanting.[64]

Negotiation: The Synthesis of Discordant Views

In contrast with contract-making in civil law, treaty-making in international law,[65] or the development of religious international organizations,[66] sacramental covenants are not negotiated; nor is the salvific covenant. However, negotiation is central to the Anglican covenant debate. A critical question is how each term of a draft covenant is likely to be received in each member church. Unlike the Lambeth Commission, *Towards an Anglican Covenant* concedes that '[t]here can be no illusions: the detail of the Covenant will determine its acceptability'.[67] Several respondents agree: a covenant is 'a good model for negotiation'; negotiation would help Anglicans to distinguish essentials from *adiaphora*; and, Anglicans have 'to learn how to negotiate' their differences.[68] Negotiation is also a fundamental of dialogue: 'the development of Christian theology has always emerged out of negotiations between the perennial sources of experience, reason, tradition and scripture;' indeed, the very identity of the Anglican Communion, in its commitment to unity in diversity, is premised on the need to embrace plurality of perspectives in a common search for truth.[69] For the Inter-Anglican Theological and Doctrinal Commission, any workable covenant must

---

61 For example Ireland, Const. IX.31.

62 For example TEC, Cans. III.4; Melanesia, Can. A.7.

63 CCM, pp. 9–10: support one another; encourage expressions of our new life in Christ; meet to share common purpose and explore differences and disagreements; be willing to change in response to critique and challenge from others; celebrate our strengths and mourn over our failures; live into the promise of God's reconciliation for ourselves and the world.

64 For example, G. Huelin (ed.), *Old Catholics and Anglicans: 1931–1981* (Oxford, Oxford University Press, 1983): collaboration began in 1867.

65 I. Brownlie, *Principles of International Law* (6th edn, London) 581–3.

66 D. Korten, *Getting to the 21st Century: Voluntary Action and the Global Agenda* (West Hartford, CT, Kumarian Press, 1990) 118.

67 TAAC, para. 17.

68 MU (2004) p. 4; TEC, s. 4: LCRPR; Percy (2005) 213.

69 E. Graham, '"Our Real Witness": Windsor, public opinion and sexuality', in Linzey and Kirker (2005) 199 at 200.

reflect carefully negotiated 'content' as well as 'form' or 'methodology'; as such it should clarify and simplify both the narrative and visionary aspects of covenant.[70] While neither the Covenant Design Group nor the Primates' Meeting 2007 explicitly deal with negotiation, they recognize the need for debate, discussion and refinement.[71] Both the Joint Standing Committee of the ACC and the Primates' Meeting and the Primates' Meeting itself suggested amendments to the Nassau draft.[72]

A key issue to be settled by discussion, in this negotiation process, is neatly presented by one respondent. As they explore the idea of a covenant, the churches must do so knowing that over the centuries Anglican comprehensiveness has given the ability to include those who wish to see boundaries clearly and closely drawn and those who value boundaries that are broad and permeable. Throughout their history, Anglicans have managed to live with the tension between a need for clear boundaries and for room in order that the Spirit might express itself in fresh ways in a variety of contexts.[73] A synthesis of these views is fundamental to covenantal negotiation.[74] Within the Communion there needs to be 'a negotiation of rights and responsibilities so that each family member is able to pursue an independent and mature life while continuing to respect and support other family members'.[75] Part of the difficulty is trading off the interests of the whole against those of individual participants.[76]

---

70 RPC, para. 2.2: 'Narrative aspects of covenant recall the context and circumstances leading to the present moment, while visionary aspects of covenant point to the goals and future directions towards which we move in hope.'

71 Report, paras 8,9: but the Group called for an early commitment to the fundamental shape of the covenant; *Communiqué*, para. 16.

72 JSC of the Primates' Meeting and ACC, Points Raised in the Discussion of the Draft Text for an Anglican Covenant; Primates' Meeting, Points Raised in the Discussion of the Draft.

73 F. T. Griswold (Presiding Bishop of TEC), Letter 18-10-2004.

74 Negotiation calls for integrity in which creative challenges are raised which could lead to 'positive re-evaluation of long held traditions and assumptions': see Ten Principles (1993), Principle 6.

75 Responses of the Windsor Report Working Group to the Requests of the Standing Committee of General Synod of the Anglican Church of Australia (2006). See also TEC, RNDC (2007): this recognizes the role of a covenant in 'negotiating the life of the Anglican Communion lived between the local and the global'; it could be a witness 'to the plurality of voices, cultures and nations' making up the Communion. See also Wales, RNDC (2007): the covenant debate raises questions about the extent to which the inherited traditions are negotiable, though Anglicans need to move away from the idea of negotiation to that of 'interchange'.

76 Bagshaw (2007). There is a parallel here with the human rights debate in secular society.

The St Andrews, Nassau and Windsor draft covenants all useful-ly illustrate the negotiability, and perhaps non-negotiability, of some matters. Some covenantal provisions, expressed with a high level of generality, seem non-negotiable, for example: that scripture is the rule and ultimate standard of faith; that each church participates in the apostolic mission; that communion is a gift of God; and that each church shall maintain and administer the sacraments.[77] Others would seem negotiable (and might be put in the category of *adiaphora*): the covenant concept itself; which issues are essential matters of common concern; and that the Instruments of Communion should continue to have their current functions.[78] The negotiability of several is ambigu-ous, for example that autonomy is fundamental to Anglican polity; and that it is to be exercised in matters of common concern with regard for the common good of the Communion.[79]

The responses to the content of the Windsor and Nassau draft covenants (outlined in Chapter 6) indicate areas of both agreement and disagreement for the negotiation process. There is common ground, for example on the need for forbearance in communion relationships; that Anglicans are called to communion; that each church has the right to order and regulate its own affairs; and that communion involves mutual edification.[80] However, the negotiation process will need to synthesize the dissonances between the responses, for example the argument that the Archbishop of Canterbury should exercise a formal global *ministry* and the counter-argument that Canterbury should exercise no extra-provincial *jurisdiction*; these may be reconciled in a covenantal agreement that Canterbury be entitled to issue *guidance* to churches in matters of controversy.[81] One method of synthesis is to employ juridical concepts of rights and duties,[82] in the context of ecclesiology as polity,[83] and consequentialism.[84]

---

77 SADC, Cls 1.1.1-3; NDC, Arts 2.2; 2.4; 2.3; 3.3; 4.1; WDAC, Arts 1.3, 6.1, 8.1, 11.1.

78 SADC, Cls 3.2.4; 3.1.4; NDC, Arts 6.3; 5.2; WDAC, Arts 17.3, 23.1, 23.3.

79 SADC, Cls 3.1.2; 3.2.1; NDC, Art. 6.1; WDAC, Arts 4.4, 18.1, 21.2.

80 See above Ch. 6.

81 SADC, Appendix, 3.2 proposes this; as did WDAC, Art. 26.3.

82 For example if for some communion imposes a precept to submit matters of com-mon concern to the Instruments of Communion, but for others autonomy prohibits this, common ground may be found in a permissive right to submit such matters or in a duty to do so for consultation.

83 M. L. Stackhouse, 'Ecclesiology and ethics', in J. F. Childress and J. McQuarrie (eds), *A New Dictionary of Christian Ethics* (London, SCM Press, 1986) 171–5.

84 H. R. Niebuhr, *Children of Light and Children of Darkness* (London, Nisbet, 1945) xiii. 'Consequentialism is the moral theory that actions are right or wrong accord-ing to the consequences they produce, rather than any intrinsic features they may have, such as truthfulness or fidelity.'

In any event, if the covenanting process involves dialogue and negotiation, this has consequences for the debate. First, several respondents propose that it must be informed by the theological virtue of patience.[85] Second, the very fact that parties negotiate means that a covenant may represent a compromise (at least with regard to negotiable matters). This is a concern with ecumenical covenants.[86] Third, the ecumenical notion of 'reconciled diversity' might assist the negotiation process.[87] The notion is used by the Community of Protestant Churches in Europe: it is perfectly acceptable to have a state of 'reconciled diversity' in which there is fellowship between churches that maintain their own distinct identity and traditions.[88] Dialogue itself is a commitment in *Charta Oecumenica*: to continue in conscientious, intensive dialogue at different levels between the churches; to examine how official church bodies can receive and implement the findings gained in dialogue; and in the event of controversies, particularly when divisions threaten in questions of faith and ethics, to seek dialogue and discuss the issues together in the light of the gospel.[89]

Education: Spiritual Preparation and Growth

Anglicanism is sometimes understood to involve cross-fertilization, which requires a willingness to learn from one another, and being

---

85 M. Percy, 'On being stretched', in Linzey and Kirker (2005) 214: 'One of the chief virtues of living within a Communion is learning to be patient' as churches negotiate their differences; the development of their global identity has involved Anglican churches in 'a process of patient listening and learning, and of evolution and devolution'.

86 A Theological Workbook on An Anglican Methodist Covenant (Archbishops' Council, London, 2002) Ch. 3: it can all too easily develop into 'a bland "lowest common denominator" form of Christianity which lacks the richness and vitality of the separate traditions out of which they come'. See also TEC-Evangelical Lutheran Relations – Concordat of Agreement (2003): 'the point of an ecumenical dialogue . . . is not to horse trade one doctrine for another, or one treasured heritage for another, but to grow into the fullness of what the Church has been and can become'; the proper question is: '"who will gain more from the Concordat?" . . . both will gain the same thing: a fuller, richer understanding of the church, and a fuller, richer realization of that understanding.'

87 ATWAMC (2002) Ch. 4 (p. 23): 'Acknowledgement is what takes place when two churches accept each other as genuine Christian churches with authentic ministries of word and sacrament. Integration is a further stage in which churches which have recognized each other develop common forms of church government and ministerial oversight.'

88 The Leuenberg Fellowship (European Lutheran and Reformed churches): *The Church of Jesus Christ* (Frankfurt am Main, 1996): ATWAMC (2002) Ch. 4 (p. 24).

89 CO (2001) II.6: 'Rather than seeing our diversity as a gift which enriches us, however, we have allowed differences of opinion on doctrine, ethics and church law to lead to separations between churches, with special historical circumstances and different cultural backgrounds often playing a crucial role'; 'consensus in faith must be continued at all costs.'

open to ideas mutually exchanged.[90] Both the Lambeth Commission and *Towards an Anglican Covenant* stress the educative aspects of the covenanting process.[91] Unlike the St Andrews and Nassau texts, the Windsor draft covenant itself provides that each church should promote in its theological education an understanding of the relationships of communion between the member churches.[92] The respondents also recognize the educational dimension of the process, which may be likened to a pilgrimage.[93] However, the educational aspect of the process, as part of a 'spiritual commitment', must occur not at the point of implementation (that is, education about what the covenant means), but in the process of discerning together what sort of covenant is needed (that is, learning together what it means to be Anglican Christians covenanting for mission).[94] Time should be made for 'study' of a covenant.[95] This could prove a positive experience, with 'fresh voices' engaged in full, reasoned, careful and faithful debate (covenanting together for something greater than that which exists currently), which might help to re-examine the basic truth, doctrine and faith which Anglicans must uphold to remain in communion.[96]

In turn, the Covenant Design Group 2007 recommends its draft covenant for 'study' by the provinces,[97] and the Primates' Meeting for study and reflection.[98] According to one respondent, the development of an Anglican covenant has to be approached in 'the right spirit'; the process should not be seen as a political contest in which there will be winners and losers or as a form of political negotiation (with attempts to broker a compromise between those who want more authority for the Instruments of Communion and those who think this will threaten provincial autonomy); rather, the process needs to be viewed as 'a spiritual exercise in which the churches of the Communion seek individually and collectively to discern the will of God through prayer and reasoned reflection on Scripture, the Christian tradition and

---

90 See the Ten Principles of Partnership (1993) Principle 5.

91 TWR, para. 118; TAAC, para. 9: a covenant could become 'a significant educational tool'.

92 WDAC, Art. 15.5.

93 See Ch. 3 for the idea that one purpose of a covenant is to develop self-understanding. Radner (2005) 610: the Anglican experience is one of 'growing into deeper unity through dynamic engagements with difference, of an ecclesiastical structure that allows the Holy Spirit to speak in the unfolding work of historical debate, experiment, and correction'.

94 Scully (2007) sect. 4.

95 Rwanda (2005) para. 7; MU, p. 3.

96 TEC, House of Bishops' Response: 12-13-1-2005, s. 4: LCRPR; Ross (2006) para. 5; Scully (2007); and IFSCCUCI (2004) p. 4; SAMS Canada (2005) p. 2: LCRPR.

97 NDC, Report, para. 9

98 *Communiqué*, paras 15, 16.

the historical situation in which God has placed us'.[99] For some, the very possibility of the covenant (rather than its actuality) has already achieved much; it is an opportunity to rediscover consensus in the midst of diversity as well as the discipline of what is entailed in journeying together within the Anglican tradition.[100] The process could be a relationship-building exercise with time for study and prayer, and the St Andrews draft covenant highlights common study and prayer as central to communion.[101]

There is a direct parallel here with sacramental covenants. A necessary prerequisite of admission to these is an understanding of their nature, significance and implications. For infant baptism, sponsors must be instructed in their responsibilities for the Christian development of the child, and adult candidates must be instructed personally, in the Christian faith or the principles of the Christian religion, in biblical doctrine, and in the meaning or significance of baptism.[102] In relation to the marriage covenant, the parties must undergo preparation which includes instruction so that they understand the nature, meaning and purpose of the covenant.[103] Similarly, candidates for ordination should be educated in listed subjects (for example scripture, theology, ministry, worship), and before priestly ordination, they must satisfy their bishop of their continuing studies, spiritual development, and growth in ministry.[104]

Needless to say, study of scripture, in particular, assists the educative elements of the process.[105] Indeed, the nine points of the Covenant for Communion in Mission 'are predicated on Scripture and the sacraments providing the nourishment, guidance and strength for the journey of the covenant partners together'.[106] That churches can be led by scripture into a covenanted relationship is particularly so in the

---

99 Davie (2007).

100 Percy (2006) para. 6.

101 Bishop Michael Doe (2006). See also Australia, RNDC (2007): a covenant consultation process should incorporate an education programme and conversation based upon it; SADC, Cl. 3.2.3.

102 See for example Southern Africa, Can. 35.4; Australia, Can. P5 1992; Chile, Can. Fic.12.

103 See for example West Africa, Can. 7.4b: this forbids a minister to solemnize a marriage unless '[h]e shall have ascertained that both parties understand that Holy Matrimony is a physical and spiritual union ... entered into within the community of faith, by actual consent of heart, mind and will, and with the intent that it be lifelong'; see also, for example TEC, Cans. I.18.2(a)–(c); Japan, Can. 16.

104 Province of the West Indies, Cans. 16–17; Scottish Episcopal Church, Can. 11.4.

105 TWR, para. 51: the Lambeth Quadrilateral commits Anglicans to 'a series of normative practices: scripture is read, tradition is received, sacramental worship is practised, and the historic character of apostolic leadership is retained'.

106 CCM, Pledge.

Southern Baptist tradition; among the four steps towards adoption of a covenant is recommendation to focus on the 'one another passages' of scripture.[107] Finally, in the ecumenical field, covenanting is commonly understood as a gathering for pilgrimage, and the invitation 'to engage in a covenanting process is another act of commitment to one another as a further stage on the way to visible unity'.[108] That covenanting is therefore part of a greater process is recognized in the Covenant Union of Anglican Churches in Concordat,[109] the Anglican-Methodist Covenant (in England),[110] and the Anglican-Lutheran Covenant (in Australia).[111] The perichoretic nature of covenanting also surfaces in *Charta Oecumenica*: this represents the churches as 'moving towards one another'.[112]

Conclusion

For those to whom a covenant is acceptable, there seem to be certain conditions which must be satisfied in the covenanting process. Evolution, vocation, collaboration, negotiation and education emerge from responses to the proposal as essential components (or even preconditions) for what may be conceived theologically as a spiritual

---

107 TCCG, p. 7; R. Stanton Norman, *The Baptist Way* (Nashville, Tenn., Broadman & Holman, 2005) 118: the development of a sensitivity to the leadership of God (the process begins at this point); a study of scripture with focus on the 'one another' passages, and the New Testament characteristics of Christian relationships; identifying the relational elements that are indispensable in the Church; and secure unanimous and personal agreement to these: to love one another, as Christ loves us (John 13.34), so that by this the world shall know that we are disciples of Christ (John 15.12); to manifest that love to all persons (1 Thess. 3.12); to be kind, tender-hearted, and forgiving of one another (Eph. 4.32); to submit one to another (Eph. 5.21); to exhort one another (Heb. 3.13; 10.25); to commit ourselves to God and to one another to be Christlike (1 Pet. 2.21); to comfort one another (2 Cor. 1.4); to consider others as more important than ourselves (Phil. 2.3); to have equal concern for each other, suffer when one suffers and rejoice when another is honoured (1 Cor. 12.25–26); to use our God-given knowledge to instruct one another (Rom. 15.14) and the Word of God to teach and admonish one another (Col. 3.16); to nurture one another toward spiritual maturity measured by the life and ministry of Jesus (Eph. 4.13); to restore gently those who sin (Gal. 6.1); not to pass judgment on one another or put any stumbling block in one another's way (Rom. 14.13); to be filled with the Spirit (Eph. 5.18): in short: let the light of godly life shine in each to bring glory to God.

108 ACCT, pp. 1, 3 (A Commitment to a Covenanting Process).

109 CUACC, Arts 1, 6: 'a process that will permit us, in due course, to enter into an agreement of full communion with a clear and common understanding of all of its implications'.

110 ACM:CS (2001) v: the covenant is a stepping stone.

111 ALCA: Our Covenant.

112 CO (2001) Preamble.

journey towards a covenant. Accordingly, the process should evolve wisely. Churches of the Communion should determine whether they are called into covenant and how to test that call. If the process is to be a meaningful act of communion, churches should be directly involved in a transparent and objective collaboration, consultative in character at the drafting stage – and the work of the Covenant Design Group goes a long way in this regard – and consensual in character at adoption. The churches must freely negotiate the terms of a covenant where negotiation is appropriate. Through an educative process of covenantal study, they should also fully understand the covenantal relationships they enter and commitments they assume. These procedural principles, or conditions, are a key feature of sacramental covenants: the canonical and liturgical evidence suggests clearly that candidates are called to, consulted about, and educated in the nature and implications of their baptismal, marriage and ordination covenants. But sacramental covenants, like the salvific covenant, are not negotiated. As well as learning ecumenically about the spiritual processes involved in covenanting in ecumenism and other global church communities, the theological challenge for Anglicans in the debate is to demonstrate that the Spirit animates their arguments in each stage of the process.

8

The Adoption of a Covenant

The fundamentals of the process preparatory to adoption of a covenant are predominantly exercises in practical theology. Evolution, vocation, collaboration, negotiation and education reflect directly the potential of a covenanting process as a spiritual journey of growth. In this journey the churches of the Communion labour together, test their call to covenant, and listen to and learn from one another about the relationships between Anglicans and their role in the mission of the Church. Spiritual preparation, if it culminates politically in an agreed text, leads finally to adoption of a covenant. The adoption stage has a mixed juridical and liturgical character. The Lambeth Commission proposed that each church should enact a law to authorize adoption of the covenant itself to be entered by means of signature in a solemn liturgical setting. This chapter examines the proposal, responses to it, and suggestions for adoption that have emerged since the *Windsor Report*, including which signatory could most appropriately act on behalf of each church. It also compares these ideas with modes of adoption in scriptural, sacramental and ecumenical covenants as well as those used for instruments of comparable international ecclesial communities.

Each Church Enacts a Communion Law

The Lambeth Commission understood that one cause of the crisis it was established to address was related to the nature of authority in Anglicanism: the principles about communion, autonomy, discernment in communion and inter-Anglican relations, enunciated at global level by the Instruments of Communion, have persuasive moral authority for individual churches; they do not have enforceable juridical authority unless incorporated in their legal systems (and generally they are not incorporated).[1] Moreover, no church has a systematic body

---

1 TWR, para. 115: this may be contrasted with the juridical experience of each church,

of 'communion law' dealing with its relationship of communion with other member churches; inter-Anglican relations are not a distinctive feature of provincial laws.[2] Consequently, how to make the principles of inter-Anglican relations more effective at the local ecclesial level is 'a persistent problem in Anglicanism contributing directly to the present crisis'.[3]

The Commission recommended, therefore, that this could be remedied by the adoption by each church of its own simple and short domestic 'communion law' to enable and implement an agreed covenant.[4] Another rationale for this is that: 'as some matters in each church are serious enough for each church currently to have law on those matters – too serious to let the matter be the subject of an informal agreement or mere unenforceable guidance – so too with global communion affairs'.[5] For the Commission the purposes of the 'brief law', to be enacted by each church, would be twofold: to authorize its primate (or equivalent) to sign the covenant on behalf of that church; and to commit the church to adhere to the terms of the covenant.[6] Using a particular church illustratively, the Commission proposed a form for

---

in which enforceable canon law, the servant of the church, facilitates and orders communion among its faithful.

2 TWR, para. 116: this may be contrasted with the increasing bodies of ecumenical law in Anglican churches facilitating communion relations between Anglicans and non-Anglicans.

3 TWR, para. 117.

4 TWR, para. 117. One version of the idea was presented to the Primates' Meeting in 2001, namely: 'A Statement or Declaration of Common Anglican Canon Law and Polity would be issued by the Archbishop of Canterbury in partnership with the Primates' Meeting, in the form of a concordat: all Primates would be signatories. The statement would not of itself be law, issuing as it would from the global moral order, but rather would set the programme for canonical revision in each church.' This was then to lead to implementation and incorporation: 'Individual churches, perhaps in groups by means of covenants . . . would begin work on incorporation of the Declaration into their canonical systems by means of canonical revision. Each church would have a body of distinctly Communion Law.' See N. Doe, 'Canon law and communion', *EccLJ* 6 (2002), 241 at 262, a paper delivered at the Primates' Meeting, Kanuga, North Carolina, USA, 6 March 2001.

5 TWR, para. 117: the Commission considers that 'a brief law would be preferable to and more feasible than incorporation by each church of an elaborate and all-embracing canon defining inter-Anglican relations, which the Commission rejected in the light of the lengthy and almost impossible difficulty of steering such a canon unscathed through the legislative processes of forty-four churches, as well as the possibility of unilateral alteration of such a law'.

6 TWR, para. 118; see also WDAC, Preamble: 'We, the churches of the Anglican Communion, in order to foster greater unity and to consolidate our understandings of communion, solemnly establish this Covenant, entered on our behalf by designated signatories and to which we shall adhere as authorized by laws enacted by each of our churches for these purposes, so that our communion may be made more visible and committed, and agree as follows . . .'

the law to be enacted by the central assembly of each church: 'The Governing Body of the Church in Wales authorizes the Archbishop of Wales to enter on behalf of this church the Anglican Covenant and commits the Church in Wales to comply and act in a manner compatible with the Covenant so entered'.[7] The form of the law would vary between each church depending on the canonical styles of its central assembly,[8] and of its primate or equivalent.[9]

In turn, *Towards an Anglican Covenant* offered at least two options for adoption. After the Anglican Consultative Council and the primates approve a final draft in 2009, their Joint Standing Committee could commend the text for juridical adoption by the central assembly of each church (in line with the Lambeth Commission suggestion) *prior* to a solemn liturgical signing.[10] An alternative would be for the Anglican Consultative Council to adopt the covenant and incorporate it into its constitution (that is, no adoption by each church); this would be subject to ratification by two-thirds of the member churches.[11] Needless to say, there are other possible modes of adoption. First, there could be synodical ratification by enactment of a brief communion law within each church *following* a solemn liturgical signing: the primate would sign on behalf of the church and a law enacted subsequently to ratify the covenant.[12] Second, the Archbishop of Canterbury could issue the covenant and request (or require) its adoption as a precondition to invitation to the Lambeth Conference.[13] Third, the Lambeth Conference could incorporate a covenant into a resolution, but then

---

7 TWR, para. 118, n. 61.

8 The formula appropriate to the Church of England, for example, could be: 'The General Synod of the Church of England authorizes the Archbishop of Canterbury to enter on behalf of this church the Anglican Covenant and commits the Church of England to comply and act in a manner compatible with the Covenant so entered.'

9 The formula appropriate to TEC, for example, could be: 'The General Convention of the Protestant Episcopal Church in the United States of America, otherwise known as The Episcopal Church, authorizes the Presiding Bishop to enter on behalf of this church the Anglican Covenant and commits the Episcopal Church to comply and act in a manner compatible with the Covenant so entered.'

10 TWR, para. 118.

11 See ACC Const., Art. 10. But this raises questions about how the covenant would bind the signatory churches themselves within their local system of government and law.

12 This would be analogous to ratification of treaties in the secular sphere of international law. In the so-called monist system, a treaty is signed on behalf of a state and then afterwards a law is passed by that signatory state incorporating the treaty into its domestic national law. A problem with this is that in some churches the primate or equivalent would require *prior* legal authority to sign, unless some form of retrospective law were enacted to cure the signature: see also n. 38 and below.

13 For the idea that invitation to the Conference lies with Canterbury, see J. Rees, 'Legal implications' (2003).

it would not enjoy a synodical basis nor would it bind the churches legally.[14] Fourth, each church could adopt a covenant by means of a non-juridical statement: this would provide a synodical foundation but the covenant would remain unenforceable. Or else, the model for the Covenant for Communion in Mission might be used; that is, adoption by a commission of the Communion without any enforceability or direct synodical participation of the churches in signing up to it.[15]

The Nassau report of the Covenant Design Group simply recommends, without further detail, 'formal synodical processes of adoption'.[16] Similarly, the Primates' Meeting 2007 refers in a general fashion to 'ratification' by the provinces and adoption or rejection by them through their synodical processes.[17] The Joint Standing Committee of the Primates' Meeting and the Anglican Consultative Council in 2007 raised the point that each church 'would have to articulate its own level of commitment to the Covenant', which suggests that it would be for each church to determine whether or not it employs a juridical adoption.[18] Unlike Windsor, but like the Nassau text, the St Andrews draft covenant makes no reference to mode of adoption;[19] nor does the Inter-Anglican Theological and Doctrinal Commission. Some have observed that the notion in *Towards an Anglican Covenant* that a covenant could be incorporated into the constitution of the Anglican Consultative Council seems to have sunk without trace.[20] The Covenant Design Group at London decided that proposals for the process of 'reception' of the covenant and 'its ultimate consideration by synodical process' will be presented to the Joint Standing Committee of the Anglican Consultative Council and Primates' Meeting in March 2008.[21]

The matter of adoption has attracted considerable attention in the responses to the covenant proposal.[22] On the one hand, some agree that each church should have a 'communion law' on its commitments

---

14 For the non-enforceability of Lambeth Conference resolutions, see N. Doe, *Canon Law and the Anglican Communion* (Oxford, Clarendon Press, 1998).

15 CCM, p. 10: it is not entirely clear to whom the 'We' refers in the expression 'We make this covenant in the promise of our mutual responsibility and interdependence in the Body of Christ'; however, ACC–13 commends the covenant 'to the churches of the Anglican Communion for study and application'.

16 Report, para. 8; see also para. 10: 'adoption through the consultative and constitutional processes of the Provinces'.

17 Primates' Meeting, *Communiqué*, 19-2-2007, para. 16.

18 Points Raised, Sect. 6.(5).

19 Compare the preambles of the two drafts.

20 Bagshaw, 'Bouncing the Covenant through the Anglican Communion' (19-6-2007).

21 *Communiqué* for SADC (February 2008).

22 Most agree that, if the covenant concept is accepted, a covenant should contain 'a mechanism for ratification': Noll (2005) 11; see also, for example, Rt Revd Dr A. J. Malik

to the Instruments of Communion.[23] Juridical adoption would reflect, for example, that Anglicans are governed by canon law as well as by 'bonds of affection', that a church desires to be part of a wider communion, and that juridical adoption could be a step toward a constitutionally governed Anglican Communion.[24] Indeed, for some, a non-binding covenant would have little impact because bishops would do the bidding of a diocese or national church.[25] Moreover, a brief law would obviate the need to establish complex legal structures, or to develop new structures of canon law at the international level.[26] Others suggest that juridical adoption symbolizes 'the true spirit of submission', or, alternatively, that a covenant could represent model legislation for adaptation by each church.[27] Juridical adoption has also attracted support from the Global South.[28]

On the other hand, it is argued that the use of law as a mode of adoption is an attempt to deliver Anglicans over to legal structures and must be resisted at all costs.[29] Within, for example, 'a marriage relationship there is a covenant without necessarily a law binding the parties'.[30] The proposal represents 'the easy road of juridical and canonical remedies' – a legislative solution – and canon law has never before succeeded in this kind of situation.[31] Others are sceptical as to whether 'a law-based system is efficient in terms of time and energy expended or indeed consonant with a gospel of grace . . . there is a cultural difference between the binding nature of canon law and the provision of a framework within which decisions may be taken

(Pakistan): he stresses 'the practical need for attention to the concrete implementation of the articles of the Covenant'.

23 Bishop Lynagh: LCRPR.

24 SAMS (Canada) (31-1-2005) p. 2; Epting, para 2: LCRPR: it is therefore 'worth serious study'.

25 Dioc. of Saskatoon: LCRPR.

26 Dioc. of Saskatoon: LCRPR; Goddard (2005) 4; see also DAZ, 54–5 (Douglas) prefers 'covenant' over 'law'; Revd Canon J. Mellis (Canada).

27 Archbishop Yong Ping Chung: otherwise the covenant would be merely 'a paper qualification'; Dioc. of Brisbane (2004) para. 4.5.

28 The preamble to its draft covenant provides that: 'We, the Churches of the Anglican Communion . . . solemnly establish this Covenant, entered on our behalf by designated signatories and to which we shall adhere as authorized by communion laws enacted for these purposes . . .'

29 FOFAD, 26: the NT notion of fellowship in a common gospel provides the model for a way forward.

30 RCW (2005) 6–7. However, see below for the juridical dimension of sacramental covenants.

31 R. A. Greer, 'No easy paths: was Trollope right?', in A. Linzey and R. Kirker (eds), *Gays and the Future of the Anglican Communion* (Winchester, O Books, 2005) 115; Dioc. of British Columbia: LCRPR: it may cause difficulties in the future; DAZ, 53 (Zahl).

within a conciliar church'.[32] Covenant is not communion law. Authority should be 'moral' not 'legislative'. Law cannot enforce affection. Thus, some consider the covenant proposal to move in the direction of international canon law.[33] In any event, whatever mode of adoption is used, a clear statement of the standing and authority of the covenant is fundamental.[34]

There seems to be no doubt that the central assembly of each church has competence to adopt a covenant by legislative enactment (even if this involves a self-limitation of its own autonomy);[35] it is common for relations with other churches, including Anglican churches,[36] to be specifically listed among the matters within the jurisdiction of central church assemblies.[37] The schedule for adoption is conditioned by the timing of the meetings of central assemblies (which typically are annual, biennial or triennial, though provision exists for extraordinary meetings).[38] It would be for each church (if minded to adopt a covenant), in an exercise of its own autonomy, to decide on the appropriate legislative mechanism to enact a 'communion law', whether by amendment of its fundamental declaration of principles,[39] its constitution (which would involve special majority procedures),[40] or its canons.[41] To the extent that a covenant touches matters of doctrine and discipline, addi-

---

32 CCW (2005) para. 2.4: LCRPR.

33 Sison (2006) 4; Dioc. of Ontario, q. 2; MacDougall (2005); M. McCord Adams, ('Faithfulness in Crisis', in Linzey and Kirker, 2005) 70; see also Jones (2005) 121.

34 MCU (2006) p. 17.

35 See, for example West Africa, Const., Art. XXIII.3: 'The Provincial Synod has the final authority in matters concerning the spiritual discipline of the Church'; Papua New Guinea, Const., Art. 6: the Provincial Council is 'the final governing body of the Church . . . on all matters affecting the life, order and discipline of this Church'; Canada, Declaration of Principles, 6: the General Synod has jurisdiction over the 'autonomy' of the church.

36 See, for example Rwanda, Const., Art. 27; Canada, Declaration of Principles, 6(d).

37 Nigeria, Const., III.23(iii); Papua New Guinea, Const., Art. 7; South India, Const., IX.15.

38 For annual meetings see, for example Scotland, Can. 52.1; South India, Const., IX.20; three years: TEC, Const., Art. I.7. For this reason, it might be that signing by a primate with subsequent juridical ratification (see above n. 12) would be helpful for those churches unable to pass a communion law, because of time constraints, prior to signature of a covenant.

39 For example, Central Africa, Fundamental Declarations, VII; Canada, Declaration of Principles, 11.

40 Most churches employ a referral model for constitutional amendment with reference to the dioceses either for consultation (for example South East Asia, Const., Art. 19), or consent (by a prescribed majority: for example South India, Const., XIV, or by all: Melanesia, Const. Art. 20); some require no referral (for example Wales).

41 For example the Scottish Episcopal Church has a Code of Canons and no formal 'constitution' (see c.52).

tional procedural norms would apply (typically reserving the initiative or final approval to the bishops).[42] In Australia, for example, adoption would involve constitutional amendment by the General Synod or each diocesan synod would have to choose to adopt the covenant; and this would doubtless not be easily achieved.[43]

Additional challenges arise with respect to the Church of England by virtue of the fact that, unlike other churches in the Anglican Communion, the church is established according to the laws of the realm.[44] Legislative adoption is likely to involve the state. As one respondent points out, a 'communion law' could be enacted by the Queen in Parliament in the form of statute (that is, primary legislation),[45] not least to overcome the terms of ancient law;[46] or else, adoption of a covenant could be achieved by the legislative enactment of a Measure of the General Synod (in so far as it might touch the constitutional rights of the subjects of the Sovereign), which to be operative requires the approval of Parliament and the royal assent.[47] However, as a possible consequence could be to narrow the national and broad popular appeal of the church, Parliament would have to think very carefully before approving such legislation.[48] But it would be difficult to predict what the

---

42 For example Wales, Const., II.36; Kenya, Const., Art. II; Ireland, Const., I.25.

43 N. Cameron, in P. G. Bolt, M. D. Thompson and R. Tong (eds), *The Faith Once for All Delivered* (Camperdown, NSW, The Australian Church Record in conjunction with the Anglican League, 2005) 52; see also R. Tong, ibid. 55 at 56: core changes to the constitution require majorities in each House and assent of three quarters of the diocesan synods (there are 23 dioceses) and metropolitical sees (of which there are five) (s. 67); and the General Synod meets every three years. If a General Synod canon were used then, as the subject matter of the covenant 'concerns the ritual ceremonial or discipline of this Church' (s. 28), a special majority is required of two thirds of the members of each house, and must be assented to by each diocesan synod; a diocesan canon requires the assent of the bishop.

44 England, Can. A.1; N. Doe, *The Legal Framework of the Church of England* (Oxford, Clarendon Press, 1996) 8–10.

45 A. Pearce, 'English ecclesiastical autonomy and the Windsor Report' (2005): 'There is only one way in which such a provision could effectively be made in England . . . To be worth making at all, the "communion law" for England would have to take the form of primary legislation. Parliament, that is, would have to pass an Act or, more likely, approve a Measure framed by the General Synod and containing the essential wording committing England to act in its public ecclesiastical affairs in a manner compatible with the Covenant (and hence with the international arbiters' interpretation).'

46 Pearce (2005): the author cites the Ecclesiastical Licences Act 1533: 'This your Grace's realm, recognizing no superior under God but only your Grace, has been and is free from subjection from any man's laws but only to such as have been devised, made and ordained within this realm . . . or to such other as, by sufferance . . . the people of this your realm have taken at their free liberty.'

47 Church of England Assembly (Powers) Act 1919, ss 3, 4.

48 Pearce (2005): adoption would alter the 'national' character of the Church of England.

response of Parliament would be.[49] Nevertheless, a Measure of General Synod could adopt a covenant to have either direct applicability in England with the organs of the church acting as final arbiters,[50] or with external arbiters having the final say in its administration.[51] Some suggest that adoption might also involve approval by a majority of diocesan synods in the Church of England.[52]

While there is something of a parallel here with sacramental covenants (each church uses law to underscore its commitment to them),[53] the adoption of a covenant on inter-Anglican relations by *legislative enactment* in each church would be an innovation for Anglicanism.[54] The constitution of the Anglican Consultative Council was 'approved' by the member churches of the Communion, but there seems to be no legal evidence that such approval was given by enactment of laws;[55]

---

49 Clatworthy, Bagshaw and Saxbee (2007) para. 5.1.

50 As with the Human Rights Act 1998 which incorporates the European Convention on Human Rights: domestic courts arbitrate on this but may consult Strasbourg jurisprudence: Pearce (2005).

51 As with under the European Communities Act 1972: Pearce (2005).

52 Clatworthy, Bagshaw and Saxbee (2007) para 5.1: they cite the Synodical Government Measure 1969, Schedule 2, Constitution of the General Synod, Art. 8: 'a scheme for a constitutional union or a permanent and substantial change of a relationship between the Church of England and another Christian body being a body a substantial number of whose members reside in Great Britain, shall not be finally approved by the General Synod unless, at a stage determined by the Archbishops, the . . . scheme or the substance of the proposals embodied therein, has been approved by a majority of the dioceses at meetings of their Diocesan Synods . . .' Clatworthy *et al.* continue, however: 'It may be argued that the purpose of this clause was to address formal ecumenical relationships and would not apply to the Anglican Communion of which the Church of England is already a part. However if the Anglican Communion is to be given juridical form it would constitute "another Christian body"'. The authors do not address the rule in Art. 8 that such other Christian bodies are those with a substantial body of members resident in Great Britain. This would apply, of course, only in relation to the Church in Wales and the Scottish Episcopal Church.

53 For example, for laws which commit churches to preserve the sacrament of baptism: South East Asia, Const., Fundamental Declaration, 1; Ireland, Const., I.2; Southern Cone, Const., Art. 1. The canonically approved liturgical books contain the ritual elements of the administration of the sacramental covenants. Moreover, though fundamentally spiritual events, the baptismal, marriage and ordination covenants all have juridical status in each church and canonical consequences flow from entry to them: see below Ch. 9.

54 DAZ, 53 (Zahl). The law of the Church in Wales to establish communion with, among others, the Spanish Reformed Episcopal Church (a member of the Anglican Communion) is rare: Can. 29-9-1966; also covenants exist between ECUSA (now TEC) and, for example, the Anglican churches in Mexico and the Philippines (with regard to mission and resources).

55 A search of the laws of the churches does not yield any law specifically enacted to adopt the constitution. One might presume that adoption was somehow 'informal'. However, laws do occasionally provide for submission of matters to the Council, for example, Tanzania, Const., IV.15: in matters of doctrine, the House of Bishops may refer the case

nor does the constitution itself provide for a legislative ratification of amendments to it in the churches.[56] Members of the Anglican Communion Network 'affiliate' through a vote of their annual conventions, but its instruments do not provide for their adoption by a law enacted by the member bodies.[57] However, not only do Anglican churches have basic ecumenical duties enshrined in law,[58] but increasingly they incorporate ecumenical agreements into their laws (Wales),[59] or otherwise adopt them formally (Australia),[60] such as by act of synod (Canada).[61] By way of contrast, the signatories to the Lutheran-Anglican-Roman Catholic Covenant (Virginia) 'recommend' the covenant to their 'respective judicatories', and *Charta Oecumenica* has 'no magisterial or dogmatic character, nor is it legally binding under church law'.[62]

Several modes of adoption are used by comparable international ecclesial communities. However, none of the global instruments studied here explicitly provides that each member church is to enact a law or other regulatory form as the mode of adoption.[63] A thorough study of the legal instruments of their member churches would be needed to determine the extent to which these churches enshrine in their own laws a commitment to the global communities to which they belong. Nevertheless, 'acceptance' of its constitution is a precondition for

---

to 'the Council of the Lambeth Conference'; Kenya, Can. II: proposed schemes for union with other churches must be submitted to the Council; New Zealand, Can. B.XVIII.10: this places a duty on the church's Ecumenical Council to represent to the ACC ecumenical matters of concern to the church.

56 Const., Art. 10: this simply provides that amendment be ratified by two-thirds of member churches.

57 ACN, Memorandum of Agreement, Note. But see Organizational Charter, Art. IV: 'We, as Dioceses and Convocations, commit ourselves . . .'; see also AGI, Draft Constitution, Art. VI: 'This organizing constitution . . . was adopted unanimously on (date) at (place) by (convening authority). Signatories' names will be provided on request.' The covenant of the Canadian house of bishops is not adopted by legislative enactment, but is a statement of goodwill: ACNS 3971 (29-4-2005).

58 Jerusalem and the Middle East, Art. 5: to maintain mutual understanding; Southern Africa, Resolution of Permanent Force of the Provincial Synod, 1 (1975): to seek unity; Korea, Fundamental Declaration, to restore unity.

59 Can. 28-9-1995 (Porvoo); Can. 1-5-1974: Covenant of Churches in Wales.

60 The Anglican-Lutheran Covenant in Australia: the 'Anglican Church formally commits itself to enter into this Covenant with the Lutheran Church'; it was 'adopted' by the General Synod and provides that '[e]ach church enacts the Covenant by whatever measures are appropriate for each church': GS Resolution, 78/04(d) and (f).

61 General Synod, Motion A164 (2001): Waterloo Declaration for Full Communion with the Evangelical Lutheran Church in Canada.

62 LARC, Preamble; OC (2001) Preamble: its authority derives from 'voluntary commitments'.

63 For example, SCOBA, Const., Art. II(a)1: but the constitution binds the conference.

membership of the Lutheran World Federation.[64] 'Acceptance' of the doctrinal statement in its constitution is a condition of membership of the World Alliance of Reformed Churches.[65] The churches of the Community of Protestant Churches in Europe 'assent' to the Leuenberg Agreement.[66] For the Old Catholic International Bishops' Conference signing by the bishops and synodical governing body of each member church 'implies acceptance of the Statute . . . by the respective Church(es)'.[67] The Anglican proposal for a synodical adoption is not, therefore, out of the ordinary.

The Signatories to a Covenant

The Lambeth Commission recognized that a covenant could be signed by the primates without formal legal authorization by each church to do so.[68] However, this would raise questions about both the authority of a primate to sign and of the covenant itself. Consequently, as we have seen, the Commission suggests that each church, through its brief communion law, might authorize its primate (or equivalent) to sign the Covenant on behalf of that church and commit the church to adhere to the terms of the covenant.[69] The preamble to the Windsor draft covenant provides that the churches of the Communion 'establish this Covenant, entered on our behalf by designated signatories . . . authorized by laws enacted by each of our churches for these purposes'.[70] The fundamental idea is that the signatories would have to be legally authorized to sign on behalf of their church. In some churches, this

---

64 LWF, Const., Art. V; see also ELCA, Constitution and Foundational Texts (2003) Chs. 1, 2, 5: the 'congregations, synods and churchwide organizations' are 'interdependent partners sharing responsibility in God's mission'.

65 WARC, By-laws, I.1: that is, acceptance of Art. II of the Constitution.

66 CPCE:LA, Preamble, 1; see also Art. 37: 'This declaration of church fellowship does not anticipate provisions of church law on particular matters of inter-church relations or within the churches. The churches will, however, take the Agreement into account in considering such provisions.'

67 Statute (2000), Guidelines, 2, 4.

68 TWR, para. 118.

69 TWR, para. 118. The formula which the Commission proposed for the 'communion law' (see above nn. 7–9), that each church should 'authorize' its primate (or equivalent) to sign the covenant on behalf of that church, might suggest that the primate (or equivalent) would then have a discretion (or right) to sign which that primate (or equivalent) could decide not to exercise. To ensure that the primate fulfils the wishes of their church, it would perhaps be more appropriate to create a duty to sign, for example: 'The Governing Body of the Church in Wales *requires* the Archbishop of Wales to enter on behalf of this church the Anglican Covenant and commits the Church in Wales to comply and act in a manner compatible with the Covenant so entered.'

70 WDAC, Preamble.

would be an innovation as primates lack a *specific* legal authority to enter such commitments on behalf of a church. However, laws often provide that one of the functions of a primate, primus, archbishop, or other presiding bishop,[71] is to act as a representative of a church in its dealings with other churches nationally and internationally. To this extent, what the Commission suggests is not radical; it would be for each church, in exercising its own autonomy, to identify the appropriate signatory.

The Covenant Design Group does not explicitly address the matter of signatories, though it speaks of the primates ultimately committing their churches (following synodical adoption) to the covenant.[72] Like the Nassau text, the St Andrews draft covenant clearly conceives of the churches as parties without specifying 'who' declares in the covenantal declaration: 'we declare our Churches to be partakers in this Anglican Covenant.'[73] However, unlike the Windsor document but like the Nassau text, the St Andrews draft covenant does not speak of designated signatories authorized to enter the covenant (by laws specially enacted for this purpose).[74] The draft covenant submitted to the Covenant Design Group by the Anglican Church of Australia refers to 'a church party to this covenant'.[75] The Primates' Meeting 2007 provided no comment on the matter of signatories,[76] though the Church of England in its response to the Nassau text raised the issue.[77]

The proposal that the primates (or their equivalents) sign the covenant on behalf of each church has attracted considerable comment. Some agree with the thrust of the Lambeth Commission proposal: 'such a document could be signed by the Primate . . . only at the behest

---

71 For example Scotland, Can. III.3: the Primus 'shall represent the Scottish Episcopal Church in its relation to all other Churches of the Anglican and other Communions'; TEC, Cans. I.2.4: the presiding bishop is 'the representative of this Church and its episcopate in its corporate capacity'; see also Korea, Const. Art. 6; Philippines, Const. Art. IV.1–2; Jerusalem and the Middle East, Const. Art. 11(i).

72 NDC, Report, para. 11.

73 SADC, Our Declaration. Compare NDC, Art. 7: 'we declare our Churches to be partners in this Anglican Covenant.'

74 The issue is raised by G. Cameron 'Baby's first steps: can the covenant ever walk?', in M. Chapman (ed.), *The Anglican Covenant* (London, Mowbray, 2008) 29.

75 Compare the ACADC, preamble: 'The Provinces of the Communion now agree to enter into an Anglican Communion Covenant'; I.1: 'member churches' means a member church of the Communion 'being a church party to this covenant'. SADC avoids the use of 'member church'.

76 Points Raised, Sect. 7: 'No comment.'

77 England, RNDC (2007): in commenting on the expression 'churches of the Anglican Communion' it asks whether the national bodies or the dioceses should be the covenant parties.

of the General Synod.'[78] However, for Australia, the primate has no authority to execute such a covenant;[79] no law authorizes the primate to represent the church 'at large' or specifically to sign a document such as an Anglican covenant; this could be remedied, but might be resisted.[80] Similar concerns have been voiced from the Episcopal Church USA.[81] With regard to the Church of England, by virtue of its established position with the monarch as supreme governor,[82] one respondent points out that the monarch is the appropriate 'treaty-partner' acting on the advice of the secular government; neither the monarch nor the bishops have authority to commit the nation internationally in spiritual matters without legislative aid.[83] For others, the proposal that the primates should be given authority to sign the covenant on behalf of their churches stems from a belief that assent would be significantly more attainable than would be the case if each legislature had to be persuaded separately; but adoption by the Anglican Consultative Council would be to misuse a consultative body to impose regulation on its members.[84] Some recognize, however, that there may be a case for the Anglican Consultative Council (on the basis of its synodical nature) or the Lambeth Conference (on the basis that in it one person from each

---

78 Ireland, Standing Committee of General Synod (25-1-2005) 8.

79 Cameron (2005) 52: Australia, Const. s. 10; Primate Canon 1985–2004: the constitution would have to be amended; its law provides for the functions of the primate, and a canon may give a specific task to the primate.

80 Tong (2005) 55 at 56: by an amendment to the constitution or by a General Synod canon or by a diocesan ordinance authorizing the primate to sign on behalf of that diocese. The response of the Windsor Report Working Group to the requests of the Standing Committee of the General Synod of the Anglican Church of Australia: alternatively, the General Synod might under s. 26 of the Constitution make a resolution to 'declare its view on any matter affecting the Church' and to 'take such steps as may be necessary or expedient in the furtherance of union with other Christian communities'; 'Arguably, the General Synod could, pursuant to such powers, authorize the adoption of a covenant by virtue of a vote garnering a simple majority of 51%'; see also 58 for resistance.

81 DAZ, 55 (Douglas): 'I am decidedly against the process suggested by the Windsor Report that gives blanket authority to the primate of the Episcopal Church to enter such a Covenant. Other churches . . . might give their primates such authority, but this is clearly not our polity. Only the General Convention, the highest legislative body of the Episcopal Church, can enter into covenants on behalf of our church.' However, see above n. 71.

82 England, Can. A7 ('Of the royal supremacy'): 'We acknowledge that the Queen's excellent Majesty, according to the laws of the realm, is the highest power under God in this kingdom, and has supreme authority over all persons in all causes, as well ecclesiastical as civil'; see M. Hill, *Ecclesiastical Law* (3rd edn, Oxford, Oxford University Press, 2007) 1.19.

83 Pearce (2005).

84 MCU (2006) p. 19.

diocese is present) to act as signatories.[85] Another idea is for the house of bishops in each church, or else individual diocesan bishops, to offer a covenant to the Archbishop of Canterbury.[86]

Nevertheless, it is a normal practice that those in episcopal office are signatories in contemporary covenant-making. The Memorandum of Agreement of the Anglican Communion Network is 'undersigned' by bishops as 'representatives' of the affiliating dioceses and convocations.[87] The Covenant Union of Anglican Churches in Concordat was entered by an archbishop and two bishops on behalf of the bodies involved.[88] The Lutheran-Anglican-Roman Catholic (Virginia) Covenant 1990 was entered by bishops.[89] However, the bishop(s) *and* the 'synodical governing body' of the respective member churches are the signatories to the statute of the Old Catholic Bishops united in the Union of Utrecht.[90] In international law, parties must have capacity under their own legal systems to enter an international treaty, and in Roman Catholic canon law today entering concordats is reserved to the pope.[91]

There are some obvious parallels here with the concept of authority for both the administration of and admission to the sacramental covenants. The laws of all churches in the Anglican Communion require that the ministers of the sacramental covenants must be authorized to administer them.[92] Churches also require that parties be authorized by law, in terms of eligibility and qualifications, to enter the baptismal covenant (for infant baptism, godparents or other sponsors must be qualified),[93] marriage (the parties must have capacity under civil

---

85 Cameron, 'Baby's first steps': the ACC because it is the most synodical body at global level; the Lambeth Conference, as its bishops are the chief pastors of their dioceses and therefore in theory most able to speak on behalf of their dioceses, and, it has been argued that the Conference is the most representative body of the Communion since there is at least one person from each diocese present.

86 John Stuart, Secretary General, Scottish Episcopal Church, Letter 5-12-2006.

87 ACN, Memorandum of Agreement; Organizational Charter, Art. IV: 'We, as Dioceses and Convocations, commit ourselves . . .'

88 CUACC (2005): ACNS 4075: the Archbishop of Nigeria, the Presiding Bishop of the Reformed Episcopal Church and the Presiding Bishop of the Anglican Province of America.

89 LARC, Preamble.

90 UOU, Guidelines (2002) 2–4.

91 I. Brownlie, *Principles of International Law* (6th edn, Oxford, Oxford University Press, 2003) 581–3; *New Advent Catholic Encyclopedia*, 'Concordats'.

92 Ordinarily, ordained ministers are authorized to administer baptism, but lay people may administer it in emergencies (e.g. Melanesia, Cans. A.1); only authorized clergy may solemnize a marriage (e.g. New Zealand, Can. G.III.25 and 2.9); only a bishop is authorized to ordain (e.g. TEC, BCP 1979, 577).

93 For example Chile, Can. F1.c.12: confirmed; Scotland, Can. 27.1: they must 'if possible' be communicants; England, Can. B23.4: the minister may dispense with the

and canon law,[94] and, in the case of minors, parental consent);[95] and ordination (the candidate must be baptized, of the requisite age and suitability).[96] In short, on the basis of comparable covenantal instruments, in ecumenism, in other ecclesial traditions, and in Anglican sacramental theology, juridical authorization emerges as a fundamental principle and prerequisite for entry to a covenant.

A Solemn Signature in a Liturgical Context

The Lambeth Commission recommends that the covenant be entered by a solemn signing in a liturgical context, which would represent 'a solemn witness to communion'. Moreover, the formality of ratification by the primates publicly assembled affords a unique opportunity for worldwide witness.[97] This aspect of adoption has attracted little attention from respondents, other than a suggestion by one that 'signing up' helpfully links the doctrinal and the relational aspects of covenanting.[98] Needless to say, a corporate signature in a liturgical context is just one possible method of solemn adoption. The laws of Anglican churches also provide models which could be adapted as a mechanism for adoption of a covenant through incorporation in certain undertakings: by bishops at consecration (or installation);[99] by clergy at ordination and appointment to a ministerial office;[100] by lay officers at their admission to office, and even by the general membership of an institutional church on admission to an electoral roll or other register.[101] In each case, the person making the declaration could undertake adherence to a covenant.[102] Neither the Covenant Design Group (at Nassau

---

requirement of confirmation.

94 For example, Papua New Guinea, Can. No.2 1995; England, Can. B31, B32; Nigeria, Cans 18.5.

95 For example England, Can. B31.

96 Ireland, Const. IX.24; West Indies, Can. 17.6; Japan, Can. II, Art. 15.

97 TWR, paras 118,119; WDAC, Preamble: 'We, the churches of the . . . Communion . . . solemnly establish this Covenant.'

98 Sharing of Ministries Abroad UK (2005) D(3): LCRPR.

99 For example Southern Africa, Can. 8.3: the bishop elect 'pledges' 'to acknowledge the Constitution of this Church' and 'to govern his Diocese in conformity with the Constitution, Laws and Canons' of the church; see also, for example, West Indies, Can. 8.10; Tanzania, Const. IV.12; Sudan, Const., Art. 44.

100 For example Scotland, Can. 12 (Appendix 12): 'I . . . promise . . . I will give all due obedience to the Code of Canons.'

101 For example Wales, Const. VI.3: 'I agree to accept and be bound by the Constitution.'

102 Each church has a system for entry of its membership on a roll or other register. A precondition for admission to the roll is that a person is to make a voluntary declaration

or London) nor the Primates' Meeting 2007 address the matter.

There is a direct parallel here with the sacramental covenants. Churches in the Communion require that admission to baptism, marriage and ordination must be administered in a solemn, public, liturgical context; entry to these covenants must also be witnessed, and registered.[103] Ritualistic covenanting, evident in the scriptural covenants (in which oath-taking is a mark),[104] also surfaces in some contemporary agreements and practices, such as the annual covenant service in Methodism,[105] or the solemn covenanting in the presence of God in the Southern Baptist tradition.[106] Solemnity is also a feature of ecumenical covenanting.[107] The Lutheran-Anglican-Roman Catholic Covenant (Virginia) ends with a prayer: 'May the Holy Spirit, who has brought us to this moment of covenanting, bring us to greater unity.'[108]

Conclusion

The adoption of a covenant through a legislative enactment by each church of its own communion law (either prior to or following a signing) would on the face of it represent a radical innovation in Anglicanism. Several respondents consider that this recommendation of the Lambeth Commission should be resisted on the basis that the use of law would unnecessarily juridify communion. On the one hand, the fear is justified. On the other hand, juridical adoption could be seen to implement the Christian principle that promises should bind (see Chapter 9). It is interesting that the Covenant Design Group and the Primates' Meeting have since Windsor spoken in general terms simply of adoption by synodical process, and the mode of adoption has not attracted systematic comment since Nassau. In any event, every church is free to employ the most appropriate instrument, including legislation,

---

or other undertaking to accept the laws of that church: a covenant could be included on the list of documents which are accepted.

103 See Doe (1998) Chs. 9, 10.

104 D. J. McCarthy, *Treaty and Covenant* (Rome, Biblical Institute Press, 1981) 294; G. P. Hugenberger, *Marriage as a Covenant* (Leiden, E. J. Brill 1994) 182–5; see also N. Lossky *et al.* (eds), *Dictionary of the Ecumenical Movement* (Geneva, WCC, 2002) 268: 'At the centre of the covenant is a solemn call to respect and maintain the integrity of all persons in the community.'

105 CPDMC (2002) para. 608.

106 TCCG, 16: Sample Constitution, IV.

107 The Covenant 1975 of the Churches in Wales: 'Accordingly we enter now into this solemn Covenant before God and with one another, to work and pray in common obedience to our Lord Jesus Christ, in order that by the Holy Spirit we may be brought into one visible Church to serve together in mission to the glory of God the Father.'

108 LARC (1990).

to authorize its commitment to the covenant, and this would most obviously be achieved by constitutional amendment. This mode of adoption of a covenant is increasingly employed in other contexts: sometimes the terms of ecumenical covenants are incorporated into the laws of Anglican churches; the instruments of comparable international ecclesial communities are 'accepted' by their member churches, and their acceptance is a condition of membership of those communities. The sacramental covenants are also adopted in the laws of Anglican churches which commit themselves juridically to the maintenance of the baptismal and ordination covenants. The recommendation of the Lambeth Commission that primates are appropriate signatories of a covenant is consistent with the canonical principle evident in the laws of many churches that a primate represents the church in its international affairs. A primate, however, has no inherent authority to enter a covenant on behalf of a church if that covenant is to be binding – prior synodical authority would have to be obtained. The recommendation for signature in a solemn liturgical context has not attracted much response, but is nonetheless a feature of biblical, sacramental and ecumenical covenanting.

9

The Effects of a Covenant

The effects of a covenant are directly related to its purposes, which include its intended effects. In this sense, the desired effects of a covenant are unity, reconciliation, recommitment, trust, identity, clarity, understanding, order, stability, mission and witness.[1] However, this chapter explores the technical effects of a covenant in terms of: membership of a covenanted Communion; its binding character; discipline and breach of covenant; changeability of a covenant; and implications for the ecclesiality of the Communion. Needless to say, the precise effects, consequences or implications of a covenant will depend on what the covenant in its final version actually says.[2] If the mode of adoption proposed by the Lambeth Commission is employed, it will be legally binding and enforceable as such. If a non-juridical model is used, theologically, it will bind morally, but legally it will be unenforceable.

Membership of the Anglican Communion

The Lambeth Commission stresses that 'the paramount model' for the Communion in any covenanted relationship must remain that of the 'voluntary association'. While the Commission does not explicitly state that membership of a church in the Communion would be conditional on its adoption of the covenant, it hints at this.[3] *Towards an Anglican Covenant* is more forthright on the implications of a covenant upon membership. It recognizes that for some there may be a 'danger' that preparedness to sign up to the covenant becomes a test of authentic membership of the Communion. However, for the covenant to work

---

1 See Ch. 3.
2 TAAC, para. 27; see also Bagshaw (19-6-07). Churches must not have 'high expectations' about its impact: Dioc. of Saskatoon (2006): LRCPR.
3 TWR, para. 120: the ACC could 'encourage full participation in the Covenant project by each church by constructing an understanding of communion membership which is expressed by the readiness of a province to maintain its bonds with Canterbury, and which includes a reference to the Covenant'; WDAC defines membership but does not relate this to adoption (Art. 7.1, 2).

there will need to be a single formulation, not subject to negotiation and opt-outs by each church, but a text around which most Anglican churches can gather. There comes a point at which churches will have to 'take it or leave it'. But it would be wrong 'to assume that failing to sign the covenant meant that a church ceased to be Anglican. The marks of Anglican identity go rather deeper.' Nonetheless, it might be expected that, as time goes on, presumptions about membership would arise between signatory churches and those that do not sign the covenant. What might emerge is a two (or more) tiered Communion, with some level of 'permeability' between churches signed up to the covenant, and those who are not.[4]

The Covenant Design Group at Nassau does not address specifically the issue of membership; but like the Nassau text, the St Andrews draft covenant proposes (somewhat ambiguously) that if churches relinquish the force and meaning of the covenant purpose relinquishment will operate 'until they re-establish their covenant relationship with *other member Churches*'.[5] Apart from this reference, the St Andrews text drops the use of the expression 'member church' – though no explanation for this is given.[6] One respondent is of the opinion that under the Nassau draft, some churches unable to ratify a covenant for reasons of conscience might become like Methodists – historically related to the Anglican Communion and bound by many common traditions, but not members of it.[7] By way of contrast, the draft covenant submitted to the Covenant Design Group by the Anglican Church of Australia is clearer: it actually defines 'member church' of the Anglican Communion by reference to whether or not a church is party to the covenant.[8]

---

4 TAAC, paras 5, 28 ('not 38 or 44 . . . variants on it', one for this and another for that group), 31, 32, and 33; para. 32: in the lengthy period when synodical bodies are considering the Covenant, prior to adoption, they 'will not be "less Anglican" during that period than they are now; and it remains to be seen in what sense they might become "more Anglican" if they decide to adopt it for themselves'; para. 33: but this does not mean that 'the present arrangements for mutual recognition and interchangeability would be swept away by . . . the Covenant'. There might be an interesting parallel here in countries where the Holy See has a concordat with the State, but other religious organizations have 'lesser' agreements with the State (e.g in Spain and Italy): see R. Puza and N. Doe (eds), *Religion and Law in Dialogue* (Leuven, Peeters, 2006).

5 SADC, Cl. 3.2.5e; compare NDC, Art. 6.6: restoration and renewal will be required to re-establish it. The use of 'other' here might suggest that a relinquishing church would still be a member church.

6 The Commentary to SADC, on the Preamble, explains that the expression 'the churches of the Anglican Communion' refers to those churches recognized in the Schedule of Membership of the ACC (including the United Churches).

7 Grieb (2007).

8 ACADC, Pt I; see also its definition of the Anglican Communion: ' "The Anglican Communion" means the member churches of the Anglican Communion, being those churches party to this covenant.'

The primates in 2007 commented that Nassau failed to mention the United Churches and asked about their place in the covenant.[9]

There are those who consider a covenant could effect redefinition of membership of the Communion: churches that refuse to 'curb' their autonomy in a covenant would place *themselves* outside the Communion; those which adopt the covenant would be more closely knit together. Some suggest that it would be difficult to argue that membership of the Communion should *not* be dependent upon agreement to abide by a covenant.[10] For others, the implications for membership are undesirable; a covenant should not be a test of membership, and where unanimity is expected those who in all conscience cannot agree will be obliged to leave.[11] However, the Archbishop of Canterbury has expressed the view that the covenant idea is necessarily an 'opt-in' matter; but this could lead to a situation in which there are 'constituent churches', which sign the covenant, and 'associate churches', which do not.[12] 'Associate' churches would have no direct part in the decision-making of the 'constituent' churches, but might well be observers whose views were sought or whose expertise was shared from time to time, and with whom significant areas of co-operation might be possible. This could mean that churches would need 'to work at ordered and mutually respectful separation between "constituent" and "associated" elements', which could be a positive invitation to clarify the meaning of a global sacramental fellowship.[13] The idea has also been proposed by some respondents;[14] if the Communion were to

---

9 Points Raised, s. 6. Australia, RNDC (2007) suggests that the Preamble formula 'We, the Churches of the Anglican Communion' be changed to 'We, as Churches . . .'. See also Wales, RNDC (2007): this finds the notion of 'member church' unhelpful and prefers 'the participation of constituent churches'. The Commentary to SADC, on the Preamble, however, refers to the United Churches.

10 Davie (2007): a key question is how it might be legitimate for one church to claim a unilateral exemption from a covenant and yet continue membership on its own terms.

11 A. Linzey, 'In defence of diversity', in A. Linzey and R. Kirker (eds), *Gays and the Future of Anglicanism* (Winchester, O Books, 2005) 185; HBTG (2005) 3.5.1; MCU (November 2006).

12 Rowan Williams, 'The Challenge and Hope of Being Anglican Today' (27-06-2006): Churches 'prepared to take this on as an expression of their responsibility to each other would limit their local freedoms for the sake of a wider witness; and some might not be willing to do this'. Consequently, the Communion could arrive at 'a situation where there were "constituent" Churches in covenant in the Anglican Communion and other "churches in association"'. The latter would still be 'bound by historic and perhaps personal links, fed from many of the same sources, but not bound in a single and unrestricted sacramental communion, and not sharing the same constitutional structures'.

13 Ibid.; this might afford 'a chance to rediscover a positive common obedience to the mystery of God's gift that was not a matter of coercion from above but of that "waiting for each other" that St Paul commends to the Corinthians'.

14 Noll (2005) 11: adoption by 'constituent members of the covenant community'; see

be composed of covenanted constituent churches, and non-covenanted associate churches, this would have implications for the membership of the Anglican Consultative Council,[15] and the other Instruments of Communion.[16] Careful thought needs to be given to those who are unable to sign the covenant.[17]

Alternatively, the covenant *itself* could provide for tiers of membership and its consequences. This is common in some, but not all,[18] instruments of comparable international ecclesial communities, several of which have explicit conditions on the recognition of churches for admission to membership.[19] The World Alliance of Reformed Churches has conditions for full and associate membership, and churches may be admitted to the Alliance by its General Council; full members have voting rights in the governing bodies of the Alliance, but associate members do not.[20] While there are 748 Reformed Churches around the world, 218 are members of the Alliance.[21] Reception into the Lutheran World Federation is decided by the Federation in its Assembly; there are elaborate rules on applications and eligibility (including the requirement that a church must be autonomous). The Federation is composed of full members and associate members, the latter entitled to participate in all the activities of the Federation including the right to send representatives to its Assembly where they have a right to speak but not to vote or hold elective office.[22]

---

also Goddard, 'Unity and diversity, communion and covenant', in M. Chapman (ed.), *The Anglican Covenant* (London, Mowbray, 2008) 74, n. 43: more work needs to be done on 'constituent' and 'associate' Anglicans.

15 ACC, Const.: currently there is no distinction between full or associate members (and the assent of two-thirds of the primates is required to alter or add to the schedule of members). Its constitution, therefore, would have to be amended, for example to enable the covenanted churches to be full members, with the right to vote, and to give the associated churches a right to observe; and this amendment would require the consent of two-thirds of the current member churches (which might prove problematic in the case of those which do not adopt a covenant).

16 It might also mean that while covenanted churches would benefit from the rights and duties contained in the covenant, non-covenanted churches would have to develop relations of communion with the covenanted churches on a church-by-church basis.

17 Bishop Brown (Dioc. of Wellington) (2006): in ministerial covenants, clergy who have not signed on are 'treated the same as everyone else'.

18 SCOBA: its constitution does not have classes of membership.

19 Some alliances have complex provisions on the recognition of churches: for example, Guidelines of the International Bishops Conference with Respect to the Recognition of a Church as an Independent Old-Catholic Church of the Utrecht Union (2002).

20 WARC, Const. Arts 1.2, 1.4, II.1; By-Laws, I.1, I.2: they may also be admitted by its Executive Committee.

21 See generally Lossky *et al.* (2002) 1217.

22 LWF, Const., Art. V.1 and 2; Bylaws, 2. The LWF 'shall exercise its functions through the Assembly, the Council, the Secretariat and appropriate instrumentalities of the member churches. In all these functions of the Federation, ordained and lay persons,

Similarly, ecumenical covenants sometimes provide for tiers of membership of different covenantal commitments as between the alliance members. For example, in the Australian Churches' Covenant fifteen churches are party to the declaration of intent and are committed to common prayer, to intercede and care for one another, and to explore Christian convictions and their application.[23] Eleven agree to support initiatives for sharing physical resources, such as buildings, and to encourage consultation between the appropriate governing bodies of the churches before new major developments are undertaken.[24] Eight agree to explore strategies for mission;[25] nine agree to mutual recognition of baptisms;[26] two churches agree to eucharistic sharing;[27] and four pairs of churches agree to work towards mutual recognition of ordained ministry.[28] All fifteen churches pledge to discuss and articulate the meaning of their involvement in the quest for more visible expression of unity and to explore further steps to make more clearly visible the unity of all Christian people.[29] The churches name each other 'as a sign of what we can covenant to do together'.[30] Such a model as this for an Anglican covenant could enable a more sophisticated range of possible relationships, affirmations and commitments within the Communion.

---

men, women and youth shall be eligible to participate' (Art. VI). The Assembly is 'the principal authority' of the LWF and consists of representatives of the member churches; it shall: be responsible for the constitution; give general direction to the work of the Federation; elect the President and the members of the Council; act on the reports of the President, the General Secretary and the Treasurer. Meetings are to be held normally every six years; and each church has 'the right to . . . at least one representative' (Art. VII). The Council is responsible for the business of the Federation between ordinary Assemblies (Art. VIII). National committees, officers, secretariat, and finances are treated in Arts IX–XIII. The constitution may be amended by a two-thirds majority vote at the ordinary Assembly (Art. XIV.1). The Council and Assembly may adopt, amend, or rescind bylaws by majority vote (Art. XIV.2).

23 ACCT, The Covenanting Document, Part B, The Proposed Commitment, a. General (e.g. Romanian Orthodox Church is not party to this; Anglicans, Lutherans and Roman Catholics, for example, are).

24 Ibid.: Anglicans, Lutherans, Greek Orthodox and Roman Catholics, for example are party to this.

25 Ibid.: the Romanian Orthodox Church, for example, is not party to this, but the Anglicans, Lutherans and Roman Catholics, for example, are.

26 Ibid.: for example Anglicans, Lutherans, Greek Orthodox, and Roman Catholics are party.

27 Ibid.: for example Churches of Christ in Australia with Uniting Church in Australia.

28 Ibid.: Anglican with Lutheran; Anglican with Uniting Church; Churches of Christ with Uniting Church; Lutheran with Uniting Church.

29 Ibid., Part C: The Future Pledge.

30 Ibid., Affirmation of Commitment.

Covenants are Binding: *Pacta Sunt Servanda*

As has already been seen, the Lambeth Commission proposed that a covenant could address the 'persistent problem' in Anglicanism of how to make the principles of inter-Anglican relations more effective at the local ecclesial level. A covenant adopted by legislative enactment of each church would bind those churches legally. This would be symbolized further at a solemn signature in a liturgical context.[31] The Windsor draft covenant clearly envisages its own binding effect on churches, and many of its provisions are cast in terms of rights and duties.[32] Most respondents recognize that if adopted by legislative enactment, a covenant would bind.[33] Moreover, for many, a covenant should bind to effect mutual accountability: a 'non-binding covenant policy . . . would have little impact'.[34] Similarly, the Archbishop of Canterbury has suggested that the Communion needs adequately developed structures and more visible formal commitments to translate the underlying sacramental communion into a more effective institutional reality; that is, 'a scheme . . . that will hold', but: 'No-one can impose the canonical and structural changes that will be necessary.'[35] In 2007, neither the Covenant Design Group nor the Primates' Meeting dealt with the matter of the binding effect of a covenant, principally because they seemed to leave open the mode of adoption beyond the acceptance by synodical process in each church 'if the covenant was to be received and have any strength or reality'.[36] The same applies to the meeting of the Group in London in 2008.

On the other hand, clear agreement on the authority of a covenant is essential.[37] Many argue that a covenant should not bind the churches: Anglicans need mechanisms 'to bind us, but not to tie us up'.[38] Consequently, they think that a binding covenant would: make the Communion less free and more coercive, at the expense of conviction and conscience; inhibit, or replace, the work of the Holy Spirit; stifle change and diversity; and oblige members to submit innovations in theology or ethics to the Instruments of Communion, thereby increasing the

---

31 TWR, paras 118, 119. See Ch. 8 above.

32 See above Ch. 6.

33 Tong (2005) 57; Pearce (2005); Wescott House: LCRPR.

34 Dioc. of Saskatoon (2006); see also Bishop Kelsey, TEC (2004); RTT (2004) para. 55: LCRPR.

35 Williams, 'Challenge and hope'.

36 CDG, Report, para. 8; under the Nassau draft itself, of course, consequences do follow in the event of breach of covenant: see below for NDC, Art. 6.6.

37 Michael Doe (2006). See also Hong Kong, RNDC.

38 TEC, s. 4: LCRPR.

likelihood of disagreement.[39] Moreover, there is a view that a covenant cannot limit the territorial authority of a bishop, or fetter discretions which laws assign to bodies or persons in the local church.[40] Similarly, if a covenant binds, some respondents fear disputes about compatibility between the laws of churches and the covenant,[41] though, a covenant could itself deal with this in a variety of ways.[42] Consequently, a non-binding model is more appropriate,[43] and some offer the baptismal covenant, with its moral authority, as an alternative model.[44] For *Towards an Anglican Covenant*, however, a binding covenant need not require uniformity in all things; it could provide for a wide range of Christian 'emphases',[45] by indicating how 'agreement to disagree' on other issues might be reached.[46]

---

39 Dioc. of Saskatoon; CIPRWR (2005), 11; RTT, para. 20; L. W. Countryman, 'Politics, polity and the Bible as hostage', in A. Linzey and R. Kirker (eds), *Gays and the Future of Anglicanism* (Winchester, O Books, 2005) 8; Greer (2005) 113; DAZ, 61 (Douglas); SECR (2005) para. 7.4; Adams (2005) 70; MCU (2006) Summary, p. 2.

40 G. Jones, 'Thy Grace shall always prevent', in Linzey and Kirker (2005) 134–5; A. Pearce 'English ecclesiastical autonomy and the Windsor Report' (2005) 8.

41 Pearce (2005) 12: for example, on the basis of the Windsor draft covenant, in the Church of England, if a cleric solemnized the marriage of a divorced person, an Instrument of Unity could hold that the cleric unreasonably became a focus of division (WDAC, Art. 13.2); but English ecclesiastical law leaves such matters to the conscience of the cleric; an English court would not be able to uphold the English position but would be obliged to subordinate it to a covenant; in this sense an Instrument of Unity could effectively override 'substantial tracts of English ecclesiastical law'; this might reduce the appeal of the church as a national church.

42 First, a covenant could incorporate the principle of law that later laws abrogate inconsistent earlier laws: in this case a covenant would prevail over inconsistent domestic church law. Second, a covenant could provide for a church body to issue a declaration of incompatibility; then the central church assembly would either have a duty or a right to alter the law to ensure compatibility. This is the position in the UK under the Human Rights Act 1998. Third, a covenant could provide that the covenant must prevail over the domestic church law: this function could be assigned either to a domestic church body or to an instrument of unity. This is the position in the UK under the European Communities Act 1972. Pearce (2005) 12: again in relation to the Church of England, such problems might narrow the appeal of the Church of England in its homeland and perhaps lead to its disestablishment.

43 M. Percy, 'On being stretched', in Linzey and Kirker (2005) 227.

44 Bishop Bruce (Ontario): Lambeth website.

45 TAAC, para. 29: 'It is part of the genius of Anglicanism that it has proved capable of embracing a wide range of Christian emphases derived from many sources. Successive Lambeth Conferences have emphasized the role of cultural diversity, social change, and theological development, and have demonstrated that there is a proper place in our life together for change and disagreement as well as for consistency and continuity.'

46 TAAC, para. 30: and 'what processes might be used to foster trust and unity during periods of extended or sensitive discernment. It could set out strategies for protecting conscientious objectors to such developments within an authentically Anglican understanding of catholicity, and propose mechanisms for handling fundamental differences of view.'

While the principles of inter-Anglican relations (typically enunciated by the Lambeth Conference) are conventional in nature, and do
not bind legally,[47] Anglicans are familiar with the concept of binding juridical agreements operative at the global level. The constitution
of the Anglican Consultative Council binds the members when they
participate in its work.[48] The Covenant Union of Anglican Churches
in Concordat seems to bind its members, but the exercise of ministry
in each church is subject to the respective regulations of that church.[49]
Somewhat less robustly, the Anglican Global Initiative proposes that
its members *respect* the historic role and authority entrusted to the
Archbishop of Canterbury, the Primates' Meeting, and the Lambeth
Conference.[50] The salvific covenant binds (but not juridically).[51] The
sacramental covenants bind (juridically).[52] By way of contrast, the
Covenant on Communion and Mission does not bind juridically.[53]
Similarly, many ecumenical covenants are merely directory,[54] not
mandatory.[55] On the other hand, when incorporated in the law of an
Anglican church, an ecumenical agreement becomes legally binding.[56]

Models from comparable international ecclesial communities are
instructive here. Some agreements bind on the basis of their formal
acceptance by churches on admission to membership.[57] Others require
member churches to take those agreements into account in making
decisions at the local level.[58] Under some agreements the decisions of

---

47 See above Ch. 2.

48 Also, see for example ACC, Guidelines for Meetings, 4.1: 'In their contributions to
discussion members shall pay proper respect to the chair of the session and in particular
shall have regard to the duties of the chair under 3.2'; 4.4: 'Members may not speak
unless called upon to do so by the chair of the session, and, if called upon to speak, shall
address their remarks through the chair.'

49 CUACC (2005) Art. 4.

50 AGI, Draft Const., Art. IV.3: the ACC is not listed.

51 And a covenant binds its successors: God's covenants include the successive generations of the person with whom he joins himself in covenant. As in the case of Adam (Gen.
1.27–28; 3.15; Hos. 6.7; Rom. 5.12–18; 1 Cor. 15.22); Noah (Gen. 6.18, 9.9), Abraham
(Gen. 17.7), Moses (Exod. 20.4–6, 8–12; 31.16), Aaron (Lev. 24.8-9), Phineas (Num.
25.13), David (2 Chron. 13.5) and people of the new covenant (Isa. 59.21).

52 These bind in the sense that juridical consequences flow from admission to them:
N. Doe, *Canon Law in the Anglican Communion* (Oxford, Clarendon Press, 1998)
241ff.

53 CCM, 9: it seeks to provide 'nourishment, guidance and strength for the journey
of the covenant partners together'.

54 AMC:CS (2001) paras 1, 44: it is not incorporated in the laws of the two
churches.

55 *Charta Oecumenica* (2001) Preamble: 'it has no magisterial character, nor is it
legally binding'.

56 Wales, Can. 28-9-1995, Sched. 1(b).

57 See Ch. 8.

58 CPCE:LA, Arts 42–46.

the central body of the community bind only that body,[59] and these decisions do not bind in relation to matters within the competence of the autonomous member churches.[60] However, in the Old Catholics' Union of Utrecht, bishops must attend meetings of the International Bishops' Conference, initiate in their churches a discussion of prescribed matters, communicate conference decisions to those churches in matters of faith and ethical behaviour, implement conference decisions on discipline, organization, and common endeavours, and bring to the attention of the conference non-reception of conference decisions; and no bishop may consecrate a bishop in another church without the consent of the conference.[61]

That a covenant will bind is a fundamental consequence of its nature as a solemn committed agreement, which itself is a feature of the contractual dimension of covenants.[62] Contractual agreements and the promises on which they are based, are legally binding. A contract is more than a statement of intention: it generates duties to fulfil promises; this is a moral and legal obligation. Promises bind, if accepted or if relied upon. The idea is summed up in the canonical principle *pacta sunt servanda*: agreements are to be performed.[63] This principle has a long canonical history.[64] Provided there is a legitimate cause for them, all promises must be observed as a matter of 'good faith', regardless of whether there has been compliance with strict formalities.[65] Indeed, the principle *pacta sunt servanda* is also central to the customary international law of treaties and, according to some authorities, the very foundation of international law: without it, treaties would be worthless; a treaty in force is binding upon the parties and must be per-

---

59 SCOBA, Const., Art. II(a)1.

60 See Ch. 5 for the protection of autonomy of member churches.

61 SOC 2000, B. Order, Art. 4(a)–(g), Art. 11.

62 See above Ch. 1.

63 E. A. Martin (ed.), *Oxford Dictionary of Law* (5th edn, Oxford, Oxford University Press, 2003) 114; A. G. Guest (ed.), *Anson's Law of Contract* (24th edn, Oxford, Oxford University Press, 1975) 2; P. S. Atiyah, *Promises, Morals and Law* (Oxford, Clarendon Press, 1981) Ch. 1; J. Finnis *Natural Law and Natural Rights* (Oxford, Clarendon Press, 1980) 288, 298ff.

64 The Roman Catholic Church today recognizes explicitly that contracts bind the Church: Code of Canon Law, c. 639: 'A juridic person which has contracted debts and obligations even with the permission of the superior is bound to answer for them.' Canon 1290: 'Whatever general and specific regulation on contracts and payments are determined in civil law for a given territory are to be observed in canon law with the same effects in a matter which is subject to the governing power of the Church, unless the civil regulations are contrary to divine law or canon law makes some other provision, with due regard for the prescriptions of can. 1547.'

65 A. W. Jeremy, '*Pacta sunt servanda*: the influence of canon law upon the development of contractual obligations', *Law and Justice* 144 (2000) 4.

formed by them in good faith.[66] This principle has been accepted by the Roman Catholic Church with regard to its church–state concordats, which override the domestic law of the church:[67] On the other hand, if a covenant is not adopted by law, but functions like the tacit covenant currently operative in the Communion (see above Chapter 2), and many ecumenical covenants, it would be similar to 'soft-obligation' agreements in the secular international sphere. These are increasingly used, and are not legally binding, but nevertheless may generate expectations of compliance. The evidence suggests that compliance with them can be effective. Such agreements are followed not because of the sacred aura of their texts but because they enable the attainment of valuable purposes.[68]

Discipline and Breach of Covenant

Enforceability of a covenant

The Lambeth Commission proposal for juridical adoption would mean that a covenant would be enforceable within the local church in the exercise of its own autonomy.[69] The Windsor draft covenant proposes a system of both local and global resolution of covenantal disputes in a communion spirit by means of (1) reconciliation, mediation or other amicable or equitable means; (2) informal liaison within the Communion; (3) guidance from the Archbishop of Canterbury; and, as a last resort (4) resolution by an Instrument of Communion.[70] However, the primates in 2005 were cautious of any development which would seem to imply the creation of an international jurisdiction which would override proper provincial autonomy.[71] *Towards an*

---

66 Martin (2003) 350; M. Evans, *International Law* (Oxford, Oxford University Press, 2003) 121-2; Brownlie (2003) 591ff; Vienna Convention, Arts, 26,42.

67 Code (1983) c.3: the Code does not abrogate the agreements entered into by the Apostolic See with nations or other civil entities; they will 'continue to be integrally honoured': *Letter and Spirit*, para. 8.

68 D. M. Johnston, *Consent and Commitment in the World Community* (New York, Transnational Publishers, 1997) xxiv; see also D. Shelton 'International law and "relative normativity"', in Evans (2003) 145, 169–171; see also: D. Shelton (ed.), *Commitment and Compliance: The Role of Non-Binding Norms in the International Legal System* (Oxford, Oxford University Press, 2000); see also M. Koskenniemi 'What is international law for?', in M. Evans (ed.), *International Law* (Oxford, Oxford University Press, 2003) 97.

69 Each church would be free to employ its own mechanism for enforcement, executive, quasi-judicial or judicial (e.g. through proceedings in its own courts or tribunals).

70 WDAC, Arts 16.2, 26.1, 26.3.

71 *Communiqué*, 24-2-05, para. 9.

Anglican Covenant recognizes similar concerns, but acknowledges that a covenant could provide an agreed framework for the prevention and resolution of conflict.[72]

The draft covenant submitted by the Anglican Church of Australia to the Covenant Design Group prior to its Nassau meeting proposes an innovative enforcement scheme on the basis that member churches acknowledge that discord and conflict will arise from time to time within the Communion and that the expectations of member churches, of themselves and of each other, will not always be met.[73] It also provides that the Instruments of Communion may be asked to mediate in situations of disagreement or conflict between member churches, but the instruments themselves should have no coercive jurisdiction.[74] The Australian draft covenant provides for its own enforceability by means of self-limitation.[75] Member churches and the Instruments of Communion may advise a church whether a matter is suitable for a process of reception but the latter may not require such process.[76] However, a member church should not lightly take action in a matter about which it has been advised by one or more member churches or by one or more of the Instruments of Communion that a process of reception would be inappropriate.[77] If a member church is advised that a process of reception is appropriate, it may embark upon the action proposed, taking into account the recommendations of the other churches or the Instruments of Communion.[78]

---

72 TAAC, paras 5, 10, 17: if a covenant involves 'some ceding of jurisdiction to the Archbishop of Canterbury, or to one or more of the Instruments of Communion', then many would have 'serious reservations about signing up'.

73 ACADC, Art. 28.

74 ACADC, Art. 31; see also Arts 13–16.

75 ACADC, Arts 18 and 19.

76 ACADC, Art. 23: a member church and the instruments of communion should consider whether the development or action: is one about which the Communion has not so far clearly expressed its mind; is one about which the Communion has previously expressed its mind, but in respect of which at least one member church and one of the instruments of communion are in favour of further consideration; is not explicitly against current Anglican teaching; is consistent with the fundamental declarations of the covenant; may be seen to preserve the essential principles of existing Anglican teaching; may be seen to bring about a convergence or the uniting of accepted doctrines, ideas or principles; has been subject to sustained theological debate and discussion at both provincial and Communion levels; has been the subject of consultation and advice from throughout the Communion through its instruments of communion; has been informed by ecumenical consensus, with the initiatives, debate and scrutiny of other churches having been taken into account.

77 ACADC, Art. 24.

78 ACADC, Art. 25: the actions should be followed by further consultation both within the member church and within the Communion, to assess the extent to which consensus is or is not emerging in relation to the development or action.

The Nassau report of the Covenant Design Group does not explicitly address the issue of enforceability. However, as we have seen, its Nassau draft provides that in essential matters of common concern each church must have regard to the common good of the Communion, and support the work of the Instruments of Communion. It must seek with fellow churches, through the shared councils of the church, a common mind about such matters, and heed the counsel of the Instruments of Communion in matters which threaten the unity of the Communion and the effectiveness of its mission. While the Instruments of Communion have no juridical or executive authority in (to enforce the covenant against) the churches, they do carry a moral authority commanding respect. Each church must seek the guidance of the instruments in cases of serious dispute which cannot be resolved by mutual admonition and counsel. In such cases, each church must submit the matter to the Primates' Meeting. If the primates believe that the matter is not one for which a common mind has been articulated, they will seek it with the other instruments and their councils. On this basis, the primates would offer guidance and direction.[79]

Respondents are divided on the matter. First, there is the question of whether a covenant should contain a mechanism for its enforcement. On the one hand, several consider that non-compliance and lack of mechanisms for discipline at a global level are a concern; there should be consequences for stepping outside the bounds of a covenant; indeed, discipline has strong biblical support.[80] Therefore, the covenant should be clear about which authorities are to police it, the processes involved and how these will be used and might be abused; but the covenant must not be a tool by which one side dominates or berates another.[81] One suggestion is that a covenant should provide that a church must refrain from intervention in the affairs of another except in extraordinary circumstances where such intervention has been specifically authorized by the relevant Instrument of Communion.[82] On the other hand, there are those who argue that the Communion already has the 'power' to exercise discipline: the problem is not a failure of structure,

---

79 NDC, Art. 6.1, 6.3, 6.4, 6.5. See also ACADC, Part 5. See also WDAC, Art. 19.2: each church shall be free from control by any decision of any ecclesiastical body external to itself in relation to its exclusively internal affairs unless that decision is authorized under or incorporated in its own law. See generally Doe (1998) 343–50 for the status of decisions of the instruments of communion.

80 Iglesia Anglicana del Cono Sur de America; Evangelical Alliance: Hilborn; Dioc. of Saskatoon (8-1-2006): HBTG (2005) 3.8.3: Mat. 18.15–20; 1 Cor. 5.1–5; 2 Thess. 3.14–15, 1 Tim. 1.20.

81 Michael Doe (2006): otherwise this would represent a new colonialism.

82 England, RNDC (2007).

but a failure of nerve.[83] At the other extreme, many respondents argue that a covenant should not be disciplinary: people must be allowed to follow their consciences; enforcement would lead to interventionism and the erosion of provincial autonomy, which is at odds with the dynamic of synodical government.[84] It has also been suggested that an enforceable covenant would be too Calvinist or foundationalist, representing too 'impersonal' a focus of unity which would be subject to interpretation by lawyers rather than by bishops and synods.[85]

Second, many criticized the Nassau proposal that the Primates' Meeting would be the principal body which would use the covenant as a means to bring the practices of a province holding a minority view on a contentious matter into line with the view of a majority of the primates themselves (so that the Communion speaks only with one voice).[86] Indeed, the Joint Standing Committee of the Primates' Meeting and Anglican Consultative Council concede that giving priority to the primates is controversial and that thought needs to be given to the development of the Council in this regard, particularly in a family of churches which thinks synodically.[87] Similarly, if the primates become the 'enforcers' of the covenant, this would be a dangerous and unaccountable concentration of power which could reduce the role of the Anglican Consultative Council.[88] Consequently, since Nassau, churches have suggested that the Primates' Meeting under a covenant should be permitted only to 'advise and guide' on the basis of a 'polity of persuasion'.[89]

---

83 Dioc. of Sydney (2005). See also Scully (2007): including the Chicago-Lambeth Quadrilateral; FOFAD, 39: structures already exist for withdrawal of fellowship.

84 CAS (2005) 2; Pearce (2005) 10; Church Society (2004) 6.3; SECR (2005) 1; see also Sharp (2007): it would 'derail local autonomy'; Church of North India, Minutes of 75th Meeting of the Synod Executive Committee, 17–19 February 2005.

85 MCU (Nov. 2006); moreover: 'secular courts may claim jurisdiction to interpret the Covenant if a dispute were brought before them (in the manner in which they adjudicate contracts, disputed constitutions of voluntary associations and other bodies, and may have power to determine interpretation of international law)'; see also MCU (2007) para. 4.1.

86 Grieb (2007); see also Archbishop B. Morgan, A talk to the Governing Body of the Church in Wales, September 2007, www.churchinwales.org.uk/structure/bishops/sermons/b25: implementation of the covenant will be in the hands of the Primates' Meeting and 'the way that some of the primates have behaved does not give me great hope of entrusting the interpretation and the implementation of the terms of the Covenant to them'.

87 Points Raised, s.6.5.

88 MCU (2007) paras 4.4; 4.7.

89 Australia, RNDC (2007); England, RNDC (2007): it would be unlawful for the General Synod to delegate its decision-making powers to the primates, and therefore the Church of England could not sign up to a covenant which gives the primates a power of 'direction'; Wales, RNDC (2007): 'The language of [the NDC] indicates a change of em-

THE EFFECTS OF A COVENANT

Third, some propose creation of a new body to function in cases of dispute. The Inter-Anglican Theological and Doctrinal Commission recognize that a covenant will need a body to interpret it,[90] as well as an advisory body on theological developments with a duty to report publicly to the Archbishop of Canterbury, Anglican Consultative Council, Primates' Meeting and Lambeth Conference. The functions of the body should be to clarify issues at stake, to identify the agreements and disagreements, and to shape a view of things in the light of the Anglican heritage of scriptural faith. Its reports would represent a growing corpus of wisdom on the nature of Anglican faith in relation to matters drawn out of the actual life of the churches.[91] The Commission also proposes an arbitration model for dispute resolution.[92] However, the Inter-Anglican Standing Commission on Ecumenical Relations, while it agrees that there is a need for an agreed mechanism to apply the covenant, criticizes the suggestion of the Inter-Anglican Theological and Doctrinal Commission.[93]

The St Andrews draft covenant offers a solution to these concerns in its Appendix. This contains Framework Procedures for the Resolution of Covenant Disagreements, designed to implement the principles and procedural elements of the draft covenant (consultation, evaluation, mediation, reception of requests and autonomy).[94] This provides that all processes for the resolution of covenant disagreements which threaten the unity of the Communion and the effectiveness or cred-

---

phasis from autonomous provincial government, with consultation, to a global body with central authority for leadership and powers of exclusion'; see also Southern Africa, RNDC.

90 RPC, para. 3.3; see also 5.1.

91 Ibid., para. 5.

92 IATDC: ACNS 4116 (23-2-2006): There should be structures for disputes: 'Disputes in the Church may be on many issues' (e.g. discipline); they may arise for many reasons: failure of communication, misunderstandings, jealousy and the 'sheer richness of the Gospel' and the difficulty in deciding amidst a number of possibilities as to what is the faithful way forward: 'Attention to the concerns of other churches within the Communion is important for putting those of each local church into a proper perspective'. 'At every level, the practice of koinonia requires that there are those who have responsibility to arbitrate in disputes and conflicts vital to our shared life . . . arbitration gains its force from the ties that bind us together in a worldwide communion. The church then needs to develop structures for testing, reconciliation and restraint.' Conflict resolution and 'the kinds of sanctions exercised in the church are thus primarily persuasive compared with those of a coercive or judicial kind. The church would be 'failing in its duty' if it did not work hard 'to deal with disputed matters', striving for reconciliation and implementing appropriate sanctions where necessary. 'The church needs those structures which allow such arbitration to take place. These structures will be both formal and informal and involve face-to-face relations as befits the communion of Jesus Christ.'

93 IASCER (8-12-2006) para. 9.

94 SADC, Cl. 3.2.5; Commentary to SADC: the Appendix is a 'tentative draft'; see Ch. 6 above.

ibility of its mission must be characterized by the Christian virtues of charity, humility, patience and gentleness and the canonical principles of fairness, transparency, and reasoned decision-making.[95] No process shall affect the autonomy of any church of the Communion,[96] or exceed five years.[97] Perhaps above all, any matter involving relinquishment by a church of the force and meaning of the covenant purposes must be decided solely by that church or by the Anglican Consultative Council.[98] Subject to prescribed substantive and procedural safeguards, the Framework Procedures themselves are to be supplemented by rules made by Communion bodies and Instruments involved in their administration.[99]

If a church proposes to act or acts in any way that another church or an Instrument of Communion claims to threaten the unity of the Communion and the effectiveness or credibility of its mission, then the churches involved and the instrument must engage in informal conversation, as an act of communion, to try to resolve the matter.[100] If the church which acts or proposes to act considers thereby that these might threaten Communion unity or mission, or if informal conversation fails (in the view of any of the parties), then that church must consult the Archbishop of Canterbury on the matter.[101] Within one month of being consulted, the Archbishop must either (a) seek to resolve the matter personally through pastoral guidance or (b) refer the matter to three assessors, appointed as appropriate by the Archbishop.[102] Having considered whether the matter involves a threat to Communion unity or mission, the assessors must recommend to the Archbishop, within one month of receiving the referral, one of four routes depending on

---

95 SADC, App. 1.1.

96 SADC, App. 1.2: 'church' and all terms in the Appendix take their meaning from the covenant itself.

97 SADC, App. 1.3: as from the date upon which a church consults under Para. 3.

98 SADC, App. 1.4: the ACC must act in accordance with Para. 8: see below.

99 SADC, App. 1.5: each Communion body or instrument involved in the following procedures shall make its own rules, in consultation with the other Instruments of Communion, for the transaction of its business in accordance with the Covenant, the Framework Procedures and the Christian virtues and canonical principles set out in Para. 1.1.

100 SADC, App. 2.1. However, under 2.2, any Instrument of Communion which asserts such a claim is disqualified from making under the procedures a decision as to relinquishment of the force and meaning of the purposes of the Covenant (namely, the ACC). This is designed to ensure fairness.

101 SADC, App. 3.1: the principle of consultation.

102 SADC, App. 3.2; 3.3: if after one month of its issue, the pastoral guidance of the Archbishop is unsuccessful as determined by the Archbishop, the Archbishop shall as soon as practically possible refer the matter to the Assessors who shall act in accordance with Para. 3.4.

how clear and immediate the threat is.[103] The Archbishop, having considered the recommendation, and within one month of receipt, shall either: (a) issue a request to any church involved; (b) refer the matter to another Instrument of Communion; (c) refer the matter to a commission of the Communion for evaluation; or (d) send the matter for mediation.[104]

Route 1: A request of the Archbishop of Canterbury When the Archbishop makes a request to a church, that church must within six months of receipt (a) accept or (b) reject the request. The absence of a response will be considered as a rejection.[105] If a church rejects the request, it may within three months of rejection appeal to the Joint Standing Committee of the Anglican Consultative Council and Primates' Meeting; it may appeal when it considers that there has been no threat to Communion mission or unity.[106] On appeal, and within three months, the Committee must decide whether there has been a threat to Communion unity or mission.[107] If the appeal is successful, the Committee must certify immediately that the matter is closed.[108] If the appeal is lost, the Archbishop shall submit the request, rejection and appeal decision to the Anglican Consultative Council to deal with the rejection.[109]

Route 2: A referral to another Instrument of Communion When the Archbishop of Canterbury refers the matter to another Instrument of Communion, that Instrument must within one year of receipt decide whether there has been a threat to Communion unity or mission. Having considered the matter, the Instrument shall make a request to any church involved.[110] A church must within six months of receipt

---

103 Namely: (a) if it is clear in the opinion of the Assessors that the matter involves a threat to Communion unity or mission and that time may be of the essence, a request from the Archbishop of Canterbury; (b) if it is unclear in the opinion of the Assessors whether the matter involves a threat to Communion unity or mission and time is of the essence, referral to another Instrument of Communion; (c) if it is unclear in the opinion of the Assessors whether the matter involves a threat to Communion unity and mission, if time is not of the essence, and if the case would benefit from rigorous theological study, referral to a Commission for evaluation; or: (d) if it is clear that the matter does not involve a threat to Communion unity or mission, mediation: SADC, App. 3.4(a)–(d).

104 SADC, App. 3.5.

105 SADC, App. 4.1.

106 SADC, App. 4.2.

107 SADC, App. 4.3.

108 SADC, App. 4.4: it is closed subject to Cls. 3.2.1, 3.2.4 and 3.2.5b of the Covenant.

109 SADC, App. 4.5: the ACC shall deal with it in accordance with Para. 8: see below.

110 SADC, App. 5.1.

either (a) accept or (b) reject the request. The absence of a response is deemed a rejection.[111] If a church accepts the request, the Instrument of Communion to which referral is made must as soon as is convenient certify that the matter is closed.[112] If a church rejects the request, that Instrument of Communion must at its next meeting submit the request and rejection to the Anglican Consultative Council to deal with the matter.[113]

Route 3: An evaluation by a commission When the Archbishop of Canterbury decides to refer the matter to a commission in the Communion, he shall choose which commission in consultation with the Secretary General of the Anglican Communion.[114] The commission must engage in study of the issues involved in the matter, bringing in expertise as needed, and evaluate the acceptability of the act or proposed act of any church involved.[115] Within eighteen months of the referral, the commission must submit its evaluation to an Instrument of Communion other than the Anglican Consultative Council as determined by the Archbishop of Canterbury. Having considered the evaluation, the Instrument of Communion must issue a request to any church involved.[116] If a church accepts the request, the Instrument of Communion must certify as soon as is convenient that the matter is closed.[117] If a church rejects the request, that Instrument of Communion must send the request and rejection to the Anglican Consultative Council to deal with the matter.[118]

Route 4: Mediation When the Archbishop of Canterbury decides on mediation, the assessors must work with the parties to set up a mediation process.[119] The parties must appoint an independent third party who must assist them to achieve a mutually acceptable resolution of the points of disagreement.[120] The mediator must participate actively in the mediation, offering suggestions for resolution, trying to reconcile opposing assertions, and appeasing feelings of resentment

111 SADC, App. 5.2.

112 SADC, App. 5.3: it is closed subject to Cls 3.2.1, 3.2.4 and 3.2.5b of the Covenant.

113 SADC, App. 5.4: the ACC shall deal with it in accordance with Para. 8: see below.

114 SADC, App. 6.1. Note: This is without prejudice to the entitlement of any other Instrument of Communion requesting the Archbishop to setting up Commissions or to any other Instrument of Communion likewise setting up such Commissions.

115 SADC, App. 6.2.

116 SADC, App. 6.3.

117 SADC, App. 6.4: it is closed subject to Cls 3.2.1, 3.2.4 and 3.2.5b of the Covenant.

118 SADC, App. 6.5: the ACC must act in accordance with Para. 8: see below.

119 SADC, App. 7.1.

120 SADC, App. 7.2.

between the parties.[121] The mediator has no decision-making authority and cannot compel the parties to accept a settlement.[122] On each
anniversary of the establishment of the mediation, the assessors must
report on the process to the Archbishop of Canterbury. Within three
years of establishing the mediation, the Archbishop together with the
Joint Standing Committee of the Anglican Consultative Council and
Primates' Meeting must certify the conclusion of the mediation process.[123] If a party refuses to enter mediation, it will be presumed to
have threatened the unity of the Communion and the effectiveness or
credibility of its mission, and the matter shall be dealt with at the next
meeting of the Anglican Consultative Council.[124]

Rejection of a Request from an Instrument of Communion: If a
party rejects a request of an Instrument of Communion, that Instrument must send the request and rejection to the Anglican Consultative Council.[125] At its next meeting, the Council must decide whether
the rejection is compatible with the covenant.[126] If the Council decides
that the rejection of the request is compatible with the covenant, the
matter is closed.[127] If the Council decides that the rejection is incompatible with the covenant, then during the course of that meeting of
the Council either (a) the church party may declare voluntarily that it
relinquishes the force and meaning of the purposes of the Covenant,
or (b) the Council must resolve whether the party may be understood
to have relinquished the force and meaning of the purposes of the
covenant.[128] If a declaration or resolution of relinquishment is issued,
the Anglican Consultative Council must as soon as is practicable initiate a process of restoration with the church involved in consultation
with all the churches of the Communion and the other Instruments of
Communion.[129]

With these procedures, the St Andrews draft is unlike other contemporary Anglican agreements and ecumenical covenants: these do not
generally deal with the prevention or resolution of disagreements.
Charta Oecumenica is a rarity: in the event of conflicts between
churches, efforts towards mediation and peace should be initiated

---

121 SADC, App. 7.3.
122 SADC, App. 7.4.
123 SADC, App. 7.5.
124 SADC, App. 7.6: the ACC must act in accordance with Para. 8: see below.
125 SADC, App. 8.1.
126 SADC, App. 8.2.
127 SADC, App. 8.3: subject to Cls 3.2.1, 3.2.4 and 3.2.5b of the covenant.
128 SADC, App. 8.4.
129 SADC, App. 8.5.

and/or supported as needed.[130] This seems to mirror secular systems of alternative dispute resolution: mediation,[131] conciliation,[132] and arbitration.[133] Nor is the subject usually dealt with in the instruments of comparable international ecclesial communities; certainly, no authority is given to a central body to intervene in the internal affairs of a member church.[134] However, while in the Union of Utrecht, the International Bishops' Conference has no jurisdiction within member churches to interfere in their internal affairs, it may decide in organizational or disciplinary matters (a) to maintain communion; (b) to ascertain whether a bishop has 'gravely harmed' the Declaration of Utrecht, the catholicity of ministry, doctrine, and worship, or the statute, or has seriously violated the 'moral order'; and (c) to determine whether such bishop is to be deprived of membership in the conference.[135]

Breach of a covenant

As a result of the events leading to the establishment of the Lambeth Commission, sanctions proposed in the Communion have ranged from admonition, through suspension, to expulsion, intervention, and declarations by member churches of impaired communion with fellow churches (self-help).[136] Nevertheless, the Lambeth Commission did not deal with the question of consequences of breach of a covenant, be-

---

130 CO (2001) II.6: 'in the event of controversies, particularly when divisions threaten in questions of faith and ethics, to seek dialogue and discuss the issues together in the light of the Gospel'.

131 A process whereby an impartial third party seeks to facilitate resolution of a dispute by agreement between the parties; but it is not binding: the mediator cannot impose a resolution.

132 In conciliation a third party is more interventionist and may be required to make recommendations to the parties on how to resolve the dispute.

133 I. Brownlie, *Principles of Public International Law* (6th edn, London, Oxford University Press, 2003) 672: an arbitrator is appointed as an independent third party by the parties to the dispute, under an arbitration agreement; the arbitrator must apply the law accurately and must comply with natural justice; the judgment is called an 'award' and subject to appeal; if the arbitrators fail to agree they can appoint an umpire. The award is binding. A treaty may contain an arbitration clause. Arbitration agreements are contracts. Conciliation (like mediation) does not bind. Modern origins are traced to the Jay Treaty 1794 between the US and GB.

134 See above Ch. 5. For example Southern Baptist Convention, Constitution (1845) Art. IV: 'Authority: While independent and sovereign in its own sphere, the Convention does not claim and will never attempt to exercise any authority over any other Baptist body, whether church, auxiliary organizations, associations, or convention.'

135 SOC 2000, B. Order, Arts 2,3(a)–(k).

136 See, for example D. W. Gomez and M. W. Sinclair (eds), *To Mend the Net: Anglican Faith and Order for Renewed Mission* (Carrollton, Texas, The Ekklesia Society, 2001); see also TWR, 29.

yond the statement that unilateralism would involve 'breach of obligations' owed to forty-three other churches.[137] Neither does *Towards an Anglican Covenant*.[138] Similarly, the Nassau report of the Covenant Design Group does not directly address the matter of breach of covenant. However, its Nassau draft provides that in the most extreme cases, where a church chooses to disregard the covenant, the instruments of communion will consider that church to have relinquished for itself the force and meaning of the covenant. Consequently, a process of restoration and renewal will be required to re-establish their covenant relationship with that other member church (Art. 6.6).[139] The Article has been criticized as lacking clarity.[140]

A somewhat more subtle disciplinary scheme was offered in the draft covenant submitted to the Covenant Design Group prior to its Nassau meeting by the Anglican Church of Australia. This proposes that central Communion bodies should not be able to issue sanctions, but instead have competence only to advise, warn and assist. Rather, any 'sanctions' should be in the keeping of individual churches: if a church ignores advice, the others may withdraw their fellowship from that church.[141] Thus, no member church or Instrument of Communion should be able to expel a church from the Communion. However, a church may withdraw from the Communion after first seeking the advice of other member churches and the Instruments of Communion, and such church should not withdraw against their advice.[142] Moreover, a member church may withdraw from or place constraints upon communion with a fellow church after seeking the same advice.[143]

---

137 TWR, para. 119; see also para. 157 for mediation, arbitration, non-invitation, and withdrawal.

138 See above for its consideration of membership.

139 This goes further than WDAC which did not deal with covenantal breach.

140 See, for example Wales, RNDC (2007). Compare Goddard, in Chapman (2008) 71.

141 See also Australia, RNDC (2007). Moreover: 'just as a sibling remains a family member despite not being on speaking terms with a particular fellow sibling, so provinces may remain part of the Communion, participating in Communion gatherings and events, while not maintaining a direct relationship with another province' by means, for example of not licensing clergy from another province; 'The covenant should have the flexibility to accommodate such disagreement and conflict without it necessarily amounting to a threat to the Communion as a whole.'

142 ACADC, Art. 29. See also Australia, RNDC (2007): the only sanction which should be applied to a church is one which that church chooses to apply to itself (that is, voluntary withdrawal); there should be no suggestion in a covenant that it is for an Instrument of Communion to determine either that the withdrawal is warranted or whether a church has exercised the sanction; the only possible sanction for an Instrument of Communion is not to invite a church to its meetings.

143 ACADC, Art. 30. See also England, RNDC (2007): the churches should commit themselves to 'the pattern of discipline involved in being part of the Anglican Covenant'.

That relationships of communion (and impaired communion) between churches should remain in the keeping of each church, in an exercise of its own autonomy, has found favour with other respondents.[144]

Nonetheless, some respondents suggest a system of 'mutually agreed sanctions' in the event of breach of a covenant (but they must not be unfettered); calling churches to repentance, or withdrawal of 'structural' fellowship, or 'separation' of churches from the Communion, but not punishment, are typical.[145] However, a breach of moral standards should not be treated in the same way as breach of structural standards.[146] For the majority of respondents, though, persuasion or exhortation is preferable to coercion, suspension or exclusion.[147] Others advocate a system of alternative episcopal oversight for churches which fail to comply with the covenant.[148] In point of fact, the adequacy of

---

144 MCU (Nov. 2006): 'Impaired communion is currently a matter of autonomous jurisdictions making separate decisions about the recognisability of one another's orders. With a Covenant as the unifying factor, communion will be impaired because of a failure to assent to a written document, or an unwillingness to be bound by its instruments. Impairment thus becomes a global decision, made by legal or hierarchical processes, which will, presumably, bind all those who have signed to be in the same impaired relationship to those who have not. A Covenant will not allow for progressive recognition of orders (as happened with the Church of South India) nor for progressive development of church order (as in the ordination of women). In effect the threat of impairment will progressively turn all those who remain within the Covenant from interdependent, autonomous bodies into a single centrally governed Church.'

145 Radner (2005) 617; Dioc. of Sydney (2005); Church Society (2004) 7 and 8; ECP (2005): 'Provinces that violate or do not adhere to the Covenant shall consider themselves to have separated temporarily from the Anglican Communion. Their Primates or representatives shall not be invited to participate in the affairs, councils, and representative functions of the Anglican Communion.'

146 Rwanda (2005) para. 5: LCRPR.

147 RHB (2005) para. 3(b): LCRPR; RTT (2004) para. 20; Inclusive Church: LCRPR; see also Sharp (2007): it would threaten discipline or exclusion of those 'whose Christian witness does not conform to androcentric and heteronormative values'; see also: John Paterson, Chair, ACC: Address: ACNS 3993 (21-6-2005): At the thirteenth meeting of the Anglican Consultative Council (2005), the Chairman in his address said in relation to the *Windsor Report*: 'Yet the ACC needs to take care lest such enhanced responsibility on the part of one of the Instruments of Unity move from the art of gentle persuasion to what has been called "institutional coercion"'; 'the Anglican Communion, [is a] world-wide faith community characterized since the 1963 Toronto Congress by mutual responsibility and interdependence and held together by little more than those "bonds of affection".' 'The ACC gives voice and hope and strength and dignity to those 80 million or more Anglicans who say they belong to us, and look to us to represent them, but who are not themselves Primates, Archbishops, Bishops, Priests, Deacons or ACC members. They are the *laos*, they are the people of God.' See also Archbishop Morgan, Church in Wales, Talk to Governing Body, Sept. 2007: the Nassau draft is 'more akin to a contract with punitive clauses than a Covenant which is a relationship of grace'.

148 ECP (2005): 'Congregations or Dioceses that disagree with the decisions of their respective Diocese or Province and refuse to be under the Pastoral Oversight of their Bishop or Primate but still want to remain Anglican/Episcopalian shall be placed tempo-

extraordinary schemes for delegated or extended episcopal oversight was the subject of the work of the Panel of Reference established by the Archbishop of Canterbury in 2005.[149]

However, under the St Andrews draft covenant, and the Framework Procedures appended to it, no Instrument of Communion is empowered to impose a sanction on a church which fails to comply with the covenant. This is in line with the results of the provincial consultation of 2007. As we have seen, if a church rejects a request from an Instrument of Communion and the Anglican Consultative Council decides finally that the action or proposed action of a church is incompatible with the covenant, two possible consequences ensue: namely, either voluntary relinquishment of the covenant purposes by that church or a declaration of relinquishment by the Council, both of which must be followed by a process of restoration of covenantal relationships.[150] There is no formal suspension or expulsion of churches from the Communion.[151]

---

rarily under the Pastoral Oversight of the Archbishop of Canterbury. The Archbishop may delegate the actual oversight to any bishop in the Communion in consultation with the concerned Primate.'

149 The *Windsor Report* recommended the establishment of a body to monitor extended episcopal oversight. In May 2005 the Archbishop of Canterbury 'directed' the establishment a Panel of Reference; its functions are: (1) at the request of the Archbishop, 'to enquire into, consider and report on situations drawn to [his] attention where there is serious dispute concerning the adequacy of schemes of delegated or extended episcopal oversight or other extraordinary arrangements which may be needed to provide for parishes which find it impossible in all conscience to accept the direct ministry of their own diocesan bishop or for dioceses in dispute with their provincial authorities;' (2) 'With [his] consent to make recommendations to the Primates, dioceses and provincial and diocesan authorities concerned, and to report to [him] on their response;' and (3) 'At the request of any Primate to provide a facility for mediation and to assist in the implementation of any such scheme in his own province.' The direction empowered the panel to determine which 'classes or categories of cases fall within its competency to consider'; it functions for five years; the Archbishop called upon: primates to provide copies of their schemes (and to notify changes); each bishop to respect fully and in accordance with its spirit any scheme of delegation or extended oversight established in their province; each parish which considers that in all conscience it cannot accept the direct oversight of its bishop to work with that bishop in the first instance towards finding some appropriate means for delegated or extended episcopal oversight within the province and diocese in which the parish is situated; and the Instruments of Unity to work tirelessly towards reconciliation and healing 'that the world may believe': ACNS 3977 (11-5-2005); for its membership see ACNS 3986 (8-6-2005).

150 SADC, Cl. 3.2.5e; Commentary to SADC: 'there is no intention to erect a centralised jurisdiction' and the Instruments of Communion 'cannot dictate with juridical force on the internal affairs of any Province'; but: 'we recognise that [communion] cannot be sustained in extreme circumstances where a Church or Province were to act in a way which rejects the interdependence of the Communion's life.'

151 It would, however, be helpful to have a clearer idea of what 'relinquishment' involves: does it mean (a) that a church is no longer party to the covenant; (b) that a church is no longer in communion with other covenanting churches (as SADC, Commentary

Meaningful parallels with breach of the salvific covenant are not obvious, though scripture indicates that both spiritual and material curses fall on Israel from God for disobedience to the covenant, which is violated by infidelity.[152] But breach of covenant does not result in its repudiation: the faithfulness of God to his covenantal commitment 'is manifested in his refusal, of free choice, to regard the breach of the covenant by the other party as a cause for . . . rescission on his part'.[153] Breach of the commitments of the baptismal covenant does not generally result in disciplinary sanction (and God remains faithful).[154] In the marriage covenant, difficult questions arise as to whether breach by one party allows the other to rescind or rather to continue to manifest the steadfast love which God shows humankind.[155] Breach of the ordination covenant, though, can lead to imposition of disciplinary sanctions.[156]

In contrast to ecumenical covenants, the instruments of comparable international ecclesial communities contain disciplinary provisions for censure. In the Lutheran World Federation, the Assembly may suspend or terminate the membership of a church by a two-thirds vote of the delegates. The suspended church is allowed to send representatives to the Assembly with a right to speak but not to vote or hold elective office. However, the membership of a suspended church must be reinstated upon an agreement by a two-thirds vote of the Assembly that the reasons for suspension no longer exist and that full membership should be reinstated. Termination of membership may occur voluntarily, or if the Assembly so decides by a two-thirds majority vote, or if the church ceases to exist as an autonomous body.[157] Associate membership or recognition may be terminated or withdrawn.[158] The Federation suspended the memberships of two churches in 1977 (which have since been restored),[159] as did the World Alliance of Reformed

---

suggests: see n. 150 above); or (c) that the other churches and Instruments of Communion must determine their own relationship with that church?

152 Exod. 19.5; Lev. 26.1–13; Deut. 29.9; Lev. 26.14–39; Deut. 29.18–28; P. A. Lillback, 'Covenant', in S. B. Ferguson and D. F. Wright (eds), *New Dictionary of Theology* (Leicester and Illinois, Inter-Varsity Press, 1988) 174.

153 T. G. Watkin, 'The concept of commitment in law and legal science', in P. R. Beaumont (ed.), *Christian Perspectives on Human Rights and Legal Philosophy* (Carlisle, Paternoster Press, 1998) 96.

154 Though the consensual compacts of each church make provision for excommunication.

155 Watkin (1998) 98–9.

156 Doe (1998) 88ff.

157 Const., Art. V; Bylaws, 2.

158 Bylaws, 2.4.4, 2.4.5: their 'relationship to the LWF' is subject to 'periodic review'.

159 S. Oppegaard and G. Cameron (eds), *Anglican–Lutheran Agreements: Regional*

Churches in 1982 (though it was lifted conditionally in 1997).[160] In 2003, the international Old Catholic Bishops' Conference 'effectively expelled' the (US-based) Polish National Church from the Old Catholic Union of Utrecht.[161] In the canonical tradition, breach of faith (*fidei laesio*) was the subject of disciplinary action.[162] International law also provides for a system of sanctions in the event of treaty-breaches and reparation.[163]

The Changeability of a Covenant

The Lambeth Commission did not deal with the issue of the amendment of a covenant, other than recognizing that unilateral alteration would not be possible, and that change might occur through practice and interpretation.[164] Beyond its provision on periodic reviews of the administration of the covenant, nor did the Windsor draft covenant expressly deal with its amendment;[165] the same applies to *Towards an Anglican Covenant*. This defect was highlighted by some respondents. As in time covenantal relations develop, so consideration must be given to allow the covenant to evolve as the Communion itself changes; thus more explicit attention as to how a covenant might be altered over time could be useful.[166] One respondent anticipates 'considerable unease' about enacting a commitment to a document over which a church has almost no control, and may endorse but may not amend.[167] Including a means of amending the covenant is essential, as is more discussion about the details of the procedure for amendment.[168] The Covenant Design Group and its Nassau and St Andrews draft covenants do not

---

and International Agreements 1972–2002 (Geneva, 2004) para. 224: the matter related to racial discrimination.

160 Lossky (2002) 1218.

161 L. J. Orzell, 'Disunion of Utrecht: Old Catholics fall out over new doctrines', *Touchstone* (May 2004): http://www.touchstonemag.com/archives/article.php?id=17-04-56-r

162 R. H. Helmholz, *The Canon Law and Ecclesiastical Jurisdiction from 597 to the 1640s* (Oxford, Oxford University Press, 2004) 362–5.

163 Brownlie (2003) 594.

164 TWR, para. 119: 'some provisions of a Covenant will be susceptible to development through interpretation and practice: it cannot predict the impact of future events. For this reason the draft Covenant is designed to allow the parties to it to adjust that relationship and resolve disputes in the light of changing circumstances.'

165 WDAC, Art. 27.3

166 MU (2004) p. 5; Dioc. of Brisbane (2004) para. 4.2: LCRPR.

167 CIPRWR (2005) 8: LCRPR.

168 MCU (2007) para. 4.11.

address amendment (nor in point of fact did most responses to the Nassau document).[169]

However, the Inter-Anglican Theological and Doctrinal Commission considers that the covenant envisioned for the Communion would not be static. It is a dynamic process like a marriage covenant. As the marriage partnership grows as it is tested by unforeseen circumstances and new situations, so the churches of the Communion will change and grow in ways they might never have expected.[170] There never has been a time when the Church did not experience conflicting interpretations of the gospel and the need to renegotiate its life together by some form of covenant renewal or ecclesiastical settlement.[171] Under the scheme proposed from the Scottish Episcopal Church, of each church having its own covenant with Canterbury, these covenants would be subject to critical examination and response by all other churches; this would allow for mutual accountability and interdependence with, in turn, each church assessing and revising its own (original) covenant resulting in the evolution of covenants involving all provinces acting in 'a covenanting framework'.[172]

Various procedural models for covenantal amendment are possible. Above all, amendment should be a Communion act. Amendments to the constitution of the Anglican Consultative Council must be submitted to the constitutional bodies of the member churches and ratified by two-thirds of such bodies.[173] The constitution of the World Alliance of Reformed Churches may be amended by a two-thirds affirmative vote of the delegates in attendance at any meeting of the General Council, providing the proposed amendment has been transmitted to each member church and to members of the Executive Committee, at least one year before it is submitted for approval.[174] This is typical.[175] While the sacramental covenants are indissoluble, presumably some terms of their commitments contained in the liturgical texts may be altered by legislative process.[176] In international law, a church–state covenant may be altered only by mutual agreement, it may provide for its own amendment and termination, or it may be discontinued because of

---

169 See, however, Southern Africa, RNDC; and Bishop Beisner, Dioc. of Northern California (2007).

170 RPC, para. 2.4.

171 Ibid., para. 3.1.

172 Scottish Episcopal Church, letter from J. Stuart (2006).

173 ACC, Const., Art. 10.

174 WARC, Const., Art. XII.1.

175 LWF, Const., Art. XIV; SCOBA, Const., Art. 6: both require a two-thirds majority.

176 If changes involve doctrine, the normal rules for liturgical reform apply: Doe (1998) 223.

desuetude, supervening impossibility, or unforeseen circumstances.[177] Ecumenical covenants sometimes provide for their own development as part of the spiritual pilgrimage towards greater unity.[178] The Inter-Anglican Theological and Doctrinal Commission has explored the changeability of covenants in scripture.[179]

A Covenant and Ecclesiality

The Lambeth Commission and *Towards an Anglican Covenant* fail to comment on the implications of a covenant for the ecclesiality (the self-understanding of an institutional church) of the Anglican Communion itself. The Archbishop of Canterbury has observed that currently, institutionally speaking, the Communion is an association of local churches – it is not a single organization with a controlling bureaucracy and a universal system of law – though, he adds, an isolated local church is less than a complete church.[180] The Covenant Design Group also sees its St Andrews draft covenant (like the Nassau text) as enabling the churches to grow together as a worldwide Communion to the full stature of Christ, and a worldwide family of interdependent *churches*;[181] but there is no express mention of the idea that a covenant will enhance the ecclesiality of the Communion.

By way of contrast, several respondents point out that the Windsor draft covenant, as seems also to be the case with the Nassau text (and by implication the St Andrews draft), tended towards making the Anglican Communion into a church which can regulate its parts.[182] A juridical covenant which might make the Anglican Communion into a church rather than simply a communion of churches may well promote

---

177 J. A. Coriden, T. J. Green and D. E. Heintschel (eds), *The Code of Canon Law: Text and Commentary* (New York, Paulist Press, 1985) p. 740; J. Werckmeister, *Petit Dictionnaire de Droit Canonique* (Paris, Les Editions du Cerf, 1993) 136; Brownlie (2003) 592–3.

178 ACCT, p. 3; CO (2001) II.3.

179 RPC, para. 1.4: 'It is at this point that there emerges the promise of a new covenant through which (this is the point) God will at last do in and through Israel what the earlier covenants intended but did not bring about.'

180 Williams, 'Challenge and hope' (27 June 2006).

181 SADC, Cl. 2.1.2; NDC, Preamble, and Art. 4.2.

182 C. Lewis, 'On Unimportance', in A. Linzey and R. Kirker (eds), *Gays and the Future of Anglicanism* (Winchester, O Books, 2005) 154. See also Australia, RNDC (2007): this suggests that a covenant should not place commitments on the Communion as a whole. See also TEC, RNDC (2007): this expresses the fear that the Communion itself will grow into a single global church governed by a constitutional statement rather than a communion of churches (though growing into the full stature of Christ is important).

formal schism; and a covenant which further demarcates Anglicans from other Christians could damage ecumenical dialogue.[183] Be that as it may, ecumenical partners do not uncommonly speak of the 'Anglican Church', and many Anglicans include 'The Anglican Church' in the titles of their own churches.[184] The perception is that it is possible to speak of the 'Anglican Church' although Anglicanism is really a communion of autonomous, provincially based churches.[185] Whether the Communion is 'a church' is similar to debate about the ecclesial character of the World Council of Churches; while it has ecclesiality in its goal (the unity of churches), it cannot, for example, hold its own Eucharist.[186] If implemented, an Anglican covenant would enhance the notion of a global Anglican church. It would also alter the ecclesiality of each church, and for the Church of England some have suggested it would have implications for its position as an established church.[187]

In what senses, if at all, would a covenant touch the ecclesiality of the Communion? First, the geographical dimension of understandings of 'a church', employed by Anglicans and shared by ecumenical partners around the concept of *locality* (Roman Catholic, Orthodox and Lutheran), suggest that the Anglican Communion is not 'a church': the Communion is not obviously 'the church in a place'; it is a global body. On the other hand, the globality of the Communion represents its territoriality, which may also be found in the sum of the ecclesiastical territorial boundaries of its constituent churches. In any event, lack of territoriality is not detrimental to ecclesiality: that their own local churches are dispersed around the globe is no bar to other comparable global ecclesial communities considering themselves as, for example, 'The Orthodox Church' or 'The Lutheran Church'. An Anglican covenant will not alter this lack of locality.[188]

---

183 Affirming Catholicism, Response to TAAC (13-12-2006) para. 6; see also Davie (2007) and Clatworthy *et al.* (2007) para. 1: the Communion would become 'a single juridical body'.

184 It would be interesting to explore the typology 'church' in sociology: M. Hill, *A Sociology of Religion* (New York, Basic Books, 1973) Ch. 4.

185 G. R. Evans, *The Church and the Churches: Towards an Ecumenical Ecclesiology* (Cambridge, Cambridge University Press, 1994) 78, 215: Anglicans do not speak of 'the Church of Canterbury' or 'the Church of York'; 'the Anglican Communion, which is not coextensive with the Church'.

186 'The Church, the Churches and the World Council of Churches', in L. Vischer (ed.), *A Documentary History of the Faith and Order Movement: 1927–1963* (St Louis, Bethany Press, 1964) 168; A. Keshishian, 'Growing together towards full koinonia', in G. Limouris (ed.), *Orthodox Visions of Ecumenism: Statements, Messages and Reports on the Ecumenical Movement 1902–1922* (Geneva, WCC, 1994) 235 at 244; Evans (1994) 301.

187 MCU (2007) para. 5.2: these are not spelt out.

188 Occasionally, in context, TWR seems to use 'the whole church' or 'the church' as synonyms for the Communion: TWR, paras 65, 70.

Second, the social dimension of 'a church', employed by Anglicans and shared by ecumenical partners (Roman Catholic, Orthodox and Lutheran), that a church is a community (a local community or a community of churches) with a defined membership (and gathered at the Eucharist) is clearly a feature of the Anglican Communion. This aspect of ecclesiality, when applied to the Anglican Communion, is found in its unity as a 'fellowship' of local churches;[189] or as 'the Anglican family of Churches'.[190] As has been seen, the *Windsor Report* too uses the idea of the Anglican family.[191] The draft covenants seek to formalize the notion.[192]

Third, forms of church polity or governance are constitutive of ecclesiality and identity in Anglicanism – autonomy, and episcopal leadership and synodical government are essential features of Anglican polity; the same applies in Roman Catholicism, where particular churches are subject to episcopal government, and to Orthodoxy, where local churches are episcopally governed; and autonomy is constitutive of ecclesiality in Lutheranism. However, currently the Anglican Communion, as a global community, lacks an authoritative polity: Anglicans are not bound together juridically,[193] but by the moral authority of the Instruments of Communion. The *Windsor Report* recommends adjustment through adoption of an Anglican covenant to make explicit and *more forceful* the loyalty and bonds of affection which govern the relationship between the churches of the Communion.[194] A covenant, adopted through the synodical processes of each church, would supply a polity (recognizing an authority in the Communion itself). In other

---

189 LC 1930, Res. 49; see also, for example, New Zealand, Const., Preamble: it is 'a fellowship of duly constituted Dioceses, Provinces or Regional Churches in communion with the See of Canterbury, sharing with one another their life and mission in the spirit of mutual responsibility and interdependence'.

190 West Indies: 'Anglican Communion means the Anglican family of Churches and organised Churches, Provinces or extra-Provincial Dioceses which, being in communion with the Church of England, accept the Faith, Doctrine, Sacraments and Discipline of the One Holy Catholic and Apostolic Church according as that Church has received the same' (Const., Art. 4.1).

191 TWR, para. 27.

192 See for example, WDAC: 'The Anglican Communion is a community of interdependent churches' (Art. 7); its communion is 'a gift of God' and 'animated in the experience of God's work of redemption'; and its divine call to communion is inviolable: 'no member church may declare unilaterally irreversible broken communion with any fellow church' (Art. 6). Importantly, the Communion is 'a church' as Anglicans are committed to join together as one eucharistic community: under the covenant, each church shall 'enjoin its members to eucharistic sharing in a fellow church in accordance with the discipline of that host church' (Art. 11); NDC, Art. 2: 'I ... the Communion as a whole ... is part of 'the church universal'; Art. 3.2: eucharistic fellowship.

193 LC 1930, Res. 49.

194 TWR, paras 105–120; App. I and II.

words, if polity is a mark of being 'a church', then the authoritative (but non-coercive) polity of the global Communion proposed by the St Andrews draft covenant would make the Communion itself more like 'a church'.

Fourth, Anglicans and their ecumenical partners propose that a community is 'a church' when its members (particular churches in Roman Catholicism, and local churches in Lutheranism and Orthodoxy) are in a relation of communion with one another.[195] On this basis, it is possible to suggest that the Anglican Communion is 'a church' *because* its member churches are in communion with each other. The *Windsor Report* devotes considerable attention to the idea of relationality. For example, '[e]ach church has a corporate ecclesial personhood and exists in and for its fellow churches.'[196] The proposed covenant would enhance the idea.[197] If (relational) communion between (local) churches within a tradition is a mark of being 'a church', then the Communion is currently a church in this sense, and the proposed covenant will formalize this relationality as a commitment.

Fifth, Anglicans and their ecumenical partners agree that 'belonging to' (Anglican), 'the realization of' (Lutheran), 'subsistence in' (Roman Catholic) or 'the presence of' (Orthodox) the Church universal in the local church is critical for that community to be a church in the fullest sense. It is possible to conceive of the Anglican Communion as a church in this sense; Anglicans consider that the Anglican Communion is a fellowship of churches *'within* the One Holy Catholic and Apostolic Church'.[198] The *Windsor Report* too stresses universality and the Communion: when '"the Anglican Communion" describes itself as such, it is self-consciously describing that part of the Body of Christ which shares an inheritance through Anglican tradition'.[199] In turn, the Windsor draft covenant recognizes that each church belongs to and must act in a manner compatible with its belonging to the One, Holy, Catholic and Apostolic Church.[200] The Communion itself has the mark of 'church' insofar as it claims to be a manifestation of the Church as a

---

195 This may be a relationship of full communion or imperfect communion.

196 TWR, para. 84.

197 The idea is implicit in SADC but explicit in WDAC: the Communion is 'a community of interdependent churches and consists in relations between one church, the See of Canterbury, and the fellowship of member churches worldwide'; each church 'is constituted by, exists in and receives fullness of life in its relation to the other member churches'; moreover, 'ordained and lay persons in each church are in personal communion with those of other member churches' (Art. 7).

198 LC 1930, Res. 49.

199 TWR, para. 46.

200 WDAC, Arts 1, 9; NDC, Arts 2.1, 3.1: 'the Communion as a whole affirms . . . that is it part' of the Church universal.

global fellowship: the Nassau draft expressly states that 'the Communion as a whole affirms . . . that it is part' of the Church universal.[201] The concept is less evident in the St Andrews draft covenant.[202]

Finally, insofar as loyalty to catholicity and apostolicity are marks of 'the Church' and 'a church' (for Anglicans, Roman Catholics, Orthodox and Lutherans, even though, for example, Roman Catholics may not agree that Anglicans possess them in relation to the Eucharist and apostolic succession), in its own self-understanding the Anglican Communion may be classified as 'a church'. The Communion is 'church' because of its (perceived) loyalty to: catholic and apostolic faith and order; the normative record of Scripture; the sacraments (baptism and Eucharist); the creeds and the historic episcopate.[203] More so than the St Andrews and Nassau texts, the Windsor draft covenant commits each church to *recognize* in each other church a common catholicity, apostolicity and confession of faith, common sacraments and liturgical tradition, common ministry and mission.[204]

Conclusion

The St Andrews, Nassau and Windsor draft covenants do not address systematically the effects of a covenant on membership of the Anglican Communion. Nevertheless, for some respondents a covenant might necessitate two ecclesial classes: signatory constituent and non-signatory associate churches. However, a covenant itself could provide for tiered membership among its signatory churches, as do agreements in ecumenism and other global ecclesial communities. Sacramental covenants, though, do not generally distinguish parties to them. If the Windsor proposal is adopted, a covenant will bind churches legally; but the Covenant Design Group speaks only in general terms of *synodical* adoption. Some consider a non-binding covenant would unhelpfully continue the status quo; for others, a binding covenant would stifle the Holy Spirit. Recourse to comparable covenants yields seemingly divergent theological and legal models. The salvific covenant binds morally.

201 NDC, Art. 2.1.
202 SADC, Cl. 1.1.1: only each church affirms 'its communion in' the Church universal.
203 LC 1930, Res. 49; WAEEC, paras 35, 37; and LC 1998, Res. III.6 and 8.
204 WDAC, Arts 1–5, 9–12. Moreover, the ecclesiality of the Communion is reflected in its purposes: proclaiming to the world in common witness the good news of the Kingdom of God; fostering and protecting a common mind in essential matters; and achieving greater unity (Art. 7), so that communion involves 'a common pilgrimage towards truth, each church in partnership with its fellow churches learning what it means to become interdependent and thus more fully a communion' (Art. 8).

Sacramental covenants bind morally but have juridical effects. Many ecumenical covenants are non-binding, but some are incorporated in Anglican laws. Generally, other global ecclesial agreements bind their communities in common matters (but preserve autonomy). However, that a covenant should be legally binding tallies with the canonical principle *pacta sunt servanda*.

According to the Windsor draft covenant, the primary responsibility for enforcement of a covenant would lie with each church, but its draft gives the Instruments of Communion a limited authority to enforce covenantal discipline. The Nassau text denies jurisdiction to the Instruments of Communion, but assigns what seems to be a moral authority to enforce the covenant principally to the Primates' Meeting. While supported by some, for most this would alter the ecclesiology of global Anglicanism in too curial a manner. By way of contrast, the St Andrews draft forbids an exercise of jurisdiction by the Instruments of Communion to violate provincial autonomy, and a system of requests is employed procedurally to deal with covenant disagreements which threaten Communion unity and mission. Like the Windsor draft covenant, ecumenical covenants do not usually address breach; though the St Andrews and Nassau texts do not provide for suspension of churches, they enable relinquishment and restoration of covenant relationships. This may be contrasted with instruments of other global church communities which permit suspension (and restoration) of member churches. The St Andrews, Nassau and Windsor draft covenants do not treat covenant amendment, unlike other global church communities and the notion of changeability in ecumenical covenants signifying their evolution in spiritual pilgrimage. One overriding effect of the Lambeth Commission proposal is that a covenant would, theologically and legally, enhance the ecclesiality of the Communion, by giving it a polity and thereby making it more like 'a church'.

Conclusion

The recommendation of the Lambeth Commission, that the churches of the Communion enter an Anglican covenant, would if adopted represent a major historical development for worldwide Anglicanism. It raises a host of both theological and legal issues. They range from the theological nature of communion, through the legal character of provincial autonomy, to the theological and juridical implications of covenanting. Initially, the Windsor proposal and draft covenant were not universally welcomed: some accepted the covenant principle and the draft; others, the principle but not the draft; and some rejected both. However, following publication of the Nassau draft covenant by the Covenant Design Group in 2007, responses (particularly those in the provincial consultation) indicate a greater general sympathy for some form of covenant. Voices rejecting the covenant principle are fewer, but concerns persist about the authority, if any, which might be conferred upon the Instruments of Communion. The St Andrews draft covenant, published by the Covenant Design Group in February 2008, seeks to address these concerns.

The Lambeth Conference 2008 is about to discuss the St Andrews draft covenant. As it moves to Lambeth and beyond, the debate necessitates a systematic and balanced presentation of the proposals and responses. Nine key issues provide a rudimentary but practical framework for the global theological and legal debate. Three relate to foundational ideas (nature, use and purposes of a covenant); three relate to structure and substance (form, subject-matter and content of a covenant); and three relate to implementation of a covenant (process, adoption and effects of a covenant). Also, an assessment of the proposals, drafts and responses (both supportive and critical) necessitates a choice of theological and legal resources to be deployed in their evaluation. Covenants in scripture, sacramental covenants, ecumenical agreements and the instruments of comparable international ecclesial communities provide useful criteria against which to measure propositions emerging in the debate.

The Proposals

In line with the Windsor Report and like the Windsor and Nassau texts (though the Covenant Design Group does not define a 'covenant'), the St Andrews draft covenant represents a relational agreement, entered voluntarily, which consists of affirmations and commitments (if not pledges or promises). Employing a formal covenant would be novel in Anglicanism, but both the Lambeth Commission and the Covenant Design Group suggest that a covenant would articulate the relationships of covenantal affection which are already operative in the Communion. This is largely a theological understanding, but it also has a legal dimension: the norms of existing inter-Anglican covenantal relations are in the shape of (morally not legally) binding mutual commitments informally agreed at global level (principally at Lambeth Conferences). The primates see the Chicago-Lambeth Quadrilateral as typical (and this has a place in the St Andrews draft covenant). However, Anglicans are also familiar with juridical covenants in the local communion of each church (with its own laws in the form of a consensual compact). Yet, identifying the purposes of a covenant is a wholly theological task. The Lambeth Commission suggested that the covenantal purposes would be: unity (and interdependence); reconciliation, recommitment, and trust; clarity and understanding of Anglican identity (not least for ecumenical partners); order and stability (including mutual accountability); and mission and witness. Restoration of trust (following current difficulties) and mission are particularly highlighted by the Covenant Design Group as key covenant objects, and the advancement of mission is prominent in the St Andrews draft covenant; but the text does not spell out the objects of the Communion *itself* as an entity.

The Lambeth Commission proposed a detailed documentary covenant with a descriptive and prescriptive linguistic form in a canonical register, with some matters (such as the constitutions of the Instruments of Communion) to be spelt out in supplementary documents. While the St Andrews draft covenant (like Nassau) is shorter than the Windsor text, its register is less canonical and more theological but seems equally prescriptive, and it is supplemented by an Appendix with framework procedures for the resolution of covenant disagreements. Like Windsor and Nassau, the St Andrews draft covenant in its provisions on faith, mission and unity deals with five basic subjects: common identity; relationships of communion; commitments of communion; autonomy and its exercise; and the management of communion issues. Like Windsor and Nassau, its terms are derived by and large from sources of classical Anglicanism (such as the Chicago-Lambeth

Quadrilateral) and spell out through affirmations and commitments the meaning of ecclesial communion. Pivotal is the Windsor principle of autonomy-in-communion, absent from the Nassau text, but now included in the St Andrews draft covenant. However, its clauses on the maintenance of communion are innovative, especially as to testing developments in matters of essential concern through common discernment, including those which threaten the unity and mission of the Communion. Communion-wide collaboration is proposed, provincial autonomy protected, and the Instruments of Communion collectively given a moral authority commanding respect. Gone is the Nassau focus on the Primates' Meeting.

The Lambeth Commission suggested a long-term process to formulate a covenant carried out in an educative context in which the whole Communion participates in the evolution of an agreed text. The Commission proposed that each church enacts prior to signature (but it could equally be ratification after signature) a brief communion law authorizing its primate (or equivalent) to sign the covenant, and committing that church legally to adhere to the covenant, a process culminating in a solemn liturgical signature. The Covenant Design Group (perhaps somewhat imprecisely) has proposed 'synodical adoption' in each church. For the Lambeth Commission a covenant could clarify Communion membership and it would bind the churches to comply with its terms; but its Windsor draft did not address consequences of non-compliance. The Covenant Design Group does not deal with the issue of membership. However, while a covenant would bind churches, the decisions of the Instruments of Communion would not. To preserve provincial autonomy, the St Andrews draft covenant employs a system of requests from the Instruments of Communion (attracting respect) in cases which threaten Communion unity and mission. If churches reject those requests (in the course of four optional procedural routes) they would relinquish (by their own declaration or by resolution of the Anglican Consultative Council) the covenant purposes thereby necessitating a process of restoration. Like the Lambeth Commission, the Covenant Design Group does not deal with covenant amendment (though the Windsor draft provided for periodic review of the administration of the covenant).

The Responses

The Archbishop of Canterbury, primates and Joint Standing Committee of the Primates' Meeting and the Anglican Consultative Council insisted from the outset on as wide a debate as possible about the covenant proposal. As the proposals and draft covenants have evolved since Windsor, so have responses to them. The first round of responses followed the *Windsor Report* in 2004: once again, some accepted the covenant principle and draft; others, the principle but not the draft; and some rejected both. Round two followed publication of *Towards an Anglican Covenant* in 2006; these largely mirrored the initial responses. By the third round, after Nassau early in 2007, and including the provincial consultation later that year, arguments for and against had become somewhat standardized, with most debate centred on the authority of the Instruments of Communion under a covenant – though opponents to the covenant principle seem to have become less vociferous.

In all three rounds, respondents generally agree about the voluntary and relational character of a covenant, though several dislike analogies between covenant and contract as too juridical (despite the canonical influence on the development of contract). There has been little comment on the promissory dimension of covenants, but there is consensus that a covenant should consist of affirmations and commitments. There seems to be a groundswell of opinion that the employment of a covenant would be consistent with the idea that Anglicans already share covenantal relationships, and that a covenant accords with the notion of the Communion as a family of churches. A minority counter-argument, however, is that a covenant *per se* is at odds with the spirit of Anglicanism and would translate the bonds of affection into formal commitments. Most consider that a covenant could help to unify, reconcile, clarify, stabilize and enhance the mission and witness of the Communion; but the critics reject its capacity to achieve these strategic objects: a covenant would disunite, destabilize and frustrate the mission of the Communion – although the covenant principle did not generate such fears in the provincial consultation of 2007.

It is axiomatic that the inner life of Communion relationships cannot itself be reduced to a document; but it is generally accepted that the public administration of visible ecclesial relations is capable of treatment in a formal instrument. Nevertheless, whether a written covenant should be descriptive or prescriptive remains a key issue; and the matter of form exercised churches in the provincial consultation after Nassau. While covenants appear by nature to be prescriptive (being based on commitments), the consensus seems to be that a covenant should codify fundamental expectations, but without being legalistic, detailed and rigidly confessional. Clarity, coherence and conciseness are critical values for the covenantal form. As to topics, there seems to be general agreement that common identity, mission, relationships, commitments, autonomy and the management of matters of common concern are proper subjects for a covenant. Sensitivity is commonly advocated over reference to the historic Anglican formularies; emphasis on their historical role is preferred by those anxious about their adverse impact on ecumenical dialogue. The St Andrews draft covenant seeks to accommodate these concerns. Few suggest that reception, *adiaphora*, interpretation of scripture, and the role of reason should be treated in a covenant.

Roughly one third of responses expressed general support for the content of the Windsor draft covenant. The critics questioned, for example: whether churches could honestly recognize the Church universal in each other; the workability of the commitments of communion; how agreement on interpreting the covenant could be reached; whether its understanding of autonomy-in-communion was correct; and, whether assigning a jurisdiction in contentious matters to the Instruments of Communion would create too centralized a polity for the Communion. The Nassau text was welcomed because: churches should affirm the centrality of scripture, creeds, sacraments and historic episcopate; churches should uphold the catholic and apostolic faith in pursuit of a common pilgrimage, and participate in a common mission; it protects provincial autonomy; it seeks to clarify the role of the Instruments; and it attempts to provide a process for the resolution of dispute. However, while some welcome a limited ministry for the Instruments in cases of serious dispute, most (including in the provincial consultation) do not want to see a determinative authority vested in the Primates' Meeting. They prefer an advisory authority to reside with the Anglican Consultative Council as more in keeping with the principle of synodical government – and so the St Andrews draft covenant moved in this direction.

The process for a covenant has attracted little comment beyond the common view that it should not be hurried and that it should involve robust debate and widespread consultation. Remarkably, few respondents seem to visualize the process as an exercise in evolution, vocation (a call to covenant), collaboration (a communion action), negotiation (a synthesis of discordant views) and education (a journey of spiritual growth). As to the mode of adoption, the Windsor recommendation of adoption by legislative enactment was welcomed by many as essential to ensure that the churches are committed to the covenant; but others fear that legislation will take too long (which could be cured by ratification after signature). Some feel that the primates are not appropriate signatories, but this did not emerge as an issue in the provincial consultation. The Covenant Design Group recommendation of 'synodical adoption' has not attracted comment (even in the provincial consultation). Finally, from the outset responses have been divided as to whether a covenant should: establish grades of membership of the Communion, dependent on the willingness of churches to accept all its articles; bind each church legally; be enforceable either at all or at the local or global level (by an Instrument of Communion); contain a system of sanctions in the event of breach of covenant. The consensus in the provincial consultation was that the Instruments should have no coercive authority – and the St Andrews draft covenant implements this. The lack of proposals for covenant amendment causes concern in some quarters, but few comment on the potential of a covenant for the ecclesiality of the Communion itself.

The Comparators

The covenant proposals, drafts and responses should not be seen in isolation. As this book seeks to demonstrate, they may be usefully measured against covenant models in scripture, sacramental theology, ecumenism, and comparable global ecclesial communities. First, many are sceptical that scripture offers a practical model for an ecclesial covenant. However, on the basis of the Windsor assumption that the existing covenantal relationship in Anglicanism has biblical foundations, there are those (notably the International Anglican and Doctrinal Commission) who consider that some scriptural covenants provide an *inspiration* for the development of an Anglican covenant. Covenantal theology (at least in the Protestant tradition) certainly holds that scriptural covenants may legitimately function as a model for ecclesiastical covenants. The salvific covenant is initiated by God to whom the people respond voluntarily in faith, in their relations with God and one another. It involves pledges, commitments and steadfast faithfulness. Its objects are reconciliation, unity, stability and order, marking out the Christian in a life of mission and witness. It is a profound spiritual relationship articulated in the record of scripture – but the covenant is not negotiated, it does not bind (in the sense of human law) and it is not changeable. In these senses scriptural covenant could inspire Anglicans in their thinking about the shape of a covenant for the Communion.

Second, from sacramental theology, baptism, marriage and ordination are all covenantal in character. Their elements are documented in the liturgical books of churches and recognized and regulated by canon law. The parties are understood to be called to covenant. Promises are exchanged, commitments are undertaken, and a life is entered in which the autonomy of the parties is limited by the duty to have regard for others. They are entered solemnly (and are registered), bind the parties spiritually, and there may be juridical consequences in the case of non-compliance with their commitments. With the exception of their indissolubility, these theological and canonical features of sacramental covenants may represent a spirit of covenanting which Anglicans might deploy for their own ecclesial covenant.

Third, lessons might also be learnt from the increasing number of inter-church covenants in contemporary Anglicanism, such as the agreements of the Anglican Communion Network (which has a confessional statement) and the Covenant Union of Anglican Churches in Concordat. These are polemical, programmatic, prescriptive, and (generally) concise. However, while they present as having been ratified by the ecclesial communities whose signatories have entered them, it is unclear whether they are binding juridically and enforceable within those communities. They may be contrasted with the Covenant for Communion in Mission, which is short, directory (not mandatory) and general in form. The constitution of the Anglican Consultative Council is a good example of the capacity of the Communion for a juridical agreement (though the Council currently has no general jurisdiction over the Communion). It deals specifically with constitutional amendment (approval by two-thirds of the member churches), and this could be a useful precedent for those anxious about the lack of provision for amendment in the St Andrews draft covenant.

Fourth, ecumenical covenants serve as valuable theological and canonical models for the Anglican debate. Covenants, and other forms of agreement, are today normal vehicles by which churches of the Anglican Communion enter and regulate their relationships of communion or intercommunion with other churches. The ecumenical covenants are based on agreement (often after years of negotiation); they are voluntarily entered and may be bilateral or multilateral. They involve affirmations (that each church recognizes the other to belong to the Church universal – a principle absent from the St Andrews draft covenant). They prescribe commitments and seek to achieve these through pledges and other solemn undertakings. They enable shared ministry, worship and mission, and represent both a call to covenant and a witness to emulate the unity for which Christ prayed. They may provide for their own development and change, for tiered membership and for differentiated commitments (such as with the Australian Churches Covenanting Together).

However, ecumenical covenants differ in terms of their enforceability. Some are incorporated in the laws of the partner churches and enjoy juridical enforceability, to express the seriousness of the commitment (such as the Porvoo agreement or the Covenant of the Churches in Wales). Others are in the nature of guidance and generate no enforceable rights and duties (such as the *Charta Oecumenica*). Like the

St Andrews draft covenant, they protect the autonomy of the partner churches as compatible with being in communion (typified in the Anglican–Lutheran covenants). Unlike the Windsor draft covenant, they do not usually provide a mechanism for their own interpretation or for the resolution of conflict. Translation by the Communion of these principles to its own ecclesial covenant could represent a real testimony to the value Anglicans place on the ecumenical endeavour.

Fifth, the instruments of comparable international ecclesial communities serve as useful models for the Anglican covenant project – they offer helpful core principles which these instruments have in common despite their provenance from very different ecclesial traditions. The constitutions and other instruments of the Standing Conference of Canonical Orthodox Bishops in the Americas, Old Catholic Bishops in the Union of Utrecht, Lutheran World Federation, World Alliance of Reformed Churches, World Methodist Council, Baptist World Alliance, and Community of Protestant Churches in Europe are all in the nature of agreements between their member churches which seek to enable shared mission, greater visible unity and co-operation in matters of common concern. They all protect the autonomy of their member churches within the context of interdependence. They are all prescriptive and juridical in form. They all envisage the operation of supplementary instruments. Acceptance of them is a precondition for admission to the membership of the global community. They all assign authority to their global institutions to make decisions in prescribed fields and provide for their own amendment. Some operate a system of full and associate membership and contain disciplinary provisions (to suspend or terminate the membership of churches and to restore them to fellowship).

Moreover, a key assumption behind covenants, concordats and other agreements employed in church–state relations within national borders is that these are negotiated agreements which deal with the treatment in partnership of matters of common concern to church and state while also protecting the autonomy of the respective parties. They are juridical, enforceable at law, and changeable on agreement. Some agreements, notably concordats between states and the Holy See, are international treaties enforceable in international law. Indeed, political lessons could be learnt from a study of these. Unlike the so-called 'soft-obligation' agreements, which are increasingly used in the international sphere, an elaborate system of principles has been developed for entry into international treaties, as well as with regard to their administration, interpretation, effects and breach – the doctrine of *pacta sunt servanda* is fundamental to the system.

Anglicans should be reassured that the general principles being developed in the covenant proposals, drafts and responses – around the nine issues explored here – are broadly consistent with the theological and legal understandings of covenant which have been developed in scripture, sacramental tradition and the rational experiences of ecumenism and comparable global ecclesial communities. There is nothing extraordinary in the Anglican enterprise. Although the project may be driven by theology, ecclesiastical politics and pragmatism, covenanting would actually involve participation in a conventional ecclesial experience for which there are numerous enduring theological and legal principles and precedents. While an Anglican covenant would appear novel to churches of the Communion, in point of fact, spiritual, sacramental and structural covenanting is a well-trodden Christian path.[1]

---

1 A spectrum of three obvious options seems to present itself: (1) a covenant which focuses on the Communion as the primary manifestation of Anglicanism, one which recognizes the competence of the Communion to limit the freedom of its member churches in a wide (but defined) field: under such a covenant, the Communion through a representative global body (preferably synodical) would have authority to block a local development in the prescribed subject area (the 'red light' model). This would probably necessitate a juridical covenant, with clearly prescribed affirmations and commitments, and a system for enforcement in which sanctions in the event of breach of covenant would not be out of place; (2) a covenant which sees partnership between the Communion and its churches as the primary manifestation of Anglicanism, one which protects the autonomy of its churches subject to the competence of the Communion to limit the freedom of a church in a narrowly defined field; under such a covenant, the Communion through a representative global body (preferably synodical) would have authority to restrain a church in a restricted field of highly contentious common matters (the 'amber light' model); (3) a covenant which sees the local autonomous church as the primary manifestation of Anglicanism, one which recognizes an unfettered freedom on the part of each church with no control from the wider Communion; under such a covenant, the Communion through a representative body (preferably synodical) would have authority to advise a church against a course of action (in a defined field), but ultimately that church may decide freely (the 'green light' model).

Bibliography

Lambeth Commission Reception Process

Following the Lambeth Commission on Communion, and the publication of the *Windsor Report* (London, Anglican Communion Office, 2004), the Lambeth Commission Reception Process attracted responses which may be found at www.aco.org/commission/reception/report.cfm (and at the other sites included below). The following responses are examined in this study – for the sake of convenience, their titles (typically: 'A Preliminary Response to the *Windsor Report*') are generally omitted; where available, the date of the response is given.

A Statement from the Global South Primates, Nairobi (27/28-1-2005)

Anglican Frontier Mission (31-1-2005)

A Scottish Response to the Windsor Report, Changing Attitude Scotland (a network working for the full affirmation of lesbian Christians within the Scottish Episcopal Church): www.changingattitudescotland.org.uk/downloads/ScottishResponse.pdf

Covenanted Churches in Wales (17-1-2005)

Church in Wales (2005)

Church of Ceylon (Sri Lanka)

Church of England, House of Bishops, A Report (February 2005)

Church of Ireland, Standing Committee of the General Synod (25-1-2005)

Church Mission Society (31-1-2005)

Church of the Province of West Africa

Church Society (2004)

Committee of the Executive Committee of the Synod of the Church of Pakistan for the Moderator Rt Revd Dr A. J. Malik

Church of the Province of the Indian Ocean (2005)

Crosslinks (An International Mission Agency) (2005)

Diocese of Bendigo (January 2005)

Diocese of Brisbane, Response agreed by the Archbishop-in-Council (16-12-2004)

Diocese of British Columbia

Diocese of Niagara

Diocese of Ontario

Diocese of Saskatchewan

Diocese of Saskatoon (8-1-2006)

Diocese of Sydney, Standing Committee of the Synod (7-2-2005)

Epting, Bishop C. (TEC)

Evangelical Alliance (Hilborn)

Ferris, Bishop R., Algoma Anglican Synod Office (Canada)

House of Bishops Theological Group, Church of England (2005)

Hong Kong, Province of (Hong Kong Sheng Kung Hui)

House of Bishops, Salt Lake City (13-1-2005)

Iglesia Anglicana de la Region Central de America (9/10-2-2005)

Iglesia Anglicana del Cono Sur de America

Inclusive Church

Kasper, Cardinal Walter, Letter to the Archbishop of Canterbury (17-12-2004)

Kelsey, Bishop J. (TEC Bishop): Statement (19-10-2004): http://www.episcopalchurch.org/3577_53210_ENG_HTM.htm

Kirker, R., Open Letter

Lynogh, Bishop P., Diocese of North East India (2005)

MacDougall, S., 'The Windsor Report: ecclesiological departures for the Anglican Communion', General Theological Seminary of the Episcopal Church, Master of Arts Candidate Dissertation (Diocese of New York, 2005)

Marona, Most Revd J., Episcopal Church of the Sudan, Initial Response (2005)

Mellis, Canon J. (Canada)

Mothers Union, Central Trustees, Submission (2004)

Myanmar, Province of

Network for Interfaith Concerns (Anglican Communion) (2005)

Pakistan, Church of

Philippines, Province of (2005)

Repair the Tear: The Windsor Report – An Assessment and Call for Action (Anglican Mainstream – UK and the Church of England Evangelical Council, 2004)

Rwanda, Province of (2005)

SAMS Canada, Response (31-1-2005)

Scottish Episcopal Church, Doctrine Committee (27-2-2005): www.lgcm.org.uk/documents/PDF/Scots WindsorReport-SEC.pdf

Sison (2006): http://anglicanjournal.com/132/01/world09.html

Vercammen, J. A. O. L., Archbishop of Utrecht (25-1-2005)

Via Media (2004)

Via Media USA: http://www.remainepiscopal.org/Windsor1.html

Wescott House, Cambridge, England

Responses to *Towards an Anglican Covenant*

Towards an Anglican Covenant, A paper prepared for the Joint Standing Committee of the Anglican Consultative Council and Primates' Meeting (2006) may be found at: www.aco/commission/covenant/index.cfm Responses to it, used in this study, are as follows:

Inter-Anglican Standing Commission on Ecumenical Relations, Responding to the Idea of a Covenant for the Anglican Communion (8-12-2006)

Inter-Anglican Theological and Doctrinal Commission, Responding to a Proposal of a Covenant (October 2006)

Brown, Bishop T., A covenant for the Anglican Communion – a response (2006)

Bruce, George, Bishop, Diocese of Ontario, Canada, A Covenant for the Anglican Communion, A Proposal for Use as a Discussion Starter

Cameron, G. K., Baby's first steps: can the covenant proposal ever walk?

Cameron, G. K., Ardour and Order: can the bonds of affection survive?

Davie, M., The rationale for the development of an Anglican Covenant, Church of England, General Synod, Agenda Paper, July 2007, The Anglican Covenant Proposal (GS 1161), Annex 3

Doe, Bishop Michael, Response to the Anglican Covenant Design Group (11 December 2006)

Hind, Bishop J., An Anglican Covenant? (30 April, revised 11 June, 2007) Church of England, General Synod, Agenda Paper, July 2007, The Anglican Covenant Proposal (GS 1161), Annex 2

LeSueur, Revd Dr Richard, Diocese of Calgary, Seeking the language of unity: covenant in the Anglican Communion (February 2006)

McPartlan, P., Towards an Anglican Covenant (Anglican Institute Website)

Noll, Revd Prof. S., Response to Working Papers on an Anglican Communion Covenant (8 December 2006)

Percy, Revd Canon Prof. M., Letter to G. K. Cameron (7 December 2006)

Perry, A. T., From Waterloo to Windsor: the proposed Anglican Covenant in light of Anglican-Lutheran co-operation in Canada, unpublished essay for the LLM in Canon Law, Cardiff University (15 August 2007)

Ross, C., Covenant (1 December 2006)

Scully, J. E., Reflections on *Towards an Anglican Covenant* and *Responding to a Proposal of a Covenant* (Epiphany, 2007)

Draft Submitted by the Anglican Church of Australia (October 2006) to the Covenant Design Group

See also:

Affirming Catholicism, Standing Committee, Response to *Towards an Anglican Covenant* (13 December 2006): www.affirmingcatholicism.org.uk

Church of England, General Synod, Agenda Paper, July 2007 (GS 1161), The Anglican Covenant Proposal

Faith and Order Advisory Group of the Church of England (A. Goddard, C. Methuen), A Contribution to the Discussion of an Anglican Covenant (23 December 2006)

Modern Churchpeople's Union, Response to Towards an Anglican Covenant (J. Clatworthy and P. Bagshaw) (November 2006): www.modchurchunion.org

Scottish Episcopal Church, letter from J. Stuart, Secretary General, to Revd Canon G. K. Cameron, Deputy Secretary General of the Anglican Communion (5 December 2006)

Strudwick (2006b), The Revd Canon Vincent, *Towards an Anglican Covenant: A Response from Inclusive Church* (20 November 2006): www.inclusivechurch.net/articles/details.html?id=101

Responses to the Nassau Report and Draft Covenant of the Covenant Design Group 2007

Covenant Design Group, Report and Draft Covenant, Nassau (ACNS 4252, 19 February 2007) may be found at: www.aco.org/commission/d_covenant/index.cfm

As well as the other websites indicated, responses may be found at: www.anglicancommunion.org/commission/covenant/responses/index.cfm

Bagshaw, P., Bouncing the covenant through the Anglican Communion (19 June 2007): www.modchurchunion.org

Bartel, T. W., Casting off the garment of humility: a response to the Report of the Covenant Design Group (2007): http://inclusive.sqnsolutions.com/uploads/media

Beisner, Rt Revd B. L., Diocese of North California, Response to the Draft Anglican Covenant (4 June 2007)

Clatworthy, J., Bagshaw, P., and Saxbee, J., A Response to the Draft Anglican Covenant (May 2007): www.modchurchunion.org/Publications/Papers/Covenant/Summer2007/MCUCovenant responseMay07.doc

Dakin, T., Reflections on the Anglican Covenant; some ecumenical and missional perspectives (June 2007): Anglican Institute Website.

Grieb, A. K., 'Interpreting the proposed Anglican Covenant through the Communiqué [of the Primates' Meeting, 2007]' Episcopal News Service (19 March 2007)

Hensman, S., 'Love and witness in a broken world' (2007)

Noll, S., An evangelical commentary on the draft covenant (1 June 2007)

Radner, R., A presentation to the House of Bishops [TEC] on the proposed Anglican covenant: steps towards the covenant (19 March 2007): Episcopal News Service

Seitz, C, 'Covenanting in the church and in scripture – congruent or discordant?' (2007)

Sharp, C.J., Our unity is in Christ: www.sarmiento.plus.com/documents (2007)

The following may be found through: www.fulcrum-anglican.org.uk:

A Response to the draft Anglican covenant from the Standing Committee of the Diocese of Virginia

Goddard, A., The Anglican Covenant, A Briefing Paper for the Evangelical Group on the General Synod of the Church of England (2006)

Sugden, C., An Anglican Communion covenant: a personal view (2006)

Fulcrum Response to the Covenant for the Anglican Communion

Provincial Responses to the Nassau Report and Draft Covenant of the Covenant Design Group 2007

These may be found at: www.aco.org/commission/covenant/st_andrews/draft_text.cfm

Anglican Church in Aotearoa, New Zealand and Polynesia: A Submission on the Draft Covenant (undated)

Anglican Church of Australia: Initial Response to the Report of the Covenant Design Group (undated)

Anglican Church of Canada: A Preliminary Response to the Draft Covenant (19-11-2007)

Anglican Church of Southern Africa: Response to the Draft Anglican Covenant (21-12-2007)

Church in Wales: Response by the Drafting Group to 'An Anglican Covenant' (June 2007)

Church of England: Response to the Draft Anglican Covenant (21-12-2007)

Church of Ireland: Response to the Draft Anglican Covenant (November 2007)

Lusitanian Church: Response to the Draft Covenant Text (28-12-2007)

Province of Hong Kong Sheng Kung Hui: Proposed Anglican Covenant, Response to the First Draft (22-1-2008)

Province of the Episcopal Church in the Philippines, Some Observations of the Draft of 'An Anglican Covenant' (undated)

Scottish Episcopal Church: The Draft Anglican Covenant: A Response (undated)

The Church in the Province of the West Indies: An Anglican Covenant: Comments (undated)

The Episcopal Church USA: A Response from the Executive Council to the Draft Anglican Covenant (28-10-2007)

The St Andrews Draft Covenant 2008

The *Communiqué* of the Covenant Design Group, meeting at St Andrew's House London, 29 January to 2 February 2008, its St Andrews Draft Covenant, an Introduction to the Draft and a Commentary upon it, may be found at: www.aco.org/commission/covenant/st_andrews/draft_text.cfm

Anglican International Instruments

A Covenant Union of Anglican Churches in Concordat (2005), entered between the Church of Nigeria (Anglican Communion), the Reformed Episcopal Church and the Anglican Province of America (12-11-2005 (Pittsburgh)): ACNS 4075 (17-11-2005)

Anglican Communion Network, Core Purpose, Vision and Values, Memorandum of Agreement, Organizational Charter (2003), Confession and Calling (2004): http://www.acn-us.org/documents

Anglican Communion Network of Legal Advisers, Draft Statement of the Principles of Canon Law Common to the Churches of the Anglican Communion: www.acclawnet.co.uk

Anglican Consultative Council, Constitution

Anglican Global Initiative, Draft Organizing Constitution 2004 ('If it becomes necessary'): http://progressiveepiscopalians.org

Council of Anglican Provinces of Africa (2005): http://www.capa-hq.org

Covenant for Communion in Mission, Inter-Anglican Standing Commission on Mission and Evangelism (2005)

Ten Principles from Towards Dynamic Mission: Renewing the Church for Mission, Mission Issues and Strategy Advisory Group II (1993)

Laws and Regulatory Instruments of Anglican Churches

Australia: *The Anglican Church of Australia: Constitution, Canons and Rules of the General Synod* (2003); *An Australian Prayer Book* (1978); *A Prayer Book for Australia* (1995)

Canada: Anglican Church of Canada, *Handbook of the General Synod of the Anglican Church of Canada* (2004); *Book of Common Prayer* (1962); *The Book of Alternative Services* (1985)

Central Africa: Church of the Province of Central Africa, *Constitution and Canons* (1996)

Chile: Diocese of Chile, Anglican Church of the Southern Cone of America, *Estatutos de la Corporacion Anglicana de Chile* (1995) (this includes the Canons)

England: Church of England, *Canons of the Church of England* (1964–2006); *Book of Common Prayer* (1662); *Alternative Service Book* (1980)

Ireland: *The Constitution of the Church of Ireland* (1988–1996); *Book of Common Prayer* (1960); *Alternative Prayer Book* (1984)

Japan: Holy Catholic Church in Japan (Nippon Sei Ko Kai), *Constitution and Canons* (1971–1994)

Jerusalem: *Constitution of the Central Synod of the Episcopal Church in Jerusalem and the Middle East* (1976–1980)

Kenya: Church of the Province of Kenya, *Constitution* (1979)

Korea: *The Constitution and Canons of the Anglican Church of Korea* (1992)

Melanesia: Church of the Province of Melanesia, *Constitution and Canons* (1992)

New Zealand: Anglican Church in Aotearoa, New Zealand and Polynesia, *Constitution and Code of Canons* (1995); *A New Zealand Prayer Book* (1989)

Nigeria: Church of Nigeria (Anglican Communion), *Constitution* (1997)

North India: United Church of North India, *Constitution and Bye-Laws* (1986)

Papua New Guinea: Anglican Church of (the Province of) Papua New Guinea, *Provincial Constitution and Provincial Canons* (1996); *Anglican Prayer Book* (1991)

Philippines: Episcopal Church in the (Province of the) Philippines, *Constitution and Canons* (1996)

Portugal: Lusitanian Church (Portuguese Episcopal Church), *Igreja Lusitana, Catolica, Apostolica, Evangelica, Canones* (1980)

Rwanda: Church of the Province of Rwanda, *Constitution* (1998)

Scotland: Scottish Episcopal Church, *Code of Canons* (2006)

South East Asia: Church of the Province of South East Asia, *Constitution and Regulations* (1997)

South India: *The Constitution of the Church of South India* (1992)

Southern Africa: Church of the Province of Southern Africa, *Constitution and Canons* (2004); *An Anglican Prayer Book* (1989)

Southern Cone: Anglican Church of the Southern Cone of America, *Constitution and Canons* (1981)

Sudan: *The Constitution of the Province of the Episcopal Church of the Sudan* (1976: as amended, 1983)

Uganda: Church of the Province of Uganda, *Provincial Constitution* (1972: as amended, 1994)

USA: *Constitutions and Canons for the Government of the Protestant Episcopal Church in the United States of America* (2000); *Book of Common Prayer* (1979)

Venezuela: Extra-Provincial Diocese of Venezuela, *Constitucion y Canones de la Iglesia Anglicana en Venezuela* (1995)

Wales: *The Constitution of the Church in Wales* (2006) 2 Volumes; *The Book of Common Prayer* (1984), 2 Volumes

West Africa: Church of the Province of West Africa, *Constitution and Canons* (1989)

West Indies: *Constitution and Canons of the Church of the Province of the West Indies* (1991); *Liturgical Texts* (1989)

Ecumenical Agreements

An Anglican–Methodist Covenant, Common Statement of Formal Conversations, Methodist Church of Great Britain and Church of England (London, 2001)

Anglican–Lutheran Covenant in Australia 2004

Australian Churches Covenanting Together

Bonn Agreement 1931

Charta Oecumenica 2001, between the Conference of European Churches and the Roman Catholic Council of European Bishops' Conferences

Covenant of the Churches in Wales 1975

Churches Together in Britain and Ireland, Constitution (2003)

Growth in Communion, Report of the Anglican–Lutheran International Working Group 2000–2002 (Geneva, 2003)

Kilcoy Covenant (2001) http://assembly.uca.org.au/cunity/churchesjoin/cjcovags/individual/cjkilcoycov6.htm

Lutheran–Anglican–Roman Catholic Covenant (Virginia, 1990)

Instruments of Comparable International Ecclesial Communities

Baptist World Alliance, Constitution, and Bylaws of the General Council (2002): http://www.bwanet.org?About Us/Membership.htm

Community of Protestant Churches in Europe, Leuenberg Agreement (1973)

Conference of European Churches, Constitution (1992)

Constitutional Charter of the Sovereign Military Hospitaller Order of St John of Jerusalem, of Rhodes and of Malta (Rome, 1998)

Lutheran World Federation, Constitution and Bylaws (1997)

Standing Conference of Canonical Orthodox Bishops in the Americas, Constitution (1961)

Standing Conference of Canonical Orthodox Churches of Australia: this was 'a vision of Archbishop Stylianos' in 1975: http://home.it.net.au/~jgrapsas/pages/sccoca.htm

Southern Baptist Convention, Constitution (1845)
Union of Utrecht of the Old Catholic Churches, Statute of the International Conference of Old Catholic Bishops United in the Union of Utrecht (2000)
Guidelines of the International Bishops Conference with Respect to the Recognition of a Church as Independent Old-Catholic Church of the Utrecht Union (2002): http://www.utrechter-union.org/english/ibc_documents003.htm
World Alliance of Reformed Churches, Constitution (2003) and Mission in Unity Project (1999–2005): http://warc.jalb.de/warcajsp/side.jsp?news_id+445& navi+27
World Methodist Council, Constitution

Secondary Literature

A Guide to the Windsor Report, Commissioned by an International Gathering from around the Anglican Communion meeting at Oxford 19/21-10-2004 (unpublished)
Abshire, B. M., 'On the nature of ecclesiastical authority and sanctions': http:// christian-civilization.org/highlands-reformed/sanctions.html
Adam, P., 'Communion: virtue or vice', in Bolt, P. G., M. D. Thompson and R. Tong (eds), *The Faith Once for All Delivered* (Camperdown, NSW, The Australian Church Record in conjunction with the Anglican Church League, 2005) 71
Advent Pastoral Letter, Archbishop of Canterbury, ACNS 14 December 2007
Anglican Roman Catholic International Commission: *The Church as Communion* (London, Church House Publishing, 1991)
Archbishop Yong Ping Chung, Primate of the Province of South East Asia, interview: http://www.anglicansabah.org/FeaturedArticles_Lambeth_10Oct.htm
Armentrout, D. S., and R. B. Slocum (eds), *Documents of Witness: A History of the Episcopal Church 1782–1985* (New York, Church Hymnal Corporation, 1994)
Atiyah, P. S., *Promises, Morals and Law* (Oxford, Clarendon Press, 1981)
Atta-Baffoe, V., 'The Anglican Covenant: an African perspective', in M. Chapman (ed.), *The Anglican Covenant* (London, Mowbray, 2008) 143
Avis, P., *The Christian Church: An Introduction to the Major Traditions* (London, SPCK, 2002)
Baima, T. M., *The Concordat of Agreement between the Episcopal Church and the Evangelical Lutheran Church in America: Lessons on the Way Toward Full Communion* (New York, Edwin Mellen Press, 2003)
Barnett-Cowan, A. (member of the Lambeth Commission): interview (22-10-2004): hhtp://aacblog.classicalanglican.net/archives/000364.html
Barton, J., 'Covenant in the Bible and today', in M. Chapman (ed.), *The Anglican Covenant* (London, Mowbray, 2008) 193
Beal, J. P., J. A. Coriden and T. J. Green (eds), *New Commentary on the Code of Canon Law* (New York, Paulist Press, 2000)
Beatson, J., and Friedman, D., *Good Faith and Fault in Contract Law* (Oxford, Oxford University Press, 1997)
Beek, W. Van, 'Covenants' (1992): http://www.lightplanet.com/mormons/ basic/doctrines/covenants_eom.htm

Bishops in Communion, GS Misc 580 (London, 2000) [Church of England]

Boff, L., *Trinity and Society* (London, Burns & Oates, 1988)

Bolt, P. G., M. D. Thompson and R. Tong (eds), *The Faith Once For All Delivered* (Camperdown, NSW, The Australian Church Record in conjunction with the Anglican League, 2005)

Brown, F., S. R. Driver, and C. A. Briggs, *A Hebrew and English Lexicon of the Old Testament* (1907)

Brownlie, I., *Principles of Public International Law* (6th edn, Oxford, Oxford University Press, 2003)

Cameron, G., 'Baby's first steps: can the covenant ever walk?' in M. Chapman (ed.), *The Anglican Covenant* (London, Mowbray, 2008) 35

Cameron, N., 'The Windsor Report 2004: legal implications', in Bolt, P. G., M. D. Thompson and R. Tong (eds), *The Faith Once for All Delivered* (Camperdown, NSW, The Australian Church Record in conjunction with the Anglican League, 2005) 49

Canadian Anglican Bishops, Statement, ACNS 4141, 5 May 2006

Chapman, M. (ed.), *The Anglican Covenant: Unity and Diversity in the Anglican Communion* (London, Mowbray, 2008)

Chapman, M., 'Dull bits of history: cautionary tales for Anglicanism', in Chapman (ed.), *Anglican Covenant*, 81

Chayes, A., and A. H. Chayes, *The New Sovereignty: Compliance with International Regulatory Agreements* (Cambridge, Mass., Harvard University Press, 1995)

Childress, J. F., 'Promise', in J. F. Childress and J. MacQuarrie (eds), *A New Dictionary of Christian Ethics* (London, SCM Press, 1986) 505

Church of England: Ministry Division, Guidance: Summary of Criteria for Selection for Ministry (2005): www.cofe.anglican.org/lifeevents/ministry/ministryinthecofe/ministryincofe.html

Church of North India, Minutes of 75th Meeting of the Synod Executive Committee (17–19 February 2005)

Coing, H., 'English equity and the *denunciatio evangelica* of canon law', *Law Quarterly Review* 71 (1955) 223

Coleman, E. (ed.), *Resolutions of the Twelve Lambeth Conferences 1867–1988* (Toronto, Anglican Book Centre, 1992)

Congar, Y., 'Quod omnes tangit ab omnibus tractari et approbari debet', *Revue historique de droit français et étranger* 36 (1958) 210

Countryman, L. W., 'Politics, polity and the Bible as hostage', in A. Linzey and R. Kirker (eds), *Gays and the Future of Anglicanism: Responses to the Windsor Report* (Winchester, O Books, 2005) 2

Davis, J. D., *The Westminster Dictionary of the Bible* (Revised edn, London, Collins, 1944)

Deweese, C. W., *Church Covenants* (Nashville, Tennessee, Broadman, 1990)

Doe, N., *The Legal Framework of the Church of England* (Oxford, Clarendon Press, 1996)

Doe, N., *Canon Law in the Anglican Communion* (Oxford, Clarendon Press, 1998)

Doe, N., 'The principles of canon law: a focus of legal unity in Anglican-Roman Catholic relations', *Ecclesiastical Law Journal* 5 (1999) 221

Doe, N., 'Canon law and communion', *EccLJ* 6 (2002) 241–63; *International Journal for the Study of the Christian Church* 3 (2003) 85–117

Doe, N., 'Canonical approaches to human rights in Anglican churches', in M. Hill (ed.), *Religious Liberty and Human Rights* (Cardiff, University of Wales Press, 2002) 185

Doe, N., 'The common law of the Anglican Communion', *Ecclesiastical Law Journal* 7 (2003) 4

Doe, N., 'Communion and autonomy in Anglicanism': www.anglicancommunion.org/ecumenical/commissions/lambeth/documents/200402whatisitfor.pdf

Doe, N., 'The Anglican Covenant proposed by the Lambeth Commission', *Ecclesiastical Law Journal* 8 (2005) 147–61

Doe, N., and R. Sandberg, 'The "state of the union", a canonical perspective: principles of canon law in the Anglican Communion', *Sewanee Theological Review* 49 (2006) 234

Does the Anglican Communion Have a Future? An Analysis of the Windsor Report (Watford, Church Society, 2004)

Douglas, I., and P. Zahl, *Understanding the Windsor Report* (New York, Church Publishing Inc., 2005)

Eames, Archbishop R., 'The Anglican Communion', two lectures delivered at the Virginia Seminary, USA: ACNS 4041 (5-10-2005) and ACNS 4045 (6-10-2005)

Episcopal Church of the USA, Office of Ecumenism and Interfaith Relations, 'A Beginner's Guide to the Concordat of Agreement' (with the Evangelical Lutheran Church of America (2003): http://www.ecusa.anglican.org/6947_9206_ENG_HTM.htm

Erickson, J. H., *The Challenge of Our Past: Studies in Orthodox Canon Law and Church History* (Crestwood, NY, St Vladimir's Seminary Press, 1991)

Evangelical Lutheran Church of America, Constitution and Foundational Texts (2003)

Evans, G. R., *The Church and the Churches: Toward an Ecumenical Ecclesiology* (Cambridge, Cambridge University Press, 1994)

Feiss, H., *Monastic Wisdom* (San Francisco, Harper, 1999)

Fiddes, P., *Tracks and Traces: Baptist Identity in Church and Theology* (Carlisle, Paternoster Press, 2003)

Finnis, J., *Natural Law and Natural Rights* (Oxford, Clarendon Press, 1980)

Fitzmaurice, G., 'Some problems regarding the formal sources of international law', *Symbolae Verzijl* (The Hague, 1958)

Franklin, R. W., 'The Episcopal Church in the USA and the Covenant: the place of the Chicago-Lambeth Quadrilateral', in M. Chapman (ed.), *The Anglican Covenant* (London, Mowbray, 2008) 101

Fried, P., *Contract as Promise: A Theory of Contractual Obligation* (Cambridge, Mass., Harvard University Press, 1981)

Georges, B., 'The Anglican Consultative Council' (2006), LLM in Canon Law, Dissertation, Cardiff University, 2006

Gilby, T., *Between Community and Society: A Philosophy and Theology of the State* (London, Longmans, Green and Co., 1953)

Goddard, A., 'Walking together? The future shape of the Anglican Communion' (2005) 6: http://www.anviljournal.co.uk/Articles/22_1_Goddard.htm.

Goddard, A., 'Unity and diversity, communion and covenant: theological, ecclesiological, political and missional challenges for Anglicanism', in M. Chapman (ed.), *The Anglican Covenant* (London, Mowbray, 2008) 47

Gomez, D., and Sinclair, M. W. (eds), *To Mend the Net: Anglican Faith and Order for Renewed Mission* (Carrollton, Texas, The Ekklesia Society, 2001)

Gräbe, P. J., *New Covenant – New Community: The Significance of Biblical and Patristic Covenant Theology for Contemporary Understanding* (Carlisle, Paternoster Press, 2006)

Graham, E., '"Our real witness": Windsor, public opinion and sexuality', in A. Linzey and R. Kirker (eds), *Gays and the Future of Anglicanism: Responses to the Windsor Report* (Winchester, O Books, 2005) 199

Greer, R. A., 'No easy paths: was Trollope right?', in A. Linzey and R. Kirker (eds), *Gays and the Future of Anglicanism: Responses to the Windsor Report* (Winchester, O Books, 2005) 100

Griswold, F. T. (Presiding Bishop of the Episcopal Church, USA), Letter 18-10-2004: http://.www.episcopalchurch.org/3577_52922_ENG_HTM.htm

Griswold, Presiding Bishop F. T., Epiphany Message from the Presiding Bishop of ECUSA (ENS 011305-2)

Growth in Communion, Report of the Anglican-Lutheran International Working Group 2000–2002 (Geneva, Lutheran World Federation, 2003)

Guest, A. G. (ed.), *Anson's Law of Contract* (24th edn, Oxford, Clarendon Press, 1975)

Hamid, D., 'Church, communion of churches and the Anglican Communion', *Ecclesiastical Law Journal* 6 (2002) 352

Handy, C., *Understanding Organizations* (4th edn, London, Penguin Books, 1993)

Harare Declaration 1991 of the Commonwealth of Nations

Hardy, D. W., *Finding the Church* (London, SCM Press, 2001) 27

Hart, H. L. A., 'Are there any natural rights?', *Philosophical Review* 64 (1955) 175

Hefling, C., 'A reasonable development?', in A. Linzey and R. Kirker (eds), *Gays and the Future of Anglicanism* (Winchester, O Books, 2005) 81

Helmholz, R. H., *The Canon Law and Ecclesiastical Jurisdiction from 597 to the 1640s* (Oxford, Oxford University Press, 2004)

Hill, Mark, *Ecclesiastical Law* (3rd edn, Oxford, Oxford University Press, 2007)

Hill, M., *A Sociology of Religion* (New York, Basic Books, 1973)

Hillerbrand, H. J. (ed.), *The Oxford Encyclopedia of the Reformation* (Oxford, Oxford University Press, 1996)

History of the Union of Utrecht of the Old Catholic Churches: http://www.utrechter-union.org/english/history001.htm

Hooker, Richard, *Of the Laws of Ecclesiastical Polity*, ed. A. S. McGrade (Cambridge, Cambridge University Press, 1989)

Huelin, G. (ed.), *Old Catholics and Anglicans: 1931–1981* (Oxford, Oxford University Press, 1983)

Hugenberger, G. P., *Marriage as a Covenant* (Leiden, E. J. Brill, 1994)

International Anglican Theological and Doctrinal Commission: http://www.aco.org/documents/iatdc/four questions/english.html

International Federation of Red Cross and Red Crescent Societies, Constitution

International Law Commission, Provisional Draft, *Yearbook ILC* (1962) ii.161

Jeremy, A. W., '*Pacta sunt servanda*: the influence of canon law upon the development of contractual obligations', *Law and Justice* 144 (2000) 4

Jones, G., '"Thy grace shall always prevent . . ."', in A. Linzey and R. Kirker (eds), *Gays and the Future of Anglicanism: Responses to the Windsor Report* (Winchester, O Books, 2005)

Johnston, D. M., *Consent and Commitment in the World Community* (New York, Transnational Publishers, 1997)

Kalluveettil, P., *Declaration and Covenant: A Comprehensive Review of Covenant Formulae from the Old Testament and the Ancient New East* (Rome, Biblical Institute Press, 1982)

Kasper, W., *The God of Jesus Christ*, trans. M. J. O'Connell (Oxford, Blackwell, 1989)

Kelsey, J. (Bishop, The Episcopal Church USA): Statement (19-10-2004): http://www.episcopalchurch.org/3577_53210_ENG_HTM.htm

Keshishian, A., 'Growing together towards full koinonia', in G. Limouris (ed.), *Orthodox Visions of Ecumenism: Statements, Messages and Reports on the Ecumenical Movement 1902–1922* (Geneva, World Council of Churches, 1994)

Knox, D. B., 'Lambeth and reunion' and 'The church and denominations', in Bolt, P. G., M. D. Thompson and R. Tong (eds), *The Faith Once For All Delivered* (Camperdown, NSW, The Australian Church Record in conjunction with the Anglican League, 2005) 81, 111

Komonchak, J. A., M. Collins, and D. A. Lane (eds), *The New Dictionary of Theology* (Dublin, Gill & Macmillan, 1987)

Korten, D., *Getting to the 21st Century: Voluntary Action and the Global Agenda* (West Hartford, CT, Kumarian Press, 1990)

Koskenniemi, M., 'What is international law for?', in M. Evans (ed.), *International Law* (Oxford, Oxford University Press, 2003) 89

Letter and Spirit: A Practical Guide to the Code of Canon Law, The Canon Law Society of Great Britain and Ireland (Dublin, Veritas, 1995)

Lewis, C., 'On unimportance', in A. Linzey and R. Kirker (eds), *Gays and the Future of Anglicanism: Responses to the Windsor Report* (Winchester, O Books, 2005) 149

Lewis, H. T., 'Covenant, contract, and communion: reflections on a Post-Windsor Anglicanism', *Anglican Theological Review* 87 (2005) 601

Lillback, P. A., 'Covenant', in S. B. Ferguson and D. F. Wright (eds), *New Dictionary of Theology* (Leicester and Illinois, Inter-Varsity Press, 1988) 173

Lindblom, A.-K., *Non-Governmental Organizations in International Law* (Cambridge, Cambridge University Press, 2006)

Linzey, A., and R. Kirker (eds), *Gays and the Future of Anglicanism: Responses to the Windsor Report* (Winchester, O Books, 2005)

Lossky, N., J. M. Bonino, J. Pobee, T. F. Stransky, G. Wainwright, and P. Webb (eds), *Dictionary of the Ecumenical Movement* (Geneva, World Council of Churches, 2002)

Lyall, F., 'Of metaphors and analogies: legal language and covenant theology', *Scottish Journal of Theology* 32 (1979) 1

MacDougall, S., 'The Windsor Report: ecclesiological departures for the Anglican Communion', General Theological Seminary of the Episcopal Church, Master of Arts Candidate Dissertation (Unpublished, Diocese of New York, 2005)

Macquarrie, J., *Paths in Spirituality* (2nd edn, London, SCM Press, 1992)

Martin, E. A (ed.), *Oxford Dictionary of Law* (5th edn, Oxford, Oxford University Press, 2003)

Mayer, R. C., J. H. Davis and F. D. Schoorman, 'An integrative model of organizational trust', *Academy of Management Review* 20(3) (1995) 709

McCarthy, D. J., *Old Testament Covenant: A Survey of Current Opinions* (Oxford, Oxford University Press, 1972)

McCarthy, D. J., *Treaty and Covenant: A Study in Form in the Ancient Oriental Documents and in the Old Testament* (Rome, Biblical Institute Press, 1981)

McCord Adams, M., 'Faithfulness in crisis', in A. Linzey and R. Kirker (eds), *Gays and the Future of Anglicanism: Responses to the Windsor Report* (Winchester, O Books, 2005) 70

McCord Adams, M., 'How to quench the spirit', *Church Times*, 29 October 2004, 9

McGrade, A. S. (ed.), *Richard Hooker and the Construction of Christian Community* (Tempe, Arizona, MRTS, 1997)

McGrath, A. E., (ed.), *The Blackwell Encyclopaedia of Modern Christian Thought* (Oxford, Blackwell, 1993)

McPartlan, P., 'Towards an Anglican Covenant: a Roman Catholic perspective', in M. Chapman (ed.), *The Anglican Covenant* (London, Mowbray, 2008) 157

Mendenhall, G. E., *Law and Covenant in the Ancient Middle East and in Israel* (Reprinted from *The Biblical Archeologist*, 17, Pittsburgh, PA, 1954) 26

Methuen, C., 'From all nations and languages: reflections on church, catholicity and culture', in M. Chapman (ed.), *The Anglican Covenant* (London, Mowbray, 2008) 123

Morgan, B., A talk to the Governing Body of the Church in Wales, September 2007, www.churchinwales.org.uk/structure/bishops/sermonsb/b25.html

Morgan, G., *Images of Organization* (San Francisco, Berrett-Koehler Publishers, 1998)

Moss, C. B., *The Old Catholic Movement: Its Origins and History* (London, SPCK, 1964)

Motluk, D., 'The code of canons of the Eastern Catholic Churches', *Studia Canonica* 36 (2002) 189

New Advent Catholic Encyclopaedia, 'Concordat': http://www.new advent.org/caten/04196a.htm

Niebuhr, H. R., *Children of Light and Children of Darkness* (London, Nisbet, 1945)

Noll, S., 'The global Anglican Communion: a blueprint' (2005): http://titusonline.classicalanglican.net/?p=10996

O'Dea, T. F., 'Five dilemmas in the institutionalization of religion', *Journal for the Scientific Study of Religion* (1961) 30

O'Donovan, O., and O'Donovan, J. L. (eds), *From Irenaeus to Grotius: A*

Sourcebook in Christian Political Thought 100–1625 (Cambridge, William B. Eerdmans Publishing Company, 1999)

Oppegaard, S., and G. Cameron (eds), *Anglican-Lutheran Agreements: Regional and International Agreements 1972–2002* (Geneva, Lutheran World Federation and Anglican Consultative Council, 2004)

Orzell, L. J., 'Disunion of Utrecht: Old Catholics fall out over new doctrines', *Touchstone* (May 2004): http://www.touchstonemag.com/archives/article.php?id=17-04-56-r

Otero, J. C., 'Church–state relations in the light of Vatican II', *Concilium* 8 (1970) 113

Paterson, J., Chair, ACC: Address: ACNS 3993 (21-6-2005)

Pearce, A., 'English ecclesiastical autonomy and the Windsor report' (2005): http://www.lgcm.org.uk/html/PearceEssay.html

Peel, A., and L. H. Carlson (eds), *Writings of Robert Harrison and Robert Browne* (London, Allen & Unwin, 1953)

Percy, M., 'On being stretched', in A. Linzey and R. Kirker (eds), *Gays and the Future of Anglicanism: Responses to the Windsor Report* (Winchester, O Books, 2005) 213

Petre, J., 'Archbishop backs two-track Church to heal divisions', *Daily Telegraph* (19-5-2006)

Piper, J., 'Why a church covenant?' (1993): http:/www.desiringgod.org/library/sermons/93/013193.html

Poole, J., *Textbook on Contract* (8th edn, Oxford, Oxford University Press, 2006)

Pospishil, V., *Eastern Catholic Church Law* (New York, St Maron Publications, 1996)

Puza, R., and N. Doe (eds), *Religion and Law in Dialogue: Covenantal and Non-Covenantal Co-operation between State and Religion in Europe* (Leuven, Peeters, 2006)

Radner, E., 'Freedom and covenant: the Miltonian analogy transfigured', *Anglican Theological Review* 87 (2005) 617

Rees, D., (ed.), *Consider Your Call: A Theology of the Monastic Life Today* (London, SPCK, 1978)

Rees, J., 'Anglican Communion Legal Advisers' Consultation', *Ecclesiastical Law Journal* 6 (2002) 399

Repair the Tear: The Windsor Report – An Assessment and Call for Action (Anglican Mainstream – UK and the Church of England Evangelical Council, 2004)

Roberts, K. A., *Religion in Sociological Perspective* (2nd edn, Belmont, CA, Wadsworth, 1990)

Sakenfeld, K. D., *Faithfulness in Action: Loyalty in Biblical Perspective* (Philadelphia, Fortress Press, 1985)

Salier, B., 'John 17.21–23 and Christian unity', in Bolt, P. G., M. D. Thompson and R. Tong (eds), *The Faith Once For All Delivered* (Camperdown, NSW, Australian Church Record in conjunction with the Anglican League, 2005) 81

Schmemann, A., *Of Water and the Spirit* (New York, St Vladimir's Seminary Press, 1976)

Shelton, D. (ed.), *Commitment and Compliance: The Role of Non-Binding Norms in the International Legal System* (Oxford, Oxford University Press, 2000)

Shelton, D., 'International law and "relative normativity"', in M. Evans (ed.), *International Law* (Oxford, Oxford University Press, 2003) 145

Signs of the Spirit: Official Report of the Seventh Assembly of the World Council of Churches, ed. M. Kinnamon (Geneva, World Council of Churches, 1991)

Simpson, A. W. B., *A History of the Common Law of Contract: the Rise of the Action of* Assumpsit (Oxford, Clarendon Press, 1987)

Stackhouse, M. L., 'Ecclesiology and ethics', in J. F. Childress and J. MacQuarrie (eds), *A New Dictionary of Christian Ethics* (London, SCM Press, 1986) 171

Stanton Norman, R., *The Baptist Way: Distinctives of a Baptist Church* (Nashville, Tennessee, Broadman and Holman, 2005)

Statement of Commitment by the Bishops of the Anglican Church of Canada: ACNS 3971 (29-4-2005)

Statements of the Methodist Church on Faith and Order 1933–1983 (London, 1984)

Stevenson, K. (ed.), *A Fallible Church: Lambeth Essays* (London, Darton, Longman, & Todd, 2008)

Strudwick, V., 'Toward an understanding of the type of Covenant needed for the Churches of the Anglican Communion' (unpublished paper: 2-2-2006)

The Church Constitution Guide: North American Mission Board, a Southern Baptist Convention agency: see: www.namb.net

The Baptist Faith and Message, Southern Baptist Convention, Sunday School Board (Nashville, Tenn., 1963)

The Eucharist: Sacrament of Unity, An occasional paper of the House of Bishops of the Church of England (London, Church House Publishing, 2001)

The Lutheran World Federation as a Communion (Geneva, Lutheran World Federation, 2003)

'The Windsor Action Covenant: Think Before You Sign' (2005): on the website of Progressive Episcopalians of Pittsburgh, A Via Media USA Alliance Member: http://www.progressiveepiscopalians.org/httml/think_first.html

Thirlway, H., 'The sources of international law', M. Evans (ed.), *International Law* (Oxford, Oxford University Press, 2003) 117

Thomas, P. H. E., 'Unity and concord: an early Anglican "Communion"', *Journal of Anglican Studies* 21 (2004) 9

Thompson, M. D., 'The concept of adiaphora and the Windsor Report', in Bolt, P. G., M. D. Thompson and R. Tong (eds), *The Faith Once For All Delivered* (Camperdown, NSW, Australian Church Record in conjunction with the Anglican League, 2005) 103

Tong, R., 'How would the Anglican Church of Australia commit itself to an Anglican Covenant?', in Bolt, P. G., M. D. Thompson and R. Tong (eds), *The Faith Once For All Delivered* (Camperdown, NSW, Australian Church Record in conjunction with the Anglican League, 2005) 55

Treitel, G. H., *The Law of Contract* (11th edn, London, Thompson, Sweet and Maxwell, 2003)

Tretera, J., 'Concordatarian agreements and public agreements in the Czech state ecclesiastical law', in R. Puza and N. Doe (eds), *Religion and Law in Dialogue: Covenantal and Non-Covenantal Co-operation between State and Religion in Europe* (Leuven, Peeters, 2006) 33

Tripp, D., 'Covenant', in G. S. Wakefield (ed.), *A Dictionary of Christian Spirituality* (London, SCM Press, 1983) 98

Tripp, D. H., *The Renewal of the Covenant in the Methodist Tradition* (London, Epworth Press, 1969)

Turner, R., 'A holey covenant: the Lambeth Commission's proposed "Anglican Covenant" considered', the Editor, 43–4 *The Christian Challenge* (2004) 2: http://challengeonline.org/modules/wfsection/article.php?articleid=39

Vinogradoff, P., 'Reason and conscience', *Law Quarterly Review* 24 (1908) 382

Virginia Report (of the Inter-Anglican Theological and Doctrinal Commission), *The Official Report of the Lambeth Conference 1998* (Harrisburg, Morehouse Publishing, 1999)

Vischer, L. (ed.), *A Documentary History of the Faith and Order Movement: 1927–1963* (St Louis, Bethany Press, 1964), 'The Church, the Churches and the World Council of Churches', 168

Wagnon, H., *Concordats et droit international* (Gembloux, Éditions J. Duculot, 1935)

Ward, K., 'African perspectives on episcopacy and sexuality', in A. Linzey and R. Kirker (eds), *Gays and the Future of Anglicanism: Responses to the Windsor Report* (Winchester, O Books, 2005) 243

Ware, T., *The Orthodox Church* (London, Penguin Books, 1963, reprinted 1991)

Watkin, T. G., 'The concept of commitment in law and legal science', in P. R. Beaumont (ed.), *Christian Perspectives on Human Rights and Legal Philosophy* (Carlisle, Paternoster Press, 1998) 95

Webb, H., 'A new church covenant': http://www.lifeway.com/lwc/article_main_page/0,1703,A=161133&M=150036,00.html

Werckmeister, J., *Petit Dictionnaire de Droit Canonique* (Paris, Les Editions Du Cerf, 1993)

Williams, Rowan, Archbishop of Canterbury, *The Challenge and Hope of being Anglican Today: A Reflection for the Bishops, Clergy and Faithful of the Anglican Communion* (27 June 2006): ACNS 4161

Wilson, K., 'The Methodist idea of covenant', in M. Chapman (ed.), *The Anglican Covenant* (London, Mowbray, 2008) 175

Wink, W., *The Powers That Be: Theology for a New Millennium* (New York, Galilee Trade, 1999)

Witte, J., *Law and Protestantism: The Legal Teachings of the Lutheran Reformation* (Cambridge, Cambridge University Press, 2002)

World Methodist Council, Mission Statement: http://www.worldmethodist council.org/mission.html

Index

Accountability 64ff, 66n, 76, 99, 128, 129, 187, 206

Adiaphora:
essentials and 103–7, 123, 134, 158
meaning 103, 106
negotiation and 158
utility 103–104

Alternative dispute resolution 200
See also Arbitration, Conciliation and Mediation

Amber light model 221n

Anglican Church, the: *See* Ecclesiality

Anglican Communion: accountability within: *See* Accountability
Anglo-centric character 156
bonds of affection: *See* Bonds of affection
canon law in: *See* Canon law
central jurisdiction 37, 140, 143n, 203n
church, as a 207–211
clarity within 61, 74
colonialism 33, 35n
commissions 150, 198
common concerns: *See* Essential matters of common concern
common good 116, 120, 141–142
common mind 132, 142
communion in 35n, 38, 74, 100–101, 144, 187
Communion issues 121–124
community, as 32
confessionalism 77–78
conflict 63–64, 86, 142–144, 191ff
consensual 19, 31, 34
conventional principles of 3, 37, 189
covenant as first constitution 19

covenant models for 221n
covenantal character 31, 33, 34, 37, 91
culture 33, 35n
definition 37n, 183n
discerning will of God for covenanting 154
discipline 64, 193–194, 199
disputes 65n, 88, 142, 144, 195f
diversity: *See* Diversity
ecclesiality of 207–211
ecumenical consultation 11, 131n, 141
eucharistic community, as 44–45
evolution of 206
fabric 2
family, as 2, 32, 33–34, 40, 54, 64, 139, 194, 207, 209
federation and 34
fellowship, as 1
fragmentation 54, 64
globalisation 33
house rules 64, 65, 79
identity: *See* Identity, Anglican
institutionalisation 76
Instruments of Communion: *See* Instruments of Communion
inter-Anglican agreements 40–41, 219
inter-church relations: *See* Communion
interdependence: *See* Interdependence
law and inter-church relations 37, 167
listening in: *See* Listening
membership 28, 62, 75, 100, 182–184, 185

mission, and 67–69, 80, 142–143, 195ff
networks in 150
order in 37n, 63–67
over-structuralised 66n
pluralism 33
purposes 67n, 100
rights and responsibilities 159
sacramental fellowship 184
sanctions in 200f
Secretary General of 5, 150n, 151
seeking full stature of Christ 55
self-understanding 61
suspension from 123n, 203
tacit covenant 37–38, 76, 80
uniformity 65
unity 141
voluntary association, as 32, 34, 38, 207
withdrawal of fellowship 194n, 201–202
witness, and: See Witness
Anglican Communion Network:
agreements 9n, 22, 174
called to its work 154
Canterbury, and 57n
commitments 28
confessionalism 77n
covenantal 41
detail of instruments 87
ecumenical partners 57n
episcopal oversight 57n
identity 63, 96
linguistic form 85
matters of common concern 109
meeting of minds idea 22
organisation 109
Primates, and 57n
relations in 100
responsibilities 98
signatories 178
unity 57
Anglican Congress 124, 152, 157
Anglican Consultative Council:
achievements 103n
agreement idea 22
approval of covenant 152
arbiter in disputes 203

autonomy, provincial 120n
binding effect of constitution 189
character of 40
civil law, in 40
collaboration 57
communion action 40
consensus 57
constitution as covenantal 40
constitution 40, 88, 96, 173–174
constitution, amendment 22, 40, 206
constitutions, model provincial 93
controversial action and 1
covenant adoption and 168, 177
covenant detail 87
covenant enforcement 194
covenant process and 150f
covenants and 4, 6
functions 100, 122, 124, 130, 131, 141
global conventions 27n
guidelines for meetings 120n, 121n
membership 57n, 183–184, 185
Network of Legal Advisers and 89
object 57
relinquishment 196, 199
responsibilities 98
SADC Appendix proposal 197ff
unity and 56–57
Anglican formularies: See Historical formularies
Anglican Global Initiative:
church planting 69
covenant, 41
detail of instruments 87
episcopal oversight 69
mission 69
respect and 189
unity 57
Anglicanism:
authority 166, 187
being Anglican 183
character 31, 61
comprehensiveness 66, 97n, 102, n, 108, 134n
covenantal character 31–34, 37, 91
duties as dominant regime 82
genius of 188n

mutual learning 161–162
origins 128, 139
tacit covenant 37–38
theological tradition 55, 95
use of covenants 35–41
Anglican-Lutheran Commission 157
Anglican-Lutheran Covenant
  Australia:
  adoption 174n
  commitments 29
  common identity 96
  covenanting process 164
  mutual recognition 18
  national 9n, 46
  pledges 25–26, 85n
Anglican-Methodist Covenant
  (England):
  bilateral 46
  covenanting process 164
  declaratory 46
  form 18, 29, 80
  formalising practice 75
  non-binding effect 189
  relations 9n, 18n, 101n
Anglican-Roman Catholic
  International Commission 113n,
  116n, 118n, 125n
Apostolic Canon 34 130
Apostolic faith: See Faith
Appeals 197
Arbitration 195, 200
Archibishop, title 80n
Australia, Anglican Church of, draft
  covenant submission 6:
  affection, on 33n
  agreement idea, on 18
  Anglican Communion, definition
    of 183n
  autonomy and 64n, 102
  bonds of affection 32
  covenant as relational 14n
  covenant, free entry 14
  covenant undertakings 23
  definitions in 75n
  enforcement 192
  form of 79
  loyalty 55
  membership 183

no use of commitments 26
reception 104
sanctions 201
signatories 176
subsidiarity 104
Australia, local covenants 13
Australian Churches Covenanting
  Together:
  agreement 20
  biblical basis 16n
  collaboration 101n
  commitments 29n
  detail of 87
  development and 207n
  membership, tiered 186
  mission 68
  parties 47
  permissive nature 85n
  pilgrimage 20
  process 164n
  unity 58
Australian National Council of
  Churches 77n
Autonomy 38n, 57, 66, 82, 101, 107,
  121n, 129, 131, 134, 143, 160,
  162, 171, 184, 194, 196, 211
  ACC, and 107n
  autonomy-in-communion 91, 102,
    106f, 140
  Baptist World Alliance, in 50
  communion, and 112
  defined 106
  diocese, of a 107
  disciples, of 14
  Eastern Catholic Churches, in 107
  ecumenism, in 105
  exercise of 142–143
  international law, in 106
  intervention in 136n
  Lutheran World Federation, in 49,
    107
  meaning 102, 104n
  Methodism, in 49–50
  negative 65n
  Orthodoxy, in 48, 106
  principle 1, 2, 3
  responsibility, and 102
  Roman Catholicism, in 107

subsidiarity, and 103
Union of Utrecht, in 48, 63
World Alliance of Reformed
Churches, in 49, 105

Baptism, covenant of 137, 139, 140,
153n, 211
adoption 17
authority to enter 178
breach of covenant 204
canonical authority 173n
celebration 180
commitment 26, 28
confessionalism 77n
consultation prior to 157
covenant duplication 55
covenant, as 17, 33n
fidelity 25
identity 63
liturgical texts 75
mission 69, 140
moral authority 188
nature 44
order 66–67
preparation 163
profession 98
promissory 25
reconciliation 60
registration 180
stability and permanence 67
undertakings 25
unity 56
vocation 154–155
Baptist tradition 50n
Baptist World Alliance 50, 58, 156
Belief, identity in 94
Benedictine tradition 14, 35n
Bible 21, 27, 77, 94, 126, 127, 138
See also Scripture
Bishop:
pressures on 98
role of 99, 117, 138, 140, 157–8,
178n, 194
territorial authority 188
Bonds of affection 14, 31, 33, 59, 62,
63, 66, 74, 86n, 144, 170, 202n,
209
Bonn Agreement 1931 45n, 86, 114n

Book of Common Prayer 1662 95,
126
British Council of Churches,
covenant of 45n
Burial office (covenantal
character) 45
Bylaws (global ecclesial
communities) 87

Canon law 24, 29, 79, 142
absence of on inter-church
relations 167
agreements, on 20, 53
breach of faith and 205
causa in 24
communion and 93
consideration in 24
covenant in 20
ecumenism 167n
fidei laesio in 205
good faith and 190–191
international 34, 170, 171
no global system 1, 3, 207
oaths in 27
pacta sunt servanda 190f
pactum 24
principles of (common to the
churches) 89–90, 95n, 142n
promises in 27, 179
recourse to 154n
servant of church 39
theology and 82
undertakings to comply with 179
Canterbury, Archbishop of:
affection for (the See of the) 34
Anglican Communion, on 207
appointment of 107–108
call to covenant 154
canon law, on 207
commitments, on 26–27
communion with (the See of
the) 16n, 37, 141
covenant adoption, on 168
covenant as opt-in matter, on 16,
187
covenant debate, on 4, 149
covenant, on 5, 16, 104n
covenant process, and 150f

covenants (individual) with 157,
178, 206, 207
effective structures, need for 187
functions of 122, 123, 130, 133,
141, 160, 196f
guidance from 83, 122, 160, 191
jurisdiction 123n
membership of Communion, on 184
requests of 197ff
unity and 54
Windsor Report, on 4-5
Catholic order 28
Catholicity 29, 85, 86n, 92, 116,
125, 211
Causa 24
Charta Oecumenica:
authority 174
commitments 29, 85n
conflict resolution 67, 100n
detail of 87
development and 207n
dialogue 160
form (mischiefs) 85n
non-binding effect 189n
parties 9n, 47
process 164n
voluntary 17
See also Conference of European
Churches
Chicago-Lambeth Quadrilateral 4n,
28, 36, 40, 62, 80, 86, 114n, 126,
129n, 137n, 163n, 214
Christian discipleship, constraints
on 26
Church, an Anglican (provincial,
national, regional etc):
apostolicity and 211
authority to adopt covenant 171f
autonomous units within 93
buildings in, covenants to share 51
catholicity 29, 211
church planting in 69
church universal 29-30
communion within 93
communion law in: *See* Communion
law
community 38, 209
conscience of 102n

consensual compacts of 38-39
ecclesiality: *See* Ecclesiality
household, as 38
identity 96
intent of 19
laws of 38-39, 89, 107, 118, 140,
188
legislative competence 171f
locality 37n, 120, 208
member 183
partakers of a covenant 144
polity 38-39, 209
province: *See* Province
relationality 210
relations with States 39, 64, 66
voluntary association, as 39
Church universal 29, 37n, 63, 80,
87n, 96, 125, 137, 140, 209,
210-211
Churches Together in Britain and
Ireland 77n
Church-state concordats: *See*
Concordats
Code, covenant not a 76, 84
Codification 75, 76
Collaboration 57, 101n, 108, 150,
156, 158
Collegiality 109n, 130, 140, 141
Commission of Episcopal
Conferences in Europe (Roman
Catholic) 9n, 47
Commitments 26ff
Common concern, matters of 107-
110
See also Essential matters of
common concern
Common discernment 104, 134-135,
156
Common life 140
Common mind 133, 135-136, 142
Communion (theological
concept) 55n
act of 149, 150
autonomy and, relationship 112
calling, as 32, 115
Communion, Instruments of: *See*
Instruments of Communion
covenant and 55n

ecclesial 14, 60, 187
eucharistic 74, 83, 138
full 26, 86, 99, 101
gift of God, as 59, 80, 100
highest degree of 33, 144
impaired 2, 202
meaning of 94, 102n, 153n
mission and 68
mutual relations as 14
obligations of 26, 97–100, 141–143
personal 14
purpose of 167
realisation of 138
relationships of 100–101
sacramental 86n
threats to 83, 142–144, 195ff
Trinity and 3, 15, 32, 74, 115, 125
visible foundation of 61
withdrawal from, voluntary 201
Communion law 166–175
criticism of formula in 175n
original suggestion 167n
provincial mechanisms 171f
signatories and 175ff
terms of 168
WDAC and 175n
Community of Protestant Churches
in Europe (Leuenberg Agreement):
agreement concept 20, 22, 49
assent to agreement 175
confessionalism 77n
descriptive 80
detail of agreement 87
identity 96
mission 69
relations within 101
supplementary instruments 87
taking agreement into account 189n
trust 61
vision 155–156
Compromises 55
Conciliarism 102, 156, 171
Conciliation 200
Concordat 1784 8, 24, 35, 56n, 80, 84
Concordat Union of Anglican
Churches in Communion, A:

discipline 67n
call to covenant 154
covenantal 9n, 20, 41
covenanting 164
detail of 87
linguistic form 85
organisation of institution 109
pledges 25
regulations of church parties 189n
relations within institution 100–101
responsibility and 98
signatories 178
undertakings 26
Concordats (church-state relations):
affirmations 26
amendment 206–207
binding effect 191
conflict resolution 61, 67
cooperation 58
declaratory 80
discord and 61
form 85
guarantees 30
incidence 50–51, 183n, 220
union of wills 22
voluntary 18
Conference of European
Churches 9n, 47, 58
See also Charta Oecumenica and
Commission of Episcopal
Conferences in Europe
Confessing churches 78
Confessionalism 77–78
Confirmation and
confessionalism 77n
Conflict resolution 63n, 65n, 67, 104, 109, 191ff
Conscience 55, 66, 67, 68, 97, 102, 114, 160, 188n
Consensual compact 38–39, 76, 77
Consensus fidelium 103n
Consequentialism 160
Considerations for global covenant
debate:
ponder the proposals 214–215
respect the responses 215–218
consult the comparators 218–220
Consultation 109n, 143, 156

See also Provincial consultation
Contract 13n, 15, 19, 21, 24, 27, 158, 190
Controversial issues 142
Council of Anglican Provinces of Africa:
functions 101
relations within 100–101
responsibility and 98–99
unity in diversity 57
Covenant:
accountability: *See* Accountability
adoption 3, 150, 166–181, 183, 215, 217
affirmations 79, 137f
agreement, as 18ff, 35n
amendment 205–207, 214
armistice 55
articulates existing principles 74
aspirational 79, 81, 82
authorisation for entry 167, 171–2, 175–178
authority 187
autonomy as subject-matter 101–107
binding character 187–191
bond 14n
breach 200–205
call to 153–156
canon law and 20
changeability 64, 205–207
clarity 61
classes of member 185
code 84
coercion 66
commitments 26ff, 79, 81, 97–100
common identity 94–96
communion relations 56, 100–101
concept in churches 38
confessionalism 77–78
consensual compact as 38–39
content 112–145, 215, 217
contract and: *See* Contract
covenant service in Methodism 180
Covenant Statement TEC 28n, 40
debate, principles for 213–221
declaration 79
definition 13, 75

descriptive 79–81
detail 86–90, 158
diachronic 74
discipline 191–205
discretion to adopt 183
documentary 73–78
duress 15n, 16
ecclesiastical organisation 42, 56
ecumenical: *See* Ecumenical agreements
educational 79
effect 182–212, , 215, 218
employment of 31–52, 214, 216
enactment of communion law 166–174
enforceability in local church 164f, 182, 191–200
enforcement by undertakings 179
evolution 205–207
exchange of promises 22ff
exclusion 68
expectations 62
family 16
foedus 14n
form 73–90, 214, 216
gift of God 33n
horizontal relationships 15, 17
identity 61, 183
incorporation in law 169, 188n
individual, with Canterbury 157, 178, 206, 207
institutionalisation, and 76
intention 19
interdependence 59n
interpretation: *See* Interpretation
introversion 68
juridical adoption 187
language 79–85
lapidary 79
local congregations 98n
matters of common concern 107–110
membership of 185
minimalist 86
mission 67–69, 98
models 221n
motivational 79, 81, 82
nature of 13–30, 214, 216

negotiability 160
negotiation 158–161
non-binding model 170, 188
not a code 76
oath 24
obligation 17
optional draft texts 151
order and stability 63–67
original suggestion 167n
penitence and 61
periodic review 205
personal declarations to comply
 with 179
personal 69
prescriptive 81–85
process 149–165, 215, 216, 217
process, criticism of 152
process, divisive 157
process, educative 79, 161–164
process, elements of 149, 166
process, evolution of 150–153
process, phases 150f
process, pneumatic aspects of 153–
 156
promissory 37, 81
proposals (significance) 213–215
provincial consultation 151–152,
 157
purpose 53–57, 182, 214, 216
reason and experience 45–51
reception of 169
recommitment 59ff
reconciliation 17, 59ff
relational 16
relinquishment 199, 201
rites 16
sacramental 8
sacrifice 155
scripture in: See Scripture
self-limitation 192
self-understanding 162n
signatories 175–178
signature 150, 168, 179–180
signature and membership 183
signature as witness 150
signature prior to legal
 adoption 168
signing, authority for 175–178

stability 66–67
steadfastness 28, 67
structure of 73–90
study 162
subject-matter 91–111, 214–215,
 216–217
subsequent ratification 168
supplementary instruments 88
synchronic 74
synodical 38
theology: See Covenantal theology
Trinity: See Trinity
trust 59ff
understanding 61
uniformity 65
union 16
vertical relations 15
vocation 153–156
voluntary 14ff
Covenant Design Group:
 accountability, on 66
 adoption by synodical process 187
 Anglican Communion nature 207
 articulation of broad principles 79
 autonomy 104
 centralised jurisdiction 143
 communion and covenant 88
 communion responsibilities 26
 communion 32
 composition of 150
 confessionalism, and 78
 conflict, on 64
 consultation 157
 covenant adoption 169
 covenant amendment 205–206
 covenant and unity 54–55
 covenant binding effect 187
 covenant binds churches
  together 54–55
 covenant detail 86
 discipline 64
 divine call to communion 154
 documentary covenant 74
 does not address form 79
 does not define covenant 13
 establishment of 5
 identity 62
 Instruments of Communion 140ff

meetings 56, 149, 151f
membership of Anglican
  Communion, on 183
mission 68, 98
Nassau Draft Covenant: *See* Nassau
  Draft Covenant
negotiation 159
promises, on 23
proposal for 150
renewal 60
reports 151–152
signatories 176
stability 64
study of covenant drafts 162
theological introduction 88
titles for covenant 13n
Trinity 74
trust 59
See also Nassau Draft Covenant and
  St Andrews Draft Covenant
Covenant for Communion in
  Mission 7, 9, 41
adoption model 169
aspirational 79n, 84–85
call to mission 154
collaboration 158
detail of 87
matters of common concern 109
mission 69
mutual responsibilities 100n
non-binding character 189
pledges 25, 84
prescriptive 84–85
spiritual nourishment for
  covenanting 163
See also Inter-Anglican Standing
  Commission on Mission and
  Evangelism
Covenantal theology 8, 56, 60, 69
Covenanting:
God and 14
negotiation 158–161
negotiation virtues 160
pilgrimage 164
pneumatological aspects 153f
prayer in 163
process, common discernment 156–
  158
spiritual process 161–164
vocational models 154–156
Covenants, individual with
  Canterbury 157, 178, 206, 207
Creeds 33n, 36, 55, 137, 211
Cross, theology of the 74n
Custom 80, 84n

Deaconess 84n
Debate 108, 142, 150
Decision-making, arbitrary 74
Desuetude 207
Diachronic covenant 74
Dialogue 62, 64, 158, 160
Diocese(s):
autonomy of 93n, 107
companion 37, 38n
union of 38–39
Discipline 171n
Christ, of 39
Church, in a 38
Disputes 65n, 68, 132, 134, 158n,
  195f
Dissent 66n, 69
Diversity 65, 66, 68, 101, 102, 108,
  134, 160–162, 188n
defined (in ecumenism) 105
See also Conscience
Doctrine 38, 39, 78
See also Faith and Historical
  formularies
Duties 82

Eastern Catholic Churches 107
Ecclesiality 29n, 38, 207–211
Ecclesiology 29, 61, 63, 153, 210
Ecumenical agreements 13, 17–18,
  20, 22, 25, 29, 45–47, 137n,
  219–220
acknowledgements 80
alternative dispute resolution 200
amendment 207
autonomy 105
biblical model 47
binding legal effect 189
canonical adoption 174
caution over labels 46
collaboration 158

commitments 186
common identity 96
cooperation 109
detail of 86
discipline 199–200
full communion 99, 101
identity 63
juridical language 85
law and 174
linguistic form 85
matters of common concern 109
membership (tiered classes) 186
negotiation 160
new relationships 61
non-binding effect 189
penitence 61
pilgrimage 164
Primates' Meeting, on 45
provincial consultation and 46
reconciliation 61
solemnity 180
source for WADC 113
TAAC on 45
written 75
Ecumenism:
consensus 192n
law and 167n
partners 57n, 61, 62n, 64, 105, 131,
    157
sacramental communion 86n
See also Inter-Anglican Standing
    Commission on Ecumenical
    Relations
England, Church of:
adoption of covenant 172–173
adoption process 177–178
delegation to Primates'
    Meeting 194n
effect of covenant in 188
established 38n
incorporation in law 188
signatories issue 177–178
Episcopacy, nature 36, 37, 38, 83,
    129, 137, 140, 211
See also Bishops
Episcopal Church, The, USA:
Concordat with Lutherans 20n, 46,
    58, 69

Covenant Statement 28n, 40
missionary covenants 35n, 36n
Episcopal consecrations 85
Episcopal oversight 69, 202
Equality, ecclesial 14, 22
Equity 118
Eschatology 100, 127n, 154
Essential matters of common
    concern 107–110, 121–124, 132,
    134, 142, 193
Ethics 160, 190
See also Moral reasoning and
    Morals
Eucharist, the 137, 140, 211
communion, and 83, 138
community 140
covenantal relations 55
covenantal, as 44–45
nature 17
order and 67
Evaluation, principle of (SADC) 143,
    198
Evangelical faith: See Faith
Evangelisation 139: See also Gospel
Evolution of covenant process 150–
    153, 205–207

Fairness 196
Faith, the:
apostolic 80, 113, 126, 138, 211
common 77, 105n
confession of 77, 92, 116
evangelical 28
good 190–191
inheritance of 57, 126, 136–138,
    140
instruments of 37
order and (Anglican) 29–30
Family:
ACC as 40
a church as 38
Anglican Communion as 2, 32, 33–
    34, 40, 54, 64, 139, 194, 207, 209
Federal concept and covenant 49n
Federal theology 14n
Federation 34, 38
Fidei laesio 205
Fiduciary duty (good faith) 82n, 191

Foedus 14n, 56
Forbearance 160
Freedom 16, 54
  churches, of 66
  ecumenism, in 105
  freedom-in-relation 91, 106

Global ecclesial communities
  (comparable):
  binding effect of instruments 189
  comparators as 47ff, 220
  constitutional amendment in 206–
  207
  instrument adoption methods 174ff
  membership 185
  sanctions in 204–205
Global South 5, 6, 18n, 33n, 170
Globalisation 33
Good faith 191
Gospel 20, 67–69, 78n, 80, 81, 94n,
  97n, 98, 115, 124, 130, 135, 139
Green light model 221n

Hermeneutics 94
  See also Scripture, interpretation of
Historic formularies (Anglican) 28n,
  77, 78, 87, 95, 126, 137
Holiness 32, 68, 69n, 138
Holy Spirit 66n, 74, 129n, 130, 137,
  140, 153, 155, 187
Hooker, Richard 8, 34n, 35, 44, 56n,
  94n, 114n
Household, a church as 38
Human rights 49, 188n

Identity (Anglican) 33n, 94–96, 183
Incorporation of covenant in law 188
Instruments of Communion (formerly
  Instruments of Unity):
  additional 131
  advisory 201
  authority of 108, 133–136, 166
  constitutions for 88
  disputes 181, 192, 193
  expectations about 97
  generally 37, 40, 57, 83, 129–131,
  134–136, 140–144, 196f
  guidance from 132

heed counsel of 132
matters of common concern 107–
111
more collaboration between 108
relations 88
requests from 197ff
sanctions 203
support for their work 131
withdrawal of fellowship 201
Instruments of faith 37
  See also Faith
Inter-Anglican Standing Commission
  on Ecumenical Relations:
  communion 74
  communion-breaking matters 104
  confessional covenant 78
  consulted 150n
  covenant compliance 195
  covenant detail 86
  Trinity 74
  See also Ecumenism
Inter-Anglican Standing Commission
  on Mission and Evangelism:
  bonds of affection 62
  clarity in relations 62
  consulted 150n
  covenant as agreement 19
  covenant as comparator 9n, 219
  covenant as voluntary 15
  Covenant: *See* Covenant for
  Communion in Mission
  covenantal pledges 25
  covenanting as free 15
  mission 69n
  scriptural covenant models 42
Inter-Anglican Theological and
  Doctrinal Commission:
  advisory body, proposal for 195
  Anglican theological tradition 95
  arbitration 195
  biblical covenants and 17, 20,
  43–44, 79, 207
  bonds of affection 33
  communion vocation 154
  consulted 150n
  covenant adoption mode 169
  covenant amendment 206
  covenant and commitment 28

covenant and unity 54
covenant and voluntary
  relations 16–17
covenant detail 86
covenant form 79
covenant negotiation 158–159
covenants in Anglicanism 35–36
future conflict 86
Instruments of Communion on 108
mission 67
reconciliation 60
relational covenants 79
renewal 60
scope of covenant 86
scripture, interpretation of 206
subsidiarity 104
trust 59
work of 2n
Interdependence, principle of 14, 32,
  59n, 63, 100n, 112n, 128, 129,
  139, 142, 169, 202n, 206
International law (secular):
autonomy in 106
covenants 21, 51
obligations 63
pacta sunt servanda 190
soft law agreements 85n, 191
treaties 27, 168n
treaty amendment 206
treaty incorporation 168
treaty negotiation 158
treaty signatories 178
treaty breach 205
undertakings 85n
Interpretation of covenant 75, 108–
  109, 123, 133, 194
secular courts and 194n
Interpretation of Scripture: See
  Scripture, interpretation of
Intervention in provinces 1, 121,
  136n

Joint Standing Committee of the
  Anglican Consultative Council and
  Primates' Meeting:
amendments to draft covenants 159
covenant adoption 168
covenant process and 149, 150f

form 84
ministry 97
role in process 4, 5, 6
Jurisdiction:
debate as to 135
supra-provincial 108ff

Kilcoy Covenant 47n

Laity 40, 109, 152, 156
Lambeth Commission:
communion, nature 26
covenant and promises 22–23
covenant negotiation 158
covenant proposal 2
covenant process 149, 150
covenant purposes 53
covenant, reasons for 3
drives behind covenant 35
establishment 2
mandate 4
reception process (post-Windsor) 4
See also Windsor Report
Lambeth Conference 122, 124, 141,
  168
Lausanne Covenant 80, 98n
Laws of churches, subjects
  treated 93: See also canon law
Legal Advisers Network: See
  Network of Legal Advisers
Legalism 81, 90n
Leuenberg Agreement: See
  Community of Protestant Churches
  in Europe
Listening 81, 86, 102, 135, 142,
  161n
Liturgy 44, 137, 150, 179–180
See also Worship
Lutheran-Anglican-Roman Catholic
  Covenant (Virginia):
adoption 174
call to covenant 155
prayer 180
relationality 18
signatories 178
tripartite 46n
Lutheranism 208–211
Lutheran World Federation:

acceptance of confessions 85
acceptance of constitution 20,
174–175
autonomy in 49, 107
bylaws 87
character 49
constitution as agreement 20
constitution 49
constitutional amendment 206n
detail of constitution 87
identity 96
joint action in common tasks 109
membership 185
mutual commitments 100
organisation 67
purposes of 49
pulpit and altar fellowship 49
relations within 101
restoration 204
sanctions in 204
suspension 204
unity and 58
Word of God 49

Marriage, covenant of:
authority to enter 178–179
binding 170
breach of covenant 204
canonical authority 173n
celebration 180
change 206
consents 157–158
consultation 157-8
covenantal 17, 45
identity 63
keeping vows 67
liturgical texts 75
preparation 163
promises 25
registration 180
stability and permanence 67
trust 60
unity 56
vocation 154–155
witness 69
Mediation 118, 143, 192, 198, 200
Membership of the Anglican
Communion 100

critical approaches to 184
compared with global ecclesial
communities 185
tests for 182–186
tiers 184
Methodist Covenant Service 180
Metropolitan, title 80n
Ministerial covenants 57, 86
Ministries, reconciliation of 26
Ministry, interchangeability 97, 99n,
117
Missio dei: See Mission.
Mission 28, 37, 54, 66, 67–69, 97n,
98, 125, 128, 134, 139, 140, 141
credibility and effectiveness 142–
143, 195
Models for covenant debate 213,
221n
Monastic tradition 28n
See also Benedictine tradition
Moral reasoning 126n, 138
Morals 75, 98, 100, 126, 141, 200,
202,
Multilateralism, procedural 63
Mutual expectations 62, 97

Nassau Draft Covenant:
absence of central authority 129–
130
ACC 131–132
accountability 129
affirmations 24
Anglican Communion as family 128
anxieties over Art 6 133–136
apostolic mission 125
Archbishop of Canterbury 130
Art 1 14, 55n, 68n, 124–126
Art 2 92, 94n, 95n, 125–126
Art 3 26n, 78n, 92, 105n, 126–127
Art 4 26n, 32n, 68n, 81n, 92,
127–128
Art 5 32, 92, 129–131
Art 6 55n, 89n, 92, 131–136, 193
Art 7 55n, 133
autonomy and 102, 129, 131
baptism 125
Bible 126–127
Book of Common Prayer 1662 126

catholicity 125
Chicago-Lambeth
  Quadrilateral 125nn
church universal 125
common mind 132
common pilgrimage 127
communion gift of God 127
confession of faith 125, 126f
confessionalism, and 78
consent to 18
content 123–136
context 126
covenant as relational 14n
covenantal relations 14
creeds 125
declaration 133
disputes 132
ecclesiality 207–211
enforceability 193
eucharist 125
eucharistic obligation 127
finance 99
historic formularies 126
hospitality 127
humanity, vision of 126
Instruments of Communion 129–
  131
Instruments of Communion, heed
  counsel of 132
Instruments, no legal authority 132
interdependence 128, 129–131
jargon in 87
juridical elements 82, 83
Lambeth Conference 131
matters of common concern 132
membership of Anglican
  Communion 183
mission 68, 128–129
moral values 75, 126
negotiability 160
origins of Anglicanism 128
Preamble 55n, 68n, 92, 124, 207n
Primates' Meeting 6, 131
principles, rules, rights, duties,
  norms in 83–84
provenance of provisions 123–136
provincial consultation 6
purposes 124–125

Reformation 128
relinquishment by churches 132–
  133, 201
revelation 125
sacraments 125
sanctions 200, 201
scripture references 124n, 125,
  126n, 127n, 129, 131n
signatories 176
subject-matter 92
support for Art 6 133
Thirty-Nine Articles 126
title 14
Trinity 125
trust 60
unity and common life 129–136
witness 127
worship 125
Negotiation about covenant 158–161
Network of Legal Advisers 64, 89,
  150n
  consultation leading to 64n
New Testament and covenant 16, 17,
  42–44
  See also Scripture, covenants in
Norma Normans 81
Norms 82

Old Catholics: See Union of Utrecht
Old Testament and covenant 16, 17,
  41–42
  See also Scripture, covenants in
Ordination, covenant of:
  breach of covenant 204
  canonical authority 173n
  celebration 180
  confessionalism 77n
  consents and consultation 158
  general 17
  identity 63
  liturgical texts 75
  mission 69
  preparation 163
  registration 180
  stability and permanence 67
  trust 60
  undertakings 25
  unity 56

vocation 155
Orthodox Church:
  admission to holy communion 84n
  autonomy in 106
  church universal and 210
  ecclesiality 208–211
  global fellowship 48
  Orthodox-Anglican dialogue 100n,
    104n

Pacta sunt servanda 187–191, 220
Pactum 14n, 24, 56
Panel of Reference 203
Partnership 38
Patience 160
Perichoresis 115n, 164
Persuasion 202
Pilgrimage 20, 116, 138, 164
Pluralism 33, 158
Pneumatology 153
Polity 34n, 40, 81
  definition 60n
  persuasion, of 194
Porvoo agreement 101n, 114n, 118
Prayer 83, 97, 98, 137, 142, 154,
  163f
Primate:
  functions under canon law 176
  representative 176
  role in provinces 133
  signatory to covenant 175–178
Primates' Meeting 1, 2, 3, 6, 130
  caution about WADC 112n
  Chicago-Lambeth Quadrilateral 62
  clarity about relations 62
  committee of Lambeth Conference,
    idea about 134
  covenant adoption 169
  covenant process and 150f
  covenant signatories and 176
  covenant 149
  creeds 36
  decision-making and 108
  does not define covenant 13
  enforcer of covenant 194
  functions 122, 123–124, 141
  in SADC Appendix 197ff
  morals 75

points raised concerning NDC 6,
  55n
polity of persuasion 194
powers 132–133
principles of canon law 89–90
scripture 36
scripture, tradition and reason 94
veto over ACC membership 57n
Windsor Report 4
Principles 82
  See also Considerations for global
    covenant debate
Process (condition for acceptability of
  covenant) 149
Promises 24, 190
Protestant tradition on covenants 42,
  56
Provincial consultation (2007) 6, 45,
  46, 94, 150–152, 157, 203, 205
Provinces 38–39
  autonomy: *See* Autonomy
  intervention in affairs of 2, 121,
    136n, 193
  competence (to enter covenant) 171f
Punishment, unacceptability of 202

Quod omnes tangit principle 83, 120

Reason 8, 94, 114, 158
Reception Reference Group 4, 8n,
  149
Reception, doctrine of 103–107, 192
  defined 103, 104n, 105–106
Recommitment 59ff
Reconciled diversity 160
Reconciliation 59ff
Red light model 221n
Referrals (under SADC
  Appendix) 197
Reformation churches 36
Reformation 128, 139
Regional agreements 46
Religious alliances 76
Relinquishment of covenant
  purposes 132f, 183, 199, 200, 201,
    203
Repentance 202
Requests, rejection 143

Resources, spiritual and material 142
Responses to covenant proposals,
  summary 215–218
Responsibility, mutual 66n
Restoration of churches 132, 201
Rights 82
Roman Catholic Church 47n, 48
  church universal and 210
  code of canon law 42
  communion within 101n
  concordats 191
  contracts 190n
  ecclesiality 208–211
  ecumenism and 47n
  See also Lutheran-Anglican-Roman
    Catholic Covenant (Virginia)
Rules of engagement 81
Rules 82

Sacramental covenants 158, 186,
  204, 218–219
Sacramental devotion 86n
Sacramental theology 28
Sacramental tradition, covenant
  in 44–45
Sacramental worship is practised 28
Sacraments 20, 36, 39, 137, 211
Saint Andrews Draft Covenant:
  Anglican Communion as family 32,
    139, 207
  Anglican Consultative Council 141
  Anglican inheritance of faith 136–
    138
  apostolic faith 138
  apostolic mission 137–138
  Appendix 88, 108–109, 144, 160n,
    195–200
  authority 140
  autonomy 102, 140, 142, 143
  baptism 140
  biblical texts 138
  bishops, role of 140
  bonds of affection 144
  canon law 142
  Canterbury, Archbishop of 141ff
  Chicago-Lambeth Quadrilateral 36,
    137n
  Church of the Apostles 139

clarity 62
Clause 1 23n, 26n, 36n, 78n, 94,
    95n, 105n, 136-138
Clause 2 23n, 26n, 32n, 68n, 78n,
    81n, 98, 139
Clause 3 23n, 26n, 88n, 89n,
    140–144
collegiality 140, 141
commitments 23
common discernment 142
common good of Anglican
    Communion 141–142
common identity 94, 96
common mind 142
common pilgrimage 138
common prayer and liturgy
    form 137
common standards of faith 142
communion and the Trinity 15
communion as gift of God 139
communion 138
confessionalism and 78
consultation 143
content 136–144
contentious issues 142–144, 195
creeds 137
declaration 19, 144
descriptive form 81
disputes 144, 195–200
ecclesiality 207–211
ecumenical dimension 139
enforceability 193
eucharist 140
eucharistic communion 138
evaluation, principle of 143
evangelisation 139
finance 99
Framework Procedures: See
    Appendix
generally 6f, 18f
historic episcopate 137
Instruments of Communion 88,
    108, 140–144
interdependence 139, 142
Introduction 15
juridical elements 82, 83–84
Lambeth Conference 141ff
leadership 138

life Anglicans share with others 139
mediation 143
membership of Anglican
  Communion 183
mission 68, 98, 139
moral reasoning 138
morals 75
mutually recognised common
  identity 96
origins of Anglicanism 139
pledges 23
prayer 98
Preamble 15, 55n, 68n, 136, 207
Primates' Meeting 141
principles, rules, rights, duties,
  norms in 83–84
procedural principles 143–144, 195
provenance of provisions 136–144
purpose 136
Reformation 139
relinquishment 143, 183
requests 143
restoration of ecclesial relations 143
sacraments 137
salvation 137
scripture covenants 15
scripture 137, 138, 142, 144
shared liturgical patterns 97–98
signatories 176
spiritual and material resources 142
subject-matter 92–93
synodical government 140
Thirty-Nine Articles 137n
threefold ministry 140
Trinity 32
understanding 62
unity and common life 140
use of NDC as source 136–144nn
use of WDAC as source 136–144nn
witness 138
worship 137
Salvation, things necessary for 103n,
  104, 113, 137
Salvific covenant: See also Scripture,
  covenants in
conditionality debate 81n
effect 189
generally 16, 19, 23, 158

moral authority 189
order 66
sanctions 204
unity 56
Sanctions 136, 200ff
Schism 55, 208
Scotland National
  Covenant 1638 36n
Scripture 142, 211, 218
authority of 37n, 81, 94, 211
criterion, as 8
interpretation of 94, 97, 105, 114,
  206
one another passages in 18
reading of 28
reason and tradition, and 8, 94,
  114, 158
supremacy of 94
ultimate standard 28n, 137
See also Bible
Scripture, covenants in 33n, 41–44
agreement 19
breach 204
change and 207
contract and 21
covenanting, ritual 180
cutting a covenant 155
documentary 75
exchange of promises 24
form 79
human covenants 43
identity 63
mission 69
models 42–44
models in ecumenism 47
obligation 27
pledges 25
prescriptive 81
promises 23, 25, 27
relational 16
salvific covenant: See Salvific
  covenant
sanctions 204
secular covenants 20
stipulative 28
treaty-like 21
trust 60
undertakings 25

unilateral 20
words 13–14
Sociology of religion 76
Southern Baptists:
agreement idea 22
Bible 77n
call to covenant 156
Convention and autonomy 105,
    200n
Convention and unity 58
Covenanting, spiritual aspects 164
local covenant relations 18
solemnity 180
written covenants 76
Sovereignty 106n, 121n, 134n
Standing Conference of Canonical
    Orthodox Bishops in the Americas:
autonomy 105
bylaws 87
character 48
commitments 29
conference decisions bind 190n
conference meetings 85
conflict prevention 67
constitution as agreement 20
constitution binds conference 174n
constitutional amendment 206n
decisive action by 85
detail of 87
generally 9n, 22n
juridical language of 85
matters of common concern 110
membership 185n
relations within 101
unity and 58
Standing Conference of
    Canonical Orthodox Bishops of
    Australia 156n
St John, of Jerusalem, Rhodes
    and Malta, Sovereign Military
    Hospitaller Order of 88n
Subsidiarity 64n, 103, 104, 109
Synchronic covenant 74
Synod meetings (provincial),
    frequency 171
Synodality, principle of 37
Synodical government 114, 124, 134,
    140, 169, 194

Ten Principles of Partnership 40, 97,
    156n, 159n
The Windsor Report:
accountability: See Accountability
autonomy 106f
call to communion 153n
canon law principles 89
canon law 39
clarity, on 61, 62
commitments 26
common discernment 156
Council of Advice 122
covenant amendment 205
covenant and identity 61
covenant and unity 54
covenant articulates existing
    principles 79
covenant as relational 14
covenant as voluntary 17
covenant breach 200
covenant enforceability 191
covenant figure 31
covenant process 150, 156
covenant purposes 53
covenanting as educative
    process 162
diversity: See Diversity
documentary covenant 73–4
does not address covenant detail 86
ecclesiality 207
ecumenical partners 61, 64
family of churches 209
membership of Anglican
    Communion 182
membership 62
mission 61
moratoria 2n
promises 22–23
provincial communion law 166–174
responses to 2, 4
signatories 175
signature of covenant 179–180
stability 63
trust 59
witness 67
Theological debate, matters of 142
Thirty Nine Articles 17n, 36, 77, 95,
    126, 137n

Threefold ministry 117, 140
Towards an Anglican Covenant:
agreement concept 19
agreement to differ 19, 104, 188
biblical covenants 153n
binding covenant and
  uniformity 188
bonds of affection 59
collaboration 156
commitments 26
confessionalism 77
conflict 191–192
covenant amendment 205
covenant and sacrifice 155
covenant and unity 54
covenant as educational 79, 162
covenant as relationships 14, 32
covenant detail 86, 158
covenant form 73
covenant, lapidary 79
covenant process and 150
covenanting negotiation 158
covenants in Anglicanism 35
descriptive form 79
documentary covenant 74
ecclesiality 207
ecumenical covenants 45
form 79
general 5, 7
identity 61n
membership of Anglican
  Communion 182–183
mission 67
need for a single covenant 183
options for adoption 168
prescriptive form 81
prevention of conflict 64
promises and 23
sanctions and 201
scriptural covenants 42
self-understanding 62
subject-matter 92
trust 59
Tradition 8, 28, 38, 94, 114, 126n,
  158
Transparency 97, 99, 150, 156, 196
Trinity 15, 32, 74, 115, 125, 133
Trust 59ff, 76, 188n

Trustworthiness 60

Ubhuntu 68
Undertakings 179
Uniformity 65
Unilateralism 64, 108n
United Churches 95n, 184
Unity 54ff, 140
Unity-in-diversity 57n, 81, 98, 158
Union of Utrecht (Old Catholic):
autonomy and communion 105
autonomy 63
catholicity 85
character 48
common tasks 110
communion 58
detail of statute 87
discipline 190, 200
doctrine and 85
ethics 190
identity 63, 96
interdependence 63
maintenance of communion 110
membership 185n
non-reception of conference
  decisions 190
sanctions in 205
signatories to statute 178
statute 9, 48
statute adoption of 175
statute binds 190
statute, juridical language 85
statute similar to a covenant 48
unity 58
worship 85

Virginia Report 115nn, 116, 119n,
  120n
Virtues, Christian 60, 161, 196

Wales, Church in 61n
Wales, Covenant of Churches in 47n,
  67, 96n, 101, 174n, 180n
Windsor Preliminary Draft
  Covenant:
agreement idea 18
Anglican Communion as
  community of interdependent
  churches 32, 115

Anglican Communion liaison officer (provincial) 122
Art. 1 81n, 94n, 97n
Art. 3 97n
Art. 4 61n
Art. 6 32n, 81n, 181n
Art. 7 32n, 67n
Art. 9 82n
Art. 10 105n
Art. 23 88n
Art. 26 191n
Arts 1–5 61n, 113–114
Arts 5–8 115–116
Arts 9–17 116–118
Arts 18–22 119–121
Arts 23–27 121–124
as source for NDC 124–136nn
autonomy 102
autonomy-in-communion 119–121
baptism 114
biblical texts 116
binding effect 187
bishops as sign of unity 117
bishops 116
canon law, principles of 118
canonical register of 81
catholicity 116
Chicago-Lambeth Quadrilateral 113
church universal 113, 116
classical Anglicanism 112n
common good 116, 120
common identity 113–114
common membership 115
common pilgrimage 116
common sacraments 114
communion commitments 26
communion law 175
communion with Canterbury 115
communion 14
communion, divine foundation 115
confessionalism 77
content 113–123
covenant amendment 205
creeds 113
descriptive form 80
dialogue 120
dissent 114

diversity 121
ecclesial fullness 116
ecclesiality 115, 207–211
ecumenism 118
enforcement mechanism in local church 191
equality 116
eucharist 114
fiduciary duty 120
finance 99
forbearance 114
good order of Anglican Communion 121–122
hospitality 117–118
inadequate on mission 98
Instruments of Communion 118, 121, 122–124
interpretation of covenant 75, 123
intervention in provincial affairs 121
juridical forms in 82–83
laity 114, 124
language 74–75
listening 114
liturgical tradition 114
management of communion issues 121–124
matters of common concern 118
membership of Anglican Communion 182n.183
ministry 117
ministry, threefold 114
mission 113
monitoring administration of covenant 123, 205
morals 75, 116
negotiability 160
periodic review of covenant 123, 205
personal communion 115
Preamble 18n, 62, 167n
precepts in 83
principles, rules, rights, duties and norms in 82–83
process and substance of communion 116
prohibitions in 83
proposal for 2

provenance of provisions 113–123
purpose 3
purposes of Anglican
  Communion 115
reasons for subjects treated 91–92
relationships of communion 115–
  116
resolution of disagreement 122
resources 118
responses 7
sacramental commitments 116f
sacraments 117
salvation 113
scriptural covenant 44
scripture 113
scripture, interpretation of 114
scripture, tradition and reason 114
source for SADC 136–144nn
status as preliminary draft 73–74
structure 91–92
subject-matter 91–92
theological education 162
Thirty-Nine Articles 113n
threats to fellowship and
  mission 121
too canonical 75
too detailed 87
Trinity 115
understanding, on 62
Windsor Report: See The Windsor
  Report
Withdrawal from fellowship 201
Witness 34, 138, 150
Witness, signature as 179
Word of God 20, 29, 80–81, 94,
  114
See also Bible, and Scripture

World Alliance of Reformed
  Churches:
agreement idea 9, 22
autonomy 105
bylaws 87
character 49
commitments 29
common service 109
constitution acceptance of 175
constitutional amendment 206
cooperation 99
detail of constitution 87
ecclesial relations 18
financial responsibilities 99
identity 96
membership 185
Mission in Unity Project 49
mission 69
purpose 49
restoration 204
sanctions 204
scripture 22
spiritual obligations 99
suspension 204
unity and 58
Word of God 29
World Council of Churches: 77n,
  114n
covenantal 29n
ecclesiality and 208
World Methodist Council 49–50:
autonomy 105
commitments 100
unity 58
Worship 35n, 38, 55n, 97, 137, 163n,
  170
See also Liturgy